Literature and the Law in South Africa, 1910–2010

The Fairleigh Dickinson University Press Series in Law, Culture, and the Humanities

Series Editor: Caroline Joan "Kay" S. Picart, M.Phil. (Cantab), Ph.D., J.D., Esquire Attorney at Law; Adjunct Professor, FAMU College of Law; former English & HUM professor, FSU

The Fairleigh Dickinson University Press Series in Law, Culture, and the Humanities publishes scholarly works in which the field of Law intersects with, among others, Film, Criminology, Sociology, Communication, Critical/Cultural Studies, Literature, History, Philosophy, and the Humanities.

On the Web at http://www.fdu.edu/fdupress

Publications

Ted Laros, *Literature and the Law in South Africa, 1910-2010: The Long Walk to Artistic Freedom* (2017)

Peter Robson and Johnny Rodger, *The Spaces of Justice: The Architecture of the Scottish Court* (2017)

Doran Larson, *Witness in the Era of Mass Incarceration: Discovering the Ethical Prison* (2017)

Raymond J. McKoski, *Judges in Street Clothes: Acting Ethically Off-the-Bench* (2017)

H. Lowell Brown, *The American Constitutional Tradition: Colonial Charters, Covenants, and Revolutionary State Constitutions 1578–1786* (2017)

Arua Oko Omaka, *The Biafran Humanitarian Crisis, 1967-1970: International Human Rights and Joint Church Aid* (2016)

Marouf A. Hasian, Jr., *Representing Ebola: Culture, Law, and Public Discourse about the 2013–2015 West Africa Ebola Outbreak* (2016)

Jacqueline O'Connor, *Law and Sexuality in Tennessee Williams's America* (2016)

Caroline Joan "Kay" S. Picart, Michael Hviid Jacobsen, and Cecil E. Greek, *Framing Law and Crime: An Interdisciplinary Anthology* (2016)

Caroline Joan "Kay" S. Picart, *Law In and As Culture: Intellectual Property, Minority Rights, and the Rights of Indigenous Peoples* (2016)

Literature and the Law in South Africa, 1910–2010

The Long Walk to Artistic Freedom

Ted Laros

FAIRLEIGH DICKINSON UNIVERSITY PRESS
Vancouver • Madison • Teaneck • Wroxton

Published by Fairleigh Dickinson University Press
Copublished by The Rowman & Littlefield Publishing Group, Inc.
4501 Forbes Boulevard, Suite 200, Lanham, Maryland 20706
www.rowman.com

Unit A, Whitacre Mews, 26-34 Stannary Street, London SE11 4AB

Copyright © 2018 by Ted Laros

All rights reserved. No part of this book may be reproduced in any form or by any electronic or mechanical means, including information storage and retrieval systems, without written permission from the publisher, except by a reviewer who may quote passages in a review.

Fairleigh Dickinson University Press gratefully acknowledges the support received for scholarly publishing from the Friends of FDU Press.

British Library Cataloguing in Publication Information Available

Library of Congress Cataloging-in-Publication Data

Names: Laros, Ted, 1978– author.
Title: Literature and the law in South Africa, 1910-2010 : the long walk to artistic freedom / Ted Laros.
Description: Madison : Fairleigh Dickinson University Press ; Lanham, Maryland : The Rowman & Littlefield Publishing Group, Inc., 2018. | Series: Series in law, culture, and the humanities | Based on author's thesis (doctoral - Carl von Ossietzky University of Oldenburg, 2013) issued under title: Long walk to artistic freedom : law and the literary field in South Africa, 1910–2010. | Includes bibliographical references and index.
Identifiers: LCCN 2017036974 (print) | LCCN 2017038299 (ebook) | ISBN 9781683930167 (electronic) | ISBN 9781683930150 (cloth : alk. paper)
Subjects: LCSH: Censorship—South Africa—History—20th century. | Obscenity (Law)—South Africa—History—20th century. | Sedition—Law and legislation—South Africa—History—20th century. | South African literature—Censorship—History—20th century.
Classification: LCC KTL3483 (ebook) | LCC KTL3483 .L37 2018 (print) | DDC 344.68/097—dc23
LC record available at https://lccn.loc.gov/2017036974

∞™ The paper used in this publication meets the minimum requirements of American National Standard for Information Sciences Permanence of Paper for Printed Library Materials, ANSI/NISO Z39.48-1992.

Printed in the United States of America

Contents

Acknowledgments	vii
Abbreviations	ix
Introduction: Literature in Law	1
Part I: Legal Groundwork, 1910–1955	**21**
1 Preparing the Ground for Autonomization	23
Part II: Hesitant Legal Recognition, 1955–1975	**47**
2 The 1965 Trials: Wilbur Smith's *When the Lion Feeds* and Can Themba's "The Fugitives"	49
3 The 1974 Trial of André Brink's *Kennis van die Aand*	85
Part III: Despite Rollback Efforts, Ongoing Recognition, 1975–1980	**125**
4 The 1978 Case of Etienne Leroux's *Magersfontein, O Magersfontein!*	127
Part IV: Decisive Legal Recognition, 1980–2010	**163**
5 (The Road to) Constitutional Autonomy	165
Conclusion: Long Walk to Artistic Freedom	193
Bibliography	203
Index	217
About the Author	231

Acknowledgments

This book is a revised and extended version of my PhD thesis, which was written between October 2010 and December 2013 at the Institute of Dutch Studies of the Carl von Ossietzky University of Oldenburg (Ger.) and approved by its School of Linguistics and Cultural Studies in early 2014.

Earlier versions of chapters 2, 4, and 7 have already appeared elsewhere: chapter 2 as "Preparing the Ground for Artistic Freedom: Judicial Censorship of Publications in Pre-Apartheid South Africa, 1890–1948" in *Journal of Dutch Literature* 5.2 (2014), pp. 35–61; chapter 4 as "Literary Autonomy on Trial: The 1974 Cape Trial of André Brink's *Kennis van die Aand*" in *The Courtroom as a Space of Resistance: Reflections on the Legacy of the Rivonia Trial*, edited by Awol Allo, Surrey: Ashgate, 2015, pp. 283–303; chapter 7 as "Law and the Literary Field in South Africa, 1910–2010" in *Literary Trials:* Exceptio Artis *and Theories of Literature in Court*, edited by Ralf Grüttemeier, New York: Bloomsbury Academic, pp. 69–87. I kindly thank *Journal of Dutch Literature*, Taylor and Francis Group, and Bloomsbury for giving me permission to reuse my material.

I would also like to thank a number of institutions for their financial support: The *Deutsche Forschungsgemeinschaft* (German Research Foundation) for providing such generous funding for this project, the Carl von Ossietzky University of Oldenburg, Radboud University of Nijmegen (Neth.), and Open University of the Netherlands for financing additional stays abroad for research purposes.

While working on this project, I greatly benefited from the comments and other kinds of collegial support that I received from my colleagues at Oldenburg University's Institute of Dutch Studies and its School of Linguistics and Cultural Studies. Therefore, many thanks goes out to all these former colleagues. Special thanks goes out to Prof. Sabine Doering, Prof. Anton Kirchhofer, and my supervisor Prof. Ralf Grüttemeier.

I also benefited greatly from feedback I received from a number of people outside of Oldenburg University. I want to thank the organizers and sharp audiences of a number of conferences in Belgium, Germany, the Netherlands, Poland, South Africa, and the United States where I presented results from my research. I especially want to thank Prof. Martin A. Kayman (Cardiff), Prof. Peter D. McDonald (Oxford), Prof. Greta Olson (Giessen), and the anonymous reviewers who commented on an earlier version of (parts of) this book.

While doing research in South Africa, I was supported very kindly at Stellenbosch University, Stellenbosch University Library, the Western Cape Archives and Records Service, and the National Library of South Africa, Cape Town Campus. Many thanks to all the people who helped me at these institutions, and especially to Dr. Ewa Dynarowicz, Prof. Siegfried Huigen, and Prof. Andries Visagie: their warm hospitality made all the difference to my stays.

I want to thank everyone at Fairleigh Dickinson University Press for believing in this project and for handling the publishing process so carefully. Special thanks goes out to Megan DeLancey, Harry Keyishian, Zach Nycum, and Dr. Caroline Picart. Also, I want to thank Josie Dixon for her advice regarding *inter alia* the title of the book, and Dr. Katherine Bird for correcting my English so thoroughly.

Writing a book is obviously a time- and energy-consuming activity. In writing this book, I was lucky enough to enjoy the constant support of my parents and parents-in-law, and especially that of my wife Gieske and daughters Lotje, Noor, Fiene, and Aafke. Since I learned a little Afrikaans along the way, I want to say to them: baie dankie my skatties, ek is lief vir julle!

Abbreviations

AD	Appellate Division of the Supreme Court of South Africa
CPD	Cape Provincial Division of the Supreme Court of South Africa
DOP	Directorate of Publications
FPA	Films and Publications Act, 1996
FPB	Film and Publication Board
FPRB	Film and Publication Review Board
NGK	Nederduitse Gereformeerde Kerk (Dutch Reformed Church)
NP	Nasionale Party (National Party)
PA	Publications Act, 1974
PAB	Publications Appeal Board
PCB	Publications Control Board
PEA	Publications and Entertainments Act, 1963
TPD	Transvaal Provincial Division of the Supreme Court of South Africa

Introduction

Literature in Law

In 1994, artistic freedom pertaining *inter alia* to literature was enshrined in the South African Constitution. Clearly, the establishment of this right was long overdue compared to other nations within the Commonwealth. Indeed, the legal framework and practices regarding the regulation of literature that were introduced following the nation's transition to a nonracial democracy seemed to form a decisive turning point in the history of South African censorship of literature. This book employs a historical sociological point of view to describe how the nation's emerging literary field helped pave the way for the constitutional entrenchment of this right in 1994. On the basis of institutional and poetological analyses of all the legal trials concerning literature that were held in South Africa during the period 1910–2010, it describes how the battles fought in and around the courts between literary, judicial, and executive elites eventually led to a constitutional *exceptio artis*[1] for literature. As the South African judiciary displayed an ongoing orientation toward both English and American law in this period, the analyses are firmly placed in the context of developments occurring concurrently in these two legal systems.

Four cases are central in all this: the 1965 trials around Wilbur Smith's debut novel *When the Lion Feeds* and Can Themba's short story "The Fugitives"; the 1974 trial regarding André Brink's novel *Kennis van die Aand* (translated by himself as *Looking on Darkness*); and the 1978 case concerning Etienne Leroux's novel *Magersfontein, O Magersfontein!* Yet close attention is also paid both to literary censorship and trials during the Union period (1910–1961) and to a number of important *administrative* censorship cases of the apartheid and post-apartheid periods, e.g., the cases of Ayi Kwei

Armah's *Two Thousand Seasons* (1980), Anthony Burgess's *Man of Nazareth* (1979, 1984, and 1992), Oswald Mtshali's *Fireflames* (1981), and Salman Rushdie's *The Satanic Verses* (2002).

Law and literature have a long and complex relationship in the West, a relationship that has intensified and become more interactive since the rise of positive law in the seventeenth and eighteenth centuries and the emergence of autonomous literary fields (*sensu* Bourdieu) in the nineteenth century.[2] The same holds true, indeed *a fortiori*, for the relationship between the two phenomena in colonial and postcolonial South Africa. Especially since the second half of the nineteenth century, literature has always been intensively regulated in this territory through legal concepts such as obscenity, blasphemy, state security, and defamation.

Quite some research has been done already on the administrative regulation of both imported and domestically produced literature in South Africa during the period between roughly 1870 and 1990 (see, e.g., Coggin; de Lange; Ehmeir; Geldenhuÿs, *Obseniteit*; Geldenhuÿs, *Pornografie*; McDonald, *Literature Police*; Silver, *Guide*). Of all the studies that have been written on South African censorship, McDonald's groundbreaking book titled *The Literature Police* (2009) is undoubtedly the most valuable one, not least because of the range it covers and because it, unlike most of the studies cited, was written at a time when the proverbial "fog of war" had cleared. Most of all, however, the merits of this study are a consequence of the fact that McDonald, in contrast to the other mentioned scholars, was able to benefit from the full disclosure of the files that had been kept by the apartheid censorship bureaucracy since its establishment in 1963. Yet, in all of its pioneering qualities, the book does leave at least two very important desiderata. Firstly, it touches but briefly on the period before 1963; and secondly, it also touches but superficially upon the *judicial* treatment of literature during apartheid. McDonald focuses almost exclusively on the administrative side of apartheid censorship, i.e., on the way in which literature was treated by the consecutive censorship boards that were established as of the early 1960s; he barely discusses the appeals against the censorship bureaucracy's decisions that were heard by the nation's Supreme Court. It is, however, highly unlikely that apartheid censorship was left completely unaffected by either the nation's pre-1963 tradition of regulating literature or the contemporary judicial treatment of the medium—indeed, apartheid censorship did not emerge in and neither did it operate in a vacuum. Hence, by mapping out both the earlier period and the contemporaneous judicial dimension of literature control, one might be able to describe and explain the behavior of the apartheid censorship boards more accurately.

Another advantage of taking the judicial regulation of literature into account would be that it can increase the comparatist potential of research on South African censorship and thus enable us to more adequately assess the nature of both this nation's history of censorship at large and of this history's constituent period of apartheid censorship. As law is generally internationally oriented and inclined toward weaving foreign legal concepts into its own fabric—and South African law certainly is, with its decisive orientation toward particularly English, but also U.S. law—the added dimension of the judicial treatment of literature would enable us to better assess, for instance, just how aberrant—or not—the legal and administrative regulation of literature during apartheid really was.

Yet a systematic historical analysis of the judicial treatment of literature in South Africa would not only facilitate a better understanding of the nation's censorship history, it could also provide us with valuable knowledge about another subject, pertaining to another area of research. For it appears that a particular type of analysis of the history of the judicial treatment of literature in a particular country can yield insights into the emergence of an autonomous literary field in the nation in question—knowledge that can both be sharpened and lifted to a supranational level when one compares it to the results of analyses of the judicial treatment of literary texts in other countries. Systematic historical research on Belgian, Dutch, and French literary trials in the nineteenth to twenty-first centuries (see Hupe; Beekman and Grüttemeier; Sapiro, *Responsabilité*) and synchronic and diachronic research that compares the judicial treatment of literature in Germany to the treatment of the medium in the Netherlands (see e.g., Grüttemeier, "Law") have demonstrated this. Departing from an interdisciplinary standpoint combining theories and methods derived from cultural sociological and literary studies, this kind of research has shown that literary trials might serve as a barometer registering the presence—or absence—of a relatively autonomous literary field in a nation (cf. Grüttemeier and Laros 205, 217). One might categorize this particular kind of research as "literature-in-law," i.e., as a type of law-and-literature research distinct from "law-in-literature" and "law-as-literature." The latter two kinds of research are generally distinguished when an attempt is being made to characterize this interdisciplinary "movement" (cf. Peters 443) that took off in the United States in the 1970s. While law-in-literature is generally aimed at examining how law is being represented in works of literature and law-as-literature at analyzing the operations and constructions of the law by means of linguistic or poststructuralist methodologies (cf. Olson and Kayman 5, 9, 10), literature-in-law seeks to examine how law, departing from its own institutional premises, deals with literature—whether through copyright laws, or through penal or civil laws regarding obscenity, blasphemy, state security, defamation, and so on (Grüttemeier and Laros 204).[3]

The examination of literary trials with the aim of gaining insights into the literary field of a particular nation, and/or the phenomenon of the literary field (*sensu* Bourdieu) at large constitutes an example of what might—in analogy to the well-known cultural anthropological notion of "participant observation"—be termed "participant objectivation."[4] This means the act of both identifying disciplinary problems, in this case literary scholarly ones, and attempting to solve them from an extra-disciplinary standpoint, in this case from the outside perspective of the law (Grüttemeier, "Interdisciplinariteit" 71–72; cf. also Grüttemeier and Laros 205). The above-mentioned studies on the Belgian, Dutch, French, and German literary fields have proven to be fruitful examples of this method: they demonstrated that the attainment of a relatively autonomous status of the four mentioned fields in, respectively, the nineteenth century (France and Germany) and around 1900 (Belgium and the Netherlands) was accompanied by the rise of a concept of *exceptio artis* in the law of these respective nations. That is to say that literature was granted a special legal status. This status, however, did not represent a general guarantee of immunity for the individual author from prosecution. Rather, it guaranteed a relative *institutional* autonomy of literature vis-à-vis the law, i.e., a protection of literature, as an institution, from intervention by other institutions such as the government, the Church, and so on. In the Netherlands and Germany, the establishment of this relative legal autonomy for literature was *inter alia* underpinned by contemporary poetological variants of idealist aesthetics. The quite similar constellation that arose in Belgium, France, Germany, and the Netherlands appears to have remained stable to this day, both with regard to its institutional and its poetological dimension (see Hupe; Sapiro, *Responsabilité*; Grüttemeier, "Law").[5]

It is plausible to hypothesize that the findings of the research on the Belgian, Dutch, French, and German fields will provide an apt description for the situation in other countries whose political, legal, and literary systems are based on ideologies that predominantly stem from the (Western) Enlightenment. In this respect, it seems that they might thus also possess validity for the situation in twentieth-century South Africa. On the other hand, however, there are some particularities to the history of this latter country—such as the (post)colonial interconnectedness of its literary and legal systems with those of the (former) mother countries and the anomalous political development which the country underwent—that might necessitate at least an adaptation of the above-described model. By way of systematically analyzing all judicial proceedings (both civil and criminal) concerning literature that were conducted during the period 1910–2010, this book will attempt to determine whether or not such research findings from other countries can be transferred to the South African case. The choice of 1910 as point of departure is motivated by a historical fact: in this year, South Africa became a self-governing Dominion of the British Empire. It is, moreover, highly unlikely that one can speak of an autonomous literary field (in the Bourdieuian sense) before this year.[6]

The analysis of the South African case will be guided by the following question: how did the South African judiciary treat literature institutionally and poetologically during the period 1910–2010, and how does this correlate with the structuralization of a literary field within the nation? In attempting to answer this overall question, the analyses of the separate trials will each be guided by two clusters of (sub)questions, one pertaining to the institutional dimension of the trial in question and one pertaining to the poetological dimension. The main questions that guide the analyses of the institutional dimension of the trials are: What degree of institutional autonomy is being claimed for literature in court, and what degree is being granted to it by the court? How might one explain the position-takings of the various actors with regard to this issue in light of synchronic developments regarding the production of South African literature? The main questions that guide the poetological analyses are: Which conceptions of literature—even if only rudimentary (cf. Edelman and Heinich 151ff)—are employed by the actors involved in the judicial proceedings, and which are legally legitimized? What is the relationship between these conceptions of literature and contemporary poetological debates held within the literary field?

The overall analysis will roughly be structured around the statutory shifts in literature regulation that occurred in the mentioned period—a century encompassing the birth of the Union of South Africa (1910), the rise to power of Afrikaner Nationalism via the Nasionale Party (1948), the birth of the Republic of South Africa (1961), and the decline of Afrikaner hegemony, resulting in the birth of a nonracial democratic South Africa (1994).[7] Another aspect of the structuration of the analysis needs mentioning, namely the fact that the judicial proceedings are being discussed chronologically. The reason for this procedure lies in the nature of the South African legal system. South African law operates according to the principle of *stare decisis*, or binding precedent, and a consequence of this is that an important part of the judicial treatment of literature evolves on the basis of earlier judgments made in court. A final point that should also be mentioned is that only trials that focused on texts are being analyzed in this study; criminal cases centering on literary authors (such as the case against Alex La Guma, which formed a part of the so-called Treason Trial [1956–1961], or the trials against Breyten Breytenbach in 1975 and 1977) are not discussed. The reason for this is that in the latter kind of trial different actors are involved (unlike in the former kind, literary expert witnesses do not play an important role in this kind of trial) and different problematics are central (cf. Grüttemeier, "Zo")—certainly, the question of literary autonomy will not be battled over in this kind of trial. In other words, it does not appear that these criminal cases can fulfill the barometer function that trials around texts seem to be able to.

FIELD THEORY

When one seeks to systematically research the way in which legal actors dealt with literature within a professional setting, one needs to find a theoretical model that makes it possible to analyze professional legal behavior within a social context. A context, that is, which reveals the societal role of literature as one that changes over time. Such a model might be found in the field theoretical model created by Pierre Bourdieu (see Bourdieu, *Field*; Bourdieu, *Rules*) and developed further by others, for example by scholars in France (see e.g., Sapiro, *Guerre*; Viala, *Naissance*), Germany (see e.g., Joch and Wolf; Magerski) and the Netherlands (see e.g., Dorleijn and van Rees, *Productie*; van Rees and Dorleijn, *Impact*). Let us, before looking at the applicability of the model for studying legal dealings with literature, first discuss its more general characteristics. These characteristics are lucidly set forth by Gisèle Sapiro in her 2003 article "The Literary Field between the State and the Market."

The Bourdieuian Model of the Literary Field

Sapiro opens her article by stating that "[c]ontrary to the ideology of the uncreated creator, the concept of 'literary field' forged by Pierre Bourdieu implies that literary activity does not escape the constraints governing the social world" (441). Yet, she continues, "unlike the Marxist theory of art as pure reflection of reality, the concept of field suggests that the cultural universes have a specific logic of functioning and their own rules, which means that they enjoy a certain degree of autonomy" (441). What the concept of autonomy is meant to signify here is freedom from various types of external constraints related to the conditions of production that are exercised either by the state or the market. In most Western European nations, this freedom appears to have been attained sometime in the nineteenth century.[8] This development was catalyzed by the liberalization of the book market, which, in turn, was brought about by the rise of economic and political liberalism (442, 450): motivated by political and economic liberal principles, the state ceased its strict regulation of the production of cultural goods and left it in the hands of producers (442). Facilitated by this economic and political liberalization, a quickly expanding publishing industry appeared, producing books for a public that was ever growing as a result of the generalization of school attendance (450–51). In this rapidly evolving book market a new type of writer could emerge: the *professional* writer (450). It was not long before professional organizations arose that furthered the interests of this kind of writer (450). Another development that accompanied the rapid growth of the book market was that a shift occurred in the position of literary genres: the novel became the dominant genre at the expense of poetry, which became marginalized (448).

As the professional author emerged, the literary field became organized around two poles: one being a "pole of large production," at which "the law of the market and ... the sanction of the large public (measured according to sales)" prevails, and the other a "pole of restricted production," at which "the judgment of peers as opposed to the taste of the profane public" is the norm (450–51). The dual development of the rise of professional authorship and book production becoming structured around these two poles represents the main phase in the process of the autonomization of the literary field (451). An important marker of this autonomization process is the increase in the number of literary magazines and reviews, which form privileged sites for dialogue among peers, relatively secure from administrative and economic constraints (451). At a certain point in time, the judgment of peers and literary experts gets to be recognized by both the state and the market, the two "poles that determine literary activity" (451). The observation regarding state recognition is particularly relevant for the present study, as literary expertise clearly played an important role in twentieth-century trials throughout the West (see e.g., Beekman and Grüttemeier; Conter; de Grazia; Grüttemeier, "Law"; Grüttemeier and Laros; LaCapra; Ladenson; Sapiro). The fact that juridical elites started to (legally) recognize literary elites—in practice, often literary academics—at a certain point in time, might be explained through Bourdieu's concept of homology (see Bourdieu, *Field* 44, 84, 97 et passim): this recognition might indicate that as of such a point, one might speak of a homology between the (authoritative) position that the juridical and literary elites occupy within their respective fields. The fact that this recognition is known to have also manifested itself in judiciaries' adoption of conceptions of literature dominant among contemporary literary elites (see Grüttemeier, "Law" 193f et passim; Grüttemeier and Laros 215 et passim), or the fact that one can point out homologies between the aesthetic norms adhered to by both elites, might be regarded as further evidence of such structural homology. In the light of these observations, this book seeks to investigate *inter alia* what role literary expertise played in South African law during the period 1910–2010.

Another important effect of the "economic law of the market" should be mentioned here, namely that it contributed to modifying the literary landscape (457). Among other things, it led to certain genres rising to prominence (the thriller, romantic fiction, the novel), and others becoming marginalized (poetry, drama) (457). With this development taking place, however, that other pole determining literary activity, the state, was given a chance to once again interfere in the production of literature, though this time not in a negative sense, but in a positive one. For it could go on and become instrumental in "saving the rights and freedom of creation from the merciless sanction of the market and the risks of the cultural producers of being exploited" (457). By means of the creation of authors' rights and policies aimed at aiding literary creation through, for example, awarding prizes and scholarships and subsidizing authors, publishers, libraries, and magazines, it could start acting in support of the pole of restricted production, i.e., the autonomous pole (457–58). As the existing research on the legal treatment of literature in Belgium, France, Germany, and the Netherlands suggests, the *exceptio artis* pertaining to literature that arose in these countries was for a considerable part a result of the emergence of this kind of benevolence toward the medium on the part of the state (see Hupe; Sapiro, *Responsabilité*; Grüttemeier, "Law"). The present study will therefore also be directed at finding out whether the South African state began displaying this type of benevolence at any point and, if so, whether this had consequences for the legal status of literature.

The Concept of Autonomy

The most important feature of the Bourdieuian model for this particular study is the concept of autonomy. Dorleijn, Grüttemeier, and Korthals Altes distinguish three distinct but interrelated domains that the concept can refer to within a field theoretical framework: the first is the autonomy of the literary field with respect to other fields; the second is internal field autonomy, i.e., "[t]he autonomy of the field as self-regulative, through the presence of its own internal institutions and actors" (xiii); and the third is the autonomy of the norms that are dominant within the field (xiiiff), that is, poetological norms. This book follows Dorleijn et al.'s conceptualization of the term and thus distinguishes two dimensions to which the concept of autonomy can pertain: an institutional and a poetological dimension.

External Autonomy

The first kind of autonomy that Dorleijn et al. distinguish is crucial to this study. As to this dimension of the concept, they observe that Bourdieuian theory regards the history of the literary field, as it does that of other social fields, to be a process of progressive autonomization with respect to external powers and influences—heteronomous powers, in short (xiii). They distinguish four main types of heteronomous forces: (1) economic forces in the sense of market pressures; (2) political forces, i.e., "political parties, state power and authorities grounded in political power" (xiv); (3) religious and moral forces; and (4) concurrent media forces such as journalism (xiv). Although Dorleijn et al. speak of the history of the literary field in terms of "progressive autonomization," they emphatically issue two warnings in this respect: Firstly, that one should not think it possible for a literary field to ever become absolutely autonomous; there will always be heteronomous forces at work, even though the actors operating within the field tend to contend otherwise (xv). In other words, the institutional autonomy of literature will always be but a relative one (cf. also Dorleijn, "Autonomy" 124; Dorleijn and van den Akker 99; van Rees and Dorleijn, *Impact* 15). Secondly, that the process of "progressive autonomization" with respect to the market, the state, religion, and so on by no means represents an irreversible and homogenous process: it is indeed very possible, they observe, that the autonomy of the literary field decreases in certain respects and due to certain causes (e.g., war, economic developments) during a specific period (xvi).

A third emphatic statement that Dorleijn et al. make in their discussion of what might be labeled "external" field autonomy (cf. xxiii), is that an important premise of field theory is that literary fields function as *national* fields (xvii). "This is already implied," they state, "by the description of the autonomization of the field by Bourdieu (the field of cultural production is situated within the field of power) and Sapiro (economic and political liberalization, which is a national phenomenon [*sic*], establishes the preconditions for an autonomizing field)" (xvii). Although I tend to partly disagree with Dorleijn et al.—I believe that especially economic pressures will often prove to be of an international nature—the focus of this book will also be on the national, as it will analyze the actions of national actors and institutions (both legal and literary).

Internal Autonomy

When it comes to the second kind of autonomy, internal field autonomy, Bourdieuian theory looks at the extent to which specific bodies are involved in the material and symbolic production and distribution of literature (xvii). "In line with Bourdieu," Dorleijn et al. contend, "it can be stated that in addition to the book market, specific institutions of production, consecration and legitimation and distribution also constitute preconditions for a relatively autonomous field" (xvii). Furthermore, Bourdieuian theory advances that the rise of the literary field in the nineteenth century can be described in terms of differentiation, specialization, and professionalization: the emergence of modern authorship, publishers with an exclusively literary list, specialized literary criticism, academic criticism, a prize system, literary education—all of these phenomena represent manifestations of these processes (xvii). It is evident, though, that depending on the period and the country being analyzed, processes of differentiation, specialization, and professionalization vary (xvii). The Bourdieuian model, which has of course often been criticized for its Francocentricity, can indeed not be considered to be universally valid: it will often need to be tailored so that an adequate analysis of foreign, i.e., non-French, fields might become possible (xviii; cf. Dorleijn and van

Rees, *Productie* 24). It certainly appears to be in need of adaptation when one seeks to analyze "small" literary fields (cf. Kohler, "Feld" 35–36 et passim; Kohler, "Institutional Autonomy" 13, 27; Kohler, "National Disposition" 36–37), or postcolonial ones (cf. van der Waal 15 et passim). Indeed, the way in which a field is structured—i.e., the overall size and number of specialized bodies it has and the way in which these bodies relate to one another—has consequences for the extent of its field-internal autonomy (xviii). Furthermore, the relationship between the degree of internal and external autonomy, or, put differently, between "the degree of internal structuration and the degree of independence from external heteronomous powers" (xviii)—the state and the market—is not homologous, but varies according to the situation, and should, therefore, be assessed historically and empirically for each case anew (xviii). As the aim of this book is first and foremost to determine what the court cases concerning literature conducted in South Africa during the period 1910–2010 might tell us about, precisely, the degree of independence the South African literary field enjoyed vis-à-vis the external heteronomous power that the law represents, the internal structuration of the field will only play a secondary role in the analyses. This second dimension of the autonomy concept will only be foregrounded—i.e., data concerning the literary field collected in the past will only be brought in—to verify the findings that this study will yield.

Aesthetic Autonomy

The third kind of autonomy, finally, concerns the autonomy of aesthetic norms. Like the dimension of external autonomy, this dimension also plays a crucial role in this study. Whereas the two kinds of autonomy that have just been discussed pertain to the institutional dimension of the literary field, aesthetic autonomy concerns the level at which "literature" is conceptualized (xix). Yet this conceptual dimension is strongly related to the institutional dimension—and both its "internal" and "external" components. As Dorleijn, Grüttemeier, and Korthals Altes succinctly put it:

> In differentiating and specializing fields, with their own institutions and their own dynamics, specific rules of conduct are developed, along with specific social practices, and hence specific systems of communication, mechanisms of value assessment and internal criteria for evaluation and legitimation. The power of disposal that the producers of culture hold over their own means of production and distribution, and over their own authorities for evaluation and consecration, highly coincide. In this respect, conceptions of literature and actual institutions are two sides of the same coin. (xix)

In fact, Dorleijn et al. contend that the autonomy of a literary field is in part constituted by "[t]he existence of specific principles of classification and ranking," as they are being applied by "specific consecration authorities" (xix; cf. also Kohler "Institutional Autonomy" 7ff; Sapiro, "Literary Field" 449). The degree to which principles of hierarchization can be considered to be autonomous represents the degree to which such principles are independent from both external and internal heteronomous hierarchizations, such as political or religious norms (external) and the principles of actors that are part of the field yet at the same time listen to the demands of the market (internal) (Dorleijn, Grüttemeier, and Korthals Altes xix). Indeed, Bourdieu found that the autonomous sector of the field, i.e., the subfield of restricted production, operates through what he conceptualized as a mechanism of reversed economy (cf. Bourdieu, *Field* 29ff; Bourdieu, *Rules* 81ff). He explains exactly how this mechanism works as follows:

> [I]n the most perfectly autonomous sector of the field of cultural production, where the only audience aimed at is other producers . . . the economy of practices is based, as in a generalized game of "loser wins," on a systematic inversion of the fundamental principles of all ordinary economies: that of business (it excludes the pursuit of profit and does not guarantee any sort of correspondence between investments and monetary gains), that of power (it condemns honours and temporal greatness), and even that of institutionalized cultural authority (the absence of any academic training or consecration may be considered a virtue). (Bourdieu, *Field* 39)

In this "loser wins" economy, failure in terms of "ordinary economics" indeed forms a requisite for symbolic success (Dorleijn, Grüttemeier, and Korthals Altes xx).

With respect to Bourdieu's conceptualization of the two major categories of hierarchization principles (autonomous and heteronomous) structuring the literary field and the way in which these categories are incorporated into his overall model of the cultural/literary field, two things should be noted. The first is that although the categories are sometimes taken to be placed in direct opposition to one another in Bourdieu's scheme (cf. Kohler, "Institutional Autonomy" 13), this book follows Dorleijn et al. in their contention that they are better not understood in terms of a binary opposition, but rather as denoting *gradual* positions. This book thus departs from the premise that literary conceptual autonomy represents but a relative autonomy (Dorleijn, "Autonomy" 144; Grüttemeier, "Law" 176), just like its institutional counterpart. It therefore does not take at face value conceptions of literature that lay claim to being of an absolute autonomous character (e.g., *l'art pour l'art*). Rather, and here we come to the crux of this study's theoretical starting point, it regards such conceptions to be representing manifestations of strategic position-taking: looked at from an analytical viewpoint—or "meta-perspective" (Dorleijn, "Autonomy" 144; cf. also van Rees 104ff; van Rees and Dorleijn, *Impact* 2)—these conceptions will be revealed as being inextricably tied up with a literary and a societal field (Dorleijn, "Autonomy" 144; van Rees and Dorleijn, *Impact* 2ff).[9] Yet this book not only takes each utterance concerning literary conceptual issues it encounters as representing manifestations of strategic position-taking, it also takes utterances regarding institutional matters (e.g., "the arts are free") thus. These latter utterances, which just like their literary conceptual counterparts are also made on the "object level"[10] (Dorleijn, "Autonomy" 144), should not be taken as representing analytical descriptions either—in this case: of the degree of institutional autonomy present at the time of utterance.

The second point that should be noted is that according to Bourdieu, the appearance of autonomous principles of hierarchization (or autonomous poetological norms) runs parallel to the emergence of an autonomous literary field, that is to say, to the later stages of such an emergence (*Rules* 61 et passim). As he himself put it:

> The degree of autonomy of a field of cultural production is revealed to the extent that the principle of external hierarchization there is subordinated to the principle of internal hierarchization: the greater the autonomy, the more the symbolic relationship of forces is favourable to producers who are the most independent of demand, and the more the break tends to be noticeable between the two poles of the field, that is, between the *subfield of restricted production*, where producers have only other producers for clients (who are also their direct competitors), and the *subfield of large-scale production*, which finds itself *symbolically* excluded and discredited. (*Rules* 217; Bourdieu's emphasis)

The validity of this position has also been questioned though: it has been argued that in certain countries—*nota bene* including France—a great degree of field autonomy was attained in a historical period that long preceded the emergence of autonomist poetological norms in these fields (Dorleijn, Grüttemeier, and Korthals Altes xx; Dorleijn and van den Akker 22). In this light, research aimed at analyzing the exact relationship between poetological and institutional autonomy, such as the present study, becomes all the more relevant.

INSTITUTIONAL AND POETOLOGICAL ANALYSIS

Yet even though it seems that Bourdieu's position is in need of qualification, there seems to be great consensus among contemporary literary, cultural, and sociological scholars that it is necessary to always study literary and poetological phenomena in relation to the social context in which they appear: when one disregards this context, one cannot come to meaningful conclusions—i.e., conclusions reached from a meta-perspective—about such phenomena (cf. Dorleijn, "Plaats" 4). Since the societal or, more specifically, institutional, and poetological dimensions of the literary field are so intricately connected, Dorleijn and van Rees argue that they ought to be conceptualized in relation to each other (*Productie* 25; cf. also Dorleijn, "Autonomy" 134; van Rees 108 et passim). Indeed, they state that it is necessary to come up with what might be termed an "institutional reading" of literary theoretical and critical texts, to be able to understand just what such texts really represent (Dorleijn, "Plaats" 7; van Rees 108).[11] At the same time, they hold that such textual interpretation forms an essential element of (literary historical) institutional research (Dorleijn, "Plaats" 7, 15; van Rees 108).[12]

Just as analyses of literary theoretical or critical texts can reveal something about the literary field in which they circulate (cf. Dorleijn, "Niet" 3ff; cf. also Dorleijn, "Plaats" 6ff), so can analyses of literary theoretical utterances of actors involved in judicial proceedings concerning literary works (cf. Grüttemeier and Laros 205 et passim). For as much as poetological position-taking in the literary arena is always tied up with a societal/institutional context, so too is such positioning in court. Thus, the employment of a conception of literature, or a part thereof, in court can, for example, represent the making of an alliance with an actor, or group of actors, from within the literary field (cf. Grüttemeier, "Law" 180, 184, 192)—an actor, or group of actors, that enjoys a certain, in most cases powerful, status within the field. The application of (elements of) a conception of literature in a courtroom can also reveal the (societal) reach of such (elements of) a poetics (cf. Grüttemeier and Laros 205 et passim). In these and other ways, the appearance of poetological precepts in a literary trial might reveal something about the degree of institutional autonomy enjoyed by the literary field from which the work that is on trial emanates.

Taking into account the inherently *normative* status of conceptions of literature (cf. Dorleijn, Grüttemeier and Korthals Altes xi; van Rees 103 et passim), i.e., "the set of ideas held by a (group of) author(s) or reviewer(s) on the nature and function of literature" (van Rees 103), the analysis of the literary theoretical principles employed in court can only serve an instrumental purpose: it can only stand in service of an *institutional* analysis, just as the analysis of conceptions of literature employed in field internal settings (cf. Dorleijn, "Autonomy" 123–24; Dorleijn, "Plaats" 11; van Rees 114). By analyzing conceptions of literature as if they appeared in a vacuum, one would run the risk of confusing the self-positioning of actors with objective-analytical scholarly observation. Instead of taking self-positionings at face value, a scholar should ask themselves: why does actor *x* place text *y* in a specific poetological frame at the moment of utterance? In other words, they should seek to analyze conceptions of literature as they relate to the *context*—i.e., first and foremost, the *institutional* context—in which they appear.

LITERATURE IN LAW

The method of combined institutional and poetological analysis as described above has proven to be fruitful for analyzing literary trials. The application of this method enabled Klaus Beekman and Ralf Grüttemeier to describe the rise of the concept of *exceptio artis* in both early twentieth-century Dutch law (see e.g., Beekman and Grüttemeier) and nineteenth and early twentieth-century German law (see e.g., Grüttemeier, "Law"). Moreover, it enabled Katharina Hupe to track the emergence of an artistic freedom pertaining to literature in Belgium around 1900 (see Hupe).

As was mentioned at the outset of this chapter, the concept of *exceptio artis* represents the idea that an utterance that in itself constitutes an offense might be judged otherwise if it occurs in a work of art. In Germany, that is to say, Prussia, the concept first emerged in a legal context in a bill of 1847 created to "organize matters concerning art" (Grüttemeier, "Law" 182; Knies 209ff). The bill never entered the statute books, but what it clearly evidenced was that the special status that it intended to grant art through this concept was meant to represent a guaranteed substantial degree of *institutional* freedom—i.e., a freedom from intervention by other institutions (politics, Church, government, etc.)—not an individual freedom that would allow the artist to do whatever he pleased (Anschütz 659ff; Grüttemeier, "Law" 181–82; Knies 27; Petersen 36f et passim). As it turns out, the concept of an expressly *limited exceptio artis* remained stable in German legal thinking throughout the nineteenth and the first third of the twentieth century (Grüttemeier, "Law" 182; Petersen 187), although it was not until 1919 that the concept was incorporated into statutory law—namely into the constitution of the Weimar Republic (Grüttemeier, "Law" 180–81; Polak 55ff). In fact, leaving aside the period 1933–1945, one can observe that the concept of the relative *exceptio artis* has remained stable until this very day: it entered the statute books once again in 1949, namely in the *Grundgesetz für die Bundesrepublik Deutschland* (Basic Law for the Federal Republic of Germany) and has remained part of German law—indeed, with the same meaning it had acquired before it temporarily disappeared from the legal arena—ever since (Grüttemeier, "Law" 191–92).

In the sense that German law acknowledges artistic freedom as an institutional freedom of art, to be distinguished from individual freedom in the name of art, it regards freedom of art and freedom of speech as two different kinds of freedoms that pertain to two different kinds of human activities and are treated differently by law (Grüttemeier, "Law" 181, 188; Knies 214ff). However, no hierarchy is intended between the two, nor is one systematically possible (Grüttemeier, "Law" 188–89; Knies 214ff). Indeed, both represent (equipollent) constitutional values. This status does not render these freedoms absolute though: both can be limited by other constitutional values when they come into conflict with each other (Grüttemeier, "Rechter" 44). Artistic freedom in Germany is thus intrinsically relative in that it, as a matter of principle, can always be outweighed by other constitutional values (Grüttemeier, "Law" 188–89). It can, however, not be outweighed by general laws (189).

The relative institutional autonomy that was bestowed upon literature within German law was brought into being by two major developments in eighteenth- and nineteenth-century Germany: firstly, the so-called "Wende zum Kulturstaat" (cultural state-turn) and, secondly, the rise of idealist aesthetics (Grüttemeier, "Law" 182–83; Huber, *Problematik* 8ff; Huber, *Deutsche Verfassungsgeschichte* 275; Knies 148ff; 207ff; Petersen 191). The former concept, which is especially connected with the name of Wilhelm von Humboldt, refers to a cultural political shift that took place in Prussia in the first decades of the nineteenth century (Grüttemeier, "Law" 182). In this period, the Prussian sovereign's position toward art changed dramatically. Whereas traditionally, the sovereign had approached art as a potentially subversive medium that should be keenly regulated, the head of state now came to regard it as something that had specific potential for the general good of the state and that therefore deserved to be protected and fostered (182–83; Huber, *Problematik* 8ff; Huber, *Deutsche Verfassungsgeschichte* 275; Knies 148ff; 207ff; Kulhoff 248). As some of the findings presented in Sapiro's article discussed in the previous section suggest, this development might be part of a more general trend occurring in the West at the time (see Sapiro, "Literary Field" 457–58).[13] Thus, the first form of *exceptio artis* came to be embedded in an instance of active state involvement in art, whose main objective was the promotion of cultural unity (Grüttemeier, "Law" 183). In this sense, one can not only define artistic freedom as a negative freedom, i.e., as a freedom from direct political, religious, or moral interference, but also as a positive one, namely as a freedom that enables art to play an important role in shaping a national culture (184). The second development, the rise of idealist aesthetics, formed a catalyst for the emergence of an institutional autonomy of literature in that the law used this particular aesthetics to underpin the newly created artistic freedom—clear evidence of this can *inter alia* be found in late nineteenth-century judgments of the *Reichsgericht*, the highest German court between 1871 and 1933 (183; Knies 148ff). Apparently, the law was looking for established allies, that is to say, authoritative poetics, in the field of art and literature so as to stabilize the newly formed autonomy for art and literature vis-à-vis the law (Grüttemeier, "Law" 180, 184; Knies 148ff).

Systematic historical analysis of the situation in the Netherlands has revealed that a similar development occurred there. There too literature and art were given a special status by law, that is to say, a relative institutional autonomy, and there too this status was brought into being through both the emergence of a general benevolence of the law with respect to art and literature and the rise of a variant of idealist aesthetics (Beekman and Grüttemeier 76ff; Grüttemeier, "Law" 180). This development started a few decades later than it had in Germany, though: in Germany/Prussia, one can find the earliest traces of an emerging concept of *exceptio artis* in 1847, the first judicial employment of the concept in an 1893 case of the *Reichsgericht*, and the concept entering the statute books in 1919 and once again in 1949. The Dutch case shows that the concept first emerged in legal debates in 1900, that it subsequently—albeit merely in passing—was employed in a 1908 trial concerning certain picture postcards, and that it in 1920 became part of the judicial treatment of literature, namely through a precedent set in a trial concerning a translation of Henri Barbusse's *L'enfer* (Beekman and Grüttemeier 59ff; Grüttemeier and Laros 206). Another similarity between the German and Dutch cases lies in the fact that the position of the law concerning literature as it arose in these two countries has remained stable throughout the last century. This despite the fact that since roughly 1950, several attempts have been made in courts in both nations to get more far-reaching autonomous positions accepted with regard to both aesthetics and literature's institutional status and that some Dutch and German judges showed themselves willing to adopt such positions, as well (Grüttemeier, "Law" 186–89, 191–92; Knies 24f et passim). Consistently, both German and Dutch law grant literature a relative institutional autonomy—not the literary writer an *individual* freedom (Grüttemeier, "Law" 181–82)—and underpin this position with (elements stemming from) relatively autonomous conceptions of literature, i.e., conceptions of literature that do not really cut the link between reality and the work of art, but rather hold that the latter can only be separated from the former to a lesser or greater *degree* (184, 191–92). The idealistic notion that a work of art ought to transform empirical reality into a separate higher unity formed a crucial catalyst in the position-taking of the law in both countries (184).

LITERATURE AND THE LAW IN SOUTH AFRICA

On the basis of the comparatist research on the German and Dutch cases, further supplemented with the research into the French and Belgian cases, one can formulate hypotheses of which might be expected—precisely because of the comparatist nature of the research—that they will also possess validity for other countries whose political, legal, and literary systems are based on ideologies emanating to a large extent from the Enlightenment. For the South African case, the following hypotheses appear plausible:

1. The formation of an autonomous literary field (*sensu* Bourdieu) is accompanied by the granting of a special legal status to literature (*exceptio artis*) that can be characterized as a relative institutional autonomy. This legal recognition might be regarded as representing a decisive step in this formation.
2. If the juridical actors that collaborate in the development of a relative legal autonomy of literature take a poetological stance, they can generally be shown to have adopted/be adopting the conceptions of literature that are being legitimized by contemporary literary experts as being dominant and up-to-date.
3. The relative legal autonomy of literature which accompanies the emergence of an autonomous literary field is robust: its fundamental characteristics remain unaltered, even though in the course of time more far-reaching positions may be defended in court and some judges might reveal themselves willing to accept such positions.

The present study will investigate to what extent these hypotheses are valid for the case of South Africa.

In order to determine the validity of these hypotheses, the institutional and poetological analyses will for an important part be aimed at reconstructing the criteria that came to guide the judiciary's approach toward literature. That is to say that the overall analyses will be directed at determining which criteria were being employed by the judiciary, and how, when, and why they were being used. An example would be the admission of literary expert evidence. As we saw above, literary expertise appears to have played an important role both in the internal and external autonomization of literary fields, notably in the autonomization of literary fields vis-à-vis juridical fields. What this book will attempt to find out is whether this criterion came to play a role in juridical debates concerning literature in South Africa. If it did come to play a role, the analysis will subsequently be directed at determining what strategical function could be ascribed to the employment of the criterion at the moment of usage, and what the application of the criterion might tell us about the degree of institutional and poetological autonomy that literature enjoyed in relation to the law at that particular point in time.

At points where the observations made concerning the judicial treatment of literature will be linked to available data regarding the South African literary field[14] —both with respect to the institutional and poetological levels—the focus will lie on data concerning the Afrikaans and English subfields. The former was, and is, mainly comprised of actors from what during apartheid was called the "Coloured" section of the population and Afrikaners; the latter mainly of both English-language whites and "non-whites," notably "Blacks," writing in English. In those two parts of the South African field, autonomization processes appear to have emerged earliest. In the case of the Afrikaans subfield *inter alia* because of impulses that were given by the state (cf. Willemse 429–30, 446)—impulses that indeed were motivated by a nation-building philosophy that seems comparable to the above-described *Wende zum Kulturstaat* in nineteenth-century Germany. Those two parts of the field, moreover, seemingly reached a (relatively) autonomous status earliest—in fact, if one conceptualizes the South African field as consisting of three subfields, namely an African language,[15] an Afrikaans, and an English one,[16] the latter two subfields are the only subfields that have as yet come to reach a relative institutional autonomy (cf. van der Waal 78–79).

A few remarks are in place here: firstly, that until the 1940s, even well into the 1970s, the English-language subfield was to a considerable extent bound up with the metropolitan literary centers of London and New York (McDonald, "Book" 804, 810; van der Vlies 707ff; van der Waal 51). Secondly, that the South African literary field, as a consequence of *inter alia* its multilingual, multicultural, and postcolonial character, is a highly complex field (cf. van der Waal 15ff). This complexity should fully be accounted for when one sets out to describe an aspect or aspects of the field from an "inside perspective," i.e., through the analysis of inner field phenomena. As this book focuses on the way in which *extra-literary*, namely judicial, institutions positioned themselves vis-à-vis the field, and on what the judicial positioning might tell us about the stage of the field's institutional development, it is not necessary to theoretically untangle all the complexities of the South African field. Indeed, it would be quite redundant to do so. The "barometer" function that the judicial treatment of literature can form is necessarily somewhat crude. It will only enable one to more roughly measure the overall amount of institutional autonomy a literary field has reached at a certain time and the societal reach that poetological positions might have. It is not an instrument that can be applied to describe the internal structure of the field in a detailed manner.

This book will proceed as follows: chapter 1 will present the analysis of the early trials concerning literature conducted in South Africa in the period 1910–1955—and in fact, it also deals with two pre-Union cases. Chapters 2 and 3 discuss the trials of the period 1955–1975: chapter 2 analyzes the trials against Can Themba's short story "The Fugitives" and Wilbert Smith's novel *When the Lion Feeds*; chapter 3 that of André Brink's *Kennis van die Aand*. Chapter 4 deals with the period 1975–1980, first and foremost with the review case of Etienne Leroux's *Magersfontein, O Magersfontein!* Chapter 5 focuses on the semi-judicial treatment of literature in the period 1980–2010. The conclusion formulates an answer to this book's main question.

NOTES

1. The principle of *exceptio artis* implies that utterances that constitute an offense—in the legal sense of the word—per se can be judged otherwise when they occur in a literary context (Grüttemeier and Laros 204n4; Janssens 349).
2. One should perhaps note here that various scholars have observed that tendencies toward autonomization manifested themselves one or two centuries earlier in countries such as France (see Viala, *Naissance*; Viala, "Bourdieu"), England (see Kayman; Williams, *Culture*; Williams, *Long Revolution*), and Germany (see Schmidt; Stockhorst; Mix).
3. For some more recent examples of law-in-literature research, see Kader and Stanford; Lockey; Nabers; Visconsi. For an example of this kind of research that specifically pertains to South Africa, see Schalkwyk. One could also count studies of aesthetical position-takings in which the relationship between literature and the law is specifically being focused upon as law-in-literature research (see e.g., Biko; Coetzee, "Into"; Coetzee, "Jerusalem Prize"; Ndebele, *Rediscovery*; Ndebele, *Fine Lines*; Sachs, "Art"). For some examples of law-as-literature research, see Brooks; Kayman; Schneck. For examples of this kind of research that especially relate to South Africa, see Sanders, and also Clarkson. For other examples of literature-in-law research, see Conter; de Grazia; LaCapra; Ladenson.
4. The term was coined by Bourdieu (see *Schwierige Interdisziplinarität* 172ff).
5. For the emergence of *exceptio artis* in German law, see also Knies.
6. A systematic historical analysis of the South African literary field or of any of its constituent parts, i.e., its African-, Afrikaans-, and English-language subfields, has not been carried out yet (cf. van der Waal 3n8). In her 2006 dissertation titled "The Battle over the Books: Processes of Selection in the South African Literary Field," Margriet van der Waal gives an initial impetus to such an endeavor, but her focus is on the 1980s and 1990s only. Furthermore, as she acknowledges herself, the analysis she presents cannot really be called systematic—she herself describes it to be "cursory, incomplete and reductionist" (34). Yet even though no systematic research into the South African literary field or its subfields exists, there is of course much good research available that delivers data on the basis of which one might formulate hypotheses regarding the institutional development and the current state of this field and its subfields. For data regarding the institutions realizing both the material and symbolical production and the distribution of literature in South Africa, see e.g., Attwell and Attridge, and especially the pieces of Driver, Johnson, Masilela, McDonald, Swanepoel, and Willemse therein; Barnett; Cronjé; Galloway and Venter; Kunene; le Roux, Struik and Labuschagne; McDonald, *Literature Police*; Sandwith; Senekal; van Coller and Odendaal; van der Waal.
7. For a comprehensive history of South Africa, see Hamilton, Mbenga, and Ross; and Ross, Kelk Mager, and Nasson. For a comprehensive history of Afrikanerdom, see Giliomee.
8. As already stated, however, various scholars have observed that tendencies toward autonomization manifested themselves one or two centuries earlier in some of the larger European countries.
9. Coming to realize this connection, one might conclude that conceptions of literature are not only gradual, but also polydimensional (Kohler, "Institutional Autonomy" 13).
10. As opposed to the "meta-level."
11. An institutional reading of literary theoretical or critical texts can demonstrate that such texts contain manifestations of behavior. In a recent article, Dorleijn, for instance, showed that when one takes account of what he calls the "institutional valences" of the elements mentioned in a literary theoretical or critical text, i.e., when one looks at the relevant relations that the elements have with other elements that are connected in one way or another to positions in the field and consequently to its history—examples of valences would be publishing houses, fellow critics, literary prizes, genre classifications, poetological debates and so on—one can observe that the text displays certain forms of (textual) behavior—such as classifying, hierarchizing, legitimizing, positioning (Dorleijn, "Niet" 3ff; cf. also Dorleijn, "Plaats" 6ff). At the same time, an analysis of a given corpus of theoretical or critical texts can provide us with information about the institutional context that surrounds them (it can, for example, tell us something about the field internal status of actors and institutions comprising a field at a particular moment in time).

12. For a general, English-language introduction into the method of institutional and poetological analysis as proposed by Dorleijn and van Rees, see van Rees and Dorleijn, "Eighteenth-Century Literary Field."

13. Leerssen's research into nineteenth-century European "cultural nationalism" also appears to provide evidence for this hypothesis (see Leerssen 31–32 et passim).

14. That it is fruitful both to conceptualize a South African literary field in the Bourdieuian sense and to analyze the South African field according to Bourdieuian methods has been demonstrated by van der Waal (see van der Waal 78–79 et passim).

15. Comprising the actors and institutions involved in producing and distributing literature in any of the nine official African languages of South Africa (i.e., Sepedi, Sesotho, Setswana, siSwati, Tshivenda, Xitsonga, isiNdebele, isiXhosa, and isiZulu).

16. It is true that such a conceptualization would not do justice to the complexity of the South African field. Considering *inter alia* the fact that South African literary activity was increasingly organized along racial lines in apartheid South Africa, with blacks, Afrikaners, and Anglophone whites all channeling their activities largely through their own institutions, the conceptualization of the field in the three mentioned subfields is indeed not very accurate.

Part I

Legal Groundwork, 1910–1955

Chapter One

Preparing the Ground for Autonomization

The laws of the Union of South Africa, the state that was established on May 31, 1910,[1] were always for a large part based on English law. Indeed, it was not until the 1930s that the Union became legislatively independent from England.[2] The Union's court system was organized hierarchically and consisted (from lowest to highest authority) of Magistrates' Courts; Provincial[3] and Local Divisions of the Supreme Court; and an Appellate Division of the Supreme Court. This system would remain in force until 1997.

When we seek to describe the judicial treatment of literature in the Union, it is best to go back to the end of the nineteenth century, because in the latter quarter of that century the statutory and precedential foundations were laid for the legal regulation of the medium within the Union. Until 1963, the regulation of literature in South Africa, indeed, the regulation of all possible types of publications, took place through a dual system of control that employed a different set of statutory provisions for the control of imported publications to that for domestically produced ones. The act underlying the regulation of the former kind of publications was the Customs Act that came into force in the Cape Colony in 1872. This act was heavily inspired by the British Customs Consolidation Act of 1853 (Kahn, "*Lion*" 280). As far as publications were concerned, the act was aimed at keeping "indecent or obscene" publications from entering the Colony. The Cape Act, in turn, formed the statutory model for customs laws adopted in the Transvaal (the Customs Management Ordinance of 1902) and Natal (the Customs Consolidation and Shipping Act of 1899). Orange Free State did not create any similar legislation (van der Poll 198).

As of 1913, there would be a uniform system of control of imported publications in what had then already become the Union of South Africa, as in that year the Customs Management Act came into force (Kahn, "*Lion*" 280). This act took over the Cape Act's provision prohibiting the import of "indecent or obscene" articles word for word, albeit that the latter formula was changed into "indecent or obscene or objectionable" (280). Moreover, it stipulated that "in the event of any question arising as to whether such articles are indecent, obscene, or objectionable, the decision of the Minister shall be final" (Customs Management Act, 1913 qtd. in Kahn, "*Lion*" 280). The Minister referred to was the Minister of Finance (Geldenhuÿs 24). Unlike in later years, as we will see further on in this and later chapters, there were no art or literary experts involved in judging publications (cf. Kahn, "*Lion*" 281)—an indication, or so it seems, that literary texts did not enjoy a special status. As the regulation of imported publications in principle remained an entirely administrative affair throughout the period 1910–1963—in the latter year a new act was passed that was designed to regulate both imported and domestically produced publications: the Publications and Entertainments Act, 1963—it does not fall within the scope of this study to go into this any further.[4]

Taking statutory measures so as to direct the regulation of domestically produced publications was a colonial and, as of 1910, provincial affair up until the aforementioned Publications and Entertainments Act of 1963 came into effect, making it a national issue (Dean 78; Kahn, "*Lion*" 283, 285; Marais 50–51). J. F. Marais, judge of the Transvaal Division of the Supreme Court and a patron of literature and the arts (Kahn, "*Lion*" 292), commented that this did not mean that the legislation in this area was inadequate though, as the standard that was being prescribed was essentially uniform, as was the body responsible for prosecution: the Attorney General (Marais 50–51).[5] In this area of publications control too, the Cape Colony was the first of the four regions to pass legislation. Its Obscene Publications Act, 1892 combated "indecent or obscene" publications on two fronts: firstly, it incorporated the provisions of the Obscene Publications Act, 1857 of England, which were aimed at supplementing the common-law misdemeanor of publishing obscene matter by vesting a magistrate with the power to order the seizure and destruction of such matter (Kahn, "*Lion*" 284; Obscene Publications Act, 1892 3109). Yet it went further than the English Act in stating that the owner, printer, maker, publisher, distributor, and so on of the obscene matter was guilty of an offense (Kahn, "*Lion*" 284). Secondly, it made it an offense to sell, distribute, offer for sale, or exhibit any indecent or obscene publication (284).

Roughly a decade later, the other colonies began to follow suit. In the Transvaal, the Criminal Law Amendment Act of 1909, whose provisions largely resembled those of the Cape Act (Geldenhuÿs 26), stipulated, among other things, that it was an offense to "sell, make, print, circulate, exhibit, or publish any indecent book, paper, pamphlet [etc.]" (Criminal Law Amendment Act, 1909 qtd. in Kahn, "*Lion*" 285). The Orange Free State made it an offense to sell, distribute, or exhibit any "profane, indecent or obscene" publication through the Police Offences Ordinance of 1902 (Kahn, "*Lion*" 285). The only relevant legislative measures that were taken in Natal were local government ordinances that empowered authorities to prohibit the exhibition or sale in a public place or in the public view of any book or other material which they considered to be "indecent, offensive, unseemly, or objectionable" (285; Marais 51).[6] In contrast to the legislation regarding imported publications, which made their regulation an entirely administrative affair in which customs functioned as the penultimate and the Minister as the ultimate arbiter in matters concerning allegedly obscene publications, the statutory measures taken by the provinces regarding locally produced publications all stipulated that it was up to the courts to decide whether a publication was obscene (Marais 52).[7] No sanctions could be imposed outside of the court (52).

Although apparently little use was made of the statutory provisions to suppress domestically produced books or other publications (Hepple 35; Kahn "*Lion*" 286; Marais 52), four cases were taken to court that in a more indirect manner tell us something about the institutional status of literature within the law during the period that South Africa formed a Union (namely *Rex* v *Shaw* [1910]; *Rex* v *Meinert* [1932]; *Rex* v *Webb* [1934]; and *Goeie Hoop Uitgewers* v *CNA and Another* [1953]). Two cases concerning allegedly obscene publications that were heard in the decades immediately preceding the birth of the Union (*Q* v *de Jong* [1894] and *G. W. Hardy* v *Rex* [1905]) are of concern too, as they by common law logic would go on to form precedents on which later cases would be built. These six cases form the only cases indicative of the legal status of literature that were treated in court in pre-Union South Africa and in the actual Union since the Obscene Publications Act, 1892 entered the statute books.[8] Let us proceed with examining the pre-Union legal prologue that the last mentioned pair of cases comprises. After we have examined these, we will go on to scrutinize the other four cases in order to see how the precedential situation evolved in the Union.

THE PRE-UNION TRIALS: SOME KEY ISSUES

The Isolated-Passage Criterion

The first pre-Union case, that of *Q* v *de Jong*, was about a publication titled "Teekenen des Tyds" (Signs of the Times[9]). The publication was pseudonymously authored by "Door Opmerker" ("By Observer") and had appeared in the *Worcester Advertiser*, a newspaper published in the town of Worcester, on August 11, 1894. In the Supreme Court, the piece of writing was referred to as a "doggerel" both by the defense and by the Bench (*Q* v *de Jong* 327, 328, 329). It was thus apparently not claimed—not in the latter court in any case—that the piece had any literary value.

The Resident Magistrate of Worcester had judged the publication to be "indecent and obscene" in terms of the Obscene Publications Act, 1892. Moreover, he had sentenced de Jong, "the lawful proprietor or editor" of the newspaper (*Q* v *de Jong* 326), to a fine of £10 or two months' imprisonment. The case formed the first prosecution under the Obscene Publications Act of 1892 (*Q* v *de Jong* 327). De Jong appealed to the Supreme Court of the Colony of the Cape of Good Hope, and the latter court dealt with the case on November 2, 1894. As the focus of the appellant was on procedural matters, not on the Magistrate's judgment that the publication was "indecent and obscene" (cf. *Q* v *de Jong* 326–28), and as the case apparently did not involve a piece that purported to be a work of literature, there is not very much to learn about either the institutional status that literature might have been allotted nor about the weight that might have been given to poetological issues by the appealing and responding parties and the judges hearing the case.

There is however one aspect of the judgment that is worth mentioning, namely that it touched upon an issue that seems to be crucial to the judicial treatment of literature in general (cf. *PCB* v *Heinemann* 140), to wit the question whether or not a publication might be judged on the basis of the so-called isolated-passage criterion. When applying this criterion, a publication might be deemed to be constituting an offense on the basis of a single passage occurring in it, without taking the publication as a whole into consideration. The direct opposite way of judging a publication, a way that for a certain time coexisted with the isolated-passage criterion in English law but that in time would come to replace it (see St. John-Stevas 134–36)—as it would in the laws of various other nations as well—is to judge a publication on the basis of a contextual approach, that is, to judge it "as a whole." This leaves the possibility open that the context of passages—that in themselves would offend in terms of the law—might redeem such passages. St. John-Stevas states that the coexistence of the two tests of obscenity was a consequence of the fact that in the case of a prosecution, an indictment should either specify certain passages or be accompanied with a submission of a copy of the work complained of. In the former case, the incriminated work would be judged on the specified passages; in the latter case, the work would be judged as a whole (134).

The contextual approach is known to have represented a fundamental judicial instrument for creating an institutional autonomy for literature vis-à-vis the law in early twentieth-century Netherlands (Beekman and Grüttemeier 198; Grüttemeier, "Law" 178). Moreover, this approach—which appears to have gone by different names such as the "dominant effect" or "dominant theme" test (cf. Lockhart and McClure 88; "Obscenity and the First Amendment" 119; *PCB* v *Heinemann* 140; J. Williams, "Obscenity" 645; St. John-Stevas 134), the "internal necessities test" (Dyzenhaus, Reibetanz Moreau, and Ripstein 975–76) and the "dirt for dirt's sake" test (Ladenson xx; Sova 95–96)—appears to have been instrumental in the institutional autonomization of literature vis-à-vis the laws of other countries such as Canada, England, and the United States, too—developments which appear mainly to have taken place from the 1930s to 1950s (cf. Ladenson 152ff; Lockhart and McClure 88ff; McDonald, "Old Phrases" 299; cf. also Robertson 61ff; St. John-Stevas 135; J. Williams, "Obscenity" 636).

Yet although the Cape Bench touched upon the issue in the case of *Queen* v *de Jong*, it cannot definitely be determined whether it had applied the isolated-passage criterion, nor whether it held it to be a valid instrument for judging a publication or not. Toward the end of its unanimous judgment the Bench stated that the "whole tenour [of the doggerel] is somewhat indecent and that some of the lines are offensively indecent" (*Q* v *de Jong* 329), and that it on this basis concluded that the publication was obscene. Yet this judgment can be read both ways. One could hypothesize that the judgment was arrived at by an application of the isolated-passage criterion, for on the basis of some *offensively* indecent lines the whole piece, of which the "whole tenour" was held to be only *somewhat* indecent, was deemed obscene. On the other hand, one could also interpret the quote as containing the ghost of a contextualist argument, for the Court might have judged the publication to be obscene because it felt that the whole tenor, being of a "somewhat indecent" nature, could not *save* the "offensively indecent" lines—in the way a work of literary merit might. Unfortunately, no further clues can be gathered from the judgment that might tip the balance in favor of one of these interpretations. Yet for the Cape Bench the question of the validity of the isolated-passage approach is not likely to have been an issue at all: first of all, the text it had to deal with in de Jong's case represented a newspaper piece, not a lengthy book; secondly, English law was still sovereign in the region at that time, and the validity of the isolated-passage approach appears not to have become an issue in English law before the twentieth century was already long underway (cf. Robertson 61ff; St. John-Stevas 135f).

The Arguments of the Classics and the "Ordinary Man"

In the other pre-Union case, that of *G. W. Hardy* v *Rex*, two other key issues were taken up. The case was treated by the Supreme Court of Natal on April 3, 1905, and represented an appeal against a decision of the Magistrate's Court of Durban. This lower court had charged a certain G. W. Hardy with the offense of "public indecency" in that he, being the editor, printer, and publisher of a newspaper called *Prince*, had published and disseminated an "indecent, lewd, scandalous, and offensive article or writing" titled "The Black Peril" in the October 7, 1904, issue of that newspaper (*G. W. Hardy* v *R* 166). Apparently, Hardy was charged with public indecency because more befitting legislation for dealing with allegedly obscene publications was lacking in the Colony of Natal at that time (cf. *Hardy* v *R* 167). Just as in *Queen* v *de Jong*, the publication at issue in Hardy's case did not purport to be a work of literature, and neither was it received as such. It rather represented a journalistic article that described the "peril" of black men and white women engaging in sexual relations with each other, a "peril" that was supposedly "threatening" Durban at the time (cf. Geldenhuys 22).

The first aspect of the case that is of interest to our discussion is that the appealing party, in regard to the contents of the publication, argued that the article was not indecent, because "[f]ar worse matters are published in England and elsewhere with impunity. The works of standard authors and translations from the classics are freely allowed publication" (*G. W. Hardy* v *R* 168). This strategy of the appealing party to argue that the incriminated article was no more "indecent" than any of the classical literature that was free to circulate in England, among other countries, seems first and foremost to have been applied in order to downplay the allegedly offensive character of the article—indeed, to stress that the article was acceptable in the light of contemporary public morals. More interesting than the particular function of the classics argument in the defense of the newspaper article, however, is the principled stance the court took vis-à-vis the argument. For just like the contextual approach, the argument of the classics is known to have played an important role in the legal autonomization of (modern) literature in certain Western countries. It played such a part in the Netherlands in the 1910s (see Beekman and Grüttemeier 65), but also in twentieth-century America, as Felice Flanery Lewis has pointed out in her study *Literature, Obscenity, and Law*. As Lewis observed in her work, "literary value, as established by centuries of acclaim, was the crack in the door through which unusually erotic fiction first squeezed past the censors [in the U.S.]. Once an exception was made of classic art, the next logical step was the granting of this privileged status to outstanding contemporary art" (45).

The judges in the Hardy case stated that they did not "appreciate the negative argument addressed to us by Mr. Hillier [i.e., the appellant's attorney], which was founded upon illustrations from literature," and explained that

> [i]t would be impossible to deny that in the works of many writers of ancient times, as well as in those of standard authors of a later period, passages of an extremely indecent and obscene character are to be found, the publication of which in the newspaper press of the present day would be an offence against good morals amounting to public indecency, inasmuch as the indiscriminate

circulation of such matter would undoubtedly tend to deprave and ‹ minds of some into whose hands it might come. (*G. W. Hardy* v *R* 17

Therefore, they concluded, Mr. Hillier's classics argument was Quite categorically they added that "the fact that indecent public .... in the past have not been made the subject of prosecution cannot relieve the Court of the duty of considering such a publication upon its own merits when brought before it in a criminal prosecution" (171).

The Court's rejection of Hillier's classics argument was congruous with the position taken on this issue by Chief Justice Cockburn in the English appeal case of *Regina* v *Hicklin* in 1868. The judgment that Cockburn had handed down in this case had set a foremost precedent not only for obscenity trials held throughout the last third of the nineteenth and the first half of the twentieth century in territories that belonged to the British Empire, South Africa included, but also for such trials held in that same period in the United States. With regard to the argument of the classics, Cockburn had emphatically advanced in his judgment that "[i]t is perfectly true . . . that there are a great many publications of high repute in the literary productions of this country the tendency of which is immodest, and, if you please, immoral, and possibly there might have been subject-matter for indictment in many of the works which have been referred to" (*R* v *Hicklin*)—reference had been made to the sixth satire of Juvenal and to more modern classics such as Chaucer, Milton, and Byron. However, Cockburn continued, "it is not to be said, because there are in many standard and established works objectionable passages, that therefore the law is not as alleged on the part of this prosecution, namely, that obscene works are the subject-matter of indictment" (*R* v *Hicklin*).

By dismissing the classics argument as it was used in Hardy's case, the Natal Bench seemed first and foremost to be aimed—just as Cockburn had apparently been in Hicklin's case—at protecting the kinds of potential readers that were considered to be vulnerable, in this case especially "the young and inexperienced" (*G. W. Hardy* v *R* 172) and, even more so, the "native population" (172–73). Such a position did not necessarily rule out the granting of a certain amount of freedom to stronger readers though. And it does indeed not appear that the judges in Hardy's case were of the position that it would. The word "indiscriminate" in the above-quoted passage from this latter case seems telling in this respect: it appears that when it came to the more principled question of "passages of an extremely indecent and obscene character" occurring in literary classics, the Bench was merely of the position that the *indiscriminate* circulation of such matter ought to be prevented so that it would not reach vulnerable readers. The medium through which the dissemination occurred apparently played a crucial role in this regard: "publication . . . in the newspaper press of the present day" of such passages (n.b.

taken out of the context of the whole work) would constitute an offense against good morals, the Bench explicitly stated, a statement that appeared to imply that matters would lie differently when such passages were disseminated (n.b. *within* the context of the whole) through the medium of an expensive book—which indeed would mean: disseminated much more *discriminately*.

The second aspect of interest to our discussion is that the Natal Bench adopted the test of obscenity that had been formulated in Cockburn's judgment in the Hicklin case. According to the Chief Justice, what had to be determined was "whether the tendency of the matter charged as obscenity is to deprave and corrupt those whose minds are open to such immoral influences, and into whose hands a publication of this sort may fall" (*R* v *Hicklin*). Yet the Natal judges did not simply adopt Cockburn's test. Importantly, they added a new component to it by stating that "[t]he point of view which we think should be adopted in estimating the tendency of an article . . . is not that of a Puritan on the one hand, or of a profligate on the other, but that of an ordinary man possessed of an average sense of decency" (172).[10] By adding this component, the Natal Bench introduced a less harsh test of obscenity for South Africa: not any reader, notably the "weak" or the "Puritan" reader, had to be taken into account when judging a publication, only the "ordinary man" thus conceived should.

Now we have established this "prehistory," let us turn to the period 1910–1955 in order to see how the regulation of literature took form in the first decades after South Africa had become an independent nation.

THE UNION TRIALS: THE TOOL KIT FOR AUTONOMIZATION

Testimony, the Contextual Approach, and Tolerance Concerning Changing Norms

The first case on printed matter that was dealt with in court since the colonies of the Cape, Natal, Transvaal, and Orange River had been united to form the Union of South Africa was the 1910 case of *Rex* v *Shaw*. The case was about an imported book titled *The Grip* that had appeared under the pseudonym of Flaneuse. In Bourdieuian terms, the work appears not to have been written for an "intellectual" audience but rather for a mass audience. It represented a work of fiction and its central theme was a tragic love affair between a young philosopher called Duncan Heriot and a woman called Elena Geisthardt. The author, or authors, that sheltered behind the name Flaneuse—or Flâneuse, as it was spelled on other works—is/are thought to have written a number of works dealing rather extensively with female sexual desire and works with an apparently somewhat feminist import, as do other authors published by the same publishing house—A. M. Gardner & Co. of London—of which the most notable is the bestselling author Elinor Glyn (Castagna; Kemp, Mitchell, and Trotter 131, 155, 427). This might give us a somewhat clearer idea both of the kind of genre that *The Grip* was held to represent at the time, and of the reason why the book might have become the subject of a court case.

In the first instance, the book was the subject of a case that was brought before the Resident Magistrate for Cape Town. That is to say, an individual called Robert Shaw, the Cape Town manager of the Central News Agency, Ltd., was accused of violating a section of the Obscene Publications Act of 1892 in that he had sold, and exposed for sale, the mentioned book, which was considered to be obscene.[11] The Magistrate also found the publication to be obscene and therefore convicted Shaw for contravening the Act. Subsequently, Shaw appealed to the Cape Provincial Division of the Supreme Court, and on October 24, 1910, the Court heard the case. As in the *Queen* v *de Jong* case, the appealing party focused on procedural matters rather than on the Magistrate's finding that the publication was obscene. Yet here too there were aspects to the case that were of significant precedential value.

Firstly, witnesses were allowed to testify in the case as to the nature of the book in terms of the law. What is especially noteworthy in this regard is that it does not seem that the witnesses who testified in court employed the "literature" argument nor that they had any special expertise concerning books or literature. The witness who declared the book to be indecent was an agent of the Social Reform Association (*R* v *Shaw* 428), a South African antivice organization equivalent to the notorious New York Society for the Suppression of Vice of Anthony Comstock and late eighteenth- and nineteenth-century English prototypes of such organizations (cf. Kahn, "*Lion*" 284–85).[12] An undefined number of witnesses called to support the defense of Shaw "took a very different view of the book," according to the judgment handed down in the case (*R* v *Shaw* 429). It is nowhere indicated that any of these defense witnesses were book or literary experts, so it appears that either they were not, or that if they were, their expertise was not considered relevant in the eyes of the Court.

Secondly, the Cape Court took a more univocal stance with respect to the isolated-passage criterion than it had in the case of *Q* v *de Jong* of a decade and a half earlier. Toward the end of the judgment it indeed stated that "[i]t may be that if the objectionable parts of the book had been pointed out [no such parts had been pointed out], other parts might have been pointed out which, reading the one with the other, would show that the general tendency of the book was not corrupting" (429). It seems, thus, that the Court believed that it was desirable to apply a contextual approach when assessing books (cf. *PCB* v *Heinemann* 140).

Thirdly, the Court seemed to be of the opinion that a general tolerance had to be observed with regard to changing societal norms relating to certain themes—in this case, or so it seems, (female) sexuality. Quite categorically, its unanimous judgment declared that "[i]t might have been shown that the book was dealing with problems which some people do not like to be discussed, and which to a certain extent might be indelicate to discuss; but the law was not meant to meet cases of that kind" (*R* v *Shaw* 429).

In sum, the Court displayed a degree of benevolence toward contemporary works of fiction that appeared to go further than the judiciary had been willing to go in the pre-Union cases we examined.

A Colonial *Exceptio Artis*

After Shaw's case, it took some two decades before the next case that tells us something about judicial attitudes toward literature was brought to court. This case was not brought before a Union court, however, but before the High Court of South-West Africa. The case is of interest to our discussion though, because, as mentioned, South-West Africa fell under South African jurisdiction at the time and the judgment might therefore be held to be representative of the judicial climate that prevailed within the Union also.[13] The case I am referring to is the case of *Rex* v *Meinert*, which was dealt with by the mentioned Court on August 10 and 12, 1932. This year is significant in at least two respects: a year earlier, the Statute of Westminster had been passed by the British Parliament, effectuating legislative independence for South Africa; a year later, moreover, the *Ulysses* case, which appears to have heralded a paradigm shift regarding publications regulation in the Anglophone world (cf. Ladenson 78ff et passim; Lewis 44; "Obscenity and the First Amendment" 119; J. Williams, "Obscenity" 645), was first brought to court in the United States.[14]

Again, the case did not deal with a literary work, yet it does tell us something about judicial attitudes toward literature and the role that arguments with respect to its institutional position could play in court at the time. The case represented an appeal against a judgment handed down by the Magistrate of Windhoek. The Magistrate had convicted a certain Mr. Meinert of having contravened the Obscene Publications Suppression Ordinance 5 of 1926—an ordinance that did not essentially differ from the laws that were applicable in South Africa (cf. *R* v *Meinert* 57–58; cf. also Marais 50–51)— in that he both had had copies of a German magazine called *Die Schönheit* (Beauty) that contained some photographs of nude males and females in his possession for sale and had sold a copy of the issue in question. The first page of the magazine gave an impression of the genre that it belonged to, as it said that the magazine represented a "Mit Bildern geschmückte Monatschrift für Kunst und Leben, Mit Beiblatt 'Licht, Luft, Leben' vereinigt mit 'Der Mensch,' Monatschrift für Schönheit, Gesundheit, Geist, Körperbildung: Begrundet [*sic*] 1902" ("Monthly magazine for art and living adorned with pictures, With supplement 'Light, Air, Living' merged with

'Man,' Monthly magazine for beauty, health, mind, physical education: Established 1902'").

The main strategy of the appealing party lay in emphasizing that the nature of the publication in terms of the law had to be measured on the basis of the actual standards of the community, and that these standards ought to be determined in an empirical fashion on the basis of *inter alia* the kind of literature that was circulating within the community. The report telegraphically records the attorney of the appellant to have stated:

> Question to be decided in the first instance: What is the state of morality at the particular time and place? Court has to enquire into the actual state of moral notions of population on the whole. Impossible to assume some imaginary ethical standard which does not prevail and to say that this is an offence against that standard. (*R v Meinert* 56)

The appealing party implied that to determine the community standards relevant to this particular case and others that would be similar to it, one had to investigate what the "cultural notions" of the people comprising the community—in this case, the inhabitants of Windhoek—were, and what kind of literature was being read by these people. It furthermore stressed that the moral standards of a community were subject to "constant progress and evolution" (57).

In reaction to the argument of the appealing party, the attorney for the responding party stated, firstly, that "[t]he current literature in Windhoek does not establish anything. It does not reflect the standard generally applicable in this community" (57); and secondly, that "[m]any books current in Windhoek might be indecent, but, because these have not yet been the subject of a prosecution it cannot be contended that the present publication is no worse and should therefore not be declared indecent" (57). The latter contention was of course rather congruous with the way in which the argument of the classics had been handled, in both the judgment delivered in Hardy's case and the one handed down in the English case of Hicklin.

In his decision, the judge handling the case, Bok, evidenced to be not just adopting the Hicklin test—as the obscenity test formulated by Chief Justice Cockburn was baptized at some point—in order to judge the case, but also to give his own twist to it, just as the judges had done in Hardy's case. Yet in doing so, Bok went further than the Natal judges had. He emphatically stated, as the Court had done in Shaw's case, that themes regarding sexuality were not off-limits per se. Such themes, he added,

> are discussed with ever increasing freedom in the literatures of all civilised peoples and to hold that all such books are obscene within the meaning of the law in this territory, because on the minds of immature, uneducated or uncivilised persons they might have a deleterious affect [*sic*], would mean to deprive

> educated people from contact with modern literature and thought in other countries and I cannot think that such could have been the intention of the Legislature. (60)

What is most remarkable about Bok's position-taking here is not so much that he was evidently breaking a lance for a certain amount of thematic freedom. As we saw above, this position had already been defended in Shaw's case based on the premise that tolerance had to be observed with respect to changing public norms. As becomes clear at other points in Bok's judgment, his tolerance regarding thematics was underpinned by this belief too, albeit only partly (61). What is much more noteworthy, however—and this becomes evident in the statement quoted above—is that Bok's positioning was also based on the contention that a certain amount of tolerance had to be observed with regard to evolving norms regarding modern literature. In fact, with his statement, Bok was taking a rather unprecedented standpoint vis-à-vis the institutional status of literature. The institutional position awarded by Bok to literature might indeed best be described as a colonial *exceptio artis*: a very early form of *exceptio artis* in Southern Africa—indeed, the first time it seems to have appeared in South(ern) African law—which also represented a very specific form of the concept, *inter alia* because it was based solely on the valuation of *imported* literature.

Evidently, Bok respected that a certain amount of freedom to depict or write about sexual matters had been conquered by literature and the arts internationally, and what is more is that he also allowed for literature to enjoy this amount of autonomy vis-à-vis South-West African law. Bok quite clearly gave priority to the right to read of literary socialized readers, or "educated people" (60), at the expense of the right of nonliterary-socialized readers, or "immature, uneducated or uncivilised persons," to be protected from potentially harmful material. By granting literary socialized readers this special right, he at once, albeit implicitly, bestowed upon "modern literature"—n.b. Bok was solely speaking of modern literature *from abroad*—a(n) (relative) *exceptio artis*. A few lines further, Bok again, and possibly even more unequivocally, underlined his point by declaring that he felt that "the test [of obscenity] cannot be whether there are persons who, incapable of understanding the real spirit of the writing, might suffer morally by being allowed to read it" (60).

It might be telling that a distinctive feature of Bok's particular application of the Hicklin test was that he did not apply the concept of the ordinary man, as introduced in Hardy's case, but that he employed the notion of the reasonable man instead,[15] and that in doing so he appeared to be applying a somewhat different standard than the judges in Hardy's case had. Obscenity had to be determined by estimating what the "reasonable man" would deem to have the tendency to deprave and corrupt (cf. 60). Bok's emphasis being more on defending the right to read of educated audiences than on defending the right of "immature, uneducated or uncivilised" audiences to be protected appears to imply that his concept of the reasonable man did not equal that of the ordinary man as laid down in Hardy's case. Indeed, it seems rather certain that Bok's priority was not to defend public morals on the basis of criteria of the "ordinary" man as he was defined in *Rex* v *Hardy*. Rather, his priority lay with defending the literary norms that had arisen in "modern literature and thought in other countries," that is to say, *European* countries, for he first and foremost seemed to be thinking of countries of that latter continent (cf. 63).

In conclusion to our discussion of the Meinert case, two more things should be noted: Firstly, that in the peroration of his judgment Bok somewhat qualified the position he had taken throughout it, a position in which judicial "realism" and a favoring of some kind of autonomy vis-à-vis the law for art in general and modern literature in particular so clearly formed a part. Concerning the latter, one only has to point toward the repeated references to and indeed concern for literature that can be discerned in the judgment on this case that did not revolve around a work of literature at all. Bok slightly toned down his position by stating that he should add that he arrived at his conclusion "with considerable hesitation bearing in mind the large uncivilised class of our population" (63) and that his conclusion "must not be understood as implying that conditions peculiar to a country like this do not necessitate a stricter view of what is permissible in this respect in the interests of art and culture, than might possibly be accepted in European countries" (63). In this respect, Bok proved himself to be a child of his time: quite clearly he regarded the indigenous peoples of South-West Africa to represent intellectually weak peoples—peoples in need of protection. His position represented the politically dominant one in Southern Africa at the time, and it quite clearly echoed the thought of earlier colonial governors and administrators such as Earl Buxton, who had been Governor-General of the Union of South Africa from 1914 to 1920. In his presidential address at the annual meeting of the Royal African Society in London on March 15, 1921, Buxton had literally spoken of the Bantu peoples of Africa as the "child races" of the empire.[16] Bok's prioritization of the right to read of the "civilised" over the right to protection from harm of the "large uncivilised class" of the South-West African population was thus not categorical; it did have to be balanced against the latter right and at some point, it seemed to be implied, the scales would tip in favor of the "uncivilised class." It is, however, quite evident that Bok considered it vital for those living in Southern Africa to be able to keep in touch with "civilised" thought.

The second thing that should be noted is that with all the emphasis laid on *foreign* literature, both by the appealing party and the judge, it seems that literature in Southern Africa, i.e., South-West Africa and South Africa, was not really a factor of importance yet, institutionally speaking. Indeed, what

Bok's judgment was clearly demonstrating was rather a worry that Southern Africa might become isolated from literary and intellectual developments taking place in the former mother countries, than a concern for an emerging Southern African literature. When one adds up these two distinctive features, i.e., the sole emphasis on foreign literature and the relatively weak form that the institutional freedom for literature as conceptualized by Bok took because of the colonial context in which the medium had to operate—or, put differently, the racialized dimension that Bok's conceptualization clearly had—the term "colonial *exceptio artis*" appears to be quite adequate for describing the institutional position that literature should be granted according to this judge.

An *Exceptio Scientiae*

Some two years after Meinert's case was dealt with by the High Court of South-West Africa, the case of *Rex* v *Webb* was handled by the Appellate Division of the Supreme Court of the Union of South Africa. This case would go on, as we will see in later chapters, to remain a crucial precedent for years to come—it for instance played a significant part in the major 1974 trial of André Brink's novel *Kennis van de Aand*. Webb's case was first brought before the Magistrate's Court of Johannesburg, where the accused, a certain Mr. Webb, was charged with the crime of blasphemy for publishing a very short story titled "A Nun's Passion: A Xmas Story," a piece which had appeared in the December 30, 1933, issue of a newspaper called *The Ringhals*, of which he was the editor. The piece read as follows:

> Sister Angelica knelt before her bed in the convent, her body trembling with sublime love. She closed her eyes and got ready to pray. She was tired of the Ave Marias and the Misereres and the old formulas. She thought of the Mother Superior and the way she spoke about Christ and love. What did a shrivelled woman with tight lips and a cold, austere heart know about love?
>
> Sister Angelica, her bosom pressed against the iron rail of her bed, poured out in spiritual ecstacy the fervent things of her warm body and her passionate soul.
>
> "Oh, Christ Jesus, I love thee; I love thee only. Put thy hands on my breasts. Clasp each of my breasts with the tenderness of thy love. Come yet more near to me Jesus. I do not fear thee.
>
> "I was sinful once, Jesus. I loved a man. He kissed me, and I lay in his arms, and I pressed my lips on his mouth, and there was blood on my lips after the passion with which I had kissed him. It was red blood, Christ, and it was very beautiful. But it was also very sinful, Lord. Yea, Lord, it was very sinful.
>
> "And then he left me.
>
> "And now I only love thee, O Jesus.
>
> "I love thy body that bore all those cruel wounds for me. I wash the blood off thy body with my tears. Thy wounds are all healed now, Jesus.

"I love thy black hair. Come closer to me Jesus. Let me put my hands on thy black hair. Let me kiss thy crimson lips. See how my mouth trembles with my love for thee. Let me know more of thy beauty, Jesus.

"So thou hast come to me Lord. Thou hast answered my prayer and thou hast come to me. Oh, the white fragrance of thy breath. Like the sweet perfume of the little night flowers. Thy presence is like a green place on the earth where two lovers have lain.

"Jesus, I feel thou art tender because thou art strong. Kiss me Jesus, kiss me. Behold, I have kept my loveliness for thee. Put thy hand here, Jesus. Here . . . Here . . . I love thee and am not ashamed."

Afterwards, when she came out of her cell, with flushed cheeks and her brow very pale, Sister Angelica looked to the Mother Superior like a woman who had sinned. ("Nun's Passion")

Not only was Webb charged with the crime of blasphemy for publishing this short story, he was also charged with contravening sec. 2 (7) of the Criminal Law Amendment Act of 1909, the principle act aimed at combating indecent and obscene publications in the Transvaal which we already encountered at the outset of this chapter. The grounds for this latter charge were that he had also published a letter in the same issue of *The Ringhals* which was supposed to be indecent and therefore constitute an offense in terms of the mentioned subsection of the act. Webb was convicted by the Magistrate and subsequently appealed to the Transvaal Provincial Division of the Supreme Court. The latter Court dismissed the appeal, and therefore Webb finally brought an appeal against the decision of the Transvaal Court to the Appellate Division of the Supreme Court. This Division dealt with the case on April 18 and 20, 1934.

The appealing party based its case primarily on the arguments that "[t]he essential of the crime of blasphemy is to revile" and that "[t]he idea of the poem was to display the sentiments of the nun, not to revile Christ" (*R v Webb* 494). Ergo, the piece could not be regarded blasphemous in terms of the law. As seems to already become apparent from this quote, the appellant also seemed to have applied a literary defense of sorts. Indeed, the appealing party at some point referred to the piece as a "prose poem" (494–95). This literary defense appears to have been a somewhat half-hearted one though, as it was not recorded in the law report as having constituted an essential point of the appellant's argument. The basic point of the respondent's argument was that the story was blasphemous as "Christ [was] associated with indecent ideas" in it (494).

In its unanimous judgment, the Court gave evidence of finding the appellant's apparent claim of literariness questionable: at one point it read in the judgment that "[t]he applicant calls it a 'prose poem'" (494–95) and elsewhere it referred to "the so-called story" (498). The Court itself referred to the piece as "publication or story" (494), or simply "publication" (494).

As to the question of intent, the Court stated: "The intent . . . is not of the essence of the crime of blasphemy and none of the authorities cited to us say so. They all agree that the question of intent is important in determining the punishment but that is all. If the words are blasphemous the intent is inferred" (495). Indeed, the rules that prescribed that intent was automatically inferred when the fact of an offense had been established and that intent could only be relevant in determining a matching punishment were applicable in all criminal cases (cf. *Hardy* v *R* 169–70; *R* v *Meinert* 60). The only question that was thus still to be answered was whether the publication, "objectively" judged—i.e., on the basis of the facts as appearing in the publication itself and disregarding the alleged authorial intent—was blasphemous.

Having presented a summary of the story, the Court stated that "there is not the slightest doubt, that the whole publication suggests that the nun in her erotic ecstasy or hallucination had a vision and imagined that she had had carnal connection with Jesus. That it is a crude, vulgar and indecent production admits of no doubt, but the question is whether it is blasphemy according to our law" (*R* v *Webb* 495). Evidently, the Court had some, though not too substantial difficulties in determining whether it did. Was it blasphemy, the Court asked, "to portray an erotic nun as having a vision of Christ appearing to her and imagining that she has carnal connection with the subject of the vision?" (496). In answering the question, the Bench observed that "the idea of a woman having a vision or dream that she has carnal connection with a godhead is not uncommon in Greek literature and in that of other countries"; one only had to refer to "the vision of the mother of Alexander the Great" (496). Essentially, however, the question was whether the fact "that the vision [wa]s that of Jesus ma[d]e the publication blasphemy" (496).

As the Court's unanimous judgment unfolded, it became clear that it was based on some of the same crucial criteria regarding publications control as had been formulated in Shaw's and Meinert's respective cases. First of all, the Court was eager to stress that community standards were subject to change (see 496).[17] Secondly, the Court made it clear that it was not the story's theme, but the manner in which the theme was treated that mattered in this case (cf. *R* v *Webb* 497–98). Thirdly, the Bench evidenced to have read the work according to the contextual approach. For in its conclusion with regard to the question whether the story was blasphemous it stated: "There is no doubt if we read the so-called story as a whole, we can come to no other conclusion than that it was designed to hurt the feelings of professing Christians. It is therefore a blasphemous publication and on this part the appeal fails" (498).

Although the Court's judgment thus largely effectuated continuity in publications control, it also introduced a new criterion. For the judgment in so many words instituted an *exceptio scientiae* of sorts when it, in coming to its conclusion regarding the story, declared that "if the erotic passion of a nun for the eidolon of Jesus were dealt with in a book on psychology or in a medical treatise or even in guarded language in some other publication, I do not think that a statement to the effect that a nun imagined that she had had carnal connection with Jesus would *per se* constitute blasphemy" (497). A remarkable aspect of this passage is that although the Court, through the hypothetical examples it gave, came to formulate a fairly explicit support of science exemption, it did not expressly entertain the hypothetical possibility of "the erotic passion of a nun for the eidolon of Jesus" being dealt with in a work of literature, in non-guarded language that is—in other words, it did not address the question of art exemption. Yet the fact that it did support science exemption is at least as remarkable. Indeed, it could well be that the Court's position-taking in this matter represents the first time that the concept emerged in South African law. It would take two more decades before the concept entered the statute books, for it was only in 1953 that the concept was incorporated into the Customs Management Act. With regard to domestically produced publications, the concept would not be statutorily introduced before 1963. On the constitutional level, finally, the concept would not be employed until 1993.

It should be noted, however, that the remarkableness of the Court's support for science exemption does not lie in the support per se. On the contrary, from an institutional point of view, the emergence of an *exceptio scientiae* within South African law through the 1934 case of *R v Webb* might be taken to result from the fact that the development of the Union's academic field seemed to have reached a quite advanced stage by that time and the state had manifested a keen interest in further promoting this development (cf. Dubow, *Scientific Racism* 11ff; Dubow, *Commonwealth* 7ff). The legal recognition of the academic field in the form of an *exceptio scientiae* can, then, partly be explained as a manifestation of structural homology (*sensu* Bourdieu) between the judicial and the academic field: the judicial elite recognizes the existence of an academic elite and acts on this recognition by granting the latter elite the (relative, institutional) autonomy to discuss matters according to the professional norms that prevail within this newborn elite. Indeed, the recognition implies ascribing a far-reaching authority to (dominant) experts who are part of this elite when it comes to dealing with matters that fall within their scientific/scholarly "jurisdiction."[18]

New Legislative Developments

Apart from Webb's case there was another important development taking place in 1934, for in that year the Customs Management Act of 1913 was amended to the effect that the Minister's decision on publications that allegedly were "indecent" or "obscene" or "objectionable"—the responsible Minister was no longer the Minister of Finance, but the Minister of the Interior (cf. Geldenhuÿs 24)—were to be given after consultation with the so-called Board of Censors. This board had initially been appointed under the Entertainments (Censorship) Act, 1931 for the purpose of "regulat[ing] and control[ling] the public exhibition and advertisement of cinematograph films and of pictures and the performance of public entertainments" only (Entertainments [Censorship] Act, 1931 132).

With the new provision requiring a censorship board to be involved in the regulation of imported publications, the seeds were sown, as we will see in the coming chapters, of a type of publications control that would be used in South Africa throughout the whole of the twentieth century and indeed also the first decade of the twenty-first century (see also McDonald, *Literature Police*). Yet although the Board of Censors thus became involved in publications regulation as of 1934, it appears not to have been policy for it to be comprised, in any part whatsoever, of literary experts (cf. "Note" 46; Hepple 37)—this very much in contrast to the period after 1963, during which literary experts would form an integral part of the state's censorship system as a matter of principle. Unlike in later periods—notably the period 1963–1990, in which censorship of both domestic and imported literature was fierce (see McDonald, *Literature Police*)—literary expert knowledge did thus seemingly not play a significant part in the censoring of imported publications while South Africa formed a Union (cf. Hood 39), not as a rule anyway. And although the standards that were to be applied by the Minister and the Board of Censors were nowhere defined (37) and reasons for bans were never given (40), it seems to become clear from the lists of titles that were banned that neither the Minister nor the Board were informed by up-to-date literary principles in their daily decisions, let alone scholarly ones. With apparent perplexity, contemporary commentators published lists of imported works which they considered to be of literary merit that ended up getting banned (see Hepple 40; Hood 39; Kahn, "*Lion*" 300ff). As neither the way in which South Africa's consecutive Ministers of the Interior of the period 1934–1963 dealt with literature, nor the manner in which the subsequent Boards of Censors did, represented a *judicial* treatment of literature, we need not delve deeper into this matter here—and indeed, it would take a separate study to adequately reconstruct the way in which the Ministers and boards precisely approached the vast number of literary titles they dealt with in those three decades.[19]

In 1939 the act was again amended, allowing the Minister to ban entire series of publications (Kahn, "*Lion*" 282). Three more legislative changes followed before the 1963 law governing both domestically produced and imported publications came into effect, namely, one in 1944, one in 1953, and one in 1955 (cf. 282–83). The only amendment made by all the changes that is worth mentioning in the light of our discussion, and quite relevant indeed, is the above-referenced provision made in 1953 that instigated a statutory *exceptio scientiae*. The provision made an exemption from the prohibition to import matter which was "indecent or obscene or on any ground objectionable" for those goods that were imported for research purposes by educational institutions under permit of the Minister of the Interior (cf. 283). While this specific form of *exceptio scientiae* would be preserved in the apartheid period, an *exceptio artis*—that is to say, an *exceptio artis* pertaining to domestically produced modern literature—would not be incorporated into South African law for years and years to come. Judging from both the statutory amendments of 1953 and the 1934 Webb case it seems, thus, that by the early 1950s, at the latest, the executive, legislative, and judicial elites were all willing to grant both domestically produced and imported scientific or scholarly texts a significant degree of institutional autonomy. As we will see below, this observation is further underpinned by the judgment delivered in the last case we will be examining in this chapter, the 1953 case of *Goeie Hoop Uitgewers* v *Central News Agency and Another*.

The situation of an *exceptio scientiae* being instigated in a certain nation's law long before an *exceptio artis* does not seem anomalous, though. When one looks at the cases of Germany and the Netherlands, one can discern the same pattern. In Germany, a science exemption first emerged in the Paulskirche constitution of 1849, while an art exemption did not emerge in jurisprudence until 1893 and was only adopted statutorily in the 1919 constitution of the Weimar Republic (Grüttemeier, "Law" 180–81). In the Netherlands, where neither an art nor a science exemption ever made it into statutory law, the origins of an *exceptio scientiae* can be traced to 1847, whereas an *exceptio artis* with respect to visual art only emerged for the first time in 1900, and with respect to literature not until 1920 (177).

Entrenching the Contextual Approach and the *Exceptio Scientiae*

One last relevant case that the Supreme Court dealt with before the legislative changes of 1963 were made was the 1953 case of *Goeie Hoop Uitgewers (Eiendoms) Bpk* v *Central News Agency and Another*. It was dealt with by the Witwatersrand Local Division of the Supreme Court on February 10 and 12, 1953. We can be brief about this case, which in essence concerned a copyright issue but in which the concept of obscenity played a major role. There are two aspects to the case that are especially noteworthy: one is that it appeared to affirm that domestically produced publications also fell under the *exceptio scientiae* rule; two is that the Court firmly entrenched the contextual approach.

As to the latter point, Justice Price, the single judge handling the case, indicated that he had come to one of his major conclusions in the case—i.e., the conclusion that the article that had been copied was obscene and that, therefore, no copyright existed in it (cf. *Goeie Hoop* v *CNA* 846)—on the basis of "several portions of the article" (847). At the same time, however, he revealed to be of the position that the contextual approach represented the only right approach for judging publications. Quite unambiguously, he declared:

> Mr. Hanson [the attorney of the appealing party] has argued that I must not look at one sentence, but at the whole article in order to judge whether it is of a scandalous character or not. That is certainly the law. One cannot judge an article by one sentence. The writing must be looked at as a whole, and its effect must be judged in that way. (847)

This rather unequivocal position-taking by Price not only represented continuity in the South African legal context, it also appeared to harmonize with the trend within Anglo-American law that appears to have begun with the 1933 *Ulysses* trial and really set in during the 1950s, that is to say, the trend to consider the contextual method of testing whether a publication is obscene as the "correct" alternative to the "invalid" isolated-passage method ("Obscenity and the First Amendment" 119; Robertson 61; St. John-Stevas 135).[20] The rise to dominance of this position had been evidenced *inter alia* by the 1949 case of *Commonwealth of Pennsylvania* v *Gordon and Others*[21] ("Obscenity and the First Amendment" 119, 119n16), a case that was referenced by the appealing party in the *Goeie Hoop Uitgewers* v *CNA* case so as to underpin its contention that the article around which the trial revolved was not obscene.

As to the other point, the *exceptio scientiae* rule, Price seemed to be stating in so many words that this rule, which had statutorily been introduced to exempt imported publications from the provisions regarding obscenity, also applied to domestically produced publications. In this way, he thus seemed to be fortifying the position taken in the Webb case. In reaching the conclusion to his discussion of the (domestically produced) article around which the case of *Goeie Hoop Uitgewers* v *CNA* revolved, Price stated that considering the medium in which the article appeared—a magazine—and the target audience of the medium—according to him, it consisted of "men and women, . . . youths and maidens, and . . . boys and girls of tender years without any discrimination whatever" (847)—the article had to be considered to be "likely in a great number of cases to corrupt the morals of young and inexperienced people" (847). Crucially, however, he added to this that "[i]t might be a different matter if an article of this kind were published in a scientific journal directed to sociological work only, and read only by scientific people, but that is not the case here" (847). Just as the Appeal Court had done in Webb's case, Price thus revealed himself to be a proponent of science exemption, and considering the context in which he made his statement, it appears that he felt that the rule should apply to domestically produced publications too—just like the Bench dealing with the Webb case seemingly felt.

The judgment that Price eventually came to seemed to have had a quite paradoxical consequence: as the article with which the copyright supposedly rested had to be deemed obscene and therefore *not* protected by law, the interdict of the sale, publication, and distribution of its copied version, which would probably have been considered just as obscene as the original[22]— Price did not go into this—had to be ruled invalid and the article had therefore to be released. It appears, thus, that due to Price's judgment, not one, but two "obscene" publications were now free to circulate within the Union. In any case, his judgment did not go unnoticed: it contributed to the emerging of a broad public debate regarding "obscene" periodicals and books in Afrikaans[23] (Geldenhuÿs 27; Kahn, "*Lion*" 286; van der Poll 202), a debate that would eventually result in new censorship legislation. We will go into this in greater detail in the next chapter.

CONCLUSION

No works were put on trial in the period 1910–1955 that would have been characterized by literary experts or the literary socialized public as representing works of literary merit. This notwithstanding, through the discussed cases that sometimes involved works of fiction or verse, the judiciary did come to introduce several concepts and practices that could and would also be applied to works of literature in ensuing decades. Furthermore, the judiciary did refer to and take a position on literary institutional issues on some occasions in this period. Both the concepts and the methods introduced and these latter position-takings are quite revealing of the stance of the judicial elite vis-à-vis literature during this period.

Already in the 1910 trial revolving around the book *The Grip* by Flaneuse, i.e., the case of *Rex* v *Shaw*, three important parameters for approaching texts were set. Firstly, witnesses were allowed to testify as to the nature of the book in terms of the law. No witnesses with literary expertise appear to have been called upon to testify in the mentioned case, however. Secondly, the Court held that a general tolerance had to be observed with respect to changing societal norms regarding certain themes—in the concrete case at hand, regarding (female) sexuality. Thirdly, the Court employed the contextual method of assessing publications. The latter two aspects would also be applied in the cases tried in the 1930s and 1950s. With all three aspects, South Africa proved itself to be in step with developments taking place in Anglo-American law. As these concepts and procedures played a crucial role in the autonomization of literatures within this wider legal sphere, one might observe that during the period 1910–1955 the ground was prepared for a legal autonomization of literature in South Africa.

Furthermore, as of the 1930s, i.e., in the case of *R v Webb* of 1934, the judicial elite started to prove itself to be in favor of an *exceptio scientiae*. In the 1950s Parliament followed suit. Moreover, the early judicial stance vis-à-vis science exemption was affirmed in the 1953 case of *Goeie Hoop Uitgewers v CNA and Another*. Evidently, the academic field had reached a mature stage by that time—which is something that in all probability cannot be said of the contemporary literary field. True, there is an indication that a judicial inclination toward the conceptual twin of the science exemption, the *exceptio artis*, existed, an inclination that became manifest in the 1932 case of *Rex v Meinert*. Yet the institutional autonomy that the judge handling the case was willing to grant literature solely pertained to *imported* literature. The judge's only concern seemed to be modern European literature and thought, not literature produced in Southern Africa, which would make sense, as no elaborate and differentiated literary infrastructure and activity seems to have been present in the region at that point. Apart from providing us with an indication that no relative autonomous literary field in terms of Bourdieu had developed in Southern Africa in the 1930s—no signs for this can be gathered from the later cases either—the tendency of the judge in the case of Meinert toward what might be termed a *colonial* art exemption also reinforces the other observation just made: that in the South Africa—and South-West Africa—of the period 1910–1950, the ground was prepared for a legal autonomization of literature. Indeed, a relative tolerance appeared to exist among the South (and the South-West) African judiciary regarding the written word, classic literature, scientific and scholarly texts, and modern European art and literature—a tolerance that was accompanied with a relative intolerance for "Puritan" positions, and also, in Meinert's case at least, with a racialized view of Southern African society.

NOTES

1. On this date the South Africa Act, which was passed by the British Parliament the previous year, came into force.

2. Through the Statute of Westminster of 1931 and the Status of the Union Act of 1934. Another way in which South Africa's legal independence from its former motherland had been established by that time was through the rise of domestic academic institutions that provided legal education. Until the late 1910s, when the first academic law schools were established in the country, many jurists working in South Africa had received their legal training in England (see Corder 46; Van Rooyen, "Centenary Law Faculty"; Visser).

3. The provinces being the Cape of Good Hope, Orange Free State, Natal, and Transvaal.

4. McDonald tentatively deals with administrative censorship in South Africa prior to 1963 in his *Literature Police* (see 104–5 et passim).

5. With regard to this latter point, Natal formed an exception (Marais 51).

6. On top of the local measures, the Post Office Act of 1911 prohibited the sending by post of "indecent or obscene" publications in the Union. The provisions of this act were later on

repeated in the Post Office Act of 1958 (Kahn, "*Lion*" 283), which apart from consolidating the mentioned prohibition in the Union also introduced it in South-West Africa (Marais 51–52). By that time, the latter area had long since become a mandated territory with the Union responsible for its administration. In 1919, Germany had been forced to relinquish its subject territories through the Treaty of Versailles and at that point South-West Africa was placed under the supervision of the Union (van der Poll 202n57).

7. Again, Natal formed the exception.

8. On the basis of systematic research on Supreme Court decisions in cases concerning literature, decisions on literary works and memos of the Publications Appeal Board—the administrative body of appeal that was created through new censorship legislation in 1975—and all of the major South African law journals and existing studies on South African censorship, I would argue that ten cases have been treated by the South African judiciary from pre-Union times until today that either directly or more indirectly pertained to literature and its status before the law: two cases before 1910 (namely *Q* v *de Jong* [1894] and *G. W. Hardy* v *Rex* [1905]); four cases during the period 1910–1963 (namely *Rex* v *Shaw* [1910]; *Rex* v *Meinert* [1932]; *Rex* v *Webb* [1934]; and *Goeie Hoop Uitgewers (Eiendoms) Bpk* v *Central News Agency and Another* [1953]); and four cases between 1963 and today (namely *Publications Control Board* v *William Heinemann, Ltd and Others* [1965]; *S* v *Insight Publications (Pty) Ltd and Another* [1965]; *Buren Uitgewers (Edms) Bpk en 'n Ander* v *Raad van Beheer oor Publikasies* [1975]; and *Human & Rousseau Uitgewers (Edms) Bpk* v *Snyman NO* [1978]). One of these trials (namely *Rex* v *Meinert*) took place in South-West Africa, which at that point fell under South African jurisdiction.

9. All translations in this study are mine, unless otherwise noted.

10. The legal fiction of the "ordinary man possessed of an average sense of decency" that is introduced by the Natal Bench here, seems to be a variant of the concept of the "reasonable man," which was introduced in English law in the early nineteenth century and has formed an important concept within it ever since (see Gardner).

11. Apparently, the book had managed to pass customs.

12. For a characterization of both Comstock's organization and its English prototypes, see Craig 36–37; 138–39.

13. That the case is indeed quite relevant to our discussion is further underlined by the multiple references that were made to the case in the landmark trial against Wilbur Smith's novel *When the Lion Feeds* that was held in 1965 (see *PCB* v *Heinemann* 139, 142, 143, 144, 151).

14. It was brought to Court twice: It was heard by the District Court for the Southern District of New York on November 25–26, 1933. On December 6, 1933, the one judge dealing with the case, Judge Woolsey, handed down his decision. Woolsey cleared Joyce's work of the charge of obscenity and, furthermore, effectuated a greater institutional autonomy for literature vis-à-vis U.S. law, *inter alia* by advancing that literary works had to be judged in their entirety. An appeal was subsequently made against the judgment to the Court of Appeals for the Second Circuit. On August 7, 1934, the appeal was dismissed by a 2–1 majority. The judgment of the majority also affirmed that a literary book had to be judged as a whole.

15. A notion that appears to have been more established than the notion of the ordinary man (see Gardner).

16. In his 1921 address titled "The Exclusion of the Bantu," two-time ANC president Z. R. Mahabane presents a clear analysis of this kind of thinking and the reasons that lay behind it (see Tafira 150).

17. That the Appellate Division clearly held this to be an important point was evidenced further in later cases tried on the basis of laws that fall outside of our focus of attention, e.g., in a 1936 case in which two newspaper editors had been convicted by a lower court on a charge of *crimen laesae venerationis* in that they had dishonored the Majesty of the King and his government and injured their dignity and power (see Corder 53–54). It is also worth noting that in *inter alia* this latter case, the Court, which was composed of three of the four judges that had sat on Webb's case, also gave clear evidence of being quite strongly committed to South Africa's institutionalized democratic values in general and to freedom of thought and speech in particular (Corder 53; cf. also 54). Its wording of the judgment in the case indeed seems telling:

"under the conditions of our modern civilization and development and of our political liberty and freedom of thought and speech," it declared, the Court "cannot be expected to accept the narrow and restricted views" of earlier centuries (*R* v *Roux and Another* qtd. in Corder 53).

18. What should perhaps also be mentioned in this conclusion to our examination of Webb's case is that no facts relevant to our discussion appeared from the part of the judgment that dealt with the indecent letter, the other component of the indictment.

19. It would depend on how well this period of censorship has been archived whether such a study could be carried out at all. As mentioned already, McDonald tentatively dealt with administrative censorship in South Africa before 1963 in his *Literature Police*, particularly with censorship in the 1950s (see 104–5 et passim).

20. Incidentally, the 1868 Hicklin case has often been referred to as authority for the isolated-passage criterion, but the actual report of the case gives no support to this view, as St. John-Stevas pointed out (134). Indeed, Chief Justice Cockburn, who, in the latter case, formulated the test of obscenity that would be fundamental to obscenity trials for decades and decades to come, declared in the 1878 case of *R* v *Bradlaugh* that "[t]he book must be looked at as a whole and . . . its effects as a whole are to produce obscenity" (Cockburn qtd. in St. John-Stevas 135).

21. The case concerned books by Erskine Caldwell, James Farrell, William Faulkner, Harold Robbins, and Calder Willingham, and a famous opinion was delivered in it by judge Curtis Bok, who declared that Pennsylvania could not deem the books concerned to be obscene (Boyer 274; Newman 58). Importantly, Bok had reached his decision on the basis of the premises that, firstly, First Amendment guarantees imposed limitations upon obscenity proceedings, that, secondly, account should be taken of a book's artistic status, and that, thirdly, a book should be judged as a whole (Sova 95–96).

22. The "original" was an Afrikaans translation of a piece that had appeared in an English periodical (*Goeie Hoop Uitgewers* v *CNA* 844).

23. The Afrikaans publishing industry was growing rapidly in the 1950s (cf. Cronjé 25 et passim).

Part II

Hesitant Legal Recognition, 1955–1975

Chapter Two

The 1965 Trials

Wilbur Smith's When the Lion Feeds *and Can Themba's "The Fugitives"*

We need to start this chapter with a fairly extensive discussion of the legal framework guiding publications control in South Africa in the period 1955–1975, because both on the national level, i.e., statutorily, and on the international legal stage, quite drastic changes occurred at the outset of this period that profoundly affected the regulation of both imported and domestically produced literature. At the end of the period, as we will see in Part III, the statutory situation changed substantially again. We will thus begin this chapter with scrutinizing the legal developments occurring on the national and international level. After that we will analyze the first and only major trial held in the period, the trial of Wilbur Smith's novel *When the Lion Feeds*, and a more minor trial, that regarding Can Themba's short story "The Fugitives." The chapter will end with a conclusion regarding the legal status of literature around 1965—inferred from the way in which the judiciary approached literature institutionally and poetologically.

Let us start with examining the developments taking place within South Africa itself. In the wake of the 1953 case of *Goeie Hoop Uitgewers* v *Central News Agency and Another*, which we examined in the previous chapter, the first of the consecutive Nasionale Party (National Party—NP) governments, that of Prime Minister D. F. Malan (1948–1954), appointed a Commission of Inquiry into Undesirable Publications. Geoffrey Cronjé, then professor of sociology at the University of Pretoria and a prominent apartheid ideologue (cf. J. Coetzee 166; McDonald, *Literature Police* 122),[1] was made chair of the commission. Quite likely, the appointment of the commission represented a reaction to the wide obscenity debate that had emerged within the Union, a debate that had seemingly been triggered by the rapid rise of popular books and periodicals in Afrikaans that were held to contain obscene content on a regular basis (cf. Cronjé et al. 28 et passim; Ehlers 40; "Note" 47)—the kind of popular publications, indeed, that had formed the center of focus of the *Goeie Hoop* case.[2] On October 3, 1956, the Cronjé Commission submitted a detailed report, and in September 1957, this report was publically released. The report, which also contained a draft censorship bill, suggested a twofold approach to the regulation of publications.

On the one hand, it argued that stricter censorship measures should be taken: the Commission proposed among other things that a system of pre-censorship be set up; that an administrative body be created that was to be called the Publications Board[3] and that was to deal with both imported and domestically produced works; that all printers, publishers, booksellers, and periodicals be formally licensed; and that a quasi-judicial[4] Publications Board of Appeal be called into existence. This latter board was to be presided over by a judge and further consist of four individuals with specialist knowledge regarding, respectively, the moral, religious, or educationist dimensions of publications control; the literary side of it; the book market in general; and the point of view of women and families. Constituted thus, it was to deal with eventual appeals against judgments made by the Publications Board (cf. Cronjé et al. 177–78; cf. also Kahn, "*Lion*" 292; McDonald, *Literature Police* 23).

On the other hand the report was echoing the nation-building philosophies and practices of many nineteenth-century Western nations—cf. the Prussian *Wende zum Kulturstaat* discussed in chapter 1—in that it proposed a program that would be aimed at improving literary standards. The proposed program would consist of creating a state-funded "South African Institute for Literature," which was basically to be the complete opposite of the Publications Board; the task of the latter was to ban "undesirable literature," the purpose of the former would be to foster "desirable" literature. Furthermore, the program would be aimed at making schools, universities, churches, and the book trade cultivate the literary taste of, notably, the "white" inhabitants of South Africa (see Cronjé et al. 256ff ; cf. also McDonald, *Literature Police* 23, 26).

The report thus clearly manifested the commission's appreciation of (white) literature (cf. also Kahn, "'Dirty' Books" 34; Kahn, "*Lion*" 287; McDonald, *Literature Police* 25). Furthermore, it evidenced that Cronjé et al. had been seeking advice from literary experts. In fact, the report showed that the commission was well-informed about the contemporary state of the art of literary theory and criticism: among the works the report cited were Roman Ingarden's *Das Literarische Kunstwerk* (1931), Jean-Paul Sartre's *Qu'est-ce que la littérature?* (1948), Cleanth Brooks's *The Well-Wrought Urn* (1947), and René Wellek and Austin Warren's *Theory of Literature* (1949) (see

Cronjé et al. 271ff). It seems quite likely that the poet and literary academic H. van der Merwe Scholtz—who would become a key literary censor in 1963 and remain so for more than two decades—formed the medium through which these scholarly up-to-date references found their way into the commission's report. Merwe Scholtz is indeed often credited with introducing formalism to Afrikaans literary studies (McDonald, *Literature Police* 27; Wiehahn 154) and was mentioned by the commission as one of the persons from whom it had received expert advice (Cronjé et al. 269).

Whereas the references to the abovementioned literary theoretical works were already a rather remarkable element in the report, the fact that the commission came to formulate a rather elaborate conception of literature is at least as noteworthy. This conception of literature was unfolded as Cronjé et al. were making their argument regarding the dual approach toward literature they envisioned. They made clear that their main reason for proposing their strict form of statutory censorship lay in their belief that "undesirable books" formed "spiritual poison" and could therefore lead to a degeneration of the "white" South African (Cronjé et al. 40). At the same time, however, they held that books could also have the very opposite effect: good literature could uplift the people, they felt (204ff)—hence the proposed promotional program. The commission's politicized and racialized scheme of "poisonous" versus "uplifting" literature was underpinned with a rather definite conception of literature that was quite elaborately sketched out and appeared to be made up first and foremost of Platonic principles and principles inspired by idealist aesthetics and formalism (see Cronjé et al. 29ff, 86–87 et passim). Platonic elements might for instance be found in passages like the following: "Undesirable publications are a cultural problem because their purpose is to drag through the gutter everything that is beautiful and good and noble" (Cronjé et al. qtd. in Kahn, "*Lion*" 291). Both idealist aesthetical and formalist influences appear to be revealed in the following passage (cf. McDonald, *Literature Police* 27)—*inter alia* in the fact that the passage in so many words states that a work of literature should satisfy a transformation principle of the kind that was described in the introduction:

> The literary work of art is a creation that is realized in language. Its building blocks are human acts, experiences, thoughts, relations, etc. These are all things that also exist in countless relationships and combinations in daily life, outside of the work of art. In the *successful* work of art, these building blocks are being rearranged for the benefit of an aesthetic goal. They are then put together in such a harmonic way and in such a dynamic relation to each other that this for the reader creates the "appearance" of real life; as such they mean new experiences and experience of life for the reader. This thus naturally implies the hand of a creator which selects and inspects, which rearranges and groups, which arranges and brings to the arranged material a certain unity or

organization. The work of art is thus an arranged whole, a building, a structure. (Cronjé et al. 86; emphasis Cronjé et al.)

Like the up-to-date references, most of the poetological principles which the commission came to formulate seemed to have found their way into the report through intermediary Merwe Scholtz (McDonald, *Literature Police* 27).

Despite the fact that the commission attributed such great value to what it regarded as serious literature, it was not willing to propose that it be given statutory exemption. Explaining their intentions regarding the draft bill, Cronjé et al. did stress, however, that they had purposely designed the functions of the proposed Publications Board in a way that would afford literature some protection. Moreover, they explicitly argued that account had to be taken of the artistic merit when judging a publication (Cronjé et al. 142), a position that was reflected in section (3) (*d*) of their draft bill (see 186). Yet just as emphatically as they advanced this latter point, they rejected explicit exemption, the ground for this being that such an absolute position would be likely to bring "inflexibility" with it (137).[5] The room that Cronjé et al. left for protecting literature lay among other things in providing that no subject matter was "undesirable" in itself, but that it was the manner in which the subject was treated that counted (29). To illustrate this point, they discussed Sophocles's *Oedipus Rex*: whereas they recognized that this work did contain "shocking" elements such as acts of incest, they argued that these facts were "presented as facts in connection with the characters and the plot, and *not for their own sake*."[6] As they occurred in a legitimate context, the commission reasoned, the details lost their offensiveness.

With its emphasis that no content was undesirable per se and with its underwriting of the contextual approach—a position-taking which they appeared to be underpinning mainly with poetological principles—the report evidenced that when it came to the criteria for judgment, the commission's proposed measures would represent continuity in the legal regulation of publications in South Africa. Another way in which the suggested criteria for judgment would have brought continuity was through the concept of the "average, civilized, decent, reasonable and responsible inhabitants of the Union,"[7] a concept that was introduced in sec. 2 (1) of the draft bill—as we saw in the previous chapter, rather similar concepts of readership constituted the norm in the pre-1950 trials. On the other hand, the commission of course also wanted to break with the past, as it proposed to sideline the judiciary and make publications control an entirely administrative affair. This latter proposal was one of the aspects of the draft bill that revealed it had been inspired heavily by the Irish Censorship of Publications Act of 1946 (cf. Cronjé et al. 114; cf. also "Report of the Commission" 114).

The Cronjé Commission made quite a few proposals that later on were effectively incorporated in a similar or even identical manner into the censorship act that would come to replace the old Entertainments (Censorship) Act of 1931, as amended. However, the Strijdom government (1954–1958), which in the meantime had taken up the baton, could not entirely agree with the approach that the commission suggested, and thus the commission's draft bill never became law. It took the Nationalist government an additional three years to present a Publications and Entertainments Bill. During this period, which saw the government of Prime Minister Hendrik Verwoerd (1958–1966) assuming power, the recommendations of the commission were extensively discussed in public.

During these same three years, several crucial international developments occurred that changed the face of the legal treatment of literature within the Anglo-American sphere. In the United States, the 1957 Supreme Court case of *Roth* v *United States* quite univocally instigated an *exceptio artis* pertaining to literature (see *Roth* v *United States*; cf. also Katz 219; Kearns 85; Ladenson 152ff; O'Neil 179). In England, the Obscene Publications Act, 1959 came into effect, also establishing an exemption for literature (cf. Obscene Publications Act, 1959 1, 4). Furthermore, the landmark case over D. H. Lawrence's *Lady Chatterley's Lover* (*R* v *Penguin Books Ltd.*) was held between October, 20 and November 2, 1960, proving the latter act adequate in this respect: Lawrence's novel, which was generally held to be of literary merit by the literary experts delivering testimony in the trial, was acquitted of the charge of being obscene, despite the fact that it contained passages and language that were found to be offensive by parts of the public. The early to mid-1960s further saw a number of obscenity trials being held over Henry Miller's *Tropic of Cancer* in different parts of the United States.[8] One of the cases was brought before the Supreme Court, which on the basis of the Roth standard decided that the book was not obscene (Bronstein 67–68). Thus, when the South African government finally introduced its bill in 1960—the year in which the referendum on becoming a republic was also held and resulted in South Africa becoming a republic on May 31, 1961—the literary field had been given definite legal recognition both in Great Britain and the United States. It was not necessarily evident that South Africa would follow suit, however.

The Publications and Entertainments Bill put forward by the Verwoerd government was based on the blueprint of the Cronjé Commission, but it went even further than the commission in the controlling measures it formulated. Moreover, it ignored the commission's recommendations for promoting literature (cf. Kahn, "*Lion*" 292; McDonald, *Literature Police* 32). Further public debate ensued, in which organizations such as the South African branch of PEN and authoritative individuals such as literary patron and Supreme Court Justice J. F. Marais, whom we already encountered in chapter 1, made strong pleas against the bill. Perhaps in part as a result of these pleas, the bill was supplanted by a modified one. The amended bill, which was titled the Undesirable Publications Bill, made a proposal that was diametrically opposed to its predecessor: whereas the original had suggested, just as Cronjé had, that censorship should become an entirely administrative affair, the second draft proposed that the courts be given the sole say (Diemont 209). After it had been read for the first time in Parliament, it was referred to a select committee. This committee, finally, came forward with yet another bill, which represented a halfway solution between the first and the second ones (209). It was called the Publications and Entertainments Bill. Having undergone some minor amendments, this third bill was passed in the 1963 Parliamentary session and thus became Act 26 of that year: the Publications and Entertainments Act, 1963.[9]

The final act reflected the same duality as Cronjé et al.'s proposed bill had. On the one hand, its spirit was as paternalistic as the commission's bill had been. This was evidenced by the remarks that the then Minister of the Interior, J. de Klerk, made when he piloted the bill through Parliament: "Let us . . . realize," he said,

> that it is the duty . . . of the whole House to ensure that this evil influence which is exerted through the medium of literature and other publications is combated and controlled . . . Let us realize that we are the guardians, and the responsible guardians, of the people outside: we must give them the necessary protection, particularly to those who are weak. You and I can judge for ourselves whether we should read this rubbish or not and that is our affair, but we must protect the weak from themselves, otherwise they will fall by the wayside. (de Klerk qtd. in Dean 79n99)[10]

What exactly it was that "people outside" had to be protected from, according to Parliament, became clear in section 5 (2) of the act. The most important provisions of this section read as follows:

> A publication or object shall be deemed to be undesirable if it or any part of it—
>
> a. is indecent or obscene or is offensive or harmful to public morals;
> b. is blasphemous or is offensive to the religious convictions or feelings of any section of the inhabitants of the Republic;
> c. brings any section of the inhabitants of the Republic into ridicule or contempt;
> d. is harmful to the relations between any sections of the inhabitants of the Republic;
> e. is prejudicial to the safety of the State, the general welfare or the peace and good order (*PEA, 1963*, 282)

Yet whereas the Act thus clearly meant to protect both South African citizens and the South African state from harm, it also showed evidence that the literary field had reached a certain amount of institutional autonomy and that Parliament had wanted to support this development: the act indeed made it possible to appoint literary experts to the Publications Control Board,[11] the censorship body—equivalent to Cronjé's Publications Board—that the act brought into being (cf. *PEA, 1963*, 278).[12] As we saw in chapter 1, the recognition of expertise represents a strong indication that the institutional autonomization of a literary field has reached an advanced stage (cf. Sapiro 450–51).

But although the PEA demonstrated that Parliament had wanted to facilitate a certain amount of autonomy,[13] it did not go so far as to grant literature the high degree of legal autonomy that the English Obscene Publications Act of 1959 had granted English literature. The primary means through which it in principle made it possible to grant literature a certain amount of autonomy—apart from the possibility to include literary experts on the board, that is—was through the concept of the likely reader, a concept which had been borrowed from the Obscene Publications Act, 1959. This concept had been introduced in the 1959 act to adapt the Hicklin test so that one no longer had to estimate what the effect of a publication would be on the *possible* reader, but what its effect would be on the *probable* reader. With the concept of the likely reader in hand, one did not necessarily always have to take "weak" readers (youth, women, uneducated people, native populations, etc.) into account when judging a publication: now it was also possible to postulate a readership comprised of "strong" readers (adults, [well-]educated citizens, literary socialized people, etc.).

Remarkably enough, the PEA did not take over the Obscene Publications Act's contextualist test, a test that had also been incorporated purposively into the latter act so as to safeguard literature—indeed, the latter act made the contextualist approach a mandatory element of the new test of obscenity which it introduced: the isolated-passage test was no longer allowed under the new act. As the above-quoted passage from section 5 (2) of the PEA quite unequivocally declared, "[a] publication or object sh[ould] be deemed to be undesirable if it *or any part of it*" was indecent, obscene, blasphemous, and so forth.

As it appears, the executive had wanted to ensure that the PEA would leave the administrative and judicial bodies involved a certain amount of flexibility in carrying out the functions it assigned them. For just as Cronjé had proposed, it avoided the "inflexibility" of an explicit statutory *exceptio artis*, and, furthermore, it chose not to make the contextualist test mandatory, but, instead, also maintain the isolated-passage test. Effectively, or so it appeared, it thus made it possible for the people it entrusted with enforcing the act to keep literature on a relatively short leash. On the other hand, by introducing a likely reader test and by apparently leaving room for the application of a contextualist test, it also made it possible to grant literature a certain amount of freedom.[14]

When it came to the concept of science exemption, the executive apparently had fewer misgivings, for the new act did contain an explicit *exceptio scientiae*: sec. 5 (4) indeed declared that "[t]he provisions of this section shall not apply with reference to [*inter alia*] any matter in a publication of a technical, scientific or professional nature *bona fide* intended for the advancement of or for use in any particular profession or branch of arts, literature or science" (*PEA, 1963*, 284).[15]

As to the procedure, the following can be said. Prosecutions brought by the Attorney General could be heard before the Magistrates' Courts or the Supreme Court (Diemont 210). If the Attorney General took no action, the Publications Control Board could declare a publication to be "undesirable" and, therefore, banned (cf. Diemont 210). Both administrative bodies (police, customs, etc.) and the public could request the PCB to judge a publication in terms of the act. In case a publication was declared "undesirable," a ban on producing and disseminating it within the territories of South and South-West Africa would be instituted. One could, however, appeal against a PCB decision to a Division of the Supreme Court. This Court would then examine both the publication and the judgment of the PCB. In turn, a decision of a Division of the Supreme Court could also be appealed: one could take such a decision to the Appellate Division of the Supreme Court. The decision of this latter judicial body would be final.

In sum, the new act clearly revealed that for the first time in its history, South Africa chose to steer its own course with regard to literature regulation and no longer follow Britain's lead. The new course that the executive had mapped out essentially resembled the course that the Cronjé Commission had envisioned: just as in the latter's draft bill, the PEA appeared to be designed to instigate a dual approach toward publications regulation: on the one hand it seemed to be aimed at (paternalistically) protecting the "weak"; on the other hand at promoting literature (so as to build a nation—first and foremost, of course, an *Afrikaner* nation). In order to attain the latter goal, the act did not establish an explicit *exceptio artis* pertaining to literature. Rather, it introduced instruments with which literature could, but not necessarily should, be granted a certain amount of institutional autonomy. The PEA was thus not necessarily as anti-literary as some contemporary juridical commentators tended to think it was (cf. Dean 112). To be sure, it contained fewer guarantees for literature than the English Obscene Publications Act of 1959: contrary to the latter act, the PEA did not establish an explicit *exceptio artis* nor did it make the contextual approach mandatory. However, it did provide the opportunity to apply the contextual approach—thereby effectively introducing it onto the nation's statute books. Furthermore, it made it possible to involve literary experts in the adjudication of literature in terms of the law—and effectively, this provision was employed to maximum effect throughout the entire period the PEA was in force: from 1963 to 1975, literary experts were de facto in control of the administrative censorship of literature (see McDonald, *Literature Police*). Lastly, the act introduced the criterion of the likely reader, in principle an empirical notion that, unlike the concepts of readership that had previously been employed by the South African judiciary, enabled differentiating between different types of audiences.

During the entire period that the PEA was in force, not many appeals were made against decisions of the PCB. This was most probably a result of the fact that very heavy costs were involved in making an appeal (cf. Diemont 213; Kahn, "Publications and Entertainments Act" 44; "'Obscenity' on Trial"; Suzman 200). Just two PCB decisions on a literary work were brought to court in the decade or so that literature was regulated by the PEA, namely the decision on Wilbur Smith's 1964 debut novel *When the Lion Feeds*[16] and the one regarding André Brink's 1973 novel *Kennis van die Aand* (cf. McDonald, *Literature Police* 56; Suzman 201ff)—the decision concerning Can Themba's 1964 short story "The Fugitives," which we will also be discussing shortly, did not represent an appeal against a PCB decision, but criminal proceedings. One should add though, with respect to the just elaborated concept "literary," that there was a rather strong consensus among both the actors who passed judgment on the Smith novel (i.e., the members of the PCB and the judges involved) and the actors who commented on the trials (i.e., literary critics and jurists) that the book could not be considered "literature" in the narrow, honorific sense.[17] Rather, it was considered an "adventure novel," i.e., "light reading" (cf. Aedilis Curulis 17; Kahn, "*Lion*" 312; *PCB v Heinemann* 152). Yet notwithstanding the fact that Smith's novel was not considered to represent a work of literature in the strict sense by the actors involved, the judgment that would eventually be passed on it by the Appellate Division of the Supreme Court would go on to become the major precedent guiding literature regulation for decades to come.

Let us now proceed with examining the mentioned cases—first the Cape trial of Smith's *Lion*; then the Cape trial concerning Themba's "The Fugitives"; and, finally, the pivotal Appellate Division trial of Smith's novel.[18]

THE CAPE TRIAL OF WILBUR SMITH'S *WHEN THE LION FEEDS*

Like most books in English that were in circulation in South Africa at the time, Smith's novel had been imported from London (cf. McDonald, *Literature Police* 104; Pienaar, "Histories-juridiese Aspekte" 245). Perhaps the words of Chief Justice Steyn, as uttered in the majority judgment of the later Appellate Division trial, offer a fairly representative picture of how the novel was generally received by the contemporaneous public: "It is a novel," Steyn stated, "which describes with many exciting episodes, life and conditions in the early pioneering days in Natal and in the Transvaal, more particularly on the Witwatersrand. It is not a publication for any select circle of mature literary connoisseurs. It provides light reading to which any literate person, in whatever walk of life may be attracted" (*PCB* v *Heinemann* 152).[19] And indeed, Smith's debut actually did attract many readers: within months 10,000 copies were sold in South Africa and some 25,000 copies abroad (Kahn, "*Lion*" 312). On July 10, 1964, some three months after the novel had appeared in South African bookshops, the *Government Gazette* reported that the PCB had judged the novel to be "undesirable," and that it therefore was banned.[20] The board had found the book to have the tendency to deprave or corrupt the minds of persons who were likely to be exposed to the effect or influence thereof; to be offensive or harmful to public morals; to be likely to be outrageous or disgusting to persons who were likely to read it; and to be dealing in an improper manner with promiscuity, passionate love scenes, lust, sexual intercourse, obscene language, blasphemous language, sadism, and cruelty (cf. van der Poll 206; cf. also Diemont 207). Nineteen passages from the novel, read in relation to the book as a whole, were considered to be violating the law (cf. van der Poll 206).[21] Of these nineteen passages, the following one would receive special attention in court. The passage describes a scene in which protagonist Sean and his girlfriend Anna have sexual intercourse:

> Now, kneeling before her, as she lay with her head thrown back and her arms half-raised to receive him, Sean suddenly bowed his head and touched her with his mouth. The taste of her was clean as the taste of the sea.
> Her eyes flew open. "Sean, no, you mustn't—oh no, you mustn't."
> There were lips within lips and a bud as softly resilient as a tiny green grape. Sean found it with the tip of his tongue.
> "Oh, Sean, you can't do that. Please, please, please." And her hands were in the thick hair at the back of his head holding him there.
> "I can't stand it any more, come over me ... quickly, quickly, Sean."
> Filling like a sail in a hurricane, swollen and hard and tight, stretched beyond its limit until it burst and was blown to shreds in the wind and was gone. Everything gone. The wind and the sail, the tension and the wanting, all gone. There was left only the great nothingness which is peace. Perhaps a kind of death; perhaps death is like that. But, like death, not an ending—for even death contains the seeds of resurrection. So they came back from peace to a new beginning, slowly at first and then faster until they were two people again. Two people on a blanket among the reeds with the sunlight white on the sand about them. (Smith qtd. in *PCB* v *Heinemann* 158–59)

Smith's British publisher, William Heinemann Ltd., appealed against the decision of the PCB, and so in early December 1964,[22] the case was brought before the Cape Provincial Division of the Supreme Court.[23] On January 15, 1965, the Court handed down its judgment, which was divided into a majority and a dissenting opinion. Let us turn to these opinions and examine, firstly, how the Court dealt with literature institutionally and, secondly, how it approached it poetologically.[24]

The institutional side of the case revolved around five major issues: (1) literary expertise; (2) contextualism; (3) (likely) readership; (4) freedom of expression; and (5) the relevance of literary merit. Let us consecutively examine what the Court had to say about these issues.

Literary Expertise

In its appeal to the CPD, the applicant Heinemann Ltd. and Others filed affidavits from six literary experts, raising five objections to the PCB's decision. The first pertained to comparisons with other books. It was meant to convince the Court that the frank way in which Smith's novel portrayed sexual matters was the rule rather than the exception in modern literature (cf. Kahn, "*Lion*" 314n89; *PCB* v *Heinemann* 148).[25] The second dealt with sales abroad. It pointed out the fact that 10,000 copies of the novel had been sold within the Republic of South Africa without any objection having been raised, and that 25,000 copies had been sold abroad with no complaints having been heard either (cf. Kahn, "*Lion*" 312). The third objection had regard to literary merit. Presupposing that this could be used as a defense—whether partial or not—it was argued that Smith's book had literary merit. The fourth objection concerned opinion evidence, i.e., the opinions of literary experts as to whether Smith's book could be deemed to be indecent or obscene, or offensive or harmful to public morals when one took into account its likely readership. The fifth objection, finally, regarded the contemporary treatment of sexual matters (cf. *PCB* v *Heinemann* 138–39). It was adduced to convince the Court that the standards of the contemporary community were such that descriptions of sexual matters had become accepted, provided that they did not represent any undue vulgarity, sensuality, or the exploitation of sex as the dominant theme (cf. Diemont 207; Kahn, "*Lion*" 314n89; *PCB* v *Heinemann* 148). Although the Court did deal with most of the issues raised by the literary experts—we will examine how they did below—the affidavits per se were of no avail: rather categorically the Court ruled that the affidavits were inadmissible. The reason for this, it explained, was that section 6 of the PEA made the Court's opinion decisive, and that the Court could and should form an opinion without the guidance of expert witnesses (cf. Diemont 207–8; *Heinemann* v *PCB* 258; Kahn, "*Lion*" 315). It appears to be rather remarkable that the Court took such a principled position, because although section 6 did indeed repeatedly indicate that it was "the opinion of the court" that mattered in the application of the section, the section did not say that the Court should form its opinion without seeking assistance from relevant actors, such as expert witnesses. What makes the position of the Court even more remarkable is that expert evidence had expressly been introduced as admissible in the English Obscene Publications Act, 1959, so as to facilitate the protection of literature. Still the Court chose not to be guided by expert evidence. Nevertheless, after having established its principled position, the Court did go on to deal with most of the themes that the literary expert witnesses had raised.

Contextualism

Counsel for Heinemann argued that the book had to be considered as a whole, not just the lewd or indelicate passages in isolation (Diemont 208). The attorney of the PCB contended otherwise: the inquiry was not whether the book as a whole was obscene, but whether any part of it was; if one passage were obscene, this damned the entire book (208). Although both the Customs Act, 1955 and the PEA, 1963 declared that "[a] publication or object shall be deemed to be undesirable if it or any part of it [is indecent etc.]," Justice van Zyl, in ruling for the majority, contended that a part could not be judged entirely divorced from the whole, and that the reference to "part" made in the relevant sections of the two acts was intended to ensure that regard was had to "the impact made by the alleged objectionable portion of the book" (*Heinemann* v *PCB* 258; Kahn, "*Lion*" 315; van der Poll 206–7). "It is the virulence of the poison and the susceptibility of the victim that determines the size of the lethal dose," van Zyl explained (van Zyl qtd. in Kahn, "*Lion*" 315). The majority judgment did declare—at first sight paradoxically so—that the board or Court had to be of the opinion that a publication, or part of it, would arouse in the reader strong feelings of sickening repugnance, or that the reader would find it shocking to his moral sensibilities or repulsive. However, for the majority this had to be in relation, not to the character or episode as such, but as part of the publication (cf. *Heinemann* v *PCB* 258; Kahn, "*Lion*" 316). Justice Diemont had a diametrically opposed view on the matter, for in his minority opinion he remarked that he regretted being driven to the conclusion that the novel represented an undesirable publication in terms of the PEA, and that if the test of the English Obscene Publications Act, 1959, could be applied that the matter be taken as a whole, he might have been able to come to a different conclusion (cf. Diemont 210; Kahn, "*Lion*" 318; van der Poll 207). Apparently, Diemont felt that the PEA called for the application of the isolated-passage test.

(Likely) Readership

As both the majority and the minority of the CPD were of the opinion that Heinemann's affidavits could not be admitted, they both had to make their own estimate of who the persons were who were likely to read Smith's novel, and what effect the book would tend to have on these persons. The estimation of the majority, Justices van Zyl and Beyers, was that the audience of the book would be made up of adults and older teenagers; they did not think that it would generally be read by the early teenager (cf. Kahn, "*Lion*" 317). Of course, circumscribing the likely audience of a book as comprising adults and older teenagers means describing an audience that is potentially very large and very heterogeneous. The majority did not believe, however, that the audience would be made up of every conceivable category of adults and older teenagers: in reference to the earlier quoted passage describing the act of oral sex, the majority apparently stated that although there were many persons who would find this passage disgusting, they were not the likely readers of the work, and that an occasional "few unsuspecting borrowers from a library" were not significant (Kahn, "*Lion*" 318).[26] Clearly, the majority thus distinguished between *possible* and *probable* readers of the novel. It also seems that the majority used the likely reader test as a means to allow Smith's novel in this particular case, yet by implication, literature in general, a certain amount of autonomy, for even though their judgment acknowledged that *many* persons would be disgusted by the passage describing oral sex, this fact alone did not make the book "undesirable": the novel's likely readers would react otherwise, in their estimation.

In his dissenting opinion, Justice Diemont again adopted a stance that was completely opposed to that of the majority: in referring to the passage describing oral sex—Diemont based his entire opinion almost exclusively on this one passage (Diemont 210; *PCB* v *Heinemann* 155; van der Poll 207)—he stated that he found that many actual readers would be likely to be shocked and disgusted by the sexual activity in the form of "animal passion" that was described therein, and in making his case, he expressly postulated "the reaction of the housewife who walks into the suburban library in Wynberg, and selects this book at random off the shelf" (Diemont qtd. in Kahn, "*Lion*" 318). Thus, notwithstanding the fact that the PEA had introduced the likely reader criterion, Diemont still took *possible* readers into account also. It appears, furthermore, that at least partly on the basis of his vision of the probable reaction of the possible reader, he felt that literature could not be granted the freedom that the majority was willing to allow it.

Freedom of Expression

With regard to the statutory test of offensiveness to public morals, i.e., whether an incriminated work was likely to be outrageous or disgustful to those likely to read it,[27] the majority concluded that "the Publications Control Board or the Court must be of the opinion that it, or part of it, will arouse in the reader strong feelings of aversion or feelings of sickening repugnance, or that the reader will find it shocking to his moral sensibilities or repulsive" (*Heinemann* v *PCB* 258). The majority further held that "[i]t [was] not sufficient if the reader [found] the character depicted, the episode recounted, the subject matter dealt with, to be such"; the mentioned test would only be satisfied if the reader found

> the publication, or part of it, *qua publication or qua* part of such publication, to be such. The degree of aversion, sickening repugnance, repulsiveness or shock to moral sensibilities . . . [would] be such as to cause the reader to want to put the book down, not want to read the book further, to throw the book away, or to throw the book from him, and these reactions . . . [would] be lasting ones and not merely those of the moment. (*Heinemann* v *PCB* 258; emphasis in the original)

Yet whereas this interpretation already postulated quite strong criteria for the public morals test, the majority raised the bar even higher by stipulating that it would be "quite fallacious to say 'but it would be disgustful to say this in the drawing-room or in company or in mixed company, and therefore it is disgustful to publish it by the printed word'" (van Zyl qtd. in Kahn, "*Lion*" 316). For "[i]t . . . always [had to] be remembered,"

> that the privacy of the reader is a very powerful conditioning factor in his reactions to what he reads, and that within the privacy of his mind the average reader will not find disgustful many matters which would be disgustful to him if uttered in public, and that the privacy of the reader also makes acceptable many things which it would be improper to utter aloud indiscriminately. (316)

Legal scholar Ellison Kahn read these words as constituting "an impressive drawing of a distinction between what is sometimes called private and public morality" ("*Lion*" 316). Yet, although the postulated "private morality" of the majority allowed for literature to treat many delicate matters which it would not have been able to deal with otherwise, the majority also stated that the test could in principle be satisfied by a lack of reticence, or too great details or peculiar selection of material (316). At the same time, however, they quite unequivocally added that it was "absurd . . . to even contemplate that the legislature intended to make any but the grossest transgressions of good taste and decorum a crime" (majority judgment qtd. in Kahn, "*Lion*" 316). It thus appears that the majority also used the test regarding offensiveness to public morals as a means to grant literature a certain amount of autonomy: by providing such strong criteria, they created considerable (legal) room to play for the medium.

In much the same vein, the majority declared in regard to the test of obscenity or indecency that "the law is not there to protect the sensibilities of the prudish at the expense of the liberty of the more frank or the more robust or even the outspoken earthy" (majority judgment qtd. in Kahn, "*Lion*" 315–16). In a passage that is quite reminiscent of the position taken by Bok in Meinert's case, the majority explained that

> [i]t should always be remembered that among the most cherished rights of our civilization and among the rights we have fought the hardest for, are the right to enquire into any matter and the right to publish and disseminate the knowledge that has been gained from any such enquiry. These rights, which have also been called the sacred right to be a heretic or to preach heresy, are part of the springs of life that have given to Western civilization that vigorous vitality that has borne that long uninterrupted period of development which has been enjoyed by almost every country and people of the Occident. It is obvious from the manner in which the legislature has drawn up the [Publications and Entertainments] Act . . . that it wished to hold with great nicety the balance between the requirements of the mores of the times on the one hand and the pursuit, publication and dissemination of knowledge—which includes experience—on the other hand, so as to ensure the South African society a healthy moral timbre and the continuation of that vigorous, spiritual and intellectual growth that has characterized the peoples of the Occident. (majority judgment qtd. in Kahn, "*Lion*" 316)

What seems to become clear from this passage is that what most fundamentally underpinned the majority's willingness to grant literature a certain degree of autonomy was not so much the idea that literature should enjoy some kind of exceptional legal status, as the belief that the freedom of expression should be protected. We cannot exclude, though, that the majority played this freedom of expression card for strategic reasons: perhaps van Zyl and Beyers felt that laying claim to the right to "the pursuit, publication and dissemination of knowledge" formed a stronger trump than claiming any (special) rights for literature would have—which, judging from the remark "which includes experience," was perhaps considered by the majority to be included in the freedom of expression.[28] The trump hypothesis becomes all the more plausible when one realizes that the South African judiciary was well aware that unlike the English Obscene Publications Act, 1959, and contemporaneous U.S. decisions regarding obscene publications, the PEA did not explicitly grant literature any special rights on the basis of it being perceived a "public good" (cf. Dean 142; Kahn, "Freedom" 48–50; Kahn, "*Lion*" 318; *PCB* v *Heinemann* 139–40).

The Relevance of Literary Merit

The majority judgment quite expressly made clear that with the PEA in force, no explicit claim could be laid to an *exceptio artis* pertaining to literature: unequivocally the judgment stated that "the literary merit or the relevancy of the matter complained about cannot be employed to take it out of reach of the statute" (*Heinemann* v *PCB* 258; cf. also Kahn, "*Lion*" 315). Interestingly enough, however, the majority declared their regret that the act made no allowances for literary merit (Kahn, "*Lion*" 315). Diemont, for his part, also critiqued the act. As we have already seen, he stated that he regretted being driven to the conclusion that Smith's novel was undesirable, remarking that if the contextualist test of the English Obscene Publications Act, 1959, were applied, a different conclusion might be reached. Yet his critique went further than this, for he added that the "South African Act [was] framed in such wide terms that much harm [could] be done to the cause of literature without any corresponding good being done to the cause of morals" (Diemont qtd. in Kahn, "*Lion*" 318).

When it comes to the question of the poetological approach of the Court, we can be quite brief. On the basis of the available sources it appears that no clear literary-conceptual position was taken either by the majority or the minority.

To conclude, both the majority and the minority of the Cape Court uttered critique of the new act. Both evidenced to be feeling that literature had not been given enough protection under the PEA. Both, moreover, seemed to regret that the PEA did not more resemble the English Obscene Publications Act of 1959 in at least certain aspects—at one point in his dissenting opinion, Justice Diemont was even explicit about this. Indeed, both the majority and the minority seemed to be of the opinion that literature should be granted a certain amount of autonomy. Yet, whereas the English Act instituted an explicit *exceptio artis* pertaining to literature through its four pillars of the contextual approach, the likely reader test, the public good test and the admissibility of expert evidence, only one of these instruments had been incorporated into the PEA: the concept of the likely reader.[29] The majority of the Cape Court seemed however to be employing a number of means it had at its disposal to effectuate a certain amount of autonomy for literature after all. Although the PEA had quite clearly not made the contextual approach mandatory, the majority of the bench, via a detour, still found a way to rule out the isolated-passage criterion and demand that a publication be judged as a whole. In the same roundabout manner, the majority seemed to be employing the concept of freedom of expression as an argument to secure an autonomous space for literature vis-à-vis the law. The likely reader test, finally, was also applied by the majority to grant *When the Lion Feeds* in this particular case, but by implication also literature in general, a certain amount of autonomy. For although Justices van Zyl and Beyers concluded that many people would be disgusted by Smith's novel, its likely readers would not and the occasional "unlikely" reader that would come to read the book were not significant. In sum, it appeared that the Cape Court was willing to guarantee a greater amount of autonomy to the literary field than Parliament had been willing to do.

The majority of the Cape Court accordingly held that none of the five passages complained of were indecent or obscene (cf. van der Poll 207), and that the novel had therefore to be released. The PCB, however, decided to appeal against this judgment to the Appellate Division of the Supreme Court, which was seated in Bloemfontein, the nation's judicial capital.

THE TRIAL OF CAN THEMBA'S "THE FUGITIVES"

During the time that lay between the Cape and the Bloemfontein trials of Smith's novel, another case concerning literature was brought before the Cape Court: the case of S v *Insight Publications (Pty) Ltd and Another*, an appeal from a conviction in a Magistrate's Court. The case centered around a short story titled "The Fugitives," which had been written by Can Themba and published in *The New African* 3.3 of March 28, 1964. The periodical was one of the leading anti–apartheid monthlies of the 1960s (McDonald, *Literature Police* 110), and was aimed at providing readers with serious journalism and literature. Themba (1924–1968), who was a journalist and literary author, was one of the leading black writers in English of the 1950s and early 1960s and an important contributor to some of the major black magazines of that period, such as *Drum* and *The Classic* (McDonald, *Literature Police* 128, 181, 324; Themba iii). His story "The Fugitives"[30] depicted—in dialogue form and in about 2,000 words—a gathering of a small group of political refugees in a Johannesburg shebeen (township bar). In this shebeen, the group is anxiously waiting for a car to transport them out of the country. Two police officers arrive on the scene, but nothing happens: they leave again after having drunk a glass of whiskey—much to the relief of the party of refugees, who immediately proceed to drink a toast to the Department of Justice. The case concerning Themba's story was not as high profile as the Smith case was, neither juridically, nor socially, yet this case too provides important evidence regarding the institutional status that was enjoyed by literature in general at the time, and literature written by blacks in particular.

The Magistrate's Case Concerning the "Fugitives"

In the course of 1964, Themba's story had prompted the Attorney General to bring a prosecution before a Magistrates' Court—which in itself seems remarkable, for one might ask oneself why this case that revolved around a short story written by a leading black literary actor and that had appeared in a serious literary and journalistic magazine was not "simply" put before the Publications Control Board and why the Attorney General immediately proceeded to prosecute. The immediate prosecution seems even more remarkable as the timing of the Attorney General's decision and the ensuing raid on the office of *The New African* as well as the home of Mrs. J. N. Block, a director of Insight Publications, the publishing house that published the magazine, came immediately after a press report had dealt fully with the refusal of the police to return what was confiscated in another raid the month before and with the failure to institute proceedings (see "Another Raid").

The state's case was built entirely on forty-seven words occurring in the text and the "combined impact which the use of the words was likely to make" on the likely readers of the text (*S* v *Insight* 778). As the Cape Court later understood it, the state case "was not that the story itself was objectionable" (778–79; cf. also 780). The state's charge thus appeared to be arrived at through application of the isolated-passage criterion, not the contextual approach. The following words, uttered by Justice van Heerden in the unanimous judgment that the Cape Bench[31] would later deliver in the appeal against the Magistrate's decision, illustrates what kind of words the case centered around:

> The language employed by the characters in the story is undoubtedly crude and coarse. Mr. Terblanche [counsel for the State] counted 47 words in all to which the State takes exception. Included in these 47 words are listed, apart from frequent repetitions of "bloody," "hell," "bastard," "damn," "bitch," etc., eight references to the Deity in one form or another [five of these were in the form of "Jeewheezus"[32] (cf. *S* v *Insight* 780)] while the following words appear on the number of occasions set out behind each of them: "shit" (6); "arse" (2); "pissed" (1). (778)

The opening passage of the story gives an impression of the context in which the quoted words appeared:

> "Where the hell is Shorty? Shorty's always late?"
> "You know he went for the booze."
> "*So* where's Mike? He's got the maps. He's the bright boy who knows all the plans. Now just when we've got to go he ain't here."
> "Look, Barnsey, you're getting jittery."
> "Shit! This isn't fun's play, cheap dramatics. *This is it!*"
> "Mama, give us another drink."
> "*IT* my arse-hole. Who d'you think you impress?"
> "But where's Shorty?"
> "Look, Barnsey, the car's not even here. You shoot your bloody nerves into all of us. Can't we have our drink without your jitteriness?"
> "T-T-To hell with you!"

"We're going there in any case."
Poo-poo-poo-poo-poo!
"That's the car, you bastard, and I haven't even slugged my first drink."
"It may be the cops. Somebody squealed. They know all about our plans. Let me out of here! Let me out of here!"
"Shut him up!"
"Quickly, somebody catch his throat!"
"His temple!"
"No, you'll kill him, you ass."
"Ahhhh!"
"Untie his shoes, his belt, his underpants, his . . . his tie."
Poo-poo-poo-poo-pooo!
"They're here . . . . !"
"Shut up, you fool!"
"Hank, you dive into that bedroom. Dive, you bastard. I don't carredam [*sic*] what instructions are, dive! Tholo, Peter, Jamesey, you, you, carry out Barnes as if he was just ordinary drunk."
"But it's only . . ."
"Shut up, and do what I tell you!"
"Shorty's delayed; I'm sure he's gone to that bitch of his, and let us get caught here. Damn his women!"
"Shut up, you guys, *shut up!* What's happened to your discipline? Has it gone to pieces so early? When the cops come, play it easy. You're only shebeeners. Hear? You're only orrinary-to-God [*sic*] shebeeners." (Themba 51; Themba's emphases)

The state's charge was that the story was "indecent or obscene, or . . . offensive or harmful to public morals, or blasphemous or offensive to the religious convictions or feelings of any section of the inhabitants of the Republic" (*S* v *Insight* 775).

In order to support its charge, the State called "a detective constable [of the Security Police, a Mr. T. Zandberg ("'Obscenity' on Trial" 2)], a telephone exchange superintendent who [was] a member of the Apostolic faith [a Mr. Swarts (*S* v *Insight* 781)], and an army chaplain belonging to the Presbyterian Church [Commandant C. S. Scott Shaw, who was also Moderator of the Cape Presbytery of the mentioned Church ("'Obscenity' on Trial" 3)]" to voice their opinions regarding the offensiveness of Themba's story (*S* v *Insight* 776). As *The New African* wrote in its March 1965 issue, "the Commandant's evidence was all the prosecution needed ("'Obscenity' on Trial" 3). And the editors went on to summarize the state's case by saying that the Public Prosecutor pointed out that

[t]he Act [i.e., the PEA] . . . was not concerned with the literary merit or integrity of the article or its writer, or with the general tone of the publication or the quality of its readership. If any part of any publication was offensive to

any section of the community, then it was objectionable by definition. This was offensive to the Cape Presbyterian Church. (3)

The defense called "an author who is also a subscriber to the said publication" to deliver testimony (*S* v *Insight* 776), Uys Krige. Krige was a prominent actor in the contemporary Afrikaans subfield at the time, and was counted among the *Dertigers* (Writers of the Thirties), a group of writers that are generally considered to be the founding fathers of modern Afrikaans literature. Krige apparently pointed out that other publications, both in English and Afrikaans, published overseas and in South Africa, used similar words ("'Obscenity' on Trial" 3). He further appears to have stated that he did not find any of the story's language offensive, and that it was used in the dialogue "to give immediacy to the situation and to reflect the personalities and emotions of the characters" (3).

Both the fact that the state did not call upon any *literary* actors to deliver testimony and the fact that a white Afrikaans and not a black English-language literary actor was called upon to deliver testimony on behalf of the defendants appears indicative of the amount of recognition that the juridical field was expected to be willing to give black literature in English at the time.

The trial ended with the Magistrate, Mr. W. F. van der Merwe, declaring that Themba's story offended against the morals section of the PEA (sec. 5 (2) (*a*)).[33] According to the judgment delivered in the Cape appeal case, he failed to make clear in what manner the story offended against this provision and merely stated that it "teemed with coarse, obscene and vulgar words and expressions and could not by any stretch of the imagination be termed highbrow reading matter" (*S* v *Insight* 776)—interestingly, the latter remark could be interpreted as indicating that the Magistrate felt that "high-brow reading matter" was entitled to be given a different treatment than non-highbrow reading matter. The Magistrate not only declared the story to offend against the moral stipulations of the PEA, however, he also deemed it to offend against the Act's religious stipulations (sec. 5 (2) (*b*)).[34] He appears to have been motivated in this decision *inter alia* by his belief that "South Africa was a religious country, and subservience to the Almighty was the corner-stone of the constitution" ("'Obscenity' on Trial" 3). On the basis of these findings, he sentenced the company to a fine of R300 and Mrs. Block, in her capacity of director, to a fine of R300 or three months' imprisonment (775).

In sum, on the basis of the Magistrate's judgment, one might be inclined to infer that the legal status of literature written by blacks was quite precarious around 1965. However, the Magistrate's decision was quite fiercely overruled by the Supreme Court.

The Supreme Court Case Concerning "The Fugitives"

The appeal against the Magistrate's decision was heard by the Cape Court on March 8, 1965; on March 24, the Court handed down its judgment. The appealing party contended that the magistrate "had misdirected himself both on the law and the facts on various aspects and that [the Cape Court] was accordingly at large to give its own decision on the merits" (776). On the authority of the CPD judgment regarding *When the Lion Feeds*, the state argued that the magistrate had erred in taking evidence into account in coming to his decision (776). In its judgment, the Cape Court basically tore the magistrate's judgment completely apart: the Cape Court had a diametrically opposed view on every fundamental issue the magistrate had dealt with. As the Court did not learn from the magistrate's judgment which factors had motivated him in forming his opinion, it stated that it was "unable to determine whether [the decision] had been reasonably arrived at and must, in the circumstances, treat the matter as a re-hearing on appeal" (776).

Although the Cape Court did not categorically want to rule out the admissibility of evidence in prosecutions under the PEA, it stated that "[h]aving regard to the evidence led in the present case, . . . this Court is satisfied that the magistrate has misdirected himself in this respect" (776). The Court found that the testimonies on which the magistrate had based his judgment represented invalid evidence, because when it came to establishing whether a publication was indecent or obscene or offensive to public morals, the matter was left to the opinion of the Court and evidence was not to be regarded at all (780)—in adopting this position, the Court was of course perfectly following the precedent which it itself had set some two months earlier in the *Lion* case. When it came to determining whether a publication was blasphemous or offensive to religious convictions or feelings, things lay different. It appeared that the Court felt that evidence would be admissible when this section had to be applied (780). However, the Court found that the evidence on which the magistrate had built his decision "ought not have carried any weight at all" (781) and could "certainly not" be used for the purpose of determining whether the words complained of were blasphemous or offensive to religious convictions or feelings (781).

The magistrate had also "misdirected himself as to the persons who would be likely to be exposed to this publication," the Court found (776). He had postulated a very wide readership, reasoning, as he apparently had, that the publication had been sold "by certain booksellers and that it was therefore likely to be read by anybody who might happen to see it" (777). Yet not only had the Magistrate "misdirected himself on the facts as to who the persons would be who are likely to be exposed to the influence of the article, or to read it," the Cape Court observed, "but [he] seem[ed] to have had a completely wrong approach to the whole question" (777). As the CPD unfolded what it held to be the right approach to the question, it put strong emphasis on the significance of the question regarding likely readership: "In a prosecution such as the present," it stated, "*it is . . . of the utmost importance* to determine who the persons are who are likely to be exposed to the effect or influence of an article" (777; my emphasis). The reason for this was that only if the Court found that a publication was likely to negatively affect—in the terms given in the act—such persons, it could judge it to be undesirable. Explaining its position further, the Court stated that it was vital that a Court carefully estimate the susceptibility of the likely readers of a publication under consideration. The question whether a publication could be deemed to be undesirable, it argued, "is relative to the impact it is likely to have on a certain class of persons, and it follows that an article which, for example, may be deemed to be indecent or obscene where it is exposed to certain persons, may not be such where other people are exposed to the influence of it" (777). Thus, quite clearly the Court revealed itself to be in favor of emancipating the "strong" reader, and by taking this position it was following the lead of both Parliament, which after all had introduced the concept of the likely reader in its PEA, and the Cape Bench that had dealt with the Smith case earlier that year. Indeed, the last-quoted statement of the Court seemed to echo the remark made in the majority judgment in the Smith trial about "[i]t [being] the virulence of the poison and the susceptibility of the victim that determine[d] the size of the lethal dose."

Coming to its own estimation of who the likely readers of the publication were and what effect the publication would have on these readers, the Court stated that "[a]n article such as 'The Fugitives,' appearing in the same publication as other articles which according to the evidence appeal largely to the intellectual classes of the community, should not be adjudged *in vacuo* as the magistrate did but according to the impact it is likely to make on the intellectual class of the community" (777). As the Court subsequently postulated in so many words that "the intellectual classes of the community" were not easily "depraved or corrupted" nor easily "outraged or disgusted," it in effect broke a lance for granting "the intellectual classes of the community" considerable autonomy vis-à-vis the PEA. The fact that it in passing referred to the strong test of disgustfulness formulated in the Cape trial of Smith's *Lion* only confirms this observation: as we observed above, this test was also meant to emancipate the "strong" reader.

The institutional position adopted by the Cape Bench in the Themba case was thus quite coherent with the institutional positioning taken in the Smith case. As far as the poetological dimension is concerned, the "Fugitives" case also revealed a similar picture to the *Lion* case: no explicit literary-conceptual position was taken in this case, either.

The eventual decision reached by the Court was that the story could not be said to offend against either the moral or the religious provisions of the act. Therefore, the appeal was upheld and the conviction and sentence were set aside. Apparently, the legal status of literature written by blacks was not as precarious as it seemed to be on the basis of the Magistrate's case concerning Themba's short story—not at the highest judicial level, in any case.

As the judgment on Themba's "Fugitives" was being delivered, the appeal against the CPD judgment in the case concerning Smith's *Lion* was still pending. Let us now turn to the pivotal Appellate Division trial of this latter work to see how this Court positioned itself institutionally and literary-conceptually.

THE BLOEMFONTEIN TRIAL OF WILBUR SMITH'S *WHEN THE LION FEEDS*

On May 13, 1965, the case was heard by a panel of five Justices of Appeal. On August 26 of that same year, the Appellate Court handed down its judgment, which was divided into a majority opinion delivered by Chief Justice Steyn with which the Justices Holmes and Potgieter concurred, a dissenting opinion formulated by Justice Rumpff,[35] and another dissenting opinion by Justice Williamson.

The institutional dimension of the judgment of the Appellate Division for the largest part centered around the same issues as the judgment delivered in the Cape trial. For the Justices of Appeal focused on the issues of (1) literary expertise; (2) contextualism; (3) comparison with other books; (4) (likely) readership; (5) freedom of expression; (6) the dynamics of societal norms; and (7) literary value. Let us proceed with examining these issues one by one.

Literary Expertise

Smith and his publisher Heinemann did not make a new attempt to get all of the affidavits they had filed when appealing to the CPD admitted and they chose to drop four of the five objections they had raised in the lower Court. They now solely concentrated on the fifth objection made in the Cape Court, i.e., the one concerning the position of the contemporary community vis-à-vis novelistic descriptions of sexual matters (cf. *PCB* v *Heinemann* 144–45, 148). The attorney representing Smith and Heinemann argued that evidence concerning this issue should be received, because, he argued,

> [t]he Court is required to form an opinion as to the likely effect of the matter objected to on the persons who are its likely readers. In order to do so, it would be relevant and necessary to know what else the average reader is reading, whether the general run of novels has contained similar passages and what the reaction of the average reader has been to them. (144–45)

Hence, the Court should allow literary experts that could enlighten the Court on these issues.

This new strategy of Smith and Heinemann had just as little success as their former strategy: the Appellate Court refused to admit the evidence that Smith and his publisher had wished to submit. Chief Justice Steyn, in ruling for the majority, remarked that the Court might receive evidence placed before it, or call for evidence to be produced. However, with regard to the nature of admissible evidence, the majority judgment declared—just as both the opinions formulated in the Cape trial of Smith's *Lion* had—that section 6 of the PEA made the opinion of the Court the determining factor in deciding whether any matter was "indecent, or obscene or offensive or harmful to public morals."[36] The opinions of others, experts thus included, should therefore be considered irrelevant and evidence as to such opinions inadmissible. The only evidence that could be admitted was evidence that could help in "establishing the identity" of the likely readers of a publication (147). The majority advanced that there was a distinction between "subjective" and "objective" evidence and stated that, unlike with questions as to the "character" of books, the identity of the persons who were likely to read them could be established objectively (cf. 147). For the benefit of establishing this "objective" fact, experts could be consulted. As far as "subjective" questions were concerned as to what the "average reader [was] reading," "whether the general run of novels ha[d] contained similar passages," or "what the reaction of the average reader ha[d] been to them," a judge had to rely exclusively on his own opinion: as the majority decision made clear, a judge should determine the "character of . . . offending books . . . by the only method by which such a fact can be ascertained, viz., by reading the books. . . . The book . . . itself provides the best evidence of its own indecency or obscenity or of the absence of such qualities" (150). True, in applying this method, the judge was not to lose sight of "contemporary standards of conduct or morality, current thought or prevailing attitudes of mind," of which he had to form his "own estimate," and which he was obliged to take into account when assessing the effect that a publication would tend to have upon its likely readers (150). Yet he was not to be guided by expert opinion in dealing with these "subjective" issues. Importantly, thus, the majority allowed literary experts to play but a minimal role in the adjudication process.

Justice Williamson could not agree with the majority on the question of evidence. In his view, a Court, in inquiring into and considering the question of the undesirability of a publication, should not "unduly restrict itself in regard to the topics on which it should receive evidence" (164). On the contrary, Williamson would "welcome evidence by informed persons which might assist [him] to become aware of any contemporary fact or circumstance or tendency material to the formation of as objective an opinion as possible" (165). He did note, however, that "[t]he affidavits filed in the present matter did not in fact seem usefully to add anything of material value to the *data* upon which the lower Court could arrive at a conclusion and the question of their admissibility or the extent thereof does not call for further consideration" (165; Williamson's emphasis). Thus, although Williamson seems to have felt that literary expert evidence could in principle be allowed and, indeed, have judicial value, he did not feel that the affidavits of the literary experts that had been filed by Smith and his publisher contained any useful information.

On the principle side, Justice Rumpff showed himself in agreement with Williamson, stating that

> [i]n view of the fact that the members of the Board are required to have certain qualifications [i.e., "hav[e] special knowledge of art, language and literature or the administration of justice" (156)] and, in view of the duty imposed on the Supreme Court to hold an enquiry, that Court, which may consist in a particular case of a single Judge, should in my view never refuse to listen to relevant and cogent evidence when it has to decide the fate of a novel, a product of the liberty of the printing press. In my view it would be wrong for the Court in every case to assume to have sufficient knowledge of the taste and sense of decency of the people who are likely to read a particular novel. (156–57)

Unlike Williamson though, Rumpff was willing to admit the affidavits regarding the contemporary novelistic treatment of sexual matters presented by Heinemann in the AD trial. In fact, not only was he willing to admit this evidence, but he also remarked that he would have been willing to admit *all* of the affidavits that Heinemann had tendered in the CPD trial, not merely the ones regarding the modern-day descriptions of sexual affairs (cf. 157).

The fact of the matter was, however, that the majority set the precedent. Williamson's and Rumpff's principled valuation of literary expert evidence did therefore not have any immediate effect for the literary field. In light of the fact that in England and the United States—after all the two shining examples for contemporaneous South African law—expert evidence had recently become a crucial component of literary trials, the decision of the majority to allow literary experts to play but a minimal role in such trials was remarkable—and telling of the amount of institutional autonomy that the majority was willing to grant literature.

Contextualism

As to the question whether the book had to be considered as a whole, the majority made the following declaration:

> [There were] . . . nineteen different passages by which, amongst others, considered "in the context of the book read as a whole," the [Publications Control] Board's decision had been motivated. In terms the Board's decision was not

> confined to particular parts of the book. Its decision was that the book was indecent, obscene or objectionable. But even if, in fact, only particular parts of the book come within that description, . . . the book as such would . . . be deemed to be indecent, obscene or objectionable. (147)

Williamson could find no fault when it came to this part of the majority's interpretation of the obscenity test as provided by the act and therefore took the same position.

Rumpff stated that "[t]o evaluate [the impugned passages of Smith's *Lion*] . . . correctly for purposes of considering whether the book should be banned, it is necessary to look at these passages in the light of what was intended to be conveyed by the book as a whole" (155–56). He thus clearly revealed himself to be favoring the Anglo-American and Cape Court's position in this respect.

The majority's stance on the issue was not as clear as Rumpff's position-taking, however. Indeed, its position could be read to be advocating both the isolated-passage criterion and the contextualist approach. Contemporary legal professionals were in fact divided on the issue (cf. *PCB* v *Republican* 291). It can thus not be determined whether the majority—and Williamson too, for that matter—was of the opinion that a book should, as a matter of principle, be considered according to the contextual approach. Whether its stance was thus markedly different from the position that had recently been taken in English and U.S. law in this respect, too, can thus not be decided.

Comparison with Other Books

Apparently, Heinemann's attorney employed the well-known classics argument, an argument that we already encountered in our discussion of the 1905 case of *G. W. Hardy* v *Rex* in the previous chapter. As the majority judgment noted: "Counsel for the respondents argued, as had been done in many other similar cases, that, if this is the purport of the expression 'deprave or corrupt,' quite a number of literary classics would have to be described as indecent or obscene" (151). Yet the majority of the Appellate Court was just as unwilling to be persuaded by this argument as the Natal Court dealing with Hardy's case had been. In his judgment, Steyn explicitly referenced the position that had been taken by Chief Justice Cockburn in the English Hicklin case (1868) and, furthermore, quoted the exact same passage from the judgment in this case that we also encountered in the previous chapter:

> It is perfectly true . . . that there are a great many publications of high repute in the literary productions of this country the tendency of which is immodest, and, if you please, immoral, and possibly there might have been subject-matter for indictment in many of the works which have been referred to. But it is not to be said, because there are in many standard and established works objec-

tionable passages, that therefore the law is not as alleged on the part of this prosecution, namely, that obscene works are the subject-matter of indictment. (Cockburn qtd. in *PCB* v *Heinemann* 151)

Steyn stated that in his view, this was still a valid answer (151). Apparently, to put it in Felice Flanery Lewis's terms, the classics would not form the "crack in the door" through which "immodest" fiction might "squeeze past the censors," as far as the majority was concerned.

(Likely) Readership

On the question of likely readership, Justices Williamson and Rumpff basically took the same position as the Cape majority had done. Williamson also made special reference to young readers. Yet, he argued, again very much like Justices van Zyl and Beyers, that if an odd teenager or adolescent should by chance get hold of a copy of the book, this did not make him "a class of person 'likely to read it'" (164). For Williamson too, a writer did not have to take every *possible* reader, into account (cf. 164). Rumpff strongly suggested that "the average adult reader," who was not a "saint," ought to be given "the peaceful right to form his own opinion" on novels (157): "If the average modern reader with a healthy mind wants to read about sex written in a manner which leaves little to the imagination," he remarked, "it is not for the Court, in giving effect to the provisions of this particular Act, to say that he should not do so" (157). He too differentiated between classes of readers that were likely to be depraved, or corrupted, or outraged, or disgusted by certain types of novels and classes of readers that were not. Concludingly, Rumpff stated that the judiciary should think twice before curtailing literature's freedoms, i.e., before declaring a novel undesirable (cf. 157).

The majority also differentiated between classes of readers that publications would have dissimilar effects on (cf. 148, 150). Furthermore, they also held that not just any possible reader of a publication could be taken into account when judging a publication; in their view, one could only take account of "a substantial number of likely readers" (150). Yet, whereas the majority of the judges in the Cape case and the minority of their colleagues in the AD case might have been inclined to apply the likely reader provision as a means for granting literature a certain amount of autonomy, the Appeal Court's majority did not appear to have such an inclination. On the contrary, they were of the opinion that it lay in the spirit of the PEA that the freedoms of a certain type of literature—namely, first and foremost, sexually explicit literature—and, hence, the freedoms of the readers of this type of literature should be curtailed: "The tendency towards what might be said to approximate to a phallic cult amongst authors and their readers may have been, and probably was, the very reason why Parliament considered it expedient to pass this legislation" (149), Steyn observed in the majority judgment. Probably in order to act in accord with this perceived spirit of the Act, he added a further qualification to his concept of the likely reader, stating that "what the Legislature had in mind in these paragraphs [dealing with the "persons who are likely to be exposed to the effect or influence" and "persons who are likely to read or see" a publication or object (150)] is the effect or influence upon or the reactions of the ordinary reader *who is neither a prude nor a libertine*" (150; my emphasis). Effectively, Steyn thus did away with the likely reader test and restored the ordinary man test as it had been laid down in the 1905 case of *G. W. Hardy* v *Rex*.

With this added clause, the emancipation of certain types of "strong" readers, e.g., the kinds of readers that allegedly had a "tendency towards what might be said to approximate to a phallic cult," could of course easily be obstructed. But there was another way in which the "strong" reader could paternalistically be withheld a right to read, namely by simply postulating that an incriminated publication was likely to have a broad readership consisting *inter alia* of "weak(er)" readers. This was exactly what the majority did in the *Lion* case. The probable readers of Smith's novel, they declared, would

> fall within a broad general category in which there would be included persons of mature and of less mature mind, persons of at least some claim to discriminating literary taste and others no more than literate, men and women of strong moral fibre and those less effectively equipped, the majority of them old enough to have acquired knowledge and experience of life but some of them also of the younger generation. Amongst all of them I have to postulate men and women who are ordinary human beings, of normal mind and reactions, the carriers of contemporary attitudes and trends of thought. (152)

Having postulated such a broad readership, it was all but inevitable that the majority would declare the novel to be undesirable in terms of the PEA, and the fact of the matter was that they did: Steyn, Holmes, and Potgieter came to the conclusion that the passages complained of indeed had the tendency to deprave and corrupt the minds of a substantial number of the likely readers of the novel, and furthermore, that they would be harmful to public morals too (154). It should, however, be noted that the (for Smith and his publisher) so very consequential postulation of such a wide readership by the majority might have resulted from the fact that there appeared to be a rather strong consensus among the judges involved that Smith's book could not be considered to represent highbrow literature. Had the case revolved around a work which they did regard as highbrow, they would perhaps have been more willing, and able, to protect it.

Freedom of Expression

Just like Justices van Zyl and Beyers in the lower Court, Justice Rumpff also played the freedom of expression card. As seen already in the plea he made in favor of the admissibility of expert opinion, he declared not without pathos that the Supreme Court should never refuse to listen to expert evidence when it had to decide on "the fate of a novel, *a product of the liberty of the printing press*" (156–57; my emphasis). In the peroration of his dissenting opinion, he again played out his trump, this time with even more rhetorical force than before:

> The freedom of speech—which includes the freedom to print—is a facet of civilisation which always presents two well-known inherent traits. The one consists of the constant desire by some to abuse it. The other is the inclination of those who want to protect it to repress more than is necessary. The latter is also fraught with danger. It is based on intolerance and is a symptom of the primitive urge in mankind to prohibit that with which one does not agree. When a Court of law is called upon to decide whether liberty should be repressed—in this case the freedom to publish a story—it should be anxious to steer a course as close to the preservation of liberty as possible. It should do so because freedom of speech is a hard-won and precious asset, yet easily lost. And in its approach to the law, including any statute by which the Court may be bound, it should assume that Parliament, itself a product of political liberty, in every case intends liberty to be repressed only to such extent as it in clear terms declares, and, if it gives a discretion to a Court of law, only to such extent as is absolutely necessary. (*PCB* v *Heinemann* 160)

Clearly, Rumpff's plea for preserving liberty in general, and freedom of speech in particular—a plea that would often be referenced in the battles over censorship that would be fought in the ensuing decades—is quite reminiscent of van Zyl's plea for protecting the freedom of expression. And in Rumpff's argument too—indeed, more explicitly so—literature is presented as a category of expression entitled to protection under this fundamental right.

The Dynamics of Societal Norms

A clear consensus can be discerned among the appeal judges as to the point that the treatment of sensitive subjects did not of itself necessarily lead to undesirable effects—"depravity," "corruption," and so on—but that it was the manner in which this kind of subject was presented that could lead to such effects. This stance seemed indeed to be in concordance with the intent the legislature had had with the act.[37] However, the majority in the AD considered a lack of "reticence as to detail and expression" (154) to constitute an improper manner to deal with delicate subjects—much as Justices van Zyl and Beyers had done in the lower Court. Furthermore, the majority estimated, and accepted, that the act was meant to have what might be called a paternalistic-interventionist purpose. As the majority declared in dealing with the issue of the comparison with other books—and a clear echo of Cockburn's opinion in Hicklin's case can be heard in its statement:

> the prevalence of similar contemporary reading matter, which may itself offend against the Act, cannot be the standard by which the effect or influence of a publication is to be measured for the purposes of the Act. It would be no answer to the prohibitions in the Act to show that what Parliament has thought fit to forbid is the very height of contemporary fashion. (149)

When it came to literature, the majority thus felt that the act rather sought to curb the institutional autonomy of (certain types of) contemporary literature than to facilitate it.

Neither Rumpff nor Williamson read the act as having a decisive interventionist purpose. In their view, the Court should not try and maintain some (static) ideal morality, but rather be responsive to the fact that the "public morals," to which the act referred, were subject to change. As Rumpff put it in his—indeed celebrated—opinion:

> The word "morality" in the Act does not connote the science of morals (which is prescriptive) or the metaphysics of morals (which is philosophic) but existing morals (sedes) which is descriptive. For purposes of the Act "morality" or "sedes" is basically a matter of taste, the prevailing taste of the community to which the Act applies, not that of a community of saints. If the average modern reader with a healthy mind wants to read about sex written in a manner which leaves little to the imagination, it is not for the Court, in giving effect to the provisions of this particular Act, to say that he should not do so. (157)

For Rumpff, the Act should be applied with the greatest caution, for he felt it was of the utmost importance that it be accepted that societal values and norms, and, hence, literature, too, were constantly changing (157). Williamson made a very similar argument to Rumpff, in very similar words (cf. 164–65).

Literary Value

The last institutional issue touched upon was the question of literary value. It was only taken up by the majority, and their position on it unfolded in a passage that was as clear as it was short: "Literary value," they stated, "is . . . not the synthesis or sum total of all human values. It has to be weighed against others, and cannot outweigh the moral values which the Act seeks to protect" (151). The position seemed quite coherent with the statement made by the majority in the Cape Court that "the literary merit or the relevancy of the matter complained about cannot be employed to take it out of reach of the statute." For the majority in the Appellate Division also, the act did not allow the Court to grant literature much institutional autonomy.

Having dealt with the issues more directly pertaining to the institutional dimension of the trial, we now come to the trial's poetological dimension. Interestingly enough, a position was taken vis-à-vis the literature of an important contemporary group of literary actors in two of the opinions. This group of actors was the *Sestigers* (Writers of the Sixties). Ellison Kahn mentions that André Brink's novel *Lobola vir die Lewe* (1963) and Etienne Leroux's novel *Sewe Dae by die Silbersteins* (1962),[38] two novels that had caused considerable controversy at the time,[39] were explicitly mentioned in the affidavits filed by Heinemann as being novels that "contained sexual episodes using more direct language and considerably more dominant than in *Lion*" ("*Lion*" 314n89). Steyn and Rumpff explicitly referenced the two works in their respective opinions, whereby Steyn in quite unmistakable terms dismissed the affidavits on the two novels (cf. *PCB* v *Heinemann* 149), and Rumpff in rather polemic fashion set out to correct the facts that Steyn had presented about the reception of Leroux's novel (cf. 157). Steyn contended that

> The mixed reception which some of these publications have enjoyed, such as "Sewe Dae by die Silbersteins," by Etienne Leroux, and "Lobola vir die Lewe," by Andre Brink [*sic*], is so well-known that judicial nescience would be mere pretence. The contention that they have been "accepted" by the "average" reader, cannot but raise an eye-brow [*sic*], and would almost of necessity invite evidence of rebuttal. (149)

Rumpff, apparently both in reaction to this and to the fact that the Cape Court had refused to admit the expert evidence tendered by Heinemann, stated that this kind of evidence "might also have shown that there was no ripple on the surface of the literary pond when 'Sewe Dae by die Silbersteins' was published but that the hullabaloo started when long after its publication it was awarded a literary prize" (157). The respective position-takings with regard to *Sestigers* Leroux and Brink appear quite clearly to be a result of the different criteria the two justices employed to judge works of literature. For Steyn, who effectively judged on the basis of the concept of the ordinary man, the two mentioned *Sestigers* fell foul of the latter's criteria. For Rumpff, who judged on the basis of the concept of the likely reader, the mentioned works—or at least Leroux's *Silbersteins*—did not constitute a problem: for "there was no ripple on the surface of the literary pond" when the work(s) had been thrown into it.

Yet as these position-takings still pertained largely to institutional issues, a poetological preference appeared to hide behind it. For Kahn also observed that Steyn regarded "certain types of contemporary literature" with "obvious distaste" ("*Lion*" 320). It is not unlikely at all that with his sharp criticism of a certain type of modern literature, i.e., with his observation that certain contemporaneous literature tended "towards what might be said to approximate to a phallic cult amongst authors and their readers," Steyn was first and foremost thinking of writers like Brink and Leroux, the two being prominent representatives of a new generation of writers that wrote openly and explicitly about sexuality. For Steyn, literature should be reticent in dealing with sexuality. Indeed, one of the reasons why he regarded Smith's novel to be undesirable was that it contained episodes that "deal[t] in an improper manner with sexual intercourse in that they violate[d] the very natural reticence as to detail and expression which may be expected to be observed in our community, however enlightened and uninhibited many of its members may be, in speaking or writing about such matters" (154). Steyn's position—i.e., the *majority's* position—thus seemed rather close to the Platonic side of the position taken earlier by the Cronjé Commission. On the contrary, Rumpff's conception of literature—however rudimentary it might have been—might have been closer to certain contemporary South African poetics, notably to that of the *Sestigers*. His remark about the "hullabaloo" created when Leroux's *Silbersteins* was awarded a literary prize—it was awarded the Hertzog Prize[40] in 1964—indeed appeared to be expressing some irritation at this reaction by part of the public. Moreover, he clearly wanted to grant the author the freedom to write and the reader the freedom to read literature that dealt with sexuality, even in an explicit manner.

CONCLUSION

When examining the judgments delivered in the three trials concerning literature that were held in 1965, we can observe that for the greatest part they revolved around the same issues that had been central to South African publications regulation in the first half of the twentieth century. Yet whereas South Africa had followed suit with England and the United States in the earlier period, the executive (endorsed by the legislature) had directed South African law onto another path with its PEA, 1963. The judiciary revealed itself to be divided as to how the new statute was to be applied in cases concerning literature.

In the Cape trial of Wilbur Smith's *When the Lion Feeds*, both the majority and the dissenting opinion delivered a critique of the new Act. Both remonstrated that literature had not been given enough protection under the PEA and that this act did not more resemble the English Obscene Publications Act of 1959. It appeared, indeed, that both the majority and the minority were of the opinion that literature should be granted a certain amount of autonomy. Yet whereas the English Act had instigated an explicit *exceptio artis* pertaining to literature through its four fundamental instruments of the contextual approach, the likely reader test, the public good test, and the admissibility of expert evidence, just one of these had been incorporated into the PEA: the concept of the likely reader. This notwithstanding, the majority of the Cape Court appeared to employ a number of the means it had at its disposal to effectuate a certain amount of autonomy for literature after all. They found a way to demand that a publication be judged as a whole and not on the basis of isolated passages; they seemed to be applying the concept of freedom of expression as an argument for securing an autonomous space for literature; and, finally, they applied the likely reader test to grant literature a certain amount of autonomy vis-à-vis the law. The Cape judgment in the case regarding Can Themba's "The Fugitives" cohered with the judgment regarding Smith's *Lion* in that it secured a considerable amount of autonomy for the intellectual reader.

The Appellate Court's judgment concerning Smith's *Lion* turned the tables, however. For although two dissenting opinions were filed that followed the same autonomy-oriented line mapped out by the majority judgment in the Cape trial of Smith's novel and the unanimous judgment in the Cape trial of Themba's "Fugitives," the majority set a quite different precedent. For among other things, they stipulated that literary experts could play but a minimal role in judicial proceedings; declared that it was invalid to compare an incriminated work with other books, whether modern or classic; and added an extra clause to the likely reader provision, thereby effectively doing away with the likely reader test and restoring the ordinary man test as it had been established in the 1905 case of G. W. Hardy. In sum, the majority interpreted the act as being aimed *inter alia* at combating contemporary sexually explicit literature, and their judgment provided the judiciary with a number of instruments with which to do this in future trials. On the poetological level, it appeared as if the position taken by the majority was rather close to the Platonic side of the position adopted in the Cronjé Report, the report that laid the foundations for the PEA.

The trials held in 1965 provide us with some clear indications that by that time the literary field had reached a considerable degree of (internal) institutional autonomy: for the first time literary expert evidence was adduced in Court. Only a minority of the judges was, however, willing to accept such evidence. Furthermore, the way in which the Cape Court positioned itself vis-à-vis literature both in the *Lion* and "Fugitives" cases might also be explained as the manifestation of a judicial recognition that the literary field had attained a significant degree of (internal) institutional development. This recognition manifested itself in a willingness to grant the field a considerable degree of autonomy. The Appellate Division's majority decision in the *Lion* case, however, represented a rollback of the degree of legal autonomy that had been established by the Cape Court. The fact that this rollback could only be realized with a 3:2 majority appears to represent further evidence that a judicial benevolence toward the literary field was present around 1965. Indeed, although the benevolent position was successfully contested by the majority in the Appeal Court, large parts of the judicial elite had evidenced a willingness to grant literature a considerably higher degree of institutional autonomy.

NOTES

1. That Cronjé apparently had credentials in the eyes of elite Afrikaner circles is further evidenced by the fact that he was later made professor and head of the Department of Drama at the University of Pretoria (see Dean 78n93; see also the entry on Cronjé in Akyeampong and Gates 1).
2. It has also been argued that the government's concern was rather the adequacy of the censorship system that had been called into existence through the Entertainments (Censorship) Act, 1931, that is to say, the censorship of *imported* publications (cf. Strydom, "Wet" 195).
3. In Afrikaans: Raad vir Publikasies.
4. For a discussion of the juridical meaning of this concept, see Eckard 175ff; Jordan 349ff; Strydom, "Ne Bis" 55–56.
5. Cf. the situation in the Netherlands, where out of "practical considerations" the legislature had also refrained from granting literature a statutory *exceptio artis* through its new obscenity law of 1911, even though it apparently found that art and science should be exempted from the new provisions (cf. Beekman and Grüttemeier 64ff). To this day, the Netherlands does not have a statutory *exceptio artis*.
6. "aangebied as feite in verband met die persone en die gebeure en *nie om hulle eie ontwil nie*" (29; Cronjé et al.'s emphasis).
7. "gewone, beskaafde, fatsoenlike, redelike en verantwoordelike inwoners van die Unie" (185).
8. For a discussion of eight of these trials, see Katz.
9. Hereafter: PEA.
10. Other evidence of the act's paternalistic nature can be found in analyses of the act carried out by contemporary jurists (see e.g., Dean, "O Tempora!" 11–12).
11. Hereafter: PCB.
12. That the state was interested in supporting the literary field also became evident through its active involvement in the production and distribution of literature, particularly Afrikaans and African-language literature (see Johnson 828; Kannemeyer 243; McDonald, *Literature Police* 263 et passim; McDonald, "Book").
13. One might perhaps also infer from the presence of a provision that made it possible for literary experts to become part of the censorship bureaucracy—and, moreover, from the additional fact that Afrikaans literary experts came to dominate the system from 1963 to 1975—that there was an intricate connection between the executive and a part of the cultural elite, i.e., the Afrikaans literary elite (cf. also Kahn, "Lion" 280).
14. There were still other ways in which the act gave the judiciary "considerable room to manoeuvre" (see Dean, "O Tempora!" 10). Most importantly, these other ways resided in the fact that the act was "set out in words and phrases of . . . [a far-reaching] degree of ambiguity and vagueness," as Dean, and other contemporary jurists pointed out (10ff). Particularly some of the most crucial concepts of the Act, such as "indecent," "obscene," "offensive," and "harmful to public morals" were subjected to this criticism (see also *Report of the Task Group* 8).
15. A wide meaning could be given to this proviso so as to make it cover literature, as was evidenced by the fact that it was effectively read in such a manner by both Prof. T. T. Cloete, one of the PCB's most prominent literary censors throughout the 1960s and 1970s, and J. J. Kruger, Chairman of the PCB from 1969 to 1974 (cf. Cloete, "Sensuur" 4 and Kruger 236). It does not appear, however, that the provision was intended to have such a wide meaning, nor that it was regularly interpreted thus (cf. Dean 145, 145n28). Indeed, when in March 1972, an

interdepartmental committee of inquiry into the application of the act was appointed, and later that year, this committee published its report, it recommended that the protection of sec. 5 (4) (b) (iii) be extended to cover "literary works of aesthetic value" (Inter-Departmental Committee qtd. in Dean 145).

16. Hereafter: *Lion*.

17. Cf. Aedilis Curulis 17; Kahn, "'Dirty' Books" 39; Kahn, "*Lion*" 312, 313, 313n85; Kahn, "Publications and Entertainments Act" 38; McDonald, *Literature Police* 51; *PCB v Heinemann* 152.

18. What is valid for the structure of the overall analysis presented in this study is also valid for the analysis presented in this chapter: the fact that South African law works with the *stare decisis* principle underlies the decision to discuss the trials in chronological order.

19. Judge Diemont, one of the judges presiding over the Cape case, apparently judged similarly on the novel's merits: he felt that Smith presented "a good story," and that he "used robust language with considerable skill to describe the quarrels of the characters"; "indeed," his conclusion was that "the story had much to commend it and was packed with action" (Diemont 210; cf. also Kahn, "*Lion*" 313). A similar conclusion was apparently reached by a book reviewer on the radio, who is reported to have said that *When the Lion Feeds* was "an exciting, pulsating story, vigorous and full of drama, deserving wide readership" (Diemont 207).

20. The PCB deemed it to be "undesirable" in terms of the Customs Act, 1955 (cf. Kahn, "Publications and Entertainments Act" 36; *PCB v Heinemann* 138), an act that interlocked with the PEA (cf. Kahn, "*Lion*" 279).

21. In the Cape trial, counsel for the PCB built his argument around a mere five passages, however (cf. van der Poll 206).

22. Actually, the case was brought before the Court in early November 1964, but since the two judges hearing the case—Judge President Beyers and Judge Diemont—could not agree on the question whether the appeal should succeed or not, they had to ask another judge to join them. Early December the three—a full bench—sat to hear the case anew (cf. Diemont 207–8).

23. Hereafter referred to as CPD.

24. It should be noted that the judgments that were handed down in the CPD trial were not reported (cf. Kahn, "*Lion*" 315). The only direct record of the majority and dissenting opinions delivered in the Cape Court that appears to be available today is to be found in the headnote which was added to the judgment and which, apparently unlike the judgment itself, can still be obtained today (see *William Heinemann Ltd and Others v Publications Control Board*). Apart from this direct source, one can also gather indirect records of the opinions in a few secondary sources dealing with the case, the most important of which are a memoir called *Brushes with the Law* by Marius Diemont, the judge that filed the dissenting opinion in the case; two juridical articles by Ellison Kahn, namely his "Publications and Entertainments Act, No. 26 of 1963" and "*When the Lion Feeds*—and the Censor Pounces: A Disquisition on the Banning of Immoral Publications in South Africa" (Kahn appears to have had access to the transcript of the Cape trial [cf. Kahn, "*Lion*" 314n77–81, 315n87–89 et passim]); and van der Poll's 2001 LLD dissertation "The Constitution of Pornography" (van der Poll also appears to have had access to the transcript of the CPD decision [cf. van der Poll 206]). Fortunately, one can get a quite adequate view of the respective poetological and institutional positions that were taken by the majority and the minority on the basis of these incomplete sources.

25. Counsel for the PCB also raised this issue: he argued that it would not assist the Court to look at other books. The fact that certain classics contained obscene passages did not mean that Smith could do so too (Diemont 208). Unfortunately, one cannot learn from the available sources whether the Court went into the issue, and if so, what position it took on it.

26. Race issues did not play a part in the discussion of this passage or any of the other passages describing sexual episodes, as there was no "miscegenation" involved in these episodes.

27. This test was laid out in section 6 (1) (b) of the act.

28. Cf. the current Constitution of South Africa, in which this is also the case (see Constitution of the Republic of South Africa, 1996, sec. 16).

29. Although with its PEA, the executive had made it possible to appoint literary experts to the PCB, and thus had given institutional recognition to literary expertise, it had only given this

recognition on the administrative level—where it could control it, as the experts it appointed were of course also subject to dismissal. As section 6 of the PEA evidenced, it had not granted this recognition on the judicial level—where it did not have any—or much, anyway—control.

30. The story can be accessed in a 2006 collection of literary work by Themba titled *Requiem for Sophiatown*: see Themba 141–48.

31. The bench was made up of Justices van Heerden and Hall.

32. According to the Cape Court, the latter were "obviously used by the same character every time as expletives to express surprise or disbelief at a certain state of events" (*S v Insight* 780).

33. That is, he ruled it to be "indecent or obscene or offensive or harmful to public morals."

34. That is, he declared it to be "blasphemous or offensive to the religious convictions or feelings of any section of the inhabitants of the Republic."

35. Rumpff would become Chief Justice in 1974.

36. That is, whether it constituted an offense in terms of sec. 5 (2) (*a*) of the act.

37. Cf. section 6 (1) of the Act (Publications and Entertainments Act, 1963, 284–86); cf. also *PCB v Heinemann* 148.

38. Both authors were, and are, counted among the *Sestigers*.

39. With regard to this controversy, see McDonald, *Literature Police* 42ff; 265–66 et passim.

40. This prize is the most prestigious prize within the Afrikaans literary (sub)field. It was established in 1915 and is named after J. B. M. Hertzog (1866–1942), an Afrikaner who had been a (Boer) general during the South African War and who had established the National Party in 1914. Later on he became Prime Minister of the Union of South Africa: he was in office from 1924 to 1939.

Chapter Three

The 1974 Trial of André Brink's *Kennis van die Aand*

Although the PEA was amended twice in the course of the late 1960s and early 1970s,[1] the amendments made did not change the way in which literary texts were to be judged: the criteria that had been laid down to judge publications remained unaltered. What did alter the superstructure guiding literature regulation was the fact that clarity was brought to the issue of contextualism. In the early 1970s, a series of battles were fought out in court between Republican Publications, the publisher of a popular men's magazine called *Scope*, and the Publications Control Board.[2] In one of these trials a work of fiction, i.e., one directed at a mass audience, was involved, namely a serialized edition of Jacqueline Susann's 1969 novel *The Love Machine*, but this case revolved around juridical technicalities irrelevant to our analysis and therefore does not call for our attention. In fact, almost none of the cases—which all centered around photos depicting (near) nude figures as well as articles dealing with problematic issues such as premarital sex, abortion, contraception, promiscuity, and marital infidelity—are of special interest to our discussion. The only case of interest here is the 1972 appeal case of Publications Control Board v Republican Publications, for in this case Chief Justice Ogilvie Thompson (in office from 1971 to 1974) came to settle the question of contextualism. In a quite elaborate discussion of the theme, in which he expressly set out to bring an end to the unclarity surrounding the majority position in the appeal case of Smith's *Lion* and, hence, of the Supreme Court at large, he ruled that where the written word was concerned, the contextual approach should be applied—not the isolated-passage criterion. As the issue was—and is—so central to judicial dealings with literature in South Africa,[3] the passage in which he came to formulate his position is worth quoting in full:

> The words "or any part of it" . . . occurring in the opening sentence of s 5 (2) make it plain that for the above-cited provisions to apply it is not essential that the whole of the "publication or object" should be "indecent or obscene": the part may vitiate the whole. For instance, the inclusion in an otherwise entirely unobjectionable book of a single outrageously lewd picture will ordinarily suffice to render the book itself "indecent or obscene" within the meaning of the Act. Where, however, the enquiry revolves around the written word, it is, in my judgment, inappropriate and incorrect to have regard solely to a particular challenged passage—that is, to apply the so-called criterion of the isolated passage—without any reference whatever to the context in which that passage appears. General principles of construction call, in my opinion, for a contextual approach in any such enquiry. To interpret the words "or any part of it" . . . occurring in the opening sentence of s 5 (2) as importing the isolated passage criterion, would, in my opinion, be to confer upon appellant Board powers even more far-reaching than those which Parliament manifestly intended the Board to have. (*PCB* v *Republican Publications* 291)

Quite univocally, the Chief Justice thus decided that the contextual approach should be followed when a work of literature was to be judged in terms of the law.

The first literary trial that was held after the appeal case of *Lion* and this latter one centered on André P. Brink's 1973 novel *Kennis van die Aand*.[4]

Kennis was the first literary work in Afrikaans to be banned by the censors (cf. Brink, Preface 10; G. Davis 116). While Brink was one of the *Sestigers*'s most controversial authors from the start, and his novels, moreover, had always formed test cases for the PCB throughout the 1960s, he seemed expressly determined to push things to the limit with his new novel (cf. Peters 25). From various pieces he had published in the course of the late 1960s and early 1970s,[5] it had become obvious that he was now expressly aiming at challenging the apartheid system. In rather unmistakable terms he stated in an article that appeared in the anti-apartheid newspaper *Rand Daily Mail* of June 20, 1970:

> If it is true that Afrikaans writers do have greater freedom vis-à-vis censorship than others . . . what have they done with this freedom? How have they used it? The depressing answer is: no Afrikaans writer has yet tried to offer a serious political challenge to the system . . . We have no one with enough guts to say: NO. . . . [I]f Afrikaans writing is to achieve any true significance within the context of the revolution of Africa (of which we form part) and within the crucible in which this country finds itself, it seems to me it will come from these few who are prepared to sling the "NO!" of Antigone into the violent face of the System. (Brink qtd. in Pienaar, "Histories-juridiese Aspekte" 243)

Quite clearly, *Kennis van die Aand* constituted Brink's own Antigonian "NO!"

The narrative of *Kennis* is told by Josef Malan, a "Coloured" person who is awaiting his death sentence in a Cape Town prison. The narrative represents his memoirs. The reader is first presented with the story of Malan's forefathers, which might be summed up as a series of ink black tragedies in which violence (both nonsexual and sexual), exploitation, and murder, all committed by whites, form the connecting thread. After Malan has told the history of his family, he starts to narrate his personal history. Malan is given the chance to receive an education by his *baas*, because the latter feels indebted to Malan's father, his erstwhile *kneg* (cf. Brink, *Kennis* 101–2). Malan goes on to study drama in Cape Town, and after completing his studies, he leaves for London to work on his acting career. During his stay there he starts to feel the urge to reconnect with his personal "prehistory"[6] though, and so he decides to go back to South Africa to start a theater group whose purpose it is to politically mobilize nonwhites. Back in his homeland he meets Jessica Thomson, a white girl of English descent. The two become romantically involved, which is illegal under apartheid law. Malan's theater group gets harassed by the authorities more and more, and eventually the group is forced to disband. Malan's relationship with Thomson is also becoming impossible to sustain. Eventually, they see no other way out than to commit suicide together. Yet their objective of the joint suicide does not end up as planned. Thomson is dead—most probably she died at the hands of Malan—but Malan is still alive. He decides to turn himself in to the Security Police, out of a certain desire to remain true to himself and to his love (cf. 392–93). He admits to have murdered Thomson and is sentenced to death.

That the work contained explosive material was obvious from the start. The South African Publisher Human & Rousseau would not publish it. This notwithstanding that Brink was already an established author at the time; that the publisher had already put out eighteen works by Brink;[7] and that it was still nonsupportive of the government at that time (McDonald, *Literature Police* 96). Buren, a publishing house that was not supportive of the government either (101), was willing to publish it though. Ampie Coetzee, a leading Afrikaans Marxist critic, who assessed the manuscript for Buren, quite strongly recommended that it be published:

> This is a document of oppression, exploitation, abuse, murder; this is a document of the story of the Coloured in South Africa. This is enough motivation for publication already; because the time has come that an Afrikaans novelist presented an image of what is really happening to a part of his people.[8]

Coetzee did, however, also stress that Buren, if it did decide to publish the novel, should take into account that the work was a likely candidate for getting banned:

> From the looks of it, the biggest problems with publishing the work will be the judgments of the Publications Board. With regard to this, writer and publisher will have to think of something, formulate a course of action. It would be tragic if the novel would be banned after appearing; tragic for the author, the publisher, and the reader.[9]

Coetzee's estimation was quite right. Shortly after the novel was published, H. J. Terblanche, chairman of the Genootskap vir die Handhawing van Afrikaans (lit.: Association for the Maintenance of Afrikaans) filed a complaint with the Security Police, while J. J. Swart, NGK[10] minister of Parow, Cape Town, sent in a request to the PCB to have the book examined (Kannemeyer 406–7). On January 29, 1974, some five months after the work had appeared in print, the PCB declared it undesirable (cf. *Buren* v *RBP* 389, 402). The ban was publicly welcomed by representatives of Afrikaner churches and conservative Afrikaner politicians: such high-ranking church and political leaders as J. D. Vorster, J. S. Gericke, D. P. M. Beukes and Minister of the Interior P. C. ("Connie") Mulder expressed their support for the ban in the media.[11] Prominent writers, critics and literary academics such as D. J. Opperman, F. I. J. van Rensburg, H. C. T. Müller, Louis Eksteen and C. N. van der Merwe spoke out against it and tried to foster understanding for this kind of literature among the conservative elements within the Afrikaner community, explaining that this literature pursued different goals and, because of this, employed a different set of values and norms—namely *aesthetical* rather than ethical ones—than the Church and the state did (Peters 62–63). To ban books by confusing these different goals and sets of values and norms would frustrate the development of South African literature (63). With an eye to a possible trial, the Johannesburg branch of the writers' group Skrywersgilde (Writers' Guild), under the guidance of John Miles, Chris Barnard, and Ampie Coetzee, created a writers' fund that could be used to help cover the expenses arising from an eventual trial (Kannemeyer 407; cf. also Brink, "Censorship" 52 and Peters 49). Furthermore, the group asked the prominent men of letters and foremost literary censors A. P. Grové, T. T. Cloete, and Merwe Scholtz to leave the PCB, as their function on this board could not be reconciled with the advancement of Afrikaans literature (Kannemeyer 407). Remarkably, Kannemeyer observed in retrospect, the Suid-Afrikaanse Akademie vir Wetenskap en Kuns (South African Academy for Science and Arts) did not issue a statement with regard to the affair, whereas in the past it had on several occasions made public statements on censorship (407; cf. also Peters 49). Amid all this public debate[12] —which according to Bourdieu provides an indication that a field has reached a high degree of institutional autonomy (see Bourdieu, *Rules* 220 et passim)—Buren appealed against the PCB's decision to the Cape Provincial Division of the Supreme Court. This Court heard the case from August 5 to 7 of 1974. On October 1, 1974, the Court passed its judgment, which was underpinned with three different rationales.

THE POSITION OF THE PUBLICATIONS CONTROL BOARD

Let us first examine the objections that the PCB raised against the book in Court, so as to see what issues were at stake. As neither the initial censorship report on Brink's novel, nor a record of the argument delivered in Court on behalf of the PCB are available today (cf. McDonald, *Literature Police* 54; cf. also *Buren* v *RBP* 381), and as newspaper reports of the trial do not offer much data regarding its argument either (cf. Peters 67, 69 et passim), the position of the Board has to be reconstructed on the basis of references made to it in the three opinions that the Cape Court delivered.

The PCB's objections can be subsumed under three main categories: moral, religious, and political (cf. *Buren* v *RBP* 411). In the first category we can place the objections that parts of the novel were "indecent or obscene or offensive or harmful to public morals"; that parts of the novel would be "outrageous or disgustful" for many readers because they contained instances of "swearing and dirty and indecent language"; and that parts of the book dealt "in an improper manner with abuse of non-whites," which would have the likely result of them being "outrageous or disgustful" for the likely readers of the book (cf. *Buren* v *RBP* 387; cf. also PEA, 1963 282, 284, 286). Under the second category, religious objections, we can classify the objection that parts of Brink's novel were blasphemous, or "offensive to the religious convictions or feelings" of "sections of the inhabitants of the Republic" (cf. *Buren* v *RBP* 387; PEA, 1963 282). The last category, political objections, then consisted in the objections that parts of the book were "harmful to the relations between sections of the inhabitants of the Republic"; that parts of the book were "prejudicial to the safety of the State, the general welfare or the peace and good order"; and that parts of the book "dealt in an improper manner with abuse of non-whites" (cf. *Buren* v *RBP* 387; PEA, 1963 282, 284, 286).[13]

The three categories of objections did not receive an even amount of attention in the argument that a Deputy State Attorney for Cape Town delivered on behalf of the PCB: the "political" and "religious" objections formed the core of the argument (cf. *Buren* v *RBP* 404, 408). As to the former category: it was contended that both parts of the book and the book as a whole were undesirable on political grounds (cf. *Buren* v *RBP* 408). The objection that the book would be prejudicial to the safety of the state was not supported by the Deputy State Attorney, however (cf. *Buren* v *RBP* 408, 421). His argument seems to have concentrated on the objection that the book was harmful to the relations between sections of the nation's population because it demonized whites (cf. *Buren* v *RBP* 397, 408–9, 421). It is not clear whether the board or its attorney marked certain passages as particularly damning. The fact of the matter is that the narrative is full of scenes in which white cruelty toward "Coloureds" is being portrayed, and that the PCB could thus have taken many excerpts to illustrate its political objections to the book.[14] Yet although one cannot tell whether or not the board found certain passages of the book particularly reprehensible, it does become clear from the law report of the case that a particular part of the narrative, namely the one in which Malan is repeatedly interrogated and tortured by the Security Police, received special attention in Court and that the PCB had also made objections to this particular part of the story (cf. *Buren* v *RBP* 399–400 and, especially, 404; Brink, *Kennis* 261–78).

In order to make the board's case regarding the "religious" objections, two theologians were called upon to deliver testimony. Both considered the book blasphemous and felt that it would offend the religious convictions or feelings of Afrikaans Christians (cf. *Buren* v *RBP* 406, 418, 421). Judging from the decisions delivered by the Cape Court, it appears most likely that the grounds for these contentions lay in the fact that the work was considered, firstly, to be taking the Lord's name in vain; secondly, to be ridiculing traditional religion; and, most of all, thirdly, to be coupling sex with religion in an affronting manner (cf., *inter alia*, *Buren* v *RBP* 400–1, 406–8, 418–21). Some of the passages that are likely to have been particularly affronting in the eyes of the PCB, as they were at the center of attention in the opinions delivered by the three judges too, were the following: Firstly, a passage in which protagonist Malan is lying in bed with a woman and this woman tells him to "[s]top acting, Joseph! Jesus! And fuck me!"[15] Secondly, a passage in which Malan explicates the feeling he is experiencing after a long night of repeated and passionate lovemaking with Jessica Thomson by saying to himself: "Now I know, without audacity, how Jesus felt when he returned from the mountain to his disciples: with that sadness and fullness in Him, with that ability to get going again."[16] Thirdly, a passage in which a "whores' wage" is compared with a church collection (cf. *Buren* v *RBP* 401, 407). Fourthly, a passage in which Malan after having described an afternoon of passionate sex with a woman, concludes:

> It was the most intense and most delightful moment of our affair when she, on that grey afternoon in the empty room on the cheap bedstead, reached an orgasm together with me, broke through it with me, and was hurled into infinity. From far away and from nearby, I heard her weep and sob and cry: "O God! O God! O God!"[17]

Fifth, and lastly, a passage at the very end of the narrative, which reads:

Jessica will lie in my arms, in the evening, in the night, in the familiar dark. And I will say to her: Come, Little Miss Muffet, come my darling: come let us go out into the streets, come let us walk hand in hand through the city, don't be afraid, no one will care, no one will stop us, and the horsemen will dismount upon seeing the water.

Come, my darling. The world is open and the laws are gone. Come, walk naked along the never ending beach with me. Stand at the puddle in the sand, so that I can wash you, your shoulders and your lovely breasts, your back and belly and legs, come let me taste your hidden darkness on my hungry tongue. And after that you will wash me, like a woman washes a corpse, with love and tender hands.

And finally you will bury me in the sand and plant a cross between my legs. They will see the cross and remember me, it will not stand there for naught.[18]

One of the issues that the debate in Court was principally concerned with was the question whether the concept of the likely reader should be read into "religious" and "political" articles 5 (2) (*b*) to (*e*) of the act. In contrast to the "moral" article 5 (2) (*a*), no mention of the likely reader was made in these articles. The issue was of course important, because—as we saw in the previous chapter—the concept of the likely reader could be employed to invalidate charges made against a book and thus increase literature's autonomy. The suggestion that the likely reader concept should be read into the articles mentioned had been made by the attorney representing Buren and Brink. In reaction, counsel for the PCB argued that it should not be read into them (cf. *Buren* v *RBP* 403).

When it came to determining the likely readership of the novel, the attorney representing the PCB argued that the work would have attracted "a wide reading circle from the general audience" (*Buren* v *RBP* 404; cf. also 411). This contention was based on the expert testimonies that had been delivered on behalf of the board. A considerable number of the experts that the board had called on to deliver testimony were chosen from its own ranks. T. T. Cloete, the poet, censor, and professor of Afrikaans-Dutch and General Literary Studies[19] at the University of Potchefstroom, had declared that *Kennis* was "smoothly written" and "easily readable"[20] and that because of its "sensational contents and easily readable style"[21] the novel would have attracted a much wider reading circle than was being contended on behalf of the appellant (cf. *Buren* v *RBP* 415). J. J. Kruger, the PCB's chairman, had stated that "because of the contents and tenor of the book and the fame of the author"[22] it was to be expected that the novel would attract great publicity and generate high sales (cf. *Buren* v *RBP* 413). Indeed, regarding the supposed fame of Brink it was contended on behalf of the board that the author was widely known, not just in literary circles, but also amongst the general audience (cf. *Buren* v *RBP* 406). A. P. Grové, censor and professor and chair of the Afrikaans Department of the University of Pretoria, had declared that the book would have a wide reading circle because it was "easily written"[23] and, notwithstanding "certain hidden and less hidden references in the main thread of the story,"[24] the narrative contained "enough sex and sensation"[25] to render the "book . . . accessible for a wide circle of readers."[26] Indeed, he had stated that the book was "chock-full of incidents of all kinds"[27] which would capture the attention of the "average reader."[28] The book's price would not prevent it from reaching a wide reading circle either, he reckoned (cf. *Buren* v *RBP* 414). Finally, a Mr. J. J. van Rooyen, managing director of C. F. Albertyn Publishers, had argued that because of the author's fame, the easy style of the book, and the themes it addressed, it would have a wide reading circle among ordinary Afrikaans readers (*Buren* v *RBP* 414–15). The PCB's strategy thus seemed aimed at convincing the Court that the novel's likely readership should not be perceived to be made up entirely of a select circle of "strong"—i.e., intellectual, literary socialized—readers, but that its readership was likely to be broad and heterogeneous and that it would by implication also be comprised of "weak" readers. It might also have been, however, that its strategy was (also) aimed at convincing the bench that the novel lacked the kind of aesthetic value that might have made the judges feel that it warranted special legal protection.

The arguments delivered on behalf of the board did not revolve solely around these more institutional matters though: outright poetological issues also played a part. These issues were taken up in response to a long testimony that had been adduced by Brink. In this testimony he had laid out the literary theory underlying the novel, i.e., the literary theoretical precepts that—according to him—had guided the conception of the novel and that generally would, and certainly should, guide the reader's interpretation of the work (cf. *Buren* v *RBP* 390–93; Brink, "*Kennis* Verbode" 90). Moreover, the expert witnesses called in by the appellants had also made statements regarding literary-conceptual matters in their testimonies. Now, in the argument that PCB member Grové delivered, he discussed the then highly current bipolar framework which situated "aesthetic novels,"[29] i.e., the novel as "hermetically sealed universe" (cf. *Buren* v *RBP* 391) at the one extreme pole, and "'engaged' novels,"[30] i.e., the novel as a form of "littérature engagée"[31] on the other. He argued that Brink was feigning to have written a non-corresponding,[32] "aesthetic" novel, while in reality he had purposely written a corresponding, "engaged" novel (cf. *Buren* v *RBP* 391–92). To put it in the terms of M. H. Abrams:[33] he was pretending to have written an "objective," or autonomist, work of literature while having expressly written a mimetic-pragmatic work—one that, moreover, contained elements that were not adequate for good literature in the eyes of the board. One of the arguments that Grové used to underpin this contention was that the narrator of the story was, contrarily to what Brink himself had argued in his testimony, a reliable one

(*Buren* v *RBP* 392). Cloete made an almost identical argument as Grové with the only difference between the two being basically that the former categorized Brink as an "engaged" writer in more implicit terms than the latter (cf. *Buren* v *RBP* 392–93, 422). The issue at stake in all this appeared to be the fictionality/transformation principle—the judicial principle which we already encountered in the introduction and chapter 2—i.e., the (judicial) question to what degree Brink's work, i.e., the sensitive parts of it, effectively distanced itself from/managed to transcend reality. The point of the PCB was that *Kennis* did not succeed in transcending reality; it failed to transform reality into a work of art.

Considering the fact that the PCB took such strong exception to the novel and found it to fall foul of the PEA's moral, religious, and political provisions, it seems not implausible to hypothesize that its conception of literature was not only made up of state of the art literary theoretical principles, but rather represented a mixture of up-to-date poetics and more traditional Platonic precepts, just as the poetics of the Cronjé Commission had.

THE POSITION OF BRINK AND HIS PUBLISHER

The argument that was delivered in Court on behalf of Brink and his publisher Buren was primarily focused on the concept of the likely reader (cf. *Buren* v *RBP* 403), i.e., both on issues of the principle of the concept and on its more practical aspects. The part of the argument relating more to the principle was constituted by the already mentioned contention that the concept of the likely reader should be read into the "religious" and "political" articles— 5 (2) (*b*) to (*e*)—of the act. On the more practical side, it was contended that the novel would (normally) have had a limited reading circle, which, moreover, would have been made up of literarily socialized individuals (cf. *Buren* v *RBP* 387–89, 404, 411)—the kind of readers that were not likely to be negatively affected by the book. The contention that the readership of the novel would (under normal circumstances) be comprised of literati was underpinned by the testimonies of expert witnesses D. J. Opperman, Ernst Lindenberg, I. D. du Plessis, Buren's founder and managing director Daantjie Saayman, Leon Rousseau, J. J. van Schaik, and G. J. Coetzee (cf. 405, 411–13). The former three were prominent figures within the Afrikaans part of the South African literary field and also linked to Afrikaans departments of South African universities; the latter four were all high-ranking individuals from within the Afrikaans literary book trade.[34]

In the testimonies delivered by these individuals, both intra- and extra-textual arguments were brought to the fore so as to make clear that Brink's book was not a book that would appeal to a mass audience but to a limited group of literati only. The intra-textual arguments all came down to the contention that because of the book's "literariness"[35] (cf. *Buren* v *RBP* 405) it would appeal to the latter category of reader only. The extra-textual arguments comprised a number of observations that mostly concerned the material side of the product *Kennis*. Firstly, it was argued that the book's length of c. 500 pages would put off the "ordinary reader" (cf. *Buren* v *RBP* 405). Secondly, it was professed that the book's blurb was "functional" and that the book as a whole was indeed presented in a "non-sensational" manner (cf. 412). In other words: Buren had not marketed the book with the purpose of reaching a mass audience. Thirdly, it was contended that the price of the novel was too high for it to appeal to a large audience (cf. 412) and that the print run of the first edition—3,000—was relatively small. Furthermore, it was stressed that the book had been distributed through very few and specialist channels (cf. 412). Fourthly, it was argued to be normal that a book's sales were relatively high in the first month—because of pre-orders and purchases by libraries—and that they would gradually decline in ensuing months. The increase in sales of Brink's novel that had started after four months was ascribed to the fact that the novel had received "abnormal" publicity some three months after it had been launched (cf. 412). By "abnormal" publicity, the witnesses were alluding to the attention that had been given to the novel after word had gotten out that the PCB was in the process of reviewing it (cf. de Lange 47). Fifth, and lastly, it was argued that none of Brink's prior works had had a strong appeal to the popular market. Indeed, it was contended that the sales of Brink's works were generally modest, unless they were prescribed by universities, and that these works were normally being bought by a "vaste eksklusieve aanhang" (413; lit. "regular exclusive following"), only consisting of individuals with a "serious interest in Afrikaans literature" (cf. 413). In sum, according to the experts delivering testimony on behalf of Buren and Brink the readership of the Brink's novel would normally have consisted of a limited number of Afrikaner literati.

Apart from the topic of likely readership, the argument delivered on behalf of Buren and Brink also focused on the question to what extent Parliament had meant for the act to have a prescriptive character when it came to moral issues, i.e., whether it had designed the act first and foremost as an instrument for decisive paternalistic intervention—as the majority of the Justices of Appeal in Smith's case evidently believed—or whether it rather, apart from providing a tool to enable certain kinds of interventions, would have wanted for certain freedoms to also be respected—as Appeal Justices Rumpff and Williamson thought. Buren's attorney argued that the latter was the case, and that a judge thus first had to establish who the likely readers of a certain work were before he could decide whether the work in question would have a detrimental effect on its readers (cf. *Buren* v *RBP* 384–85). Having taken this stance, the appellants also argued that in order to be able to judge Brink's work rightfully, it was vital to take regard to contemporary books that were comparable to his (cf. Brink "*Kennis* Verbode" 91, 95, 96; *Buren* v *RBP* 390, 422). If one were to do so, they argued, one would find that the nature of many works in circulation in South Africa could be compared to Brink's novel, and that some of these would have probably been read by the likely reader of *Kennis*. Hence, the appellant party concluded, such a likely reader would not be harmed by Brink's work; he would have already become used to works like that of Brink—he would have become "shock proof" already, as one of the judges succinctly summarized this presumption (cf. *Buren* v *RBP* 400).

A third issue that the Buren and Brink party touched upon was the principle of contextualism, i.e., the principle that parts of a publication should be considered in the light of the whole. As we have seen in the previous chapter, this concept had expressly been applied in contemporary American and British law as an instrument to grant literature a(n) (relatively) autonomous status vis-à-vis the law. Moreover, a lance had also been broken for the principle by a number of judges in the two trials of Smith's *Lion*, apparently also for the purpose of securing a certain degree of autonomy for literature. The Buren-Brink party relied on the concept to argue that the coupling of sex with religion in *Kennis* was legitimate—because it was "functional" within the entirety of the work (cf. Brink, "*Kennis* Verbode" 92, 94ff; *Buren* v *RBP* 407–8). Furthermore, they employed the concept to profess how the likely reader would regard both the work as a whole and the risqué passages that were part of it. This reader, they advanced, would see these as, respectively, a unity of "essential-functional"[36] elements, and single examples of such elements—indispensable building blocks, effectively (cf. *Buren* v *RBP* 405, 412–13, 421–22). With both arguments the appellants were in effect laying claim to a relatively high degree of institutional autonomy.

As already becomes apparent from the above-quoted references to the concept of functionality that the Buren-Brink party employed, literary theoretical issues were drawn into the debate as well. They were drawn in both through the long testimony adduced by Brink himself and by the testimonies of the expert witnesses who had been called in by the appellants. Brink took a decisive autonomist position in his testimony. "*Kennis van die Aand*," he declared,

> was conceived of as fiction from the very start, and in this respect it is vital to point out that all forms of fiction—and the novel more than any other—during the couple of decades since World War II more than ever before have been studied by Literary Studies across the globe (but most of all in Germany and the U.S., with a strong following in Britain and South Africa) as art forms in their own right, to be distinguished from "reality representation." The essential point of departure from standard works such as Booth's *Rhetoric of Fiction*, Stanzel's *Narrative Situations in the Novel* and literally hundreds of others, is that the literary work establishes a world of words in its own right, in which

correspondences with the world outside are completely irrelevant. The approach, judgment and test of such a work lies solely in the establishment of the meaningful relation between all elements within the work itself and the essential elements are usually summarized as: characters, action, space, and time.[37]

In his offensive, Brink thus also chose to rely on the fictionality/transformation principle. Indeed, he employed it as the main argument to underpin an apparently absolute autonomist conception of literature, a conception which, in turn, was meant to underpin a claim to a far-reaching degree of institutional autonomy. After having emphasized the hegemonic status of the conception of literature he adhered to, he drove home his argument as follows:

> In writing *Kennis van die Aand* I could thus *a priori* trust that the work, conceived as a novel, would be judged exactly in this context and in this manner, and not in any other. For the purpose of still more insurance that the work would only be *judged* as fiction because it only *exists* as fiction, this standpoint was printed in a foreword to the book: there it is categorically stated that everything "within the new context of the novel . . . (is) fictive"; and further, that "the demonstrable surface of the current affairs (is) not relevant as such anywhere, only the patterns and relations under it are." (Brink's emphasis)[38]

The above-quoted passages, which formed the first two paragraphs of Brink's testimony, basically contained the three quintessential elements of the defense it presented. These were (1) that with *Kennis*, he had had the intention of creating a work of literature; (2) that with *Kennis* being a novel, it by definition constituted a work of fiction, i.e., an *autonomous* "world of words," not a representation of reality; and (3) that since *Kennis* was conceived as a work of literature, it should, and normally would, be judged on the basis of the literary-conceptual standards that, according to Brink, were dominant at the time; standards, indeed, that were, in Abrams' terms, of an "objective," or autonomist, nature—not on the basis of other criteria.

Brink was backed in his literary theoretical positioning by the expert witnesses that were called in by his attorney to deliver testimony. One of the most cogent examples of this support can be found in the testimony delivered by D. J. Opperman. He declared that "[t]he function of the artwork as mirror is no longer being accepted; your likely reader sees a novel as a soap bubble which gives a spherical vision, a bent reflection of reality."[39] The purpose of the argument regarding the validity of the "objective"/autonomist way of conceptualizing literature and the invalidity of the "mimetic" way was perhaps not just to relatively straightforwardly lay claim to a high degree of institutional autonomy. More indirectly, it was possibly also applied in order to exert pressure on the judiciary. There seems to have been some anxiety among judiciaries in the West who feared embarrassing themselves when dealing with literature—the way in which the French judiciary apparently lost face in the trial of Flaubert's *Madame Bovary* appears to have formed the foremost frightening example (cf. Grüttemeier and Laros 211). By contending in so many words that anyone who knew anything of literature approached a novel as an autonomous work of art and not as a representation of reality, the appellants effectively put pressure on the judiciary to do the same—if not, they would reveal themselves to be out of touch with modern art.

THE COURT'S JUDGMENT

The Court's judgment was unanimous: on the basis of the PEA, the book was "undesirable." However, the three judges had quite different reasons for coming to this conclusion, and so each of them formulated an individual opinion. Not only did the judges have distinct opinions as to the question on which grounds Brink's work ought to be considered "undesirable"—Judge President van Wyk found it to be undesirable on religious, moral, and political grounds; Judges Diemont and Steyn considered it undesirable on religious grounds only—but more importantly, the positions they adopted vis-à-vis the literary field and their poetological stances were also markedly different. Therefore, I will discuss the individual opinions of the three judges separately.

Judge President van Wyk

The position that Judge President van Wyk took both regarding literature in general and Brink's novel in particular had many "heteronomist" traits. This applies both to the institutional and the poetological dimension of his point of view. As far as questions concerning the institutional status of literature were concerned, van Wyk was very clear, and his standpoint greatly resembled the position that the majority had taken in the appeal trial of Smith's *Lion*. First of all, he categorically held that the law was the law and that neither the prevalence of similar books, nor the acceptance of such books by certain audiences was relevant when a Court had to judge a book on the basis of the PEA (cf. *Buren* v *RBP* 382–83, 384–85, 390, 393, 400). Van Wyk's position clearly cohered with the position taken by Chief Justice Steyn and the Justices Holmes and Potgieter in the appeal case of *Lion* as their judgment declared that "the prevalence of similar contemporary reading matter, which may itself offend against the Act, cannot be the standard by which the effect or influence of a publication is to be measured for the purposes of the Act. It would be no answer to the prohibitions in the Act to show that what Parliament has thought fit to forbid is the very height of contemporary fashion" (*PCB* v *Heinemann* 149). For van Wyk too it was thus a matter of principle not to leave it up to the (likely) reader to decide what he wanted to read, but up to the PCB/a Court to decide what this reader could be allowed to read on the basis of the PEA.

As van Wyk's standpoint on the admissibility of comparisons with other books already indicates, his position also cohered with that of the majority in the appeal case of *Lion* when it came to his interpretation of the purpose of the PEA: he too held that the law had a decidedly interventionist aim—which, thus, also implied that it was aimed at keeping the institutional autonomy of literature in check. In response to a remark made by Buren's attorney that all that the legislator had meant to accomplish with article 6 (1) of the PEA was to prevent public morals from being corrupted, and that a Court could only decide whether certain matter would be corruptive if it knew who would see or read the matter in question, van Wyk replied:

> It is indeed true that the aim of the Legislator is to protect public morals, but it does not follow from this that the Legislator compels the Court because of this to establish who will see or read certain matter for the purposes of art. 6 (1) (c). *On the contrary, the Legislator wanted to protect public morals on a broader basis, namely by declaring matter undesirable if it to the opinion of the Court deals with certain subjects in an improper manner.* (emphasis mine)[40]

That van Wyk indeed employed the act as an interventionist tool became evident when he got to the concept of likely readership. As we have seen in the previous chapter, this concept could be employed both as a means to promote and as an instrument to curb the autonomy of the reader and, by implication, literature. Van Wyk quite obviously used it as a tool for doing the latter. He conceptualized likely readership very broadly: he argued that "persons whose thoughts could be exposed indirectly to the influence of the book"[41] also constituted the likely readership of the novel. "One could easily think of examples of such indirect influence," he stated, "like for example where the contents of parts of a book are being read or passed on to others."[42] Not only did van Wyk conceptualize likely readership so very broadly, he also emphasized—and in this he also followed the majority opinion in the AD case of *Lion* (*PCB* v *Heinemann* 150–51)—that it did not have to be the case that a publication would actually corrupt the mind of readers, but that it was enough when the publication had a *tendency* to do so (cf. *Buren* v *RBP* 383). Finally, van Wyk resolutely dismissed the argument of Buren's attorney that the concept of the likely reader should also be read into the paragraphs of the act in which it was not mentioned (cf. *Buren* v *RBP* 384–86). It was the opinion of the Court that mattered in these articles, he declared (cf. *Buren* v *RBP* 383–84; 386–87). Thus, especially when it came to alleged offenses on the basis of the "religious" and "political" articles of the act, but also where "moral" issues were concerned, van Wyk was not willing to grant the literary field much autonomy.

When van Wyk came to actually establish the identity of the likely reader of *Kennis*, he, not very surprisingly, did indeed postulate a rather broad readership. "In my opinion," he stated,

> this book has been read by a wide reading circle already, and if it had not been declared undesirable, the circle would have gotten bigger by now. It contains all the usual elements of a bestseller: sex and violence. On top of that there are sexual relations across the color line and also many political affairs. This is a book that would of course predominantly be read by Afrikaans-speaking people, mainly Whites, but also by many non-Whites. The largest number of readers are certainly those who have at least completed standard eight.[43] The publisher says his goal was to have the book prescribed at universities. Whether it would be prescribed or not, there can be little doubt that a large amount of students would read the book. A significant amount of other people, old and young, like teachers, businessmen, farmers and civil servants would read the book too. A very large number of these likely readers are members of the Afrikaans churches.[44]

So despite the efforts of the expert witnesses that had delivered testimony on behalf of the Buren party, van Wyk did not quite envision a limited audience consisting of literary socialized readers for Brink's novel. Furthermore, he also ignored the plea of the appealing party to take into consideration that the novel would have received less public attention and that the sales of the novel would have kept on decreasing gradually after the first month in which they were relatively high, if it had not been for the "abnormal" publicity that the novel had received after word had gotten out that it was taken up for scrutiny by the PCB. Indeed, he stated:

> It is being claimed that the initial sales confirmed the generally expected sales pattern and that this would have ensued had it not been for the excessive publicity that was given to it [i.e., to the novel]. Excessive publicity is a fact though, and one of the factors that can be taken into consideration in establishing who will be the likely readers. The reasons for large sales, whatever they may be, are no grounds for ignoring the fact of large sales. The greater the sale, the greater the groups of likely readers.[45]

Clearly, unsolicited publicity was not a mitigating factor for van Wyk. As this position was not an unavoidable one—Diemont, as we will see, adopted the exact opposite position—it appeared also to be symptomatic of van Wyk's opposition to granting a significant degree of autonomy to literature in general and to Brink's novel in particular.

Yet even though the cumulative evidence presented above makes it justified to say that van Wyk was not willing to allow the literary field much autonomy vis-à-vis the law, there was an aspect of his position that evidenced that this field had in fact already attained, and could not be denied, a certain degree of autonomy. Van Wyk indeed appeared to realize that the opinions of the expert witnesses called in by both parties carried a certain weight, for he quite extensively employed the poetological arguments delivered by some of the PCB's expert witnesses to make his own argument. Effectively, this recognition of the expert status of the actors called upon from within the literary field meant granting the literary field a certain amount of institutional autonomy vis-à-vis the law—however modest this granted autonomy might have been, both in absolute terms and in comparison to the heteronomist aspect of his position.

Indeed, van Wyk took a decisive poetological stance in his opinion. Yet before he came to reveal his conception of literature, he first invalidated the testimony that Brink had delivered. The reason for this appeared to be that in his declaration, Brink had largely focused on professing what had been his intention with *Kennis*. The act provided, however, that no regard was to be had to the purpose of the writer,[46] and apparently, thus, that a text-oriented (or objective) approach was to be applied, not an intention-oriented (or subjective) one.[47] As van Wyk declared, Brink's "long statement under oath . . . in which he attempted to set forth his perspective on his book"[48] was irrelevant in Court: "It is not necessary to go into the author's argument in detail," he stated after having briefly referred to Brink's testimony, "because his subjective motives as he has formulated them are actually not relevant. They actually have nothing to do with the question whether the book is undesirable under one or more of the provisions of arts. 5 and 6 of the Act."[49] Yet although van Wyk appeared to be invalidating Brink's testimony on the basis of the latter's focus on authorial intent, he himself based his judgment for an important part on what he professed to have been the author's purpose too, as we will see below.

Having annulled Brink's testimony, van Wyk came to his own reading of the novel. Apparently, he read novels, or at least Brink's, on the basis of a mixture of mimetic and pragmatic poetological premises. What is more is that he held that many likely readers of Brink's novel would share his conception of literature, and that they as a consequence would read Brink's novel in the same manner as he had. Referring to the remark made by Buren's witness Opperman, that the likely reader of *Kennis* saw a novel as a "soap bubble" which offered "a spherical vision, a bent reflection of reality," van Wyk declared:

> Of the soap-bubble-technique, of which Prof. Opperman speaks, in a novel which purports to be a novel which is based on reality, I was completely unaware until now. I am not a man of letters, but this also counts for most likely readers. I therefore have no reason to think that there would not be thousands of likely readers of the book who would share my "ignorance" in this respect. My impression was still that such a novel, although the narrative

itself is fictive, still to a great extent represented a reflection of reality as it is or was at a certain time.[50]

As the word "purports" in the first sentence of the quote already indicates, van Wyk held that it had been Brink's intention to write a mimetic novel. Indeed, van Wyk unambiguously declared that "[t]here [wa]s enough evidence that the book was purposely written in such a manner that the reader would get the impression that especially the more important incidents, although fictive, [we]re a mirror image of reality."[51] Approvingly, van Wyk quoted passages from the testimonies of PCB witnesses Grové and Cloete in which they explained the bipolar classificatory model in which the autonomous novel—the novel as "hermetically sealed universe" (cf. Buren v RBP 391)—formed the one extreme pole, and the pragmatic—"engaged" (cf. Buren v RBP 391)—novel the other. In great accord, van Wyk cited the analyses of these two experts witnesses, and particularly Grové's, who had stated that Brink had explicitly taken a pragmatic stance (*sensu* Abrams) in programmatic poetological texts, but now that he was up for trial, he sought to pass for an autonomous author: "[T]he difficulty with second appellant [i.e., Brink]," Grové had stated,

> [is] precisely that he wants to sit on two chairs. With *Kennis van die Aand* he writes a *roman engagé*, a novel that breaks through the walls surrounding the world of the novel in a hundred ways, for example by mentioning situations, places, persons, localities, a novel that wants to "write open" the S. A. situation, that wants to reform, that wants to expose injustices. But now that its one-sided representations and agitation are being pointed out, now he wants to hide behind the theory that regards the novel as a "hermetically sealed universe." As an assailant he wants to be a reformer; as a defender he wants to be an aesthetic. When he charges, the novel is a literary weapon to him; when he defends, the novel suddenly becomes a distinct world that has nothing to do with current events. He wants, thus, to have the best of both worlds.[52]

For van Wyk, this remark of Grové's hit the nail on the head (cf. *Buren* v *RBP* 391). And as a consequence of this, or at least partly because of this, he tested the novel *inter alia* on the basis of mimetic criteria. *Kennis* clearly did not pass this test. Van Wyk devoted a large part of his argument to discussing the way in which whites were being portrayed in Brink's novel—even though the PCB had not declared the novel to be undesirable on the basis of sec. 5 (2) (c) of the PEA, i.e., on the grounds that it would bring any section of the population "into ridicule or contempt."[53] The judge's conclusion was that the book's many episodes of crimes committed against "Coloureds" by whites did not form a truthful representation of the South African past, nor of its current situation.[54] Indeed, he stated,

> [i]t is improper to throw together such isolated crimes committed by Whites in such a manner that they are being held up as a reflection of the broad reality. By doing this a false image of Whites is being created, an image which brings Whites as a group into contempt. Art 5 (2) (c) explicitly lays down that a publication that brings a section of the population into contempt is undesirable, and therefore has to be barred.[55]

Apart from the fact that *Kennis*, because of the way in which Brink had "thrown together" his episodes of racist crimes, constituted a "political" offense, it also represented an offense in terms of some of the "moral" sections of the law, according to van Wyk. In his eyes, Brink's "distorted fiction that was being held up as a mirror image of reality" was, *inter alia*, "also undesirable on the basis of sec. 6 (1) (*b*), because it was likely to be outrageous and disgustful to a significant number of the likely readers."[56]

What was also morally affronting in van Wyk's view was the manner in which certain sexual episodes were being described. After presenting a number of passages that according to him violated section 5 (2) (*a*) read together with 6 (1) (*b*), he stated that "[i]t is true that some so-called sophisticated readers actually find nothing disgustful or outrageous, but in my opinion, the great majority of the likely readers will probably find this book disgustful and outrageous."[57] As the determinants "so-called sophisticated" indicate, van Wyk seemed to have had a certain group of actual readers in mind when making this statement, and it is not unlikely at all that with the first part of his remark he was referring to the following of the *Sestigers*—as apparently Chief Justice Steyn had done in similar fashion a decade earlier when he observed that there was a "tendency towards what might be said to approximate to a phallic cult amongst [contemporary] authors and their readers" (149). In any case, van Wyk's remark appeared to evidence that his poetics was rather coherent with the Platonic conception of literature that underlaid the majority opinion in the AD case of *Lion*.

Two final aspects of the book that, according to van Wyk, would offend the likely readers of the novel were the coupling of sex with religion and the taking of the Lord's name in vain (cf. *Buren* v *RBP* 400-01). Yet whereas van Wyk's objections to the untruthful representation of white cruelty against "Coloureds" was a direct result of the mimetic requirements he had postulated as a crucial test for judging the book, this latter objection seemed rather to have been a consequence of his conviction that the PEA was meant to have a decidedly interventionist purpose—a conviction that appeared underpinned by both institutional and literary-conceptual arguments.

In sum, van Wyk was not willing to allow the literary field a great degree of autonomy vis-à-vis the law. On the contrary, in his view, literature had to obey the evidently reactionary normative standard that Parliament had established with its PEA—a standard that cohered with the apparently Platonic conception of literature to which van Wyk adhered. However, his position also revealed that the literary field had effectively reached a considerable degree of autonomy already, for van Wyk appeared to realize that the testimonies delivered by the expert witnesses in the trial carried a certain weight. Indeed, he determinedly underpinned his opinion with both the poetological arguments and the analyses of Brink's behavior as an author—both between the covers of his novel *Kennis* and as an accused in the trial of his novel—that had been delivered by some of the expert witnesses appearing on behalf of the PCB. In doing so, he effectively confirmed that (at least some of) the expert evidence that had been delivered in Court had legal relevance: indeed, that the way in which (some of) these witnesses dealt with literature was judicially adequate. Yet although van Wyk both through validating and employing some of the adduced expert evidence thus effectively granted the literary field a certain amount of institutional autonomy vis-à-vis the law, this autonomy was not that significant when viewed in the light of the most fundamental aspect of his position: for him, law/the political field enjoyed almost absolute sovereignty over the literary field.

Judge Diemont

The second judge who formulated an opinion in Buren's case was judge Diemont, the same judge who a decade earlier had heard the initial trial of Smith's *When the Lion Feeds* and had delivered the dissenting opinion. In his opinion on *Kennis*, Diemont adopted a much more tolerant position than his colleague van Wyk, a position that allowed the literary field considerable autonomy.

Early on in his judgment, Diemont remarked that it was vital to take into account that "the Court is not free and unconfined in the exercise of its discretion. It might be that I would not have forbidden *Kennis van die Aand* if I could have exercised an uncurbed discretion, but I cannot let my own viewpoints prevail over the principles of the Law, and especially the provisions of arts. 5 and 6."[58] Clearly, Diemont's position had not changed much since the Smith trial: although he seemed to be indicating that he as a private person felt that the literary field should be granted a considerable degree of autonomy, he as a judge was well aware of the fact that he had to respect the wishes of Parliament.[59] Yet although Diemont appeared quite categorically to be upholding the principle of parliamentary sovereignty,[60] he did declare that a judge always had to try to guarantee the fundamental freedoms that he perceived to underpin the South African state as far as he could, i.e., as far as was possible within the boundaries of the law. Approvingly, he quoted the passage regarding the freedom of speech and the freedom to publish a story that Rumpff—who by now had been appointed Chief Justice—had incorporated in his minority judgment in the appeal case of Smith's *Lion* (cf. *Buren* v

RBP 402–3; *PCB* v *Heinemann* 160). In the name of freedom of speech, Diemont thus propagated a tolerant approach toward literature.

That Diemont was willing to allow the (literary socialized) reader—and hence literature—considerable autonomy seems to be evidenced by the fact that he, unlike van Wyk, did effectively hold that the concept of the likely reader ought to be read into the sections of the act that did not mention it, as Buren's attorney had advanced. Indeed, Diemont argued that he "found it difficult to understand how the Court would be able to decide whether a book would be undesirable without asking the question—for whom is it undesirable? Who is going to read the book? This question is of vital importance."[61] Surely, the question was "of vital importance" for the literary field, because when the criterion by which to measure the undesirability or otherwise of a publication was to be the likely reader in the application of every section stipulating the kinds of offenses that would make a text undesirable, the field could potentially reach a considerable amount of autonomy. For at least since the 1932 case of Meinert, the South African judiciary appears to have generally conceptualized the literary socialized, or "intellectual," reader as a reader that was not as easily affected negatively as his nonintellectual counterpart was.

When Diemont subsequently came to actually determining the identity of the likely reader, he argued that two factors should be taken into consideration first and foremost: (1) the contents of the book; and (2) the reputation of the author. As to the former aspect, Diemont stated that although sex and violence, which, he added, were both "known and usual elements of the bestseller,"[62] abounded in the book, the book was in fact not a bestseller. For, he rhetorically asked, if it had been a bestseller, why had only 2,500 copies been sold in the first five months (cf. *Buren* v *RBP* 404)? Significantly, the same figures that had led van Wyk to declare that the novel had already been read by a wide reading circle in the five months before it had been banned, were not so impressive for Diemont. The reason why sales had been modest was obvious, Diemont explained: the book was not easy to read (cf. *Buren* v *RBP* 404). Indeed, he rather unequivocally stated:

> This is a long-winded story that progresses at a slow pace until it finally comes to an end in a death cell. Personally I would have never finished the book had I not been obliged to read it for the purposes of this case. The author goes out of his way to impress the reader with his erudition, his broad knowledge of literature and philosophy and drama; I find this irritating and boring.[63]

Tellingly, Diemont's position was diametrically opposed to that of van Wyk in this matter too. For although the latter also found the book to be long-winded and tedious at certain places, he held that the book was full of incidents of all kinds and that the philosophical elements that it contained would not restrain an ordinary reader from reading it (cf. *Buren* v *RBP* 404).

Expounding on the perceived difficulty of the book, Diemont discussed some of the testimonies that had been delivered by the (literary) expert witnesses on behalf of both the Board and Buren. Disapprovingly he cited PCB witness Cloete, who, as we have seen, had declared that the book was smoothly written and easily readable. Yet in a clear effort to underpin his own argument, he extensively quoted Buren witnesses Opperman, Lindenberg, and du Plessis, who all had argued that the book was difficult to read for non-literati and that it would thus normally have had a select reading circle consisting of men of letters (cf. *Buren* v *RBP* 405). Apparently—and herein Diemont did not distinguish himself from van Wyk—he thus also recognized the value of literary expert opinion.

After having discussed the expert evidence with which he concurred, Diemont came to the conclusion regarding his first point. He declared that he was of the opinion that if he took into consideration "the literary content of the book and the complicated style,"[64] he had to conclude that its readership would largely be limited to people "with a serious interest in the art of the novel."[65] "Shallow people or those who seek titillating reading matter would quickly be discouraged," he added.[66] *A priori* Diemont thus posited that the kind of literature that Brink wrote was normally being read by literary socialized individuals only. Diemont's stance was rounded off with him taking a position on the issue whether the fact that the novel had attracted so much publicity since it became known that the PCB had begun to scrutinize the book should be taken into account. He argued that the Court's decision should not be influenced by the fact that interest in, and thus sales of, the book might have increased because of all this publicity: "This," he explained, "would be unjust towards the author and the publisher. The question is—who would have read the book under normal circumstances when it would not have been banned under the Censorship act."[67] On this matter too, Diemont thus adopted a remarkably more lenient position than his colleague van Wyk had.

As far as the second point, the author's reputation, was concerned, Diemont declared that Brink was indeed known within literary circles, but that he was also renowned among the general audience. However, Diemont argued that Brink's renown among the broad public would not result in it being potentially interested in his novel. On the contrary, he contended, the author's reputation would scare off the "ordinary reader, the man who seeks light reading matter,"[68] read: the not, or only poorly, literary-socialized reader. Potentially, a principled supposition like this could be instrumental in allowing literature a significant amount of autonomy: if books like that of Brink's—books with a "literary content" and a "complicated style"—would indeed only appeal to a select circle of literary socialized readers, i.e., to "strong" readers who would not be corrupted easily, one might argue that there would not be much need to suppress such books.

Having established his position regarding the two determining factors he had posited, Diemont came to his overall conclusion regarding the likely readership of the novel. His conclusion was that the book would have a limited circle of readers consisting for the largest part of literary socialized readers, i.e., "men of letters, persons with an education and a serious interest in matters";[69] "people with an interest in literature, philosophy, and sociological problems."[70]

After he had determined the identity of the likely reader, Diemont set forth what effects the book would probably have on this reader. As far as the "religious" component of the book was concerned, he stated that the likely reader would probably not consider the book blasphemous (cf. *Buren* v *RBP* 406). However, he argued that the book would in all likelihood offend the religious feelings of many a likely reader. The reason he gave for this was that

> [t]he reading circle might be relatively small and it might be . . . that it consists of men of letters and educated people for the largest part, but it must also be remembered that many of them, perhaps the majority, would also be Afrikaans-speaking Calvinists, or members of the Dutch Reformed Church or one of its sister churches. Most of these persons have had an orthodox Christian upbringing and although they may be sophisticated worldly-wise readers today, many of them would consider parts of this book as offensive nonetheless.[71]

With the indefinite "parts of this book," Diemont was thinking first and foremost of "incidents and descriptions in which sex was being coupled with religion."[72] As to the argument that the passages in which sex was being connected to religion made a contribution to the narrative, that they were "functional," Diemont declared:

> This may be so, but I do not think this is relevant. I have to apply the provisions of the Act. I have to decide, regardless of the part that these incidents of sex-religion play in the story, whether the provisions of sec. 5 (2) (*b*) of the Act are being transgressed. The answer is affirmative, in my opinion.[73]

Again, for Diemont, the law was the law, and neither his eventual own preferences (literary or moral or otherwise) nor literary-conceptual issues like these could therefore be of any relevance: whatever amount of autonomy could be granted to literature, there was a point where the autonomy of the literary field had to succumb to the sovereignty of the political field, and in Diemont's view, Brink had surpassed that point with his "incidents of sex-religion."

When it came to the "political" component of the book, Diemont was quite straightforward. As to the first "political" objection that was raised against the book, i.e., the objection that it would harm relations between certain sections of the South African population, Diemont declared that the likely reader, being the sensible person that he was (cf. *Buren* v *RBP* 408–9), would not react to the book, and particularly to the way in which whites were being portrayed (cf. 408–9), in such a way that it would trouble or harm "race relations."[74] As to the second objection, which was that the book would be prejudicial to the safety of the state, the general welfare, or the peace and good order, Diemont came to the same conclusion: he could not imagine that the kind of people that would read Brink's novel would react to it in such a way that any of these might become endangered (cf. 408).

As for the "moral" objections to the book: Diemont did not go into them at all.[75] His final conclusion was that the PCB's decision that *Kennis* was undesirable on religious grounds—i.e., on the grounds that it would offend the religious convictions or feelings of a section of the South African population—had been justified. The board's judgment that the book was also undesirable on political grounds—in that it would harm the relations between sections of the population, or the safety of the state, or the general welfare, or peace and good order—had not been valid, he declared.

As the way in which Diemont dealt with institutional matters might be termed quite autonomist-oriented, the manner in which he handled the key poetological question that the case posed could also be characterized thus. For Diemont accepted Brink's claim that it had been his intention to write a non-mimetic work of literature and that he might *a priori* assume that its readers would interpret it accordingly. Approvingly, he quoted a passage from Brink's foreword to the book in which the fictive character of his novel was being emphasized (see *Buren* v *RBP* 409; also Brink, "*Kennis* Verbode" 90). If the likely readers of the book "had enough sense to read and understand this type of book," the judge concluded, "they ought to realize that this is all fiction."[76] Unlike van Wyk, Diemont thus not only thought Brink's non-mimetic literary-conceptual position-taking to be relevant, he also endorsed it. Indeed, he held that the novel should not be judged on the basis of mimetic criteria, or the criteria of nonfiction, as van Wyk had done: whatever elements of reality Brink had used in his novel, the way in which he had used them had transformed them into artistic elements per se.

Concludingly, it can be observed that Diemont's approach to literature in general and Brink's novel in particular—i.e., both when it came to institutional and literary-conceptual matters—allowed the literary field a significant degree of autonomy. The aspects of his position that were most instrumental in opening up an autonomous space for literature were his principled favoring of a freedom-oriented approach, his particular conceptualization of the likely reader—both theoretically and with regard to the practical case that

Kennis offered—his acknowledgment of literary expertise, and his employment of literary-conceptual arguments advanced by a literary actor (Brink). The latter two aspects, moreover, provide us with a rather clear manifestation that a homology (*sensu* Bourdieu) was present between the nation's juridical and literary fields (cf. Grüttemeier and Laros 215).

Yet although Diemont's position did establish a considerable degree of autonomy for literature vis-à-vis the law, this autonomy remained but relative. For in the end, Diemont did feel obliged to declare Brink's novel undesirable in terms of the PEA. It is significant to observe that in Diemont's eyes, Brink had transgressed the boundaries of the permissible by his thematization of religion, or, more precisely: Christianity—not with his treatment of "political" or "moral" issues. This significance is emphasized by the fact that *Kennis* appeared to have been quite bold in its treatment of the latter kind of issues too: counsel for Buren seems indeed to have conceded that the leading case on *When the Lion Feeds* was tame compared with *Kennis van die Aand*, but that over the ten years that had passed since the former case, attitudes toward sex had changed (Diemont 214). That Brink's novel was also daring when it came to political issues became quite evident from van Wyk's judgment, and also from Ampie Coetzee's early estimation that the novel was a likely candidate for getting banned. It thus appears that the amount of autonomy that Diemont was willing to grant literature was smallest when it came to religion, but relatively large as far as morals and politics were concerned.

Judge Steyn

The last judge who formulated an opinion in the case was judge Steyn—not to be confused with the Chief Justice of the same name who was in office from 1959 to 1971 and who had formulated the majority opinion in the Smith trial some ten years earlier. The position that Steyn adopted in his judgment was rather autonomist-oriented too, in fact even more so than that of Diemont.

Steyn began his opinion by delivering a rather fierce critique of the PEA [77] and—just as Diemont had done—approvingly quoting the passage on the freedom of speech that Rumpff had uttered in the Smith trial (cf. *Buren* v *RBP* 409–11). Nonetheless, he also emphasized—again, just as his colleague Diemont had—that the law was the law, and that a judge could not use his own discretion instead of the directives laid down by the legislature (cf. *Buren* v *RBP* 411). If Parliament decreed that the autonomy of creative expression should be restricted, a judge had to act accordingly, regardless of his own thoughts on the matter.

After having set forth his principled position vis-à-vis the PEA, he came to the more practical matters that the case posed, and the first issue that he took up was that of the likely readership of Brink's novel. Steyn reached his conclusion regarding this matter after having made "a careful consideration of the various statements under oath."[78] Indeed, he quite elaborately discussed the remarks concerning the identity of the likely reader made by witnesses for both parties in their respective testimonies. As this fact already presents us with implicit evidence that Steyn found literary expert evidence to be a potential asset for the judge who had to determine whether a work of literature was undesirable in terms of the PEA, more explicit evidence that he valued such evidence—and in fact even seemed to find it indispensable in some cases—can be found a little further on in his argument. Turning to the question whether expert evidence should be allowed when applying sections 5 (2) (*b*) to (*e*) of the PEA—sections in which no mention was made of either "the opinion of the Court" or the likely reader—he stated that a judge "should not rule out evidence—and indeed sometimes can hardly fulfill his duties properly without it—when he has to decide whether a particular publication is affected by the prohibitions concerned."[79] Steyn was predominantly thinking of the religious and political sections with his remark, yet he also felt that for the application of the moral sections, "factual" evidence as to the likely readership of a publication should be welcomed (cf. *Buren* v *RBP* 417). As Diemont did, he also felt that one should always take into account who was going to read a particular publication, for he too found it absurd to ban a publication because it would offend people who were not going to read it (cf. *Buren* v *RBP* 417).

Still more evidence that Steyn attached considerable judicial weight to literary expertise was evidenced by the fact that he took all the testimonies of the witnesses that had good literary credentials—i.e., that were important actors within the literary field—seriously, but more or less disqualified the testimonies of the witnesses that in his view lacked, precisely, expertise in the field of literature. One can sense from his discussion of J. J. Kruger's testimony that he did not take very seriously the arguments presented by the PCB's Chairman—who indeed did not have the literary credibility that most of the other witnesses had (cf. McDonald, *Literature Police* 52–53; Peters 37; Kannemeyer 233). Yet even more clearly, he invalidated the testimony of J. J. van Rooyen, managing director of publishing house C. F. Albertyn. Expressly he brought to the Court's attention that van Rooyen was really not a literary expert: he was "really a newspaper man,"[80] who, despite the fact that he was now employed in a publishing house, seemed to have no experience with publishing literature—Steyn made it look as if the only types of publications that van Rooyen had obtained some experience with were encyclopedias and books on politics (cf. *Buren* v *RBP* 414). After having stated that he believed the testimonies of Buren's witnesses to be more objective than those of the witnesses testifying on behalf of the PCB, he quite unambiguously stated: "As far as [van Rooyen] is concerned, one needs only refer to his comparison between the back page of a Sunday paper and a serious novel of 500 pages[81] to realize that we perhaps should not overestimate his opinion. His experience in the field on which he delivers testimony indeed seems rather limited to me."[82]

Having weighed the expert evidence, Steyn reached his conclusion regarding the likely readership of the novel. His conclusion was that the book would have had a select reading circle. The reasons for coming to this conclusion, he explicated, were that he believed the testimonials of the appellant to be more objective than those of the respondent. Moreover, he found that the sales figures underpinned the appellant's argument that the book would have had a rather limited readership and not the respondent's opposite argument, which was substantiated with the same figures. Lastly, he held that despite the fact that Brink was a controversial figure, it was not to be expected that his novel would attract a wide public. Elaborating further on his estimation, he stated that the probable limited reach of the work would mainly be the result of the "slow narrative style"[83] and "long-winded descriptions"[84] that characterized the book. He added—much as his colleague Diemont had done too—that he himself had had a hard time reading the book, and that he had only managed to accomplish his task with some difficulty. He further added—again just as Diemont had—that he believed that anyone who read the book because he was looking for sex and sensation would be deeply disappointed by it, and that if the book had not become a subject of scrutiny for the PCB, it would not have attracted a wide reading circle among the "ordinary reading public."[85]

However, even though Steyn felt that the "ordinary" reader would not have been very interested in the novel, he did not think that its readership would have solely consisted of literati either. He contended that

> considering the contents of the book and the subjects which it treats, the reading circle would not have been limited to merely men of letters. Engaged literature in the form of the novel that deals with current national affairs, always draws a wider group of readers than the novel per se. There is not a doubt in my mind that Brink has entered the domain of engaged literature here. The amount of sex and violence—which are laid on quite thick—would indeed contribute to arouse attention.[86]

Amongst the non-literati that would also have been interested in the novel, Steyn counted "informed citizens, who have an interest in national affairs and in politics."[87] "There are many concerned South Africans," he explained, "who have a strong sense of alleged injustice in the administration of their country and who would gladly want to see how an author of the stature of second appellant deals with this matter in an engaged novel."[88]

A final aspect of the likely reader of *Kennis* as he was sketched out by Steyn, was that he was considerably less reality-oriented than the one envisioned by van Wyk. Whereas the latter believed that most of the likely readers of Brink's novel would interpret the novel—as he himself has done—in a perfectly mimetic manner,[89] i.e., as a "mirror of reality" (cf. *Buren* v *RBP* 393), Steyn held that the probable reader would read it in a non-mimetic fashion (cf. 423). We will come back to this aspect below; here, it suffices to say that it appears that although Steyn postulated a likely readership that was not solely comprised of "men of letters," he did assume that the probable readers were individuals who were literary socialized to a considerable degree.

Having established the identity of the likely reader, Steyn could carry on with determining what effect Brink's work would have on him. In doing so, he proceeded by successively discussing each of the three categories of objections that had been raised against the book—religious, moral, and political objections. In his discussion of the first kind, Steyn first set out to determine whether or not the book should be deemed to be blasphemous. He thereby focused both on the meaning that had been given to the concept in South African law and on the theological debate as it had entered the courtroom through the testimonies of the three theology professors. As far as the latter debate was concerned, he approvingly quoted Prof. Lombard, an apparently unorthodox theologian who had testified on behalf of the Buren party. Lombard, unlike the other two theology professors, had argued that the book should not be considered to be blasphemous (cf. *Buren* v *RBP* 406, 418–19, 421).[90]

When it came to the novel's alleged offensiveness to religious convictions or feelings, however, Steyn had to reach a conclusion that was not so favorable for the Buren-Brink party. Steyn did start his discussion by emphasizing that the Court ought to be liberal whenever this matter was at issue. He expressly stated that the freedom of religion ought to be respected at all times. Furthermore, he argued that "a strong meaning"[91] should be given to the term "offensive,"[92] i.e., that a publication should really be "likely to be outrageous or disgustful,"[93] before it could be deemed "undesirable"—in doing so, he was thus following the lead of the majority in the Cape Court decision on *Lion* rather than the line set by the majority in the Appeal Court's decision regarding this novel. A third reason why Steyn felt that a Court had to be liberal when assessing whether a publication was offensive to religious convictions or feelings lay in the fact that he believed that in order to promote religious life in the community, it was necessary for free speech—as an extrinsic good—to be promoted as well.[94] Lastly, Steyn declared that strictly dogmatic positions should not be protected. Yet even though he took such a tolerant position regarding "religious" matters, and indeed had found it "incredibly difficult"[95] to assess the impact on religious convictions and feelings that Brink's work would have, he still had to conclude that it should be considered undesirable in terms of the PEA. The reason for this was that he felt that the "unnecessary, crude and unfunctional coupling of sex and religion"[96] that was to be found in it would be offensive to a significant number of likely readers (cf. *Buren* v *RBP* 420–21). There were, thus, limits to the amount of autonomy that Steyn was willing to grant literature too.

As to the "moral" objections to the book, Steyn was short. He declared that it was unnecessary for him to deal with the objections that the book was indecent or obscene or harmful to public morals. He did, however, want to note that although "the author on occasion sketche[d] sexual scenes in a sensitive manner," he on the other hand, "add[ed] explicit sex on several occasions where this d[id] not seem functional to [him, i.e., to Steyn himself] at all."[97] Two things seem remarkable about this comment. The first is that Steyn's neglect of the moral objections to the book appears to confirm the hypothesis that since the 1965 case of Smith's *Lion*, literature had gained a considerable amount of autonomy when it came to treating "moral" issues, read: issues regarding sexuality. The second thing is that Steyn appeared to be taking a poetological position with this comment regarding the functionality of Brink's thematization of sexuality.[98] He appeared indeed not to have applied the concept of functionality within the framework of a more institutional discussion concerning isolated passages, whether or not seen in the light of the whole book. Indeed, he did not make clear whether his comment would have had institutional implications at all—although he did state elsewhere that he had not employed the isolated-passage criterion at any time, but that he had applied the contextual approach instead (cf. *Buren* v *RBP* 420). By adopting this latter approach, he explicated, he was following the precedent that had been set by Chief Justice Ogilvie Thompson in the 1972 Appellate Division case of *PCB* v *Republican Publications*, that is, in one of the *Scope* cases that were mentioned at the outset of this chapter.

As far as the "political" grounds were concerned, finally, Steyn, remarkably enough, did not settle the matter in a markedly judicial manner; instead, he decided it on the basis of full-fledged poetological arguments. In fact, his discussion of the "political" objections, which formed the peroration of his entire opinion, was more a defense of literature than anything else. That is to say, Steyn dealt only with the "political" dimension of the case insofar as he aimed at invalidating the central poetological premises of van Wyk's argument, these being that it had been Brink's aim to write a mimetic novel and that the majority of its likely readers would interpret it thus. Steyn countered these contentions by postulating, firstly, that one had to distinguish between books that were "directed towards reality"[99] and those that were "faithful to reality."[100] In taking a position in what he termed the "polemic" that was to be found in the testimonies of the expert witnesses "on how the novel [of Brink] should be approached,"[101] he declared:

> Engaged literature is certainly as old as man's ability to write. When an author, fired up by his worries about for instance injustices or undesirabilities in his

own community wants to employ the novel as a means for reformation, there can, as far as I am concerned, be no objection against the fact that his book, although directed towards reality, is not faithful to reality. To then always judge an engaged novel on the "truth" or to condemn it because it is "false" or "exaggerated" or conveys "a distorted image" is completely and utterly unconvincing to me.[102]

Quite obviously, Steyn was engaging in a polemic himself, for he quite harshly deconstructed van Wyk's characterization of Brink's novel here. As Steyn went on with his argument, he came to defend a conception of literature that clearly differed from the one van Wyk adhered to. "In this respect," he continued his argument,

> Henry James's well-known statement is appropriate for me when he says: "The only reason for the existence of a novel is that it does attempt to represent life . . . and the analogy between the art of the painter and the art of the novelist is so far as I am able to see, complete." As photographic art is not the only convincing art form, just as little is truthful engaged literature the only convincing literary art form.[103]

The reference to Henry James might be taken as an indication that Steyn was well acquainted with the contemporary Anglophone part of the South African literary field. For one of the most influential critics within that subfield at the time was F. R. Leavis (McDonald, "Old Phrases" 294; Johnson 828–29, 831–32), who had notoriously proclaimed Henry James to be one of the only four "great English" novelists that history had produced (Leavis 9). In any case, Steyn effectively underpinned his defense of non-mimetic pragmatic literature (*sensu* Abrams) against van Wyk's criterion of truthfulness with James's conception of literature. In itself, the fact that Steyn relied on a literary actor in this judicial polemic also goes some way toward indicating that the South African literary field had reached a considerable degree of autonomy at the time.

Steyn's second counterargument was aimed at falsifying van Wyk's presupposition that the likely reader would read Brink's novel as a mimetic work of literature. Steyn argued that the complete opposite was the case. "*Kennis van die Aand*," he stated,

> is full of "exaggerations" and "inaccuracies." The profile of the Afrikaner that it sketches is not flattering. I do not think, however, that a meaningful number of adult White readers—and more particularly Afrikaner White readers—would celebrate the opinion that this book brought them into ridicule or contempt. My own judgment is also . . . that the book does not bring the White Afrikaner (or the White man) into ridicule or contempt. The obvious exaggerations would make anyone reading the book realize very quickly, not just that he has hold of fiction, but also that he is dealing with a malicious author who is

using the novel to offend. In my opinion, the House of Assembly—which is a product of political Freedom itself—did not intend the Freedom of speech to be so curtailed that the sensitivity of the intolerant and immature would be protected. The mature Afrikaner community would deal with the attempts at caricaturing that occur here with equanimity. To ban this book on this ground would in my opinion speak of an intolerance which I would not gladly ascribe to the Legislature.[104]

Yet, as said, Steyn's peroration did not solely seek to disqualify van Wyk's central poetological premises. Even more than it was aimed at serving this purpose, it was directed at presenting a defense of literature. As the above quote indicates, Steyn held that upholding the right to free speech also entailed granting literature a fairly high degree of autonomy. For, as he declared, even novels that were written by "malicious authors" with the aim to "offend," such as *Kennis*, should be protected—indeed, when necessary, at the expense of the "sensitivity of the intolerant and immature."

Yet apart from defending literature on the grounds of free speech, he also defended it in a much more straightforward manner: he also quite clearly defended it on the basis of a "public good" argument, as known from contemporaneous British and U.S. law, i.e., on the basis of it being worthy of defense in its own right, as it made a valuable contribution to the (cultural) life of a nation. To begin with, after having declared that as far as he was concerned, there could be no objection to an engaged novel not being faithful to reality, he went on by stressing, indeed, the *importance* of engaged literature. Referring to a statement made by Cloete in his testimony, he declared that "to disqualify engagement with the contention that 'a strongly prevailing trend within literary theory these days is precisely engagement, often with a neo-Marxist literary-sociological tendency,' in my opinion merely evidences of an attempt at damnation by labeling and ignores the meaningful role that engagement plays in a living literature."[105] Not only did Steyn break a lance for engaged literature, he also took the occasion to debunk "conforming" literature: "Conforming men of letters," he stated,

> faithful to the needs of the administration of their time, seldom succeed in making contributions that enrich their language and culture. Sure, Alfred Austin was poet laureate of England.[106] He is, however, not remembered for his contributions to English literature, but for his servile doggerel verses which amongst other things praised the imperialism of his time by, for instance, elevating the Jameson raiders to heroes.[107] His most meaningless attempt in poetry which is eternalized as an obvious example of the price that the faithful literary slave pays to his lord, is his doggerel verse regarding the illness of the Prince of Wales when he versifies: "Across the wires the electric message came, he is not better, he is much the same."[108]

As both the content of the point that Steyn is advancing here—there appears to be a clear Afrikaner nationalistic undertone in this passage—and the rhetoric in which he presents it seem to reveal: Steyn's views regarding literature appear not only to have been premised on the idea that it formed a "public good"; they also seem to have been quite close to the conception of literature of the *Dertigers*, more particularly to that of preeminent *Dertiger* N. P. van Wyk Louw. Indeed, as Steyn's polemic against "conformism" indicates, his position might have been rather close to the Louwian concept of "loyal resistance" ("lojale verset"), which was very influential not only among the *Dertigers*, but also—still—among certain *Sestigers* (cf. McDonald, *Literature Police* 28). The Louwian conception of literature, with its concept of "loyal resistance" might in Abrams's terms best be characterized as an objective-pragmatic conception of literature: it was objective in its emphasis on aestheticism and, indeed, avant-gardism; and it was pragmatic in its focus on uplifting the Afrikaans *volk*.[109]

The final remarks of Steyn's judgment seem to provide further evidence for the hypotheses that he defended literature on the basis of it being a "public good" and that he adhered to a Louwian conception of literature—perhaps the former position was indeed underpinned by the latter. In these remarks he emphasized the importance of nonconformist literature anew—and again, both the content and the rhetoric appear to confirm the hypotheses: "I am aware of the fact that in our community with its diversity of peoples, languages and cultures, the freedom of speech has been curtailed to some extent so as to eliminate friction and conflict," he declared. "I am, however, not prepared," he continued,

> to accept that our Legislature would have wanted to enforce a conforming literature upon the Afrikaner, which would make him utter, like Napoleon did with regard to the decline of French literature: "People complain that we do not have literature. This is the fault of the Minister of the Interior . . . he should make sure that decent ware is being written." . . .
>
> For these reasons I have come to the conclusion that respondent on account of the provisions of the Publications and Entertainments Act, 26 of 1963, was right in judging the book *Kennis van die Aand* undesirable. This is a decision that I have taken reluctantly for various reasons; most of all, however, firstly, because of the need for a virile literature in the Afrikaans language which would indeed write fearlessly about the current affairs of the South African situation. Secondly, because I now realize the insufficiency of my own Afrikaans; reading this book with its rich language has brought this home to me so clearly. In the light of the statutory provisions, the author's malice has left me no choice, however.[110]

Even more clearly than in the other comments concerning literature that comprised the major part of Steyn's peroration, these remarks seem to evidence that he held literature to be a "public good," worthy of protection in the form of a significant amount of autonomy vis-à-vis the law. For he unambiguously declared here that there was a "need for a virile literature in the Afrikaans language," a literature that unlike "conformist" literature à la Austin *would* "succeed in making contributions that enrich[ed] [in this case: Afrikaans] language and culture"—a literature that would make one, precisely, "realize the insufficiency of one's own Afrikaans." The fact that the "virile" literature that he envisioned "would indeed write fearlessly about the current affairs of the South African situation," would surely only increase the need for a guaranteed amount of autonomy vis-à-vis the law.

In sum, Steyn was certainly willing to grant the literary field a considerable amount of autonomy. Many aspects of his position evidenced that he did: his fierce critique of the PEA; his high valuation of literary expertise—and, indeed, distrust of witnesses whose credibility as literary experts was disputable; his way of conceptualizing the likely reader; and of course his quite passionate defense of literature on the basis of it being a public good and, as it appeared, also on the basis of a poetics that carried a lot of weight within the Afrikaans part of the South African literary field, namely the Louwian conception of literature. The fact that there is some evidence that Steyn seemed to adhere to the Louwian conception of literature appears to indicate that at least the Afrikaans literary subfield had reached a considerable autonomy at the time. The fact, moreover, that he also seemed to be employing a poetological statement of a writer who was a foremost authority in the English-language subfield to underpin one of the judicial arguments he was making, i.e., to support his defense of non-mimetic pragmatic literature against the truthfulness-criterion employed by van Wyk, seems to provide further evidence that the field had attained considerable autonomy. Yet despite the field having apparently reached such a significant degree of autonomy and despite Steyn's autonomy-oriented position, there were still limits to the amount of space that Steyn was prepared to allow literature (in the light of the PEA anyway). Tellingly, the domain that Steyn would not allow literature to invade was the domain of religious convictions and feelings, the same domain that Diemont had guarded against infringement.

CONCLUSION

Although the trial of Brink's *Kennis* resulted in a confirmation of the ban that had been instigated by the PCB, the three opinions delivered in the case revealed that the literary field had effectively reached a considerable degree of institutional autonomy already. Van Wyk, despite his emphasis on the interventionist spirit of the Act, his apparently Platonic conception of literature and his resultant unwillingness to allow the literary field a significant degree of autonomy vis-à-vis the law, revealed that he realized the value of (literary) expert evidence. In fact, he determinedly underpinned his opinion with the poetological analyses that had been delivered by the literary experts called in to give testimony on behalf of the PCB. The amount of autonomy that van Wyk actually granted literature through the validation and employment of expert evidence was relatively insignificant though, when viewed in the light of the most fundamental aspect of his position: for van Wyk, the sovereignty that the political field enjoyed over the literary field was indeed far-reaching. Van Wyk's position represented the minority position, however. Diemont and Steyn were both much more autonomy-oriented.

The latter two both allowed the literary field a significant degree of autonomy vis-à-vis the law. This autonomy was created first of all because both categorically favored a freedom-oriented approach to publications regulation. Moreover, it came about because of the way in which the two judges conceptualized the likely reader, both on the more theoretical and on the more practical level. A third way in which it was brought about was through the recognition of the (judicial) value of literary expertise and the application of arguments advanced by these experts. Lastly, the legal recognition and, indeed, judicial employment of poetological arguments advanced by contemporary literary actors contributed to the creation of an institutional autonomy of literature vis-à-vis the law. Yet although both adopted a position that established a considerable degree of autonomy for literature, this autonomy clearly remained but relative. In the end, both indeed declared that Brink's novel was undesirable in terms of the PEA, because they found that it had transgressed the boundaries of the permissible by its thematization of religion, i.e., Christianity—not with its thematization of "political" or "moral" issues. It appears thus that the amount of autonomy that the two were willing to grant literature was smallest when it came to religion.

Comparing the Brink trial to the trials of 1965, it seems justified to conclude that by around 1975 the literary field had reached a significantly higher degree of development than it had in 1965. Evidence that it had might be found *inter alia* in the fact that Justice Diemont appeared to take such a markedly different stance vis-à-vis the literary field than he had in the 1965 Cape trial of *Lion*. Further evidence seems to lie in the fact that the likely reader-test was "restored" and no longer represented the "ordinary man" test that it was made into in the 1965 AD trial of *Lion*. Rather clearly, the majority of the Cape Court in effect recognized that the intellectual or literary socialized reader could lay claim to minority rights. First and foremost, however, the higher degree of institutional autonomy is evidenced by the fact that whereas literary expertise was only allowed to play a minimal role in the trials of 1965, it now played a crucial role in the judicial debates. Indeed, it not only played a fundamental role on the institutional level: conceptions of literature of contemporary South African actors appeared also to have penetrated the judicial reasoning of at least one of the judges hearing the case

(Steyn). A significant degree of structural and conceptual homology (*sensu* Bourdieu) between the juridical and the literary field appeared thus to have emerged by 1975.

The opinions delivered in the *Kennis* trial were given wide publicity in the press. "There was criticism," Diemont remarked in retrospect, "but there was no appeal" (Diemont 216). The *Kennis* case would be the last case involving a literary work that was brought before the Supreme Court and judged under the PEA. Later that year the act was repealed by a new censorship act: Publications Act No. 42 of 1974. In the next chapter we will see in what ways this new act changed the regulation of literature in South Africa.

NOTES

1. Through the Publications and Entertainments Amendment Act, no. 85 of 1969 and the Publications and Entertainments Amendment Act, no. 32 of 1971.

2. See *Republican* v *PCB* 1970 (1) SA 577 (C); *Republican* v *PCB* 1971 (2) SA 1 (D); *Republican* v *PCB* 1971 (2) SA 162 (D); *Republican* v *PCB* 1971 (2) SA 243 (D); *Republican* v *PCB* 1971 (3) SA 399 (D); *PCB* v *Republican* 1972 (1) SA 288 (A); *Republican* v *PCB* 1972 (3) SA 562 (D); *Republican* v *RBP* 1973 (4) SA 549 (D); *Republican* v *RBP* 1974 (2) SA 55 (D).

3. Indeed, as we saw in chapter 1, it seems not only fundamental to past and contemporaneous judicial dealings with literature in South Africa, but to judicial dealing with literature at large, at least in the West.

4. Hereafter: *Kennis*.

5. For example, Brink, "Antwoord"; Brink, "Op"; Brink, "Tussen."

6. "verband met [sy] voorgeskiedenis weer op te neem" (194).

7. Not including his translations and adaptations which they also had on their list.

8. Dis 'n dokument van vertrapping, uitbuiting, mishandeling, moord; dis 'n dokument van die verhaal van die kleurling in Suid-Afrika. Dit is al genoeg motivering vir publikasie; want dit het nou tyd geword dat die Afrikaanse romanskrywer 'n beeld gee van wat werklik met 'n deel van sy mense gebeur. (Coetzee qtd. in Peters 27).

9. Uiterlik gaan die grootste probleme by die publikasie van die werk die oordele van die Publikasieraad wees. Skrywer en uitgewer sal hieroor iets moet bedink, 'n beleid moet formuleer. Dit sal tragies wees as dié roman na verskyning verbied word; tragies vir die skrywer, die uitgewer én die leser. (Coetzee qtd. in Peters 28).

10. Nederduitse Gereformeerde Kerk, the largest of the three Calvinist churches in South Africa.

11. Rev. J. D. Vorster—the brother of B. J. Vorster, who served as South Africa's Prime Minister from 1966 to 1978—Rev. J. S. Gericke , and Rev. D. P. M. Beukes all held top positions within the Nederduitse Gereformeerde Kerk. Gericke also served as Vice-Chancellor of Stellenbosch University; Beukes was also chairman of the Federasie van Afrikaanse Kultuurvereniginge (Federation of Afrikaans Cultural Associations).

12. For more information regarding the *Kennis* controversy, see de Lange 46ff; McDonald, *Literature Police* 54–57 et passim; and especially Peters 38ff.

13. As the judgment explained, a single utterance could constitute an offense in terms of more than one section of the act, and the respondent had indeed listed their accusation that the book dealt with "abuse of non-whites" "in an improper manner" both as a moral and a political offense (see *Buren* v *RBP* 387).

14. Cf. the "highlights" of incidents of white cruelty depicted in the book that Justice van Wyk enumerates in *Buren* v *RBP* 394–97.

15. "Hou op toneel speel, Josef! Jesus! En naai my!" (*Buren* v *RBP* 398, 401; see also Brink, *Kennis* 192).

16. "Nou weet ek, sonder vermetelheid, hoe Jesus gevoel het toe hy van die berg afterugge-kom het na sy dissipels: met dié treurigheid en volheid in Hom, met dié vermoë om weer te begin" (*Buren* v *RBP* 401, 407; see also Brink, *Kennis* 300).

17. "Dit was die hewigste en mees verruklike moment van ons verhouding toe sy daardie grou middag in die kaal kamertjie op die goedkoop katel die orgasme saam met my bereik, saam met my deurbreek, en die eindeloosheid ingeslinger word. Ek het haar ver, naby, hoor huil en snik en roep: 'O God! O God! O God!'" (*Buren* v *RBP* 398, 420; see also Brink, *Kennis* 169).

18. Jessica sal in my arm lê, in die aand, in die nag, in die vertroude donker. En ek sal vir haar sê: Kom, Little Miss Muffet, kom my liefling: kom ons gaan uit na die strate, kom ons loop hand aan hand deur die stad, moenie bang wees nie, niemand sal omgee nie, niemand sal ons keer nie, en die ruiters sal afklim by die sien van die water.Kom, my liefling. Die wêreld is oop en die wette is weg. Kom, loop saam met my nakend oor die strand sonder einde. Staan by die poel in die sand, dat ek jou was, jou skouers en jou lieflike borsies, jou rug en maag en bene, kom laat ek jou verborge duisternis proe op my honger tong. En daarna sal jy mý was, soos 'n vrou 'n lyk was, met liefde en teer hande.En eindelik sal jy my begrawe in die sand en 'n kruis inplant tussen my bene. Hulle sal die kruis sien en my onthou, dit sal nie verniet daar staan nie. (*Buren* v *PCB* 407, 420; see also Brink, *Kennis* 401)

All passages but the third were fully quoted by the Cape Court.

19. "Algemene Literatuurwetenskap" (*Buren* v *RBP* 405, 415).
20. "vlot geskryf... en maklik leesbaar" (*Buren* v *RBP* 405).
21. "sensasionele inhoud en maklik leesbare styl" (*Buren* v *RBP* 415).
22. "Weens die inhoud en strekking van die boek en die bekendheid van die skrywer" (*Buren* v *RBP* 413).
23. "maklik geskryf" (*Buren* v *RBP* 414).
24. "sekere bedekte en minder bedekte verwysings in die hoofgang van die verhaal" (*Buren* v *RBP* 414).
25. "genoeg seks en sensasie" (*Buren* v *RBP* 414).
26. "die boek lê oop vir 'n wye leserskring" (*Buren* v *RBP* 414).
27. "propvol insidente van allerlei aard" (*Buren* v *RBP* 414).
28. "gemiddelde leser" (*Buren* v *RBP* 414).
29. "estetiese romans" (*Buren* v *RBP* 391).
30. "'betrokke' romans" (*Buren* v *RBP* 391).
31. Grové explicitly used this Sartrean concept to explain the concept of *"betrokke" romans* and to characterize Brink's novel, which in his eyes represented a full-blown "roman engagée [*sic*]" (cf. *Buren* v *RBP* 391).
32. In the philosophical sense, that is.
33. Even though Abrams's well-known model of aesthetic theories has its shortcomings, it arguably does provide an adequate tool for reconstructing poetological positions (cf. van Rees and Dorleijn, *Impact* 9–10). Abrams's four ideal types of aesthetic theories each prioritize a different dimension of literary communication: his "mimetic" theories prioritize the relation between text and reality; his "pragmatic" theories the relation between text and public; his "expressive" theories the relation text-author; his "objective" (or: autonomist) theories focus on the text itself, i.e., take it to be representing "a self-sufficient entity constituted by its parts in their internal relations" (Abrams 26). By conceptualizing each category as prioritizing a different dimension, Abrams enables one to reduce the great variety of conceptions of literature that one might encounter when doing literary research to just the four mentioned types (van Rees and Dorleijn, *Impact* 9).
34. D. J. Opperman was already a principle Afrikaans poet at the time and a professor of Afrikaans literature at Stellenbosch University; Ernst Lindenberg was *inter alia* an editor of the literary magazine *Kriterium* and a lecturer at the Afrikaans Department of the University of the Witwatersrand; I. D. du Plessis, as one of the judges in the trial described him, was a "former professor at the Department of Afrikaans and Dutch of the University of Cape Town, . . . former Secretary of the Department of Coloured Affairs, and a renowned South African man of letters" (*Buren* v *RBP* 412); Leon Rousseau, director at publishing house Human & Rousseau;

J. J. van Schaik, director at Van Schaik Boekhandel (Van Schaik Bookstore); and G. J. Coetzee, chief manager at Nasionale Boekwinkels (National Bookshops).

35. Phenomena that supposedly were to be found in the novel, such as "learned references" ("geleerde aanhalings" [*Buren* v *RBP* 405]), "slow narrative style" ("stadige verteltrant" [405]), "long-winded descriptions" ("omslagtige beskrywings" [405]), "literary references and philosophizings" ("literêre verwysings en . . . filosoferings" [405]), "fairly extensive interpretations of great dramas of world literature" ("vry uitvoerige interpretasies van groot dramas uit die wêreld literatuur" [405]), "technical [narrative] experiments" ("tegniese eksperimente" [405]), "serious tenor" ("ernstige strekking" [405]), and "philosophical undertone" ("filosofiese ondertoon" [412]), would all fall under this category.

36. "noodsaaklik-funksioneel" (*Buren* v *RBP* 405).

37. *Kennis van die aand* is uit die staanspoor gekonsipieer as fiksie en in dié verband is dit noodsaaklik om daarop te wys dat alle vorme van fiksie—en die roman meer as enige ander— gedurende die paar dekades sedert die Tweede Wêreldoorlog meer as ooit tevore deur die Literatuurwetenskap dwarsoor die wêreld (maar veral in Duitsland en die V.S.A., met 'n sterk gevolg in Brittanje en Suid-Afrika) in hul eie reg as kunsvorme bestudeer is, soos te onderskei van "werklikheidsweergawe." Die essensiële uitgangspunt van standaardwerke soos Booth se *Rhetoric of Fiction*, Stanzel se *Narrative Situations in the Novel* en letterlik honderde ander, is dat die literêre werk 'n woordewêreld in sy eie reg tot stand bring, waarin ooreenkomste met die wêreld daarbuite glad nie ter sake is nie. Die benadering, beoordeling en toets van so 'n werk lê uitsluitlik in die vaststel van die sinvolle verhouding tussen alle onderdele binne die werk self en die essensiële onderdele word gewoonlik saamgevat as: figure, gebeure, ruimte en tyd (Brink, "*Kennis* Verbode" 90).

38. By die skryf van *Kennis van die aand* kon ek dus *a priori* staatmaak daarop dat die werk, gekonsipieer as roman, juis in dáárdie konteks en op dáárdie wyse beoordeel sou word en op geen ander nie. Ter wille van nog meer sekerheid dat die werk uitsluitlik as fiksie *beoordeel* sou word omdat dit uitsluitlik as fiksie *bestaan*, is dié standpunt in 'n voorwoord tot die boek afgedruk: daar word dit pertinent gestel dat alles "binne die nuwe konteks van die roman . . . fiktief (is)"; en voorts, dat "die aantoonbare oppervlakte van die aktualiteit nêrens as sodanig ter sake (is) nie, net die patrone en verhoudinge daarónder" (Brink, "*Kennis* Verbode" 90; Brink's emphasis).

39. "Die funksie van die kunswerk as spieël word nie meer aanvaar nie; jou waarskynlike leser sien 'n roman as 'n seepbel wat 'n sferiese siening, geboë weerkaatsing aan die werklikheid gee" (*Buren* v *RBP* 392). Elsewhere in the law report, Opperman's statement is quoted slightly differently, namely as: "die funksie van die kunswerk as spieël word nie meer aanvaar nie, jou waarskynlike leser sien 'n roman as 'n seepbel wat in 'n sferiese siening geboë weerkaatsing van die werklikheid gee" (*Buren* v *RBP* 422). Cf. also McDonald's translation on p. 56 of his *Literature Police*.

40. Dit is wel waar dat die Wetgewer se doel die beskerming van die sedes is, maar dit volg nie daaruit dat die Wetgewer om daardie rede die Hof verplig om vir doeleindes van art. 6 (1) (c) vas te stel wie die bepaalde stof sal sien of lees nie. *Die Wetgewer wou juis die sedes op 'n breër grondslag beskerm, nl. deur stof ongewens te verklaar indien dit na die mening van die Hof met sekere onderwerpe op 'n onbetaamlike wyse handel* (*Buren* v *RBP* 384–85; emphasis mine).

41. "persone wie se gedagtes indirek aan die invloed van die boek blootgestel kan word" (*Buren* v *RBP* 383).

42. "'n Mens kan maklik voorbeelde van sodanige indirekte beïnvloeding bedink soos bv. waar die inhoud van dele van 'n boek aan andere voorgelees word of oorvertel word" (*Buren* v *RBP* 383).

43. It was permissible to leave school at the end of standard eight (eighth grade), which usually was at the age of sixteen.

44. Na my mening is hierdie boek reeds deur 'n wye leserskring gelees en indien dit nie ongewens verklaar is nie, sou die kring al groter geword het. Dit bevat al die gebruiklike bestanddele van 'n treffer: seks en geweld. Boonop is daar seksverhoudinge oor die kleurskeidslyn asook talle politieke aangeleenthede. Dit is 'n boek wat natuurlik veral deur Afrikaanssprekendes, hoofsaaklik Blankes, maar ook deur baie nie-Blankes gelees sal word. Die grootste

aantal lesers is sekerlik diegene wat minstens standard ag behaal het. Die uitgewer sê sy oogmerk was dat die boek by Universiteite voorgeskryf sou word. Of dit voorgeskryf sou word of nie, daar kan min twyfel wees dat 'n groot aantal studente die boek sou lees. Ook sou 'n wesentlike aantal ander mense, oud en jonk, soos onderwysers, sakemanne, boere en amptenare die boek lees. 'n Baie groot aantal van hierdie waarskynlike lesers is lidmate van die Afrikaanse kerke (*Buren* v *RBP* 390).

45. Daar word beweer dat die aanvanklike verkope die algemeen verwagte verkoopspatroon bevestig het en dit sou gevolg het as dit nie was vir die oordrewe publisiteit wat daaraan verleen is nie. Oordrewe publisiteit is 'n feit, en is een van die faktore wat in ag geneem kan word by die bepaling van wie die waarkynlike lesers sal wees. Die rede vir 'n groot afset wat dit ook al mag wees is nie 'n grond om die feit van 'n groot afset te ignoreer nie. Hoe groter die omset, hoe groter die groepe van waarskynlike lesers (*Buren* v *RBP* 389–90).

46. Cf. sec. 6 (2) of the act (see PEA, 1963 286).

47. Dutch and French law have also generally favored the text-oriented or objective approach since they instigated an *exceptio artis* pertaining to literature (see Beekman and Grüttemeier 198; Sapiro, "Legal Responsibility").

48. "lang beëdigde verklaring . . . waarin hy sy seining van sy boek probeer stel" (*Buren* v *RBP* 390).

49. "Dit it nie nodig om die skrywer se betoog in besonderhede aan te haal nie, want eintlik is sy subjektiewe motiewe soos deur hom gestel, nie relevant nie. Dit het eintlik niks te make met die vraag of die boek ongewens is ingevolge een of meer van die bepalings van arts. 5 en 6 van die Wet nie" (*Buren* v *RBP* 391).

50. Van die seepbel-tegniek, waarvan prof. Opperman praat, in 'n roman wat voorgee om 'n roman te wees wat op die werklikheid gebaseer is, was ek tot nog toe volkome onbewus. Ek is geen letterkundige nie, maar dit geld ook vir die meeste waarskynlike lesers. Ek het dus geen rede om te dink dat daar nie duisende waarskynlike lesers van die boek is wat my "onkunde" in hierdie verband deel nie. My indruk was nog altyd dat so 'n roman, hoewel die verhaal self fiktief is, tog tot groot hoogte 'n weerkaatsing is van die werklikheid soos dit op 'n bepaalde tyd is of was (*Buren* v *RBP* 393).

51. "Daar is afdoende getuienis dat die boek opsetlik so geskryf is dat die leser die indruk moet kry dat veral die meer belangrike insidente hoewel fiktief, 'n spieëlbeeld van die werklikheid is" (*Buren* v *RBP* 391).

52. die moeilikheid met tweede appellant [is] dat hy juis op twee stoele wil sit. Met *Kennis van die Aand* skryf hy 'n roman engagée [sic], 'n roman wat die muur rondom die romanwêreld op honderd maniere deurbreek, bv. met die noem van toestande, plekke, persone, lokaliteite, 'n roman wat die S. A. situasie wil "oopskryf," wat wil hervorm, wat onregte wil blootlê. Maar nou dat gewys word op sy eensydige voorstellings en opruiing, nou wil hy skuil agter die teorie wat die roman sien as "hermatically [sic] sealed universe." As aanvaller wil hy hervormer wees; as verdediger wil hy esteet wees. As hy aanval, is die roman vir hom 'n literêre wapen; as hy verdedig, is die roman skielik 'n aparte wêreld wat niks met die aktualiteit te make het nie. Hy wil dus die beste van beide wêrelde hê (*Buren* v *RBP* 391).

53. Judge Diemont felt that van Wyk was wrong for "look[ing] for additional reasons for censoring the book" (Diemont 215).

54. Cf. also Silver, "Criticism" 583.

55. Dit is onbetaamlik om sulke geïsoleerde misdade deur Blankes so aanmekaar te flans dat dit voorgehou word as 'n weerkaatsing van die breë werklikheid. Deur dit te doen word 'n vals beeld van die Blanke geskep, 'n beeld wat die Blanke as groep veragtelik maak. Art. 5 (2) (*c*) bepaal uitdruklik dat 'n publikasie wat 'n bevolkingsgroep veragtelik maak ongewens is, en dus belet moet word (*Buren* v *RBP* 394; cf. also 397).

56. "verwronge fiksie wat voorgehou word as 'n weerspieëling van die werklikheid is ook ongewens ingevolge art. 6 (1) (*b*) omdat dit vir 'n wesentlike aantal van die waarskynlike lesers waarskynlik aanstootlik en walglik sal wees" (*Buren* v *RBP* 394).

57. "Dit is so dat sommige sogenaamde gesofistikeerde lesers feitlik niks walglik of afstootlik vind nie, maar my mening is dat die oorgrote aantal waarskynlike lesers hierdie boek waarskynlik walglik en afstootlik sal vind" (*Buren* v *RBP* 399).

58. "die Hof in die uitoefening van sy diskresie nie vry en ongebonde is nie. Dit mag wees dat ek *Kennis van die Aand* nie sou verbied het nie as ek 'n onbeteuelde diskresie kon uitoefen, maar ek mag nie my eie beskouings laat geld ten koste van die beginsels in die Wet, en veral die bepalings in arts. 5 en 6 nie" (*Buren* v *RBP* 403).

59. Cf. the following remark that Diemont made as he penned down his memories of the Brink case in his *Brushes with the Law*: "Parliament made the law, and we must apply the law whether we liked it or not" (215).

60. It appears that a "tradition of parliamentary sovereignty with a concomitant emphasis upon literalism in the interpretation of statutes" was dominant among the South African judiciary throughout apartheid (D. Davis 40).

61. "Ek vind dit moeilik om te begryp hoe die Hof kan besluit of 'n boek ongewens is sonder om die vraag te stel—vir wie is dit ongewens? Wie gaan die boek lees? Daar die vraag is van kern belang" (*Buren* v *RBP* 403).

62. "bekende en gebruiklike bestaandele van die treffer" (*Buren* v *RBP* 404).

63. Dit is 'n langdradige storie wat teen 'n stadige tempo vorder totdat dit eindelik in die dodesel tot 'n eind loop. Ek self sou die boek nooit klaar gelees het nie was ek nie verplig om dit vir die doeleindes van hierdie saak te lees nie. Die skrywer gaan uit sy pad om die leser te beïndruk met sy geleerdheid, sy wye kennis van literatuur en filosofie en drama; ek vind dit irriterend en vervelig (*Buren* v *RBP* 404).

64. "die literêre gehalte van die boek en die ingewikkelde styl" (*Buren* v *RBP* 405).

65. "'n ernstige belang in die roman-kuns" (405).

66. "Die ligsinniges of dié wat prikkelleesstof soek sal gou mismoedig word" (405).

67. "Dit sou teenoor die skrywer en die uitgewer onregverdig wees. Die vraag is—wie sou die boek gelees het onder normale omstandighede as dit nie onder die Sensuurwet verbreid was nie" (*Buren* v *RBP* 405).

68. "die gewone romanleser, die man wat ligte leestof soek" (*Buren* v *RBP* 406).

69. "letterkundiges, persone met opvoeding en 'n ernstige belangstelling in sake" (*Buren* v *RBP* 406).

70. "mense wat belangstel in die letterkunde, filosofie en sosiologiese probleme" (408).

71. Die leserskring mag betreklik gering wees en dit mag wees . . . dat dit grotendeels bestaan uit letterkundiges en opgevoede mense, maar daar moet ook onthou word dat baie van hulle, miskien die meerderheid, ook Afrikaanssprekende Calviniste sou wees, of lede van die Nederduits Gereformeerde Kerk of een van die susterkerke. Meeste van hierdie persone het 'n ortodokse Christen opvoeding gehad en ofskoon hulle vandag gesofistikeerde wêreldwyse lesers mag wees, sou baie van hulle nie te min dele van hierdie boek as aanstootlik beskou (*Buren* v *RBP* 406–7).

72. "insidente en beskrywings waar seks en godsdiens gekoppel word" (*Buren* v *RBP* 407).

73. Dit mag so wees, maar ek dink nie dit is ter sake nie. Ek moet die bepalings van die Wet toepas. Ek moet, ongeag die rol wat hierdie seksgodsdiens insidente in die storie speel, besluit of die bepalings van art. 5 (2) (*b*) van die Wet oortree word. Die antwoord is myns insiens bevestigend (*Buren* v *RBP* 407–8).

74. "rasse verhoudinge" (409).

75. Strictly speaking there had not been a need for him to go into the "political" objections either, as he had already declared that the book was undesirable on religious grounds. The only reason that he did go into these charges was that a large part of the judicial debates had been devoted to it, or so he stated (cf. *Buren* v *RBP* 408).

76. "[As die waarskynlike lesers] genoeg verstand het om hierdie tipe boek te lees en verstaan behoort hulle te besef dat dit alles fiksie is" (*Buren* v *RBP* 408).

77. He held its most crucial provisions to be very vague and therefore inadequate, and this especially worried him considering the fact that something so precious as the freedom of speech was at stake.

78. "'n versigtige oorweging van die verskillende beëdigde verklarings" (*Buren* v *RBP* 415).

79. "nie getuienis sal uitsluit—en inderdaad somtyds kwalik sy pligte behoorlik daarsonder sal kan nakom—wanneer hy moet bepaal of 'n besondere publikasie getref word deur die betrokke verbodsbepalings" (*Buren* v *RBP* 416).

80. "eintlik 'n koerantman" (*Buren* v *RBP* 414).

81. Steyn was referring to van Rooyen's remark that "the book c[ould] count on a rather wide reading circle in the same way as the popular back pages of certain Sunday papers f[ound] such a reading circle" ("die boek op 'n nogal wye leserskring sal kan staatmaak op dieselfde manier as waarop die populêre agterblaaie van sekere Sondag koerante sodanige leserskring vind" [*Buren* v *RBP* 415]).

82. "Wat laasgenoemde [i.e., van Rooyen] aanbetref hoef mens maar net te verwys na sy vergelyking tussen die agterblad van 'n Sondagkoerant met 'n ernstige roman van 500 bladsye om te besef dat ons miskien nie sy mening te hoog moet skat nie. Sy ondervinding op die gebied waaroor hy getuienis lewer kom my ook as taamlik beperk voor" (*Buren* v *RBP* 415).

83. "stadige verteltrant" (*Buren* v *RBP* 415).

84. "omslagtige beskrywings" (*Buren* v *RBP* 415).

85. "gewone leserspubliek" (*Buren* v *RBP* 415).

86. "gesien die inhoud van die boek en die onderwerpe waarmee dit handel, die leserskring nie beperk sou gewees het slegs tot letterkundiges nie. Betrokke letterkunde in roman vorm wat met die aktualiteite van landsake handel trek altyd 'n breër groep lesers dan die roman *per se*. Dat Brink hier hom op die gebied van betrokke letterkunde begeef, bestaan daar by my geen twyfel nie. Die dosis seks en geweld—die pap waarvan taamlik dik aangemaak is—sou dan ook bydra om belangstelling aan te wek" (*Buren* v *RBP* 415–16).

87. "ingeligte landsburgers, wat 'n belangstelling het in landsake en in die politiek" (*Buren* v *RBP* 416).

88. "Daar is baie besorgde Suid-Afrikaners wat beweerde onregverdigheid in hulle landsbestel sterk aanvoel en wat graag sou wou sien hoe 'n skrywer van die formaat van tweede appellant met hierdie aangeleentheid in 'n betrokke roman handel" (*Buren* v *RBP* 416).

89. Cf. Abrams 8ff; 31ff.

90. It is worth noting the analogy between the way in which Steyn dealt with some of the questions concerning religion raised by the case and some of the questions concerning literature: apparently, he saw both religion and literature as specialist disciplines and some questions pertaining to these disciplines were questions that compelled a judge to seek assistance from professionals in possession of expert knowledge on these disciplines.

91. "'n sterk betekenis" (*Buren* v *RBP* 419).

92. "aanstootlikheid" (*Buren* v *RBP* 419).

93. "waarskynlik skokkend of walglik sal wees" (*Buren* v *RBP* 419; cf. also 420).

94. What Steyn literally said was that the Court should not "give such extensive protection [to religious convictions and feelings] that this would result in depriving our community of the free dialogue that is necessary for the stimulation of growth and development, also on the religious level" ("beskerming sal verleen wat so omvangryk is dat dit tot gevolg sou hê dat die vrye dialoog wat noodsaaklik is ten einde groei en ontwikkeling te stimuleer ook op godsdienstige gebied ons gemeenskap ontneem sou word nie"; *Buren* v *RBP* 419).

95. "ontsettend moeilik" (*Buren* v *RBP* 420).

96. "onnodige, kru en onfunksionele aaneenskakeling van seks en godsdiens" (*Buren* v *RBP* 420).

97. "Ek wil egter aanteken dat die skrywer met geleentheid op sensitiewe wyse seksuele tonele skets maar dat hy aan die ander hand by etlike geleenthede eksplisiete seks bybring waar dit my glad nie funksioneel voorkom nie" (*Buren* v *RBP* 421).

98. And other ones, for that matter: cf. the above-quoted comment concerning the "unnecessary, crude and unfunctional coupling of sex and religion."

99. "werklikheidsgerig" (*Buren* v *RBP* 422).

100. "werklikheids-getrou" (*Buren* v *RBP* 422).

101. "polemiek oor hoe die roman benader moet word" (*Buren* v *RBP* 421).

102. Betrokke letterkunde is seker so oud soos die vermoë van die mens om te skryf. Wanneer die skrywer, aangevuur deur sy besorgdheid oor byvoorbeeld ongeregtighede of ongewensthede in sy eie gemeenskap die roman as hervormingsmiddel wil aanwend, kan daar wat my aanbetref geen beswaar wees teen die feit dat sy boek, ofskoon werklikheidsgerig, nie werklikheids-getrou is nie. Om dan 'n betrokke roman steeds te beoordeel aan die "waarheid" of om dit te veroordeel omdat dit "vals" is of "oordrewe" is of "'n verwronge beeld" oordra is vir my geheel en al onaanneemlik (*Buren* v *RBP* 422).

103. Henry James se bekende verklaring is vir my in dié opsig gepas wanneer hy sê: "The only reason for the existence of a novel is that it does attempt to represent life . . . and the analogy between the art of the painter and the art of the novelist is so far as I am able to see, complete." Net soos fotografiese kuns nie die enigste aanneemlike kunsvorm is nie, net so min is waarheidsgetroue betrokke letterkunde die enigste aanneemlike literêre kunsvorm (*Buren* v *RBP* 422).

104. *Kennis van die Aand* wemel van "oordrywings" en "onjuisthede." Die profiel van die Afrikaner wat dit skets is nie vleiend nie. Ek dink nie dat enige betekenisvolle aantal volwasse Blanke lesers—en meer besonderlik Afrikaner Blanke lesers—egter die mening sal huldig dat hierdie boek hulle belaglik of veragtelik maak nie. My eie oordeel is ook . . . dat die boek nie die Blanke Afrikaner (of die Blanke) belaglik of veragtelik maak nie. Die klaarblyklike oordrywings sal enigiemand wat die boek lees baie gauw laat besef, nie alleen dat hy fiksie beet het nie, maar ook dat hy met 'n geniepsige skrywer wat die roman gebruik om te kwets, te doen het. Na my mening het die Volksraad—wat self 'n produk van politieke Vryheid is—nie beoog dat die Vryheid van spraak sodanig ingekort moet word dat die sensitiwiteit van die onverdraagsame en onvolwassene beskerm moet word nie. Die volwassene Afrikaner-gemeenskap sou die pogings tot karikaturing wat hier voorkom met gelatenheid verwerk. Om hierdie boek op hierdie grond in die ban te doen sou na my mening van 'n onverdraagsaamheid spreek wat ek nie graag die Wetgewer sou wou toereken nie (*Buren* v *RBP* 423).

105. "om betrokkenheid af te maak met die stelling dat "'n Sterk heersende tendens deesdae in die literêre teorie is juis betrokkenheid, dikwels met 'n nieu-marxistiese literêr-sosiologiese inslag' . . . getuig, myns insiens slegs van 'n poging tot verdoeming deur etikettering en is 'n negering van die betekenisvolle rol wat betrokkenheid in 'n lewende letterkunde speel" (*Buren* v *RBP* 422).

106. Alfred Austin (1835–1913) was an English poet who was appointed Poet Laureate in 1896.

107. The Jameson Raid was an ineffective attempt by the British to overthrow the government of the Transvaal Republic of President Paul Kruger in December 1895.

108. Konformerende letterkundiges, getrou aan die behoeftes van die bestel van hulle tyd, slaag selde om bydraes te lewer wat hulle taal en kultuur verryk. Alfred Austin was nou wel "poet laureate" van Engeland. Hy word egter nie vir sy bydrae tot die Engelse letterkunde onthou nie, maar vir sy slaafse rympies wat onder meer die imperialisme van sy tyd loof deur bv., die Jamieson (sic) invallers tot helde te verhef. Sy mees sinlose poging in die digkuns wat verewig is as kennelike voorbeeld van die prys wat die getroue letterkundige slaaf aan sy heerser betaal, is sy rympie aangaande die ongesteldheid van die Prins van Wallis wanneer hy dig: "Across the wires the electric message came, he is not better, he is much the same" (*Buren* v *RBP* 422–23).

109. For a lucid discussion of the Louwian conception of literature, see McDonald, *Literature Police* 27ff.

110. Ek is bewus van die feit dat in ons gemeenskap met sy verskeidenheid van volke, tale en kulture die vryheid van spraak in sekere opsigte ingekort is ten einde wrywing en konflik uit te skakel. Ek is egter nie bereid om te aanvaar dat ons Wetgewer 'n konformerende letterkunde op die Afrikaner sou wou afdwing nie, wat hom, dan net soos Napoleon, in verband met die terugsinking van die Franse letterkunde sou laat verklaar: "Mense kla dat ons nie letterkunde het nie. Dit is die skuld van die Minister van Binnelandse Sake . . . hy hoort daarvoor te sorg dat ordentlike goed geskryf word." . . .Om hierdie redes het ek tot die gevolgtrekking geraak dat respondent uit hoofde van die bepalings van die Wet op Publikasies en Vermaaklikhede, 26 van 1963, reg was om die boek *Kennis van die Aand* ongewens te verklaar. Dit is 'n besluit wat ek teësinnig geneem het om verskeie redes; veral egter, eerstens, vanweë die behoefte aan 'n viriele letterkunde in die Afrikaanse taal wat dan ook onbevreesd oor die aktualiteite van die Suid-Afrikaanse situasie sal skryf. Tweedens, omdat ek nou 'n besef het van die ontoereikendheid van my eie Afrikaans; die lees van hierdie boek met sy ryk taal het dit so helder aan my tuisgebring. Die skrywer se moedswilligheid het in die lig van die wetsbepalings my egter geen keuse gelaat nie (*Buren* v *RBP* 423).

Part III

Despite Rollback Efforts, Ongoing Recognition, 1975–1980

Chapter Four

The 1978 Case of Etienne Leroux's *Magersfontein, O Magersfontein!*

We must start this chapter with a rather extensive discussion of the new legal superstructure and infrastructure established by the Publications Act of 1974 to guide the regulation of publications in South Africa, as these differed substantially from those that had been established by the PEA. Let us start our discussion by looking at how the new act came into being.

Well before the Brink case was taken to court, doubts had already arisen about the adequacy of the 1963 act and the way in which it was being applied by the board and the courts. A significant part of the judicial elite complained about being involved in publications regulation, a task that in its eyes should be carried out entirely by the executive (see Kruger et al. 25–26; *PCB* v *Heinemann* 156; Snyman qtd. in Pienaar, "Sensuur" 13). Moreover, the consecutive Ministers of the Interior that served during the tenure of Prime Minister B. J. Vorster (1966–1978) seemed quite unhappy about the fact that the courts kept on overruling decisions of the PCB—especially the *Scope* trials mentioned at the outset of the previous chapter must have been a source of frustration for the successive Ministers, as they were all lost by the PCB (cf. Diemont 216; van Rooyen, *Censor's Tale* 20[1]). A prevailing thought, not only among the successive Vorster cabinets, but also among a substantial part of the judicial elite was that the board was better equipped to carry out publications control than the courts were, as the board, in accordance with the stipulations of the PEA, was made up of people with "special knowledge of art, language and literature" (see Diemont 212–13; *PCB* v *Heinemann* 156–57, 164–65; Snyman qtd. in Pienaar, "Sensuur" 13; Suzman 197–98). It was repeatedly advanced that the right to appeal to the Supreme Court against decisions made by the PCB should therefore be abolished, and that an administrative tribunal should be called into existence to deal with such appeals (see *Debatte van die Volksraad* vols. 25–27, col. 6032; Diemont 209, 212–13; Pienaar, "Sensuur" 13; Suzman 192)—just as the Cronjé Commission had suggested.[2]

There had also been constant public opposition against the Publications Control Board, especially since J. J. Kruger had been appointed Chairman in 1968 (cf. McDonald, *Literature Police* 52–53; van der Poll 209). However, there was public support for the PCB, too: importantly, the South African Teachers Union and the General Synod of the Dutch Reformed Church fiercely defended the board (van der Poll 209). The opposing viewpoints led to two petitions in 1971, which respectively became known as the "Noble anti-censorship petition"[3] —supported by such leading South African literary actors as Alan Paton, Uys Krige, Etienne Leroux, Jan Rabie, and Ernst van Heerden—and the "Rutter pro-censorship petition."[4] Both petitions were submitted to Deputy Minister of the Interior Schalk van der Merwe.

All the controversy surrounding the act led to the appointment of an interdepartmental committee of inquiry in March 1972 to assess the contemporary state of affairs (see "Notice 840 of 1972"). The committee's recommendations, which, on the whole, were approved by the government, led to a number of minor statutory adjustments, of which one of the most significant ensured that as of 1973 the Minister of the Interior would be empowered to ask the PCB to review decisions (see General Law Amendment Act, 1973 18ff). Apparently, the government was thus aiming at stepping up its interventionist possibilities.

Despite the adjustments made, matters were still not settled, however. The government therefore appointed a parliamentary committee to investigate the matter further (see Kruger et al., *Report of the Select Committee*). As this committee could not conclude its investigation before the parliamentary recess, a presidential commission was appointed in July 1973 to continue the pressing investigation (van der Poll 210).[5] J. T. Kruger, who at that time was Deputy Minister of the Interior, was appointed chair of the commission. Due to serious differences of opinion between the commission's members, it published its findings and recommendations in two separate reports in early 1974: a majority report signed by nine members, all MPs for the National Party, and a minority report signed by four members, all belonging to the more liberal United Party (van der Poll 210; McDonald, *Literature Police* 58). The majority report proposed that a new act be drawn up instead of amending the old one. It put forward a bill aimed first and foremost at bringing about an entirely different bureaucratic system and abolishing the right to appeal against censorship decisions to the Supreme Court.

Apparently, the commission's intent was to further tighten government control over the public sphere and gratify the more conservative elements within the Afrikaner community, particularly the religious elite, at the expense of the Afrikaans literary elite (cf. McDonald, *Literature Police* 58–59).

True, the commission did recognize the autonomist poetological, and by implication also institutional, aspirations of particularly the Afrikaans literary field, yet it was only willing to recognize this aspired autonomy as *one* value to be weighed against other values: "Even if art should be judged by purely artistic norms," the commission stated in its report, "care must be taken not to absolutise art: 'L'art pour l'art' at the expense of true morality and decency" (Kruger et al., *Report of the Commission of Inquiry* 5). It is quite likely that with this remark, Kruger et al. had the Sestigers in mind—as Chief Justice Steyn apparently had earlier in ruling for the majority in the AD case of Smith's *Lion*. Under the banner of an autonomous conception of literature this group of literary actors had indeed been provoking parts of the South African public with its libertarian literature for over a decade—as the blurb for Brink's first major English novel *Looking on Darkness* (his own 1974 translation of *Kennis van die Aand*) put it, the group "deliberately challenged the local tradition of petty realism and helped break down the current taboos on sex, religion and related subjects, exploring the possibilities of fiction in a highly experimental way" (inside flap of Brink, *Looking on Darkness* qtd. in McDonald, *Literature Police* 42).[6] And, indeed, as the Kruger Commission was finishing its report, the scandal over Brink's *Kennis* had been long underway (cf. Peters 38ff). As we will see later on in this chapter, the commission's principled idea that literary value should be seen as one value that had to be weighed against other values would be fundamental to the approach of the Publications Appeal Board, the highest body in the censorship system that was then yet to be created.

The Commission's draft bill[7] met great resistance both in Parliament and in the public arena.[8] However, on September 11, 1974, after a long and often heated debate, Parliament came to adopt it. The new Publications Act[9] came into force on April 1, 1975 ("Freedom of Speech and the Press: Publications Act 42 of 1974" 19). It repealed and replaced the PEA. Let us examine the features of the act most relevant to our inquiry.

To begin with, the act drastically changed the censorship bureaucracy. It replaced the old Publications Control Board with a Directorate of Publications,[10] an administrative body that consisted of a director, a deputy director, and at most three assistant directors (cf. PA, 1974 7; van Rooyen, "Aspekte" 122). The main function of the DOP was to appoint, and oversee the work of ad hoc censorship committees that were to make the actual decisions. A committee had to consist of at least three members, who should be chosen from a list compiled by the Minister of the Interior.[11] This latter fact gave the Minister great powers over censorship affairs, as professor of state and administrative law M. Wiechers commented (cf. Wiechers, "Enkele Gedagtes" 60).

The Minister's influence was further manifested in his power to order that a decision of the censors be reviewed (cf. Wiechers, "Enkele Gedagtes" 61).

Under the new act, this authority was bestowed on the Minister in his entitlement to at any time refer the judgment of a committee to the Publications Appeal Board.[12] The PAB was to take over the function of the Supreme Court as the final arbiter in censorship cases, as the new act abolished the right to appeal to this Court against decisions made by the censors. Surely, the abolishment of this right might be regarded as a crucial feature of the new law: whereas the administrative censorship bureaucracy had been kept in check by an independent judiciary[13] in the past,[14] the role of the Supreme Court in South African censorship was now greatly diminished. Indeed, while previously there had been a possibility to lodge two appeals to a division of the Supreme Court—as we have seen, one could in the first instance appeal against a decision of a Magistrate's Court or the PCB to a Local or Provincial Division of the Supreme Court and then in the second instance file an appeal against the decision of a Local or Provincial Division to the Appellate Division of this Court—it was now only possible to lodge one appeal, namely to the PAB, an executive tribunal whose members were appointed—and, indeed, subject to dismissal—by the Minister of the Interior. There was still a possibility to take a decision of this tribunal to the Supreme Court, but only so that the Court could review[15] the decision of the PAB, i.e., to make the Court determine on the basis of the evidence adduced in the appeal case heard by the board whether its decision was legally valid. If the Supreme Court judged that the PAB's decision was not legally valid, the case had to be referred back to the PAB for reconsideration, unless the Court found that the board had acted *mala fide*. In that case the Court had to substitute its own decision as to the undesirability or otherwise of the work in question for that of the PAB (cf. PA, 1974 53, 55).

Unlike previously, under the PEA, the Supreme Court thus no longer established the facts regarding a publication and then judged the publication in terms of the law—that is, considered cases entirely anew, as a "super censorship board," as Williamson put it in the AD trial of Smith's *Lion* (*PCB v Heinemann* 162[16]).[17] Furthermore, whereas there previously had been the possibility to appeal against a decision twice, nota bene to a *judicial* body, there now was only *one* possibility of appeal—to an *administrative* body—and, after that, of a *review* of the its decision (cf. van der Vyver 24–25). Those entitled to make appeals to the PAB within a limited amount of time after a decision had been made and announced[18] were parties that had applied to the DOP to have a certain matter scrutinized by a censorship committee, parties that had a direct financial interest in the case (authors, publishing houses), the DOP, and, thus, at *any* time, the Minister of the Interior.

With the regulation of publications having now become an almost exclusively executive affair, this executive was surely able to increase its powers over the literary field (cf. Dean, "O Tempora!" 12; Wiechers, "Enkele Gedagtes" 59). Indeed, as the PAB's first chairman, Johannes Hendrik ("Lammie") Snyman, a former judge of the Supreme Court,[19] did not fail to observe:

> [The] differences between the repealed Act and the current Act entail that the committees and the Appeal Board, except where the Appeal Board acts *mala fide*, have the sole authority to decide what is undesirable under the Act.[20] Although the Minister can order that certain decisions of a committee be reconsidered by the Appeal Board, even the Minister is bound to the decisions of the Appeal Board.[21]

It has to be remarked, however, that although the PAB was an executive body, it was designed to function as a semi-*judicial* one (cf. B. Coetzee 67): its chairman—and its deputy chairman also—was to be a senior legal professional with at least ten years of legal experience (cf. PA, 1974 49) and was, moreover, to determine the procedure by which the board would operate (cf. PA, 1974 51). In practice, as we will see shortly, the PAB operated precisely as it was designed, its first chair Snyman ensuring that the procedure followed by the board would closely resemble the one by which the actual judiciary worked—among other things, the board in principle applied the rule of *stare decisis*—and that it would follow the positions that had been/would be taken in Court (cf. Silver, "Who" 110; van Rooyen, "Aspekte" 126; van Rooyen, "Wet" 355; van Rooyen, *Publikasiebeheer* 53, 55).[22] This approach was later continued by his successor J. C. W. (Kobus) van Rooyen, who held office from 1980 to 1990 and had served as deputy chairman from the PAB's inception in 1975 to his own promotion to chairman in 1980.[23]

Another feature of the new act worth mentioning was the provision that made it possible for any person, or the directorate of its own accord, to have a publication that had been declared undesirable in the past to be considered anew by a committee once a period of two years had elapsed since the date of the decision. The new decision resulting from this could be appealed against in exactly the same way as the initial judgment could by any of the relevant parties (see PA, 1974 21ff). The rationale behind this provision was apparently that Parliament now recognized that community standards were subject to change (cf. "Appèlraad" 74; Kruger et al. 6; J. Snyman 195, 200; van der Poll 214). This position, coherent with that quite consistently taken by the judiciary ever since the 1910 case of *Rex* v *Shaw*, was in principle advantageous for the maintenance of a degree of literary autonomy vis-à-vis the law.

However, two ways in which the act differed from its predecessor signaled an apparent attempt by Parliament to reduce the degree of institutional autonomy that literature had come to attain under the previous act. In fact, Parliament had chosen to remove the only two instruments incorporated into the earlier statute with which literature could be granted a certain degree of autonomy. Firstly, it scrapped the concept of the likely reader from the statute books. Whereas the provisions of sec. 5 of the PEA—i.e., the section that contained the provisions regarding the moral, religious, and political grounds on which a publication could be deemed undesirable—had been incorporated into the new act in their entirety, the new act did not contain any of the provisions of sec. 6 of the old act, the section that had to be read together with sec. 5 and that contained the provisions that prescribed, among other things, the likely reader test for issues concerning public morals. As we have seen in the previous chapters, this section 6, with its concept of the likely reader, could very well be used to grant the literary field a certain degree of autonomy, or, to put it differently, to bestow upon the literary socialized reader a certain "right to read." Most probably, by taking out the autonomy-friendly concept of the likely reader, Parliament had meant to pave the way for a markedly interventionist approach, and as we will see, the first Appeal Board indeed interpreted the move thus.

The second way in which the PA apparently aimed at reducing the degree of autonomy that literature had come to achieve was by completely removing the provisions of the old act that had enabled literary experts to take central positions in the censorship bureaucracy. The PA's provisions regarding the composition of the different bodies comprising the censorship apparatus no longer stipulated that individuals could be appointed members of one of the bodies by virtue of their "special knowledge of art, language and literature" (cf. PA 7, 9, 49; PEA 278; cf. also "Publications Act 42 of 1974" 33).

A further signal that the PA was aiming to reverse the autonomization process that had taken place under the PEA was that the new act continued to lack any provision for contextualism, as most significantly its English counterpart, the Obscene Publications Act of 1959, did (cf. Geldenhuÿs 45, 120). The new act still stipulated that "any publication . . . shall be deemed to be undesirable if it *or any part of it* [is indecent or obscene etc.]" (PA, 1974 61; my emphasis). In principle, the maintenance of this stipulation did not necessarily evidence that the PA was aiming at curtailing the degree of autonomy that literature had enjoyed under the PEA; after all, it had been part of the old act as well. It did, however, certainly represent a decisive choice to lend "flexibility" to those that were to administer the act—as it had done in the case of the old act too.

In sum, it seemed quite clear that with its new act, Parliament had sought to serve the more conservative elements within the Afrikaner community instead of—and, indeed, at the expense of—the literary field. Indeed, as the very first section of the act decisively declared: "[i]n the application of this Act the constant endeavour of the population of the Republic of South Africa to uphold a Christian view of life shall be recognized" (PA, 1974 7).[24]

Let us proceed with investigating how the provisions of the new act[25] in general and the measures that so clearly appeared to be directed at increasing the executive's power over the literary field in particular worked out in practice. In order to do so, we will first examine how the PAB dealt with literature during the period 1975–1978, i.e., before the act was amended with the purpose of (modestly) facilitating the literary field again—we will assess the 1978 amendments later on in this chapter. Although the PAB was only a semi-legal body, its approach to literature is important for this study, as it does reflect juridical thinking that could be legitimized in South Africa at the time. Moreover, the second chairman of this body, Kobus van Rooyen, would go on to become a central figure in drafting the post-apartheid legislation that came to govern, *inter alia*, literature, and that still governs it to this very day. To illustrate the PAB's approach toward literature during this initial period we will use the case of Etienne Leroux's 1976 novel *Magersfontein, O Magersfontein!* The fact that the PAB was quite consistent in its approach, not only during this period, but also during the subsequent periods that can be distinguished, and that it, moreover, clearly set forth the general principles which effectively came to guide its decisions on literary works in the *Magersfontein* case, allows us to restrict ourselves to discussing just this one case for the purpose of characterizing the PAB's general approach to literature during the first period of its existence. A further advantage of providing a detailed discussion of precisely this case is that it perfectly suits our analysis of the judicial dimension of literature regulation in South Africa: the PAB's judgment in the case of *Magersfontein* was in fact the only PAB judgment that became subject to review by the Supreme Court during the entire period in which the PA had force of law, i.e., the period 1974–1996. This being the case, we will proceed, after a discussion of the PAB's approach toward literature, by examining the Supreme Court's review of the PAB's decision on the novel. Following this, we will examine the 1978 amendments and investigate the approach toward literature taken by the PAB after these amendments had been made. This latter investigation focuses on the PAB's approach up until 1980, as this year is marked by another turning point. In this year, van Rooyen became chairman of the PAB and this signaled the beginning of considerable reform—a development which we will be examining in the next chapter.

THE PUBLICATIONS APPEAL BOARD AND THE LITERARY FIELD, 1975–1978

The Case of Etienne Leroux's *Magersfontein, O Magersfontein!*

In order to be able to adequately assess the PAB's judgment on Leroux's *Magersfontein, O Magersfontein!*,[26] it is necessary to first look at some aspects of the fate that had befallen this novel since its first publication by South African publishing house Human & Rousseau in 1976.[27] By the time of the novel's publication, Leroux, son of a former NP Minister of Agriculture and apparently an avowed Nationalist (cf. de Lange 37, 41), was a leading, though not uncontroversial, Afrikaans author. Since 1965, several of his novels had already become the object of scrutiny for the censors (cf. McDonald, *Literature Police* 265ff).

The narrative of *Magersfontein* centers on a film crew setting out to reenact the 1899 Battle of Magersfontein, a battle that was—and is—of particular importance to both Afrikaner history and mythology. In this battle, which took place during the South African War (1899–1902),[28] an outnumbered Boer army achieved an important victory over the British.

Contemporaneous critics, who quite consensually were very positive in their judgments of the novel (Kannemeyer 370), did not perceive the narrative to be a particularly realistic one (370–71, 373). Indeed, as the narrative's list of *dramatis personae* is made up of such characters as the nearly blind Lord Sudden and the nearly deaf Lord Seldom, the two filmmakers leading the project; a director called Amicus Achtung; a logistician known as Mr. Shipmaster; a chauffeur called Aristophanes Pompidous; a screenwriter, Oxford G. von Waltzleben; a woman of culture called Lady Jubilance; and a nurse named Florence J. Fiskaal (lit.: fiscal)—"anti-heroes" with "comically-ironical and often allegorical names,"[29] as Kannemeyer observed (370)—it does not particularly invite a realistic reading. The episodes presented in the novel do not contribute to such a reading either. As Kannemeyer further observed: "With the phantasmagorical presentation of the matter, game of irony, satirical elements, connection of comic and tragic and grotesque situations in this novel, Leroux continues the path of his previous [also non-mimetic] works."[30] André Brink characterized the work, which eventually culminates with a great flood killing a substantial part of the cast, as "a brilliant accomplishment, a grotesque fantasy which deepens into an astonishing vision."[31]

In January 1977, an individual citizen applied to the Directorate of Publications to have the novel examined. The director appointed a committee consisting of Anna Louw, Etienne Malan, and Prof. H. van der Merwe Scholtz, three key literary censors, and entrusted them with the case. At the end of January, they came to formulate their individual conclusions and their joint decision. Let us proceed with examining these judgments, as this is necessary to be able to adequately assess the PAB's judgment on the novel later on.

The Committee's Judgment on *Magersfontein*

All three censors recognized that if any of the act's provisions did apply to the case, they would be the moral and religious provisions, not so much the political ones. But in both their individual reader's reports and in their joint judgment, the censors took great pains to emphasize that the literary mode in which the novel was written annulled all of its potential culpability. All passages that might in other cases be considered to be obscene or blasphemous, were "functional" in Leroux's work, each of the censors contended. Moreover, they argued—Malan and Scholtz literally, Louw more implicitly—that the novel was a "satire," and that precisely the application of the satirical form neutralized the potentially corrupting effect that it might have had if it had not been cast in this mold. As Scholtz wrote in his individual reader's report:

> [T]he sustained satirical assault possesses a certain built-in "protection," it forms, as it were, a pass, or passport, which allows the writer, as it already did with the Greek comedy writers of old, great freedom of speech. . . . [I]n my view, the problematical instances (that is, the *potential* problems in terms of the Act) ought to be judged [in the following way]: there is the sustained "satirical distance" which gives the potentially delicate or offensive facts an abstractness, an un-characteristicness, and even "contemplativeness," which takes from them their sting.[32]

As the passage makes clear, Scholtz attempted to strengthen his genre argument by pointing out that satire had been a bona fide literary genre since classical antiquity, and that it had always bestowed great freedom upon writers ever since this illustrious period.

Apart from their attempts at stressing that *Magersfontein* represented a work of a particular, and very bona fide, literary genre, and that, because of this, the elements of its construction should be read in a particular way, namely as serving a decisive function within the work, the committee—apparently mainly on Scholtz's initiative—also made great efforts to emphasize that the work should not merely be considered literary, but that it actually possessed great literary value. Scholtz, who after having acted as initial reader took upon himself the function of committee chairman in the examination of *Magersfontein*, wrote in his individual report that Leroux's novel formed a serious and very important work of literature.[33] In the report he drew up in his capacity as chairman of the committee, he not only opened his presentation of the committee's findings by telegraphically writing the words "serious and important literature,"[34] he also ended it by declaring that "[t]he Committee thus decide[d] unanimously that this important novel ought to be passed."[35]

The Directorate accepted the committee's decision, and by consequence, also its motivation. The novel was declared not undesirable. Later that year, *Magersfontein* won the CNA Award, a major South African literary award that was founded in 1961 and named after the CNA chain of bookstores. Shortly after it was announced that the novel had won this prestigious award, however, a pressure group called Aktie Morele Standaarde (Action Moral Standards)[36] started a campaign that had the single purpose of having Leroux's book banned. The AMS was a group linked to the leading Afrikaner churches; one of its previous actions had been to lobby the government to have the PEA replaced by a new act that would result in stricter censorship. The AMS's campaign was set up as follows: Its leader, Eddie van Zuyl, had compiled a list of all the words and expressions occurring in Leroux's novel that he considered to be immoral or blasphemous—in total, the list contained seventy-two instances of "filthiness."[37] This list was then sent to 2,500 Afrikaners along with the request that, if the recipient found the list to contain offensive material, he or she would notify Minister of the Interior Connie Mulder of his or her moral indignation in writing. Many people wrote, and in response the Minister, after having discussed the matter in the Vorster cabinet (van Rooyen, *Censor's Tale* 51), directed the PAB to consider the case anew (cf. de Lange 39; Kannemeyer 372; McDonald 271).

On October 31 and November 1, 2, and 4, 1977, the PAB heard the case.

The Position of Human & Rousseau

Human & Rousseau was represented by advocate S. A. Cilliers of Pretoria-based law firm Tim du Toit and Co. Cilliers's contention that the committee's original finding should be upheld was based on both institutional and poetological arguments. He began by setting forth which principles ought to be applied when judging the novel in terms of the PA.

Both the appealing and the responding party had adduced testimonies. Indeed, no less than thirty-six people had been called to give evidence: the PAB had filed evidence from sixteen witnesses; Human & Rousseau evidence from twenty witnesses.[38] Cilliers contended that the group of witnesses that had thus been gathered was comprised of acknowledged leaders from within the South African community, and that when it came to establishing community standards, great weight should be attached to their opinions. However, when it came to establishing the literary value of a work and the functionality of the language employed in it, the board should listen to literary experts only.

The literary expert evidence clearly established that *Magersfontein* represented a satire and that it heavily employed the stylistic device of irony, Cilliers stated (*Magersfontein: Die Dokumente* 32). Expounding on the implications hereof, he paraphrased Henry Fowler's standard reference work *A Dictionary of Modern English Usage* as observing that the goal of a satire is to reform the community, the specific field it is aimed at is moral standards and customs, the method applied is that of emphasis and exaggeration, and the target the self-satisfied within the community (32–33). In order to explain the special means employed in satires, he referred to Gilbert Highet's 1962 monograph *The Anatomy of Satire*, and quoted the following passages:

> The subject-matter of satire is multifarious. But its vocabulary and the texture of its style are difficult to mistake. . . . Most satiric writing contains cruel and dirty words; all satiric writing contains trivial and comic words; nearly all satiric writing contains colloquial anti-literary words.
> . . .
> [W]hen a satirist uses unambiguous language to describe unpleasant facts and people he intends to do more than merely make a statement. He intends to shock his readers by compelling them to look at a side they had missed or shunned. He makes them realise the truth and this moves them to feelings of protest. Most satirists enhance these feelings by careful choice of language. They employ not only accurate descriptive words, but also words which are apt to startle and dismay the average reader. Brutally direct phrases, taboo expressions, nauseating imagery, callous and cruel slang—these are part of the vocabulary of almost every satirist. (Highet qtd. in *Magersfontein: Die Dokumente* 33)

Having quoted these passages, Cilliers concluded that the PAB thus had to consider and judge a work "aimed at reforming the self-satisfied community regarding its morality and value system through emphasis and through shocking and strong language."[39] As this remark already implied that he meant to present the special techniques that were inherent to satire as justified, he explicitly presented them as such when he contended that "if these considerations would not be taken into account, this special art form would be disacknowledged and an unfair judgment would be passed on the drastic methods of the author."[40] Clearly, Cilliers was thus claiming an *exceptio artis* for the satire genre and its deviant methods.

Yet not only for the sake of literature in general, but also for the sake of Afrikaans literature in particular, should special allowance be made for the drastic methods of the author. Cilliers explicitly stated that *Magersfontein* represented the first satire of stature that had been produced in Afrikaans, and that the breakthrough of this art form in Afrikaans literature required unusual lenience. It would be unfair to judge the strong language, which is "typical to and functional in this genre of literature,"[41] by comparing it to other Afrikaans literary works in which the satirical method had not been applied. In this respect, Cilliers's argument was thus quite reminiscent of Justice Steyn's argument in the case of Brink's *Kennis*.

As a consequence of the fact that no mention of the likely reader was made in the new act, the board had come to set a new standard by which the undesirability or otherwise of a publication was to be measured, the so-called median person. Therefore, Cilliers's next and final step was to estimate how this fictive personality would react to the kind of work that *Magersfontein* represented. He contended that this median person, or "average reasonable person," as, in an apparent reference to both the English and South African legal traditions, he would rather call him, should be attributed the following qualities:

He has an average degree of knowledge; he has an average degree of humility, also with respect to his own limitations and prejudices, and an average degree of tolerance towards others who think differently than he does; and above all, he has an average degree of appreciation for the fact that there are leaders, thinkers, artists, in our community, and that they are cultural pioneers—each in a style of their own. He does not live in a cultural vacuum. He does not live on the level of the great artist either, and he will sometimes understand him only partly, but he does not deny the artist's right to existence and his role in society. He acknowledges this. He wants to keep great artists and thinkers in his community, if he feels this to be at all possible. He realizes that artists and thinkers are pioneers, and that the development and future of our culture depends on them. He knows this, because in school he has read the verses of F. W. Reitz and Pannevis, and then Eugène Marais,[42] and then the *Dertigers*, and then the *Sestigers*—or he is aware of them. And he knows that they were not immediately accepted, or he knows this from his average knowledge of the world and its cultural history. Maybe he knows that painters in the middle ages only painted impersonal Madonnas beautifully, and that when Rembrandt began to paint ugly people, The Night Watch was hung in a back corner. Or maybe he knows that van Gogh out of 800 paintings only sold one, because he painted reality not as it appears but as he saw it with his mind's eye.[43]

The board, he concluded, should not conceive of the average reasonable person as if he knew nothing about these things, or did not want to know anything about them. On the contrary, this average reasonable person would make room in his own value system, indeed, a "place of honor," for "the leaders and the artists that are the frontier thinkers of his people."[44] On the basis of these cultural philosophical/poetological principles—in which resonated a quite unmistakable echo of van Wyk Louw's poetics—the average reasonable person would want literature to enjoy a considerable amount of institutional autonomy.

There would be limits to the autonomy that this person would allow literature, however: he would not accept that artists have carte blanche to appear with the most blatant crudeness or libertarianism under the guise of art. If he thought a work to be simply pornographic, or blasphemous, or defamatory, and so forth, he would not believe that the work's constituent parts had been applied in the service of art. In such instances he would consider the work offensive. In borderline cases, where both a strong element of artistry and banal means of expression were present, he would be in doubt. But he would keep in mind that "artistic means, in the hands of the artist, knows virtually no limits: that *Finnigan's Wake* and some of van Wyk Louw's poems transgress even the acknowledged standards of syntax and grammar."[45]

Having established this, Cilliers came to set forth how the average reasonable person would react in the particular case that *Magersfontein* represented:

> With *Magersfontein, O Magersfontein!* The average reasonable reader will say to himself: This work is so deep and so difficult and directed at such a limited circle, that I accept that the banalities occurring in it are incidental, and functionally incidental, in relation to the artwork, and not the other way round. If he, as a reasonable person would, went on to seek information and clarification so that he understood the work, before he would make a judgment, he would understand that the crude language, sex references, and profane language are merely symbols of the intellectual poverty that is being represented, and that the writer uses symbols because he does not reason like a philosopher, but portrays as an artist. And if he simply does not want to read or understand the work, he will, as a reasonable person, say: it would be unreasonable if I, who do not want to read or do not understand this, should judge whether or not this is offensive in the name of those who do want to read and who can understand this.[46]

Dealing with such a "deep" and "difficult" work, the average reasonable reader would in this case pay close attention to the majority opinion among the thirty-five community leaders that had been called to deliver testimony regarding the book, and he would indeed accept it. For he was not of the opinion that literary writers should "write *for* the average reasonable person as if literature was nothing more than reading matter for the masses."[47] He did not ask this of the writers; on the contrary, he would want them to also write "great and difficult works," and indeed "be proud of that."[48]

In the peroration of his argument, Cilliers observed that the difficulty remained how to bar the really offensive, but still allow the "creative, thinking artists"[49] as much freedom as possible. The answer to the problem was that the board should regard the "median person" in the South African community as being not so low as to easily ban the artist/thinker with his chosen means out of his "field of tolerance."[50] Twenty-five community leaders, including three Hertzog Prize winners, had declared before the board that the novel should not be banned, Cilliers emphatically observed, and he trusted that the board would accept this. Yet above all he asked the board to not "regard our community to be so undeveloped that it could not appreciate the work of a Hertzog Prize winner [i.e., Leroux[51]] for what it is."[52]

The PAB's Majority Judgment on *Magersfontein*

In order to be able to judge the publication in an "objective" manner (*Magersfontein: Die Dokumente* 62), the board appointed advocate P. Krijnauw as *amicus curiae* to make the case against the publication. Unfortunately, only a rudimentary reconstruction of Krijnauw's argument can be made on the basis of the available sources. What becomes clear from the sources is that he accepted that the publication had literary value, and that he, in judging the work, had applied the contextual approach (*Magersfontein: Die Dokumente* 17). What also becomes clear is that he held the work to offend against the moral section 47 (2) (*a*) of the act in that it dealt with sex or nudity in an improper manner; in that it employed curse words, blasphemous words, and other kinds of offensive words; and in that it represented the immoral "as normal and natural, satisfying and right."[53] Krijnauw further argued that the book also offended against the religious section 47 (2) (*b*) in that it was offensive to the religious convictions or feelings of any section of the inhabitants of the Republic. Moreover, he observed that the book might also be held to offend against the political section 47 (2) (*c*) of the act in that Afrikaners and blacks were being brought into ridicule or contempt by certain passages in the book. And finally, he contended that the book might also be offending against the political section 47 (2) (*d*) in that certain passages appearing in it were harmful to the relations between any sections of the inhabitants of the Republic (see 18). In order to support his case, Krijnauw added a long list of quotations, organized in four different categories, the first three of which illustrated the offense against the moral and religious stipulations of the act; the last one—which contained considerably fewer references than the other three—illustrated the offense against the political sections of the act. The list contained well over a hundred citations, both very short and longer ones—to name only a few of the shorter ones that were held to offend against the moral and/or religious provisions of the Act: "Fuck you, you bastard!" (19); "Fuck you all" (19); "You are chickenshit" (19); "Christ!" (24); "Jesus Christ!" (24); "Goddêmit!" (25).

On November 21, the board passed its judgment, which consisted of a majority opinion that was delivered by J. H. Snyman and with which J. C. W. van Rooyen, Gideon Joubert,[54] and D. P. Wilcocks concurred, and a minority opinion delivered by A. P. Grové and C. D. Fuchs. The board had come to its judgment by considering: (1) the publication itself; (2) the reasons of the committee that had judged the publication in the first instance; (3) the affidavit filed by the applicant; (4) the arguments made by the counsel of the applicant and by the *amicus curiae*; and (5) the thirty-six testimonies gathered by both the applicant and the PAB itself. Let us first examine the majority judgment.

The decision of the majority made the PAB's (official) position regarding the institutional status of literature quite clear. The board held that in contrast to what had been the case while the PEA had been in force, the likely reader might not be taken into account in the application of the new act (cf. PAB Case of *Magersfontein* [77/77] 3–4). Under the new act, public morality was "personified in the standards of the average member of the South African community,"[55] and this average member was not a representative of a "special interest group."[56] Indeed, the board stated unambiguously that "the Act protects in section 47 (2) (*a*) the morals of the entire community,"[57] and that "public morals are based on the standards of the broad community and not on the views of a special interest group"[58] (read, in this case: literati, or "the men of letters in the community"[59]): "The views of a special interest group are merely taken as a factor in assessing the standards of the community."[60]

Expounding on its decision to disregard the likely reader from consideration when judging publications, the board stated that "the assessment d[oes] thus not take place on a literary level, but with consideration of a wide spectrum of values. The act deals with 'publications' and does not give any special preference to publications with literary merit."[61] On the other hand, the board did recognize literariness as a value, and considered it a factor that had to be taken into account (cf. 3–4), much like it understood "special interest groups" as a factor to take into consideration. At the outset of the hearing, Chairman Snyman indeed stated that it could be accepted that the publication was of "high literary standing."[62] In the light of what we have seen in the previous chapters, the board's choice to not take the likely reader into account but to take literary merit into consideration at the same time is remarkable. For literariness had always been relevant only insofar as it could reveal anything of the likely readership of a work and, hence, of the effect that a work would have on this readership. In any case, the board's careful position-taking vis-à-vis literature revealed that the literary field had attained such a degree of institutional autonomy that the board could not completely ignore it.

The same can be said of the board's position vis-à-vis literary expertise. In order to determine whether or not a given work could be regarded a work of literature, the PAB accepted evidence from literary experts. As the experts called upon to deliver testimony would, in practice, be white experts in South African literature in English and, particularly, Afrikaans, the question of the literary merits of a work would be settled on the basis of the conceptions of literature that were dominant among these groups. In practice, this meant that when it came to questions regarding literariness, the objective-pragmatic conception of literature (*sensu* Abrams) of the disciples of van Wyk Louw remained dominant within the censorship bureaucracy (cf. McDonald, *Literature Police* 63 et passim).

In the *Magersfontein* case, the board considered evidence provided by a great number of literati: the majority of Human & Rousseau's witnesses—perhaps even all of them—appear to have had literary expertise (cf. PAB Case of *Magersfontein* [77/77] 5–6). Yet although the PAB was willing to accept the opinion of literary experts when it came to settling the question whether a work could be considered literary, it apparently ascribed less importance to their opinions when it came to determining whether a work would have a negative effect—in terms of the law, that is—on its readership. The "great majority"[63] of the experts that had voiced their opinions apparently took a clear stand in favor of literature in general and *Magersfontein* in particular, and employed both institutional and poetological arguments to make their case, arguments that might be grouped under the headings "genre," "functionality," and "likely readership." They professed that the work represented mature, sophisticated literature. They stated that the work was meant to be read by literary socialized readers, not the masses, and that it would effectively only be read by a small circle of such readers and not the masses. This actual audience would interpret the work as a satire and, moreover, would consider the work didactic. The work, being a didactic satire, would have a healing and sanitizing effect and constitute a contribution to morality. The "foul language"[64] used in the novel was contended to be functional, indeed, necessary for the "shock technique"[65] employed to install the book's moral lesson into the reader's mind. And finally, it was advanced that the work made a valuable contribution to Afrikaans literature (cf. PAB Case of *Magersfontein* [77/77] 5). The PAB, however, was only willing to accept the experts' shared contention that *Magersfontein* constituted a work of literature. It considered their other arguments juridically irrelevant (cf. 4). The PAB's refusal to consider expert evidence regarding the (likely) readership of the novel or the effect that the novel would have on its readership was of course rather consistent with its standpoint that under the new act the likely reader should no longer be taken into account.

When it came to the question of comparing a book under scrutiny with other books that were being read in the South African community, the PAB apparently followed the precedent that had been set in the AD case of *Lion* and confirmed by van Wyk in the CPD case of *Kennis*, as it stated that "the fact that there is more offensive matter than the work in question circulating is juridically irrelevant because there is no pre-control of publications. Moreover it is precisely the goal of the Act to prevent the dissemination of this type of publications."[66] Significantly, the PAB interpreted the act as having a markedly (paternalistic) interventionist—or, as the board itself termed it, "idealist" [67]—purpose, just as the majority in the AD trial of Smith's *Lion* and van Wyk in the trial of Brink's *Kennis* had interpreted its predecessor, the PEA (cf. van Rooyen, *Censor's Tale* 65).[68] Thus, when it came to applying the moral section 47 (2) (*a*), the PAB did not consider it its task to determine what was held to be morally acceptable on the basis of the import of the kind of works that were being read at the time. On the contrary, it held its task to be of an interventionist nature: it felt that its duty was to intervene with what was being read, whenever it deemed this necessary and regardless of the status—literary or otherwise—of a given work.

The final institutional issue that was addressed pertained to contextualism. In fact, in the eyes of the board this issue formed the central problem of the case. The majority judgment signaled that "some men of letters and also the minority of the Appeal Board are of the opinion that when words are contextually defendable within the context of the publication, they will lose their offensiveness."[69] Furthermore, it stated, "the minority is also of the opinion that it is a *contradictio in terminis* to contend that a book of high literary standing contains a whole series of unnecessary and unwarranted foul elements."[70] These contentions now posed the central question of the case, the board felt. The point at issue, it stated, was "whether the standpoint of the men of letters on the admissibility of foul language (no matter how dirty) in a book of acknowledged literary standing is juridically justifiable."[71] In other words, whether literature should be granted a certain—in fact, *high*—degree of autonomy when it came to the employment of "foul language."

On the one hand the PAB stated that functionality was a factor that had to be considered when assessing a given text (cf. 3, 14 et passim). And indeed, the fact of the matter was that it did acknowledge that Leroux's book contained elements that "did not honor [the average man's] sense of sexual and bodily privacy"[72] but that were satirically and literarily functional (cf. 10, 12). On the other hand, however, the board professed its adherence to the principle that "[e]ven if the message of the whole is not undesirable, the parts *per se* may be undesirable."[73] With regard to the more specific case of *Magersfontein*, the board declared that one had to acknowledge that "the taking of the Lord's name in vain was something which the Christian section of the population [wa]s sensitive about" and that "this factor certainly ha[d] to be taken into account when assessing the standards of the community."[74] Furthermore, the PAB was of the opinion that the juridically conceptualized "average man," as it had conceptualized him,[75] would not read "contextually": he would consider foul language in a novel as foul language period, and would find this offensive (cf. 6; cf. also 13). What apparently was most important to the PAB's reasoning, however, was the concept of the "cumulative effect"[76] of foul elements: it was the "cumulative effect" of the "foul language" that would disgust the average man (5); it was *excessive* use of foul language and *excessive* taking of the Lord's name in vain that would offend the average man to such an extent that the novel had to be declared undesirable within the meaning of the PA (cf. 13; cf. also 8 and 9). It appears, thus, that although the board's position on the question of contextualism was not as principled as Ogilvie Thompson's conceptualization of the term, it did apply a contextualist approach of sorts.

In the end, the board thus declared the novel undesirable within the meaning of the moral and religious sections 47 (2) (*a*) and (*b*) of the act.[77] It did not hold it to contravene any of the political provisions of the act (cf. 13–14).[78] Almost apologetically, the majority judgment ended with alerting men of letters to the fact that permission to obtain the book for literary scholarly purposes could be granted by the Directorate of Publications (cf. 14–15) and that libraries remained free to obtain and keep undesirable books for the benefit of "bona fide study and research purposes" (15), as they had been under the previous act. Under the new act, as interpreted by the PAB, the *exceptio scientiae* that had long since been established thus remained in force; yet the degree of autonomy that literature had come to attain over the years was reduced considerably.

The PAB's Minority Opinion on *Magersfontein*

The minority opinion is also of interest to our analysis. This is partly because it would also be discussed in the Supreme Court's review of the PAB judgment later on—albeit not playing a very great part in it—but mostly since it throws the majority decision into relief. The argument of the minority, i.e., of Alwyn Grové, a former member of the PCB, professor of Afrikaans literature at the University of Pretoria, editor of the foremost Afrikaans literary journal *Standpunte*, and Chairman (1977–1979) of the Suid-Afrikaanse Akademie vir Wetenskap en Kuns (South African Academy for Science and Arts), and Douglas Fuchs, a former Director-General of the South African Broadcasting Corporation, was short and simple. Its basic contention was that when answering the question whether the book should be deemed undesirable or not, there were at least three important implications to the unanimous acknowledgment from all parties that the book was of high literary standing ("Minderheidsuitspraak *Magersfontein*" 1).

The first implication was reached through a particular, indeed markedly autonomist, literary-conceptual logic. When one acknowledges that a given text constitutes a work of literature, Grové argued,[79] one has to read it as such, that is, one has to read it as "a serious work of prose which novelistically creates an own world of words."[80] He drove home his argument by stating that when one is dealing with "a novel as novel,"[81] which, it was implied, was the case with *Magersfontien*, one cannot "[assess and judge] . . . the elements of it, (the language, the imagery, the dialogue, the entire satirical nature of it) out of context."[82] Quite clearly, Grové was here playing the "transformation" card, the principle that we encountered in the introduction and chapters 2 and 3. Yet his particular transformation test appeared to be more far-reaching than the transformation tests that were rooted in idealist aesthetics. Whereas the latter principally regard the fictionality of a work of art to represent a gradual phenomenon, which in referential and moral respects can distance itself from reality to a lesser or greater extent, but never completely, Grové seemed to be taking a more absolutist position: for him, it appeared, the artwork represented an autonomous work which, as a matter of principle, did not refer to reality, but rather to itself.

The second implication, Grové contended, pertained to the issue of contextualism. This part of his argument we already encountered in our discussion of the majority judgment, namely that it would be a contradiction in terms to argue that a book of high literary standing contained a whole series of unnecessary and unwarranted "foul" elements. In such a book, Grové stressed, "all elements will be contextually meaningful and defendable, and words which out of context could count as foul or offensive, will within context lose their offensiveness."[83] For Grové, deeming a work to be of high literary stature in a legal context thus implied annulling all possible sanctions that the law could impose on the work in question—a quite strong autonomist position indeed.

The third and last implication, Grové argued, was that "the fact that we are dealing with a literary work of high stature [is] of great importance in the attempt of the Appeal Board to predict the reaction of the median person."[84] This was so because "it had already been admitted by the Appeal Board that the reasonable person would display greater tolerance in his reaction to a serious book than in the case of a light, superficial, or non-literary publication."[85] The minority pointed toward the thirty-five reader's reports that had been filed in the case. They argued that these reports represented the reactions of a diverse group of people, a group that was to a great extent representative of the community.[86] About two-thirds of this group did not want to see the book disappear from bookstores, the minority stated. And they argued that "[t]his is a highly relevant fact which in our view can certainly not be ignored by the Appeal Board in its assessment of the standards of the community."[87] In the opinion of the minority, the "median person," "reasonable" and "balanced" as he had been conceptualized by the PAB (cf. "Minderheidsuitspraak *Magersfontein*" 3), would tolerate *Magersfontein*, even though he might not understand the book in its fullest essence. Thus, when it came to the question of readership, the minority, well aware as they were that the likely reader defense was no longer an option, attempted to retain as high a degree of institutional autonomy for literature as possible by advancing that the "average man" would want for it to have a certain degree of autonomy vis-à-vis the law—just as the counsel of Human & Rousseau had done.

On the basis of these three implications, the minority concluded that the novel should not be declared undesirable.

Conclusion

The PAB case of *Magersfontein* presents a clear overview of the principles applied by the Appeal Board when dealing with literature during the period 1975–1978. Crucially, the board chose to employ the criterion of the average man, not that of the likely reader, and conceptualized him in such a manner that the institutional autonomy of the literary field was seriously corroded. Another aspect evidencing that the approach of Snyman's board was rather heteronomy-oriented, was its refusal to admit evidence in which a book under scrutiny was being compared to other books circulating within the community in order to demonstrate that the contemporary public was used to reading works like the incriminated one. For Snyman, this proved nothing, as for him the act was clearly meant to be interventionist, not laissez-faireist.

On the other hand, the PAB's approach also demonstrated that the literary field had reached a degree of autonomy that the board could not entirely ignore. Firstly, the board explicitly recognized that the eventual literary value of a work should be taken into consideration when it was to be adjudged in terms of the law. At the same time, however, the board made it quite clear that literary value was but *one* value to be weighed against other values. Secondly, the board was willing to allow (literary) expert evidence in order to determine whether any literary merit was present in an incriminated work. It thus effectively attributed value to this kind of expertise within a (semi-)legal framework. Despite these manifestations of—admittedly quite weak—recognition, it is rather clear that the degree of autonomy literature had come to attain over the years was reduced considerably by Snyman's PAB. Evidently, the board was aiming at gratifying the conservative elements in society at the expense of the autonomy of the literary field, and it appeared mainly to be effectuating this by replacing the concept of the likely reader, the concept that had been so vital to the autonomization of literature vis-à-vis the law, with its own concept of the average man.

That the board was seeking to satisfy conservative forces by curbing the literary field was quite clearly also confirmed by the specifics of the *Magersfontein* case. The board indeed chose to ban the work even though the novel was not only widely supported in the public arena, but quite vehemently defended by "community leaders" and representatives of the Afrikaans literary elite on both the committee level and the level of the PAB. Yet what was most significant to the whole case was that Leroux was not just any Afrikaans author: he was regarded as a highbrow literary author by both his "friends" and his "foes" in both the committee judgment and the Appeal Board process. In fact, he was generally held by the literary elite, by representatives of both the *Dertiger* and *Sestiger* generations, to be one of the most important authors within the Afrikaans literary field at the time (cf. Brink "Censorship" 43; Kannemeyer 377–78; Smuts 73; N. Snyman 87ff). To round it off, at least part of the literary elite, but probably even a wider audience, considered Leroux to be politically, and by consequence also morally and religiously, on the "right" side of the political spectrum: he was perceived to be a nationalist Afrikaner, albeit a recalcitrant one, i.e., more in the spirit of the Louwian "lojale verset" (cf. de Lange 37, 41; McDonald, *Literature Police* 72, 265). That the PAB chose to ban a work by such a high-profile Afrikaans literary figure was a clear demonstration that this newly created semi-legal body was not willing to facilitate the literary field in the way that parts of the judicial elite had been prepared to do in the past. Quite evidently, the board attempted to reduce the relative—and indeed rather weak—autonomy that the literary field had attained vis-à-vis the law with the case of Brink's *Kennis* to a level of autonomy that more resembled the one that the majority in the AD case of Smith's *Lion* had been willing to grant the field.

Let us now turn to the Supreme Court case in order to see what the Court thought of both the PAB's more principled stance toward literature and of its position vis-à-vis Leroux's *Magersfontein* more specifically.

THE JUDICIARY AND THE LITERARY FIELD

On December 21, exactly one month after the board had passed its judgment, Human & Rousseau filed a Notice of Motion indicating its intent of making a request to the Transvaal Provincial Division of the Supreme Court to set aside the board's decision on the novel. As emerges from its supporting affidavit, Human & Rousseau chose to adopt a different strategy than it had before the board. Had its strategy before the latter tribunal been to argue that the fictive person by whom the effect of a publication was to be measured should be conceptualized in a way that would allow literature a considerable degree of autonomy, it now argued that the PAB erred in its principled standpoint that the PA prohibited taking the likely reader into account when assessing whether or not a publication should be deemed undesirable. The PAB's judgment on *Magersfontein* was therefore also flawed, as it failed to take a relevant consideration into account (cf. *H & R* v *Snyman* 838; cf. also *Magersfontein: Die Dokumente* 59).

In order to support the contention that the circle of likely readers of the publication was a relevant consideration in this case, Human & Rousseau remarked that the great majority of the persons that had delivered testimony in the PAB case had declared that the publication represented adult, sophisticated literature which would have but a limited reading circle, while the masses would not read it. The affidavit further mentioned that the work was not intended for the masses either (59). This fact was confirmed by evidence that merely 4,282 copies of the novel had been printed and that sales could thus not have exceeded this number. J. J. (Koos) Human, codirector of Human & Rousseau and representing the company in the case, confirmed on the basis of his own knowledge that *Magersfontein* constituted a publication that was difficult to read and of high literary value—he stressed this point by mentioning that it had won the CNA Award—and that it therefore would not have been read by the average reader or a mass readership (59). From the nature of the publication itself, and in the light of the irrefutable evidence regarding its likely readership, he concluded, the Appeal Board should have accepted the evidence as to who the likely readers of the publication would have been. From the PAB's decision it indeed appeared implicitly that it had accepted this, but considered it to be irrelevant (59–60).

In his opposing affidavit, respondent Snyman, who acted on behalf of the PAB, evidenced to have recognized the change in strategy of the applicant. He noted that although the board's position regarding the concept of the likely reader—i.e., that it could not take the likely reader as a standard when assessing and measuring the community's views concerning public morals—had repeatedly been documented in earlier decisions, and although every decision of the Appeal Board was open to the public, and known to the legal representatives of the applicant, the correctness of the board's view on this matter had not been contested by the applicant in his affidavit, nor by his legal representative in his argument before the board (63). The applicant's case, he noted further, had indeed been built on the foundation of the correctness of the board's position (63).

Elaborating on the PAB's position in this matter, Snyman argued that the board had indeed adopted an absolute approach to publications control as opposed to the approach relative to the likely reader or an "interest group" that the repealed act had prescribed (64). In earlier judgments, it had justified this decision with the following reasoning. The old act's section 5 had contained the moral, religious, and political stipulations that the *Board* had to apply when considering a case. The old act's section 6 had contained, firstly, the provisions that the *Courts* had to apply when assessing whether a publication violated any of the moral stipulations of section 5; and, secondly, the act's only references to the likely reader. Since the moral provisions set out in section 5 differed from the ones set out in section 6, this had caused a contradiction in the act. As section 6, unlike section 5, had not been incorporated into the new act, this section must have been left out because of this contradiction. It was now therefore no longer permitted to use the likely reader as a consideration in the decision-making process—hence its recourse to the concept of the average reader (*H & R* v *Snyman* 838).

The Supreme Court Review of the PAB's Judgment on *Magersfontein*

The case was heard by three judges of the Transvaal Provincial Division of the Supreme Court on May 8 to 10, 1978. The judges hearing the case were Boshoff, Myburgh, and van der Walt, three Afrikaner judges (cf. Comaroff 5, 28; also "Senior Judge"). On June 8, 1978, Myburgh handed down the bench's unanimous judgment. Let us examine how it dealt with the dispute over the validity of the concept of the likely reader within the new statutory dispensation. As the bench held that the dispute pertained to both the question whether the book should be deemed to constitute an offense against the moral provisions of the act and the question whether it violated the act's religious provisions—as we saw, the PAB had declared that it violated both kinds of provisions—it consecutively discussed the concept's validity within the framework of the former provisions and its validity within the frame of the latter. The Court first dealt with the question whether the likely reader had to be taken into consideration when deciding whether or not a book was undesirable in terms of the moral provisions of the new act (cf. 841), i.e., the provisions that made it an offense for matter to be "indecent," or "obscene," or "offensive or harmful to public morals."

Concerning the alleged contradiction in the 1963 act, the Court argued that section 6 had also applied for the board, not merely for the courts. It based this contention on both the majority judgment delivered in the AD case of Smith's *Lion* and the minority opinion that Justice Rumpff had handed down in that same case. Furthermore, the bench advanced, section 6 had to be seen as an elaboration of section 5. This, it explained, had already been decided by Chief Justice Ogilvie Thompson in the 1972 case of *PCB* v *Republican Publications*—the case in which the former Chief Justice had ruled out the isolated-passage criterion when it came to the written word. Moreover, the Court observed, Ogilvie Thompson's decision had been followed in later Supreme Court cases, notably by van Wyk in the case of Brink's *Kennis* (cf. 843–44). The Transvaal Bench thus concluded that effectively there had been no contradiction between sections 5 and 6 of the former act.

Further, the Court argued, the PAB's reasoning was inconsequent. This inconsequentiality was to be found in the standpoint that the board had manifestly adopted with regard to the relevance of section 6 (1) of the former act for the application of the present act. The latter section had read as follows:

> If in any legal proceedings under this Act the question arises whether any matter is indecent or obscene or is offensive or harmful to public morals, that matter shall be deemed to be—
>
> a. indecent or obscene if, in the opinion of the court, it has the tendency to deprave or to corrupt the minds of persons who are likely to be exposed to the effect or influence thereof; or
> b. offensive to public morals if in the opinion of the court it is likely to be outrageous or disgustful to persons who are likely to read or see it; or
> c. harmful to public morals if in the opinion of the court it deals in an improper manner with murder, suicide, death, horror, cruelty [etc. etc.] or any other similar or related phenomenon; or
> d. indecent or obscene or offensive or harmful to public morals if in the opinion of the court it is in any other manner subversive of morality. (PEA 1963, 284, 286)

The Transvaal Bench observed that whereas the board categorically held that the likely reader might not be taken into account in the application of the new act as section 6 (1) (*b*) of the old act was not incorporated into the new one, it did not categorically hold that sections 6 (1) (*a*) and (*d*) might not be taken into account either: as far as these latter two sections were concerned, the board merely held that the provisions that had been made in them were not *requirements* for undesirability under the new act (cf. 845). The PAB's rationale for adopting the absolute test, and, in fact, for considering the latter test to be mandatory (cf. 838), was therefore invalid in the eyes of the Transvaal Court. The Court's answer to the main question regarding the moral provisions of the PA—i.e., the provisions set out in section 47 (2) (*a*) of this act— therefore read that "considering the general tenor of the provisions of section 47 (2) (*a*) which do not contain stipulations to limit the field of examination of the Appeal Board, the Appeal Board has . . . decided unlawfully that with respect to section 47 (2) (*a*), in the assessment of the community standards, the likely reader may not be taken into account."[88]

Effectively, the juridical concept of the likely reader, which had been eliminated from the statute books and which, therefore, was considered by the PAB to be no longer lawful, was thus maintained, not to say salvaged, by the Court. This maintenance had important implications for the institutional autonomy of literature vis-à-vis the law in South Africa. Indeed, as the concept of the likely reader had proven to be one of the most important legal instruments—if not *the* most important instrument—for effectuating an autonomization of literature vis-à-vis the law in South Africa, the Court's decision delivered a quite crucial contribution to shoring up the degree of institutional autonomy that the literary field had come to attain during—particularly—the period 1963–1975.

Having dealt with the question of the relevance of the concept of the likely reader with respect to the moral section 47 (2) (*a*) of the PA, the Court came to answer the question regarding the validity of the concept within the framework of the religious section 47 (2) (*b*). This section read that a publication should be deemed undesirable if it, or any part of it, was "blasphemous or . . . offensive to the religious convictions or feelings of any section of the inhabitants of the Republic" (PA, 1974 61). In answering this question, three issues were pertinent, according to the Court: (1) the contents of the book; (2) offensiveness; and (3) religious convictions or feelings (cf. 847).

As for the first issue, the Court stressed that the isolated-passage criterion might not be applied, but that the book ought to be judged as a whole (cf. 847–48). To underpin its position, it quoted relevant passages from both the minority opinion of Justice Rumpff in the AD case of *Lion* and the judgment of Chief Justice Ogilvie Thompson in the AD case of *PCB* v *Republican Publications*. Since the contextual approach—which, as we saw in chapter 1, appears to have been employed for the first time in South Africa in the 1910 case of *Rex* v *Shaw*—had proven to be about as crucial an instrument in the legal autonomization of literature in South Africa as the concept of the likely reader had, the Court's principled position-taking regarding this issue constituted another important entrenchment of the institutional autonomy that literature had reached in—especially—the previous decade and a half.

About the second issue, "offensiveness," the Court could be brief: a strong meaning should be attached to the term (cf. 848). On this matter, the board had the same standpoint (cf. PAB Case of *Magersfontein* (77/77) 4). To attach a strong meaning to the terms that the act gave for testing whether or not a work was undesirable was also a means by which the institutional autonomy of literature could be increased, as we saw in the previous two chapters. By maintaining this principle, the Court thus secured yet another legal instrument with which the literary field could be, and indeed had been, granted a certain amount of institutional autonomy.

As for the third and final issue, religious convictions or feelings, the question was whether the test should determine whether a publication was offensive to the likely reader, or, rather, offensive to a section of the population, i.e., a section with a specific common religion. In the dispute between the appellant and the respondent, the meaning of the likely reader came to the fore in two ways, the Court observed. The first was in the assessment of the "nature or tenor"[89] of the book "taken as a whole and with making due allowance for the context in which the words were being used therein."[90] For this purpose, the Court found, the likely reader could be taken into account. In fact, the Court observed, the Board had done so, and besides, it continued, the grounds of the review did not center on this aspect of the meaning of the likely reader (cf. 850).

The second way in which the meaning of the likely reader had come to the fore pertained to who or what Parliament had intended to protect from offense with the religious section 47 (2) (b). Determining the religious convictions or feelings of a certain part of the population had to be done on the basis of the subjective belief of the section of the population in question, the Court stated; "how the likely reader would understand it [was] not relevant and it would be unlawful to determine the convictions and feelings on the basis of the likely reader and in conflict with the provisions of section 47 (2) (b)."[91] As religious convictions and feelings were not determined on the basis of the likely reader, it concluded, it could not be said that the Appeal Board had acted unlawfully in this respect (cf. 851). By taking this position, the tables suddenly turned both for the institutional autonomy of literature in general and for Leroux's novel *Magersfontein* in particular. For in the only literary trial in which the issue regarding the relevance of the likely reader concept with respect to the religious and political sections of the act had arisen, i.e., the trial of Brink's *Kennis*, two out of three judges had declared in so many words that it was relevant: both Diemont and Steyn had indeed advanced that it was of vital importance to determine who was going to read a book, when one was to adjudge it in terms of the law. As Steyn argued, it was absurd to ban a publication because it would offend people who were not going to read it. Only van Wyk had stated that the likely reader should not be read into the religious and political sections of the act. Thus, although the Transvaal Court effectively shored up the institutional autonomy of literature in three very significant ways, it actually effectuated a crucial setback when it came to the religious section 47 (2) (*b*) of the act.

Having established all of the above, the Court could come to its final conclusion. This was that although the Board had erred as far as its application of the moral section 47 (2) (*a*) was concerned, it had not made fundamental mistakes with regard to the religious section 47 (2) (*b*). Therefore, the Court could not rule that the PAB had to reconsider its judgment. The judgment that *Magersfontein* was undesirable was thus upheld.

Let us postpone our conclusion regarding the (proper) judicial position vis-à-vis the literary field within the framework of the PA for now and first examine how the semi-judicial PAB dealt with literature in the remainder of Snyman's tenure. After we have mapped out the final two years of the board's approach toward literature under this ex-Supreme Court judge's chairmanship, we will come to our conclusion regarding the judicial position toward literature, a conclusion which we will then immediately juxtapose with our conclusion regarding the PAB's approach toward literature during the periods 1975–1978 and 1978–1980.

THE PUBLICATIONS APPEAL BOARD AND THE LITERARY FIELD, 1978–1980

The whole *Magersfontein* history provoked major protests. Tellingly, the protests regarding the banning of the book emanated not just from the literary elite and progressive circles, but also from more conservative circles (cf. Brink, "Censorship" 45; de Lange, 40ff; McDonald, *Literature Police* 72, 271; van Rooyen, "1963–1988" 342; van Rooyen, *Censor's Tale* 54–55). This provides us with a quite strong indication that the literary field had indeed reached an advanced stage of autonomy (cf. Bourdieu, *Rules* 220 et passim).

When in 1978 Alwyn Schlebusch succeeded Connie Mulder as Minister of the Interior, he responded to the crisis—apparently after having been lobbied by a group of leading literary figures including the censor Scholtz—by ensuring that some amendments were made to the PA: later that year a Publications Amendment Act was passed by Parliament (cf. McDonald, *Literature Police* 72–73; van Rooyen, "1963–1988" 342; van Rooyen, *Censorship* 9; van Rooyen, *Censor's Tale* 55; van Rooyen, "Censorship" 26). The most important features of the Publications Amendment Act, 1978, in terms of the institutional autonomy of literature, was that it stipulated that the PAB might appoint a committee of experts, to be picked from a list compiled by the Minister, for the purpose of advising it on the literary merits of a work; and, furthermore, that it enabled the PAB to release a work under certain conditions, i.e., with age or display restrictions (cf. Publications Amendment Act, 1978 3–7, 9–11).

With Snyman as chair, the PAB was evidently not prepared to really change its approach though. In a newspaper interview, the chairman apparently referred to the amendments made as representing merely "a sop to the writers" (Snyman qtd. in van Rooyen, *Censor's Tale* 55). And indeed, the PAB effectively did not change its ways. It did not really listen to the advice the literary expert committees gave and it did not regard likely readership as "having any special weight" either (cf. van Rooyen, *Censor's Tale* 55–57; cf. also B. Coetzee 67; McDonald, *Literature Police* 74–75; Merrett 81; Silver, *Political Censorship* 64; Silver, "Publications Appeal Board" 276). In fact, Snyman's board provoked a new crisis when it dealt with the case of John Miles's novel *Donderdag of Woensdag* (Thursday or Wednesday) in 1978. In this case it chose to reject a report drawn up by a committee of thirteen literary experts, almost all of whom were literary academics,[92] explaining that the novel was not blasphemous, and instead accept the report of a single theologian, who had been consulted on the initiative of Snyman himself and who adopted the diametrically opposed position on this issue. Its conclusion therefore was that the novel should remain banned (cf. PAB Case of *Donderdag of Woensdag* [70/78] 2ff; Malan and Bosman 12ff; van Rooyen, "1963–1988" 342).

With respect to the battles fought over the institutional autonomy of literature between the literary field and (a part of) the political field, it is worth noting, by way of coda, that about a year after the Supreme Court case had taken place, the censors Grové and Scholtz ensured that the South African Academy for Science and Arts belatedly awarded Leroux's novel with the Hertzog Prize (McDonald, *Literature Police* 271), the most prestigious prize within the Afrikaans literary field. The awarding of this prize to *Magersfontein*—the award turned Leroux's work into the only banned prizewinning Afrikaans novel of the apartheid era (McDonald, *Literature Police* 271–72)—was warmly welcomed by prominent literary actors such as Bartho Smit, Anna M. Louw, Ernst van Heerden, E. Lindenberg, and J. C. Kannemeyer as one of the most important decisions regarding literature that the academy had ever made. According to these actors, the academy's choice "satisfied the human sense of justice,"[93] because a writer of Leroux's stature "had been groundlessly humiliated by a retarded control or censorship system."[94] At the same time, however, these actors did not believe that the accolade would prove to be "the turning point . . . that . . . writers, men of letters, and all for whom . . . Afrikaans literature is of importance, have been waiting for so long."[95]

We will see in the next chapter that change did begin to come, gradually, when van Rooyen took over as acting chairman of the PAB in October 1979, and that it really came into effect when he was elected chairman in 1980 (cf. McDonald, *Literature Police* 74–75; Merrett 81; Silver, *Political Censorship* 64; van Rooyen, *Censor's Tale* 57 et passim).

CONCLUSION

Looking at the initial phase of the PAB's existence, i.e., the period 1975–1978, one might observe that the approach toward literature of Snyman's board considerably reduced the degree of institutional autonomy that literature had come to achieve over the years. Apparently, the board was aimed at gratifying the more conservative elements in society—and especially the NGK elite—at the expense of (the institutional autonomy of) the literary field. The board's substitution of the concept of the likely reader for its particular concept of the average man represented the clearest example of this. As the former concept had repeatedly been employed as a means of granting the literary socialized reader, and hence the literary field, a considerable degree of autonomy—indeed, as this concept had proven to be one of the most important, if not *the* most important legal instrument for effectuating a significant degree of autonomy for literature vis-à-vis the law in South Africa—the implementation of the board's particular concept of the average reader effectively cut off the path to this relative freedom. Another aspect of the board's approach further emphasized its rather heteronomist orientation. It refused to admit evidence aimed at comparing an incriminated work to other works circulating within the community, as it apparently reasoned that the act had clearly been meant to be interventionist and that it, therefore, had also been aiming to reduce the institutional autonomy of literature rather than promote it. In these crucial ways, the board thus attempted to considerably reduce the degree of autonomy that the literary field had attained vis-à-vis the law during the period before the PA had come into force.

However, the PAB's approach also evidenced that Snyman et al. did realize that the literary field had become a force to be reckoned with. The board therefore acted accordingly: it very carefully stressed that literary merit was a factor that had to be taken into account when assessing a text in terms of the PA and that functionality was also a factor that had to be taken into consideration. Moreover, it admitted evidence by literary experts, and in principle it indeed left the question of the literary merits of a given work entirely up to them. In practice, this recognition did not carry much weight for its decisions, however, as the case of *Magersfontein* very clearly demonstrated. For although the literary experts delivering testimony in this case generally held this work to be of outstanding literary value, and, indeed, of great importance for the development of Afrikaans literature, the work still had to succumb to the supposed convictions and feelings of the postulated average man.

The heteronomy-oriented approach of Snyman's PAB was not held to be legally valid by the Supreme Court, however. Indeed, in the TPD's review of the board's decision on *Magersfontein*, the Transvaal Bench invalidated the most fundamental features of this approach. First of all, the bench came to salvage the concept of the likely reader, the concept that had been eliminated from the statute books and which, on the basis hereof, was considered to be no longer lawful by the PAB. It underpinned this decision by referring to opinions handed down in the trials of Smith's *Lion* and Brink's *Kennis* and to the judgment delivered by former Chief Justice Ogilvie Thompson in the case of *PCB* v *Republican Publications*. As the concept of the likely reader had proven to be of such vital importance for literary autonomization in South Africa, the Court's decision delivered a quite crucial contribution to shoring up the degree of institutional autonomy that the literary field had come to attain during—particularly—the period 1963–1975.

The Court's position regarding two other issues fundamental to the regulation of literature within the nation further underpinned the institutional autonomy that literature had come to attain. Firstly, the Court emphasized that the contextual approach was the only one valid when it came to judging works of literature. The Court again underpinned its decision by referring to the AD case of *Lion* and the judgment of Ogilvie Thompson in the *PCB* v *Republican Publications* case. Since the contextual approach had proven to be about as decisive an instrument in the autonomization of literature vis-à-vis the law in South Africa as the concept of the likely reader had, the importance of the Court's position-taking in this issue cannot easily be overestimated. Secondly, the Court ruled that a strong meaning should be attached to the all-important statutory term of "offensiveness." As seen in the previous chapters, the strategy of attaching a strong meaning to the terms that the statutes pertaining to censorship gave for testing whether or not a work was undesirable was also a means by which the institutional autonomy of literature could be increased. By maintaining this principle, the Court thus secured yet another legal instrument with which the literary field could be granted a degree of institutional autonomy.

Yet the Court's autonomy-friendly positioning was qualified significantly by its position regarding the relevance of the concept of the likely reader for the religious provisions of the act. In the only previous literary trial in which this issue had arisen, the trial of Brink's *Kennis*, the majority of the judges had declared in so many words that it was relevant, both to the religious and to the political provisions of the law. Both Diemont and Steyn had indeed quite categorically advanced that it was of vital importance to determine who was going to read a book, when one was to adjudge it in terms of the law.

The position of Diemont and Steyn thus effectively expanded the (relative) autonomy of literature to also cover the religious and the political stipulations of the law: their position-taking effectuated that the literary reader was not merely the determinate factor when it came to the moral provisions of the law, but that he was also decisive when it came to the law's religious and political provisos. The Transvaal Court, however, chose not to follow the precedent set by these two judges, but to adopt the position that van Wyk had taken instead in the same trial. The latter had stated that the likely reader should not be considered with regard to the religious and political sections of the act. In sum, one can thus observe that although the judgment of the Transvaal Court effectively shored up the institutional autonomy of literature in three very significant ways, it at the same time effectuated a crucial setback when it came to the autonomy of the literary field vis-à-vis the religious stipulations of the act. As a consequence of this principled position-taking, the Court had to uphold the PAB judgment on Leroux's *Magersfontein*. The novel thus remained banned.

The *Magersfontein* furor prompted the new Minister of the Interior, Schlebusch, to break with the heteronomy-oriented approach toward literature that had been instigated by his predecessor Mulder through the PA. By amending the act he enabled the PAB to grant literature a more autonomous position vis-à-vis the law than it had had since the PA had come into force. The Publications Amendment Act of 1978 made it in principle possible to grant literary (socialized) readers more freedom once again by allowing the board to release books under age and/or distributional restrictions. Moreover, it elevated literary experts—who had effectively, through the PA, been written out of the statutory regulations regarding censorship—to a more prominent role within the system once again. The PAB's response to these statutory amendments was quite indifferent, however. Indeed, despite the changed statutory framework and despite the fact that the majority of the cultural, judicial, and political elites apparently held that the literary field should be granted a relative autonomy vis-à-vis the law, the board chose to continue its restrictive approach. Yet with both the judiciary and the government showing support for a relative autonomy for literature, the board would not be able to keep up its line of approach very long, as we will see in the next chapter. What we will see further is how the autonomist tendencies of the judiciary and Parliament would be incorporated into the approach adopted by the new PAB in the 1980s and in which ways this approach was instrumental in the creation of a new statutory and, indeed, constitutional dispensation for literature in the 1990s. Lastly, we will investigate the dynamic status that literature came to enjoy under this new dispensation.

NOTES

1. Cf. also Dean 61–62, 122ff; Murray 4, 7, 8; Pienaar, "Sensuur" 8; Suzman 199–200; van Rooyen "1963–1988" 341; van Rooyen, *Censor's Tale* 18; Wiechers "Enkele gedagtes" 59.
2. For more discussion of the reasons behind the doubts regarding the adequacy of the PEA, see Diemont 212–13; Geldenhuys 80; Kahanovitz and Manoim 11ff; McDonald, *Literature Police* 57–58; J. Snyman 190, 191–92, 196–97, 199, 200; van Rooyen, *Censor's Tale* 20; van Rooyen, *Censorship* 14; van Rooyen, *Publikasiebeheer* 56.
3. Named after J. N. Noble, a resident of the city of Durban, who had initiated the petition. According to newspaper reports, Noble had gathered 10,000 signatures with his petition by January 1971 (van der Poll 209n103).
4. Named after G. O. Rutter, an official of the Youth for Christ Movement, Cape Town (van der Poll 210n104).
5. A noteworthy detail is that the later state president and Nobel Peace Prize laureate F. W. de Klerk was one of the members of both the parliamentary committee and the presidential commission.
6. For an apt characterization of the group, see McDonald, *Literature Police* 258ff. As McDonald describes, the group became internally divided over poetological issues as of 1968. Whereas a part of the group remained true to an autonomist conception of literature, another part of the group chose to go in a more pragmatic direction (*sensu* Abrams).
7. See Kruger et al. *Report of the Commission of Inquiry* 56ff.
8. Cf. "Freedom of Speech and the Press: The Publications Act 42 of 1974" 32; Wiechers, "Enkele Gedagtes" 59.
9. Hereafter: PA.
10. Hereafter: DOP.
11. For a discussion of the procedure regarding the appointment of committees, see Silver, "Who" 107ff.
12. Hereafter: PAB.
13. It is arguably fair to say that the South African judiciary was, to a considerable degree, independent, also during apartheid, yet at the same time it is of course debatable to exactly what extent the judiciary was effectively independent (cf. Forsyth; also Corder).
14. As we have seen, this became quite evident from the fact that all PCB decisions on the magazine *Scope* that were appealed against were set aside by the Supreme Court in the early 1970s (cf. McDonald, *Literature Police* 58; van Rooyen, *Censor's Tale* 20).
15. The Kruger Report explained that "[i]n respect of the right of review the common law principles of review [were] applied" (28).
16. Cf. also *PCB* v *Heinemann* 164; and also *Brandwagpers* v *RBP* 43; "The Judiciary" 536–37; Wiechers, "Enkele Gedagtes" 59.
17. Except, thus, in cases in which the board would have been found to have acted *mala fide*.
18. Apart from the DOP itself, concerned parties were either informed of a decision by the DOP or by an announcement made in the *Government Gazette*. The DOP had to make an appeal against a decision within seven days from the day on which it was informed about a decision; other parties within thirty days.
19. He had been a judge in the Transvaal Division of the Supreme Court from 1958 to 1975 (see Comaroff 34).
20. Yet, of course, the Appeal Board formed the "highest body" in the censorship system, as Snyman was keen to observe elsewhere (cf. PAB Case of *Magersfontein* [77/77] 1).
21. "Hierdie verskille tussen die herroepe wet en die huidige wet bring mee dat die komitees en die appèlraad, behalwe waar die appèlraad *mala fide* handel, die alleenseggenskap het om te besluit wat onder die wet ongewens is. Alhoewel die minister kan gelas dat sekere beslissings van 'n komitee deur die appèlraad heroorweeg word, is selfs die minister aan die beslissings van die appèlraad gebonde" (J. Snyman 194).
22. It should be noted, however, that the PAB did remain only a *semi*-judicial body in a double sense: apart from the fact that it did not represent a (proper) judicial body but a body that belonged to, and was controlled by, the executive, its inner structure and its procedures also diverged from those of (proper) judicial bodies in some significant respects, e.g., the PAB

was partly made up of laymen (cf. PA, 1974 49 cf. also J. Snyman 192; van Rooyen, *Publikasiebeheer* 54); although it aspired to create a system of precedents (cf. Cheh 41–42; Silver, "Who" 110), it was not *bound* by precedent (cf. van Rooyen, *Publikasiebeheer* 54; cf. also Silver, "Publications Appeal Board" 273); and applicants were only allowed to make some *limited* representations (cf. PA, 1974 51; cf. also "Appèlraad" 75; "Freedom of Speech and the Press: The Publications Act 42 of 1974" 35, 38; van Rooyen, "Aspekte" 125–26, 131; Wiechers, "Enkele Gedagtes" 61).

23. As for the power that the chairman of the PAB had within this specific body, see Silver, "Publications Appeal Board" 273.

24. For juridical comments on this provision, which from a juridical perspective was apparently quite awkward, see "Freedom of Speech and the Press: The Publications Act 42 of 1974" 33; Geldenhuys 134; J. Snyman 193n9, 196; Strauss, Strydom and van der Walt 74–75; van der Vyver 22ff; and Wiechers, "Enkele Gedagtes" 60. For the PAB's interpretation of it, see "Appèlraad" 74; PAB Case of *Magersfontein* (77/77) 2–3; van Rooyen, "Aspekte" 128–29, 130; van Rooyen, "Wet" 355–56; van Rooyen, "Review" 30.

25. Some adjustments were made to the act through the Publications Amendment Act, No. 79 of 1977, but these amendments are not relevant to our analysis.

26. Hereafter *Magersfontein*.

27. For this study I used a later edition of the novel, see Leroux.

28. Also referred to as the Second Boer War. Among Afrikaners it was—and is—also called the Tweede Vryheidsoorlog (Second War of Independence; lit. Second Freedom War).

29. "anti-held[e]"; "geestig-ironiese en dikwels allegoriese name" (Kannemeyer 372).

30. "Met die fantasmagoriese aanbieding van die gegewe, spel van die ironie, satiriese elemente, verbinding van komiek en tragiek en groteske situasies in hierdie roman sit Leroux die lyn van sy vorige werke voort" (Kannemeyer 373).

31. "'n briljante prestasie, 'n grillige fantasie wat verdiep tot 'n verbysterende visioen" (Brink qtd. in Kannemeyer 370).

32. [D]ie volgehoue satiriese aanslag [het] 'n sekere ingeboude "beskerming," . . . dit [is] as 't ware pas of 'n paspoort wat die skrywer, soos reeds die Griekse komedieskrywer van ouds, veel vryheid van spraak veroorloof. . . . [V]olgens my, [moet] die probleemgevalle (d.w.s. móóntlike probleme in terme van die Wet) [op die volgende wyse] beoordeel . . . word: daar is die volgehoue "satiriese afstand" wat aan potensieel delikate of aanstootlike gegewens 'n afgetrokkenheid, 'n on-persoonlikheid en selfs "beskoulikheid" gee wat hulle hulle byt ontneem (Reader's report on *Magersfontein* by Reader C 1–2). (Scholtz based the notion of satire which he employed in his report on the definition that was given of the term in the 1973 reference work *A Dictionary of Modern Critical Terms* [cf. Bevinding 2; Fowler 167; *Magersfontein: Die Dokumente* 103; McDonald, *Literature Police* 272; Reader's report on *Magersfontein* by Reader C 1–3].)

33. On the first page of his reader's report, he wrote: "hopelik [is] duidelik dat ons dit hier met ernstige en belangrike literatuur te make het" (Reader's report on *Magersfontein* by Reader C 1) "I hope that it is clear that we are dealing with serious and important literature here"; in the final sentence of his report, he referred to Leroux's novel by using the words "baie belangrike roman" (3) "very important novel."

34. "Ernstige en belangrike literatuur" (Report on *Magersfontein* by ad hoc committee 3).

35. "Die Komitee besluit dan ook eenparig tot deurlating van hierdie belangrike roman" (Report on *Magersfontein* by ad hoc committee 3).

36. Just like the Social Reform Association, which we encountered in chapter 1, this group might also be regarded as a South African anti-vice organization equivalent to Anthony Comstock's New York Society for the Suppression of Vice or the late eighteenth- and nineteenth-century English prototypes of this latter organization.

37. "smerighede" (Kannemeyer 372).

38. Some of the sources relevant to the case make mention of 35 testimonies: 16 filed by the PAB and 19 by Human & Rousseau (see *Magersfontein: Die Dokumente* 28 et passim).

39. "wat daarop uit is om die selftevrede gemeenskap te hervorm ten opsigte van hulle moraliteit en waardesisteem deur beklemtoning en deur skokkende en kras taal" (*Magersfontein: Die Dokumente* 33).

40. "Indien nie rekening gehou word met hierdie oorwegings nie, word die besondere kunsvorm misken en 'n onbillike oordeel oor die kras metodes van die outeur uitgespreek" (*Magersfontein: Die Dokumente* 33).

41. "besonders en funksioneel tot hierdie genre van die literatuur" (*Magersfontein: Die Dokumente* 33).

42. F. W. Reitz (1844–1934) was a high-profile judicial, political, and cultural figure in late nineteenth- and early twentieth-century South Africa: he was, among other things, chief justice of the Orange Free State from 1876 to 1889, state president of the Orange Free State from 1889 to 1895, and president of the Senate of the Union of South Africa from 1910 to 1921. As a writer he was especially renowned for his poems, and his work is regarded as exemplary for the First Afrikaans Language Movement. Arnoldus Pannevis (1838–1884) was a Dutchman who immigrated to the Cape Colony in 1866 to take up a position as teacher of Latin and Greek at the Gymnasium of Paarl. His efforts in promoting the Afrikaans language resulted in him becoming a key inspiration for the First Afrikaans Language Movement. He is also known for his poems in Afrikaans. Eugène Marais (1871–1936) was a journalist and writer who played a principal role in the Second Afrikaans Language Movement. All three are highly canonical figures within Afrikaans culture/literature.

43. "Hy het 'n gemiddelde mate van kennis; hy het 'n gemiddelde mate van nederigheid, ook oor sy eie onkunde en vooroordele en 'n gemiddelde mate van verdraagsaamheid teenoor ander wat anders as hy dink; en bowenal het hy 'n gemiddelde mate van waardering vir die feit dat daar leiers, denkers, kunstenaars, in ons gemeenskap is, en dat hulle die kulturele voorlopers is—elk in die styl wat eie aan homself is. Hy leef nie in 'n kulturele vakuum nie. Hy leef ook nie op die vlak van die groot kunstenaar nie, en hy begryp hom soms slegs ten dele, maar hy misken nie die kunstenaar se bestaansreg en sy rol in die samelewing nie. Hy erken dit. Hy wil groot kunstenaars en denkers in sy gemeenskap behou as hy voel dat hy enigsins kan. Hy besef dat kunstenaars en denkers die voorlopers is, en dat die ontwikkeling en die toekoms van ons kultuur van hulle afhang. Hy weet dit want hy het op skool rympies van F. W. Reitz en Pannevis gelees, en toe Eugène Marais, en daarna die Dertigers, en toe die Sestigers—of hy is bewus van hulle. En hy weet hulle is nie dadelik erken nie, of hy weet dit uit sy gemiddelde kennis van die wêreld se kultuurgeskiedenis. Miskien weet hy dat skilders in die middeleeue net onpersoonlike madonnas mooi geskilder het, en dat toe Rembrandt lelike mense begin skilder het, die Nagwag in 'n achterhoek gehang is. Of miskien weet hy dat van Gogh uit 800 skilderye slegs een verkoop het, omdat hy die werklikheid geskilder het, nie soos dit voorkom nie, maar soos hy dit met die geestesoog gesien het" (*Magersfontein: Die Dokumente* 38).

44. "'n ereplek, vir die leiers en die kunstenaars wat die voorste denkers van sy volk is" (*Magersfontein: Die Dokumente* 38).

45. "dat Finnigan's Wake en sommige van Van Wyk Louw's gedigte selfs die erkende maatstawwe van die sintaks en die grammatika oortree" (*Magersfontein: Die Dokumente* 38).

46. "By Magersfontein, O Magersfontein! sal die gemiddelde redelike persoon vir homself sê: Die werk is so diep en so moeilik en tot so'n beperkte kring gerig, dat ek aanvaar dat die banaliteite daarin insidenteel, en funksioneel insidenteel, tot die kunswerk is, en nie andersom nie. As hy, soos 'n redelike persoon, voorligting en verduideliking soek totdat hy die werk verstaan voordat hy oordeel, sal hy ook begryp dat die kru taal, seksverwysings en die profane taal, maar net simbole is van die geestesarmoede wat uitgebeeld word, en dat die skrywer simbole gebruik omdat hy niet soos 'n filosoof redeneer nie, maar soos 'n kunstenaar uitbeeld. En as hy die werk glad nie wil lees of verstaan nie, dan sal hy, as redelike persoon, sê: dit is onredelik dat ek, wat dit nie lees of kan verstaan nie, moet oordeel namens die wat dit wel wil lees en kan verstaan, of dit aanstootlik is al dan nie" (*Magersfontein: Die Dokumente* 39).

47. "vir die gemiddelde redelike persoon skryf asof die letterkunde niks meer as massaleesstof is nie" (*Magersfontein: Die Dokumente* 39; emphasis Cilliers).

48. "hy wil hê dat hulle ook groot en moeilike werke skryf en is trots daarop" (*Magersfontein: Die Dokumente* 39).

49. "skeppende, denkende kunstenaars" (*Magersfontein: Die Dokumente* 39).

50. "verdragingsveld" (*Magersfontein: Die Dokumente* 40).

51. As already mentioned in chapter 2, Leroux had won the Hertzog Prize in 1964 for his novel *Sewe Dae by die Silbersteins*.

52. "ons gemeenskap so onontwikkeld aan te slaan dat hy nie 'n bekroonde werk van 'n Hertzogpryswenner kan aanvaar vir wat dit werklik is nie" (*Magersfontein: Die Dokumente* 40).

53. "as normaal en natuurlik, bevredigend en reg" (*Magersfontein: Die Dokumente* 18). The phrase was a judicial one; it was employed by Steyn in the AD case of *Lion* and became a standard test in publications control (cf. van Rooyen, *Censorship* 54).

54. A General of the South African Police Force, not to be confused with the writer and *Burger* journalist of the same name.

55. "verpersoonlik in die opvattings van die gemiddelde lid van die Suid-Afrikaanse gemeenskap" (PAB Case of *Magersfontein* [77/77] 3).

56. "'n besondere belangegroep" (3).

57. "[d]ie Wet beskerm in paragraaf 47(2)(a) die sedes van die hele gemeenskap" (6).

58. "[o]penbare sedes is gebaseer op die opvattings van die breë gemeenskap en nie op die beskouings van 'n besondere belangegroep nie" (6).

59. "[d]ie letterkundiges in die gemeenskap" (6).

60. "Die beskouings van 'n belangegroep word net as 'n faktor in ag geneem by die peiling van die gemeenskapsopvatting" (6).

61. "Die peiling geskied dus nie op letterkundige vlak nie, maar met inagneming van 'n wye spektrum van waardes. Die Wet handel met 'publikasies' en gee geen spesiale voorkeur aan publikasies met letterkundige meriete nie" (3).

62. "hoë letterkundige gehalte" (cf. "Minderheidsuitspraak *Magersfontein*" 1). The PAB would go on to repeat its opinion on the status of the book in the Supreme Court, as we will see later on: before the Court it declared that it held the book to be of a "serious and high literary nature" ("ernstige en hoë literêre aard" [*H&R* v *Snyman* 847]).

63. "oorgrote meerderheid" (PAB Case of *Magersfontein* [77/77] 5).

64. "ongure taal" (5). The term was conceptualized by the PAB as follows: "Taal word as onguur beskou indien dit nie in die gemengde geselskap van opgevoede mans en vrouens gebruik word nie" (7) "Language is considered to be foul if it is not used in the mixed company of educated [in the sense of well-raised] men and women." The board did however hold that mitigating circumstances were possible in cases in which an individual was confronted in private with what was, in principle, "foul language" (cf. Rumpff's differentiation between responses in private and responses in public in the AD case of *Lion*). Thus, when it had to decide on reading matter, it might consider the eventual literary nature of the reading matter in question to be a mitigating factor. In cases in which an individual would be confronted in public with "foul language," for example in the case of a "public entertainment," such mitigating circumstances were not possible (cf. 9).

65. "skoktegniek" (5).

66. "die feit dat daar aanstootliker stof as die onderhawige werk in omloop is, [is] juridies irrelevant . . . omdat daar nie voorafbeheer oor publikasies is nie. Daarbenewens is dit juis die doel van die Wet om daardie tipe publikasie se verspreiding te voorkom" (4).

67. For a discussion of the PAB's usage of the terms "idealism" and "realism," see du Toit 114–15.

68. It appears that Snyman partly found grounds for this in the fact that the new act made no express provisions for literary experts to serve as censors, as the old act had done, but instead stipulated that the members of the committees and the DOP, and a significant part of the members of the PAB as well, would be appointed "by reason of their educational qualifications and knowledge [or "experience" (see PA, 1974 49)]," which Snyman thus concluded, meant that the "approach must be that of the educationist, not of the literary scholar" (cf. McDonald, *Literature Police* 60–61; PAB Case of *The Dawn Comes Twice* (144/76) 19; Silver, "Sex" 126; J. Snyman 193, 195, 199, 200; van Rooyen, "Aspekte" 129; van Rooyen, *Publikasiebeheer* 13, 65; van Rooyen, "Review" 30). Snyman was using the term "educate" and its derivatives in the broad sense of "raise, form mentally" here ("'Opvoed' word hier in sy breë betekenis van 'groot maak, geestelik vorm' verstaan" ["Appèlraad" 74; cf. also Silver, "Sex" 126]).

69. "Sommige letterkundiges en ook die minderheid van die Appèlraad is van mening dat as woorde konteksueel verdedigbaar is binne die konteks van die publikasie, hulle hul aanstootlikheid verloor" (5).

70. "Die minderheid is ook van mening dat dit 'n *contradictio in terminis* is om te beweer dat 'n boek van hoë letterkundige gehalte 'n hele reeks onnodige en onverantwoorde ongure elemente bevat" (5).
71. "of die letterkundiges se standpunt oor die toelaatbaarheid van ongure taal (hoe vieslik ookal) in 'n boek van erkende letterkundige gehalte, regtens te regverdig is" (6).
72. "geen eerbied vir [die gemiddelde man] sy gevoel van seksuele en liggaamlike privaatheid toon nie" (10).
73. "Selfs al is die boodskap van die geheel nie ongewens nie, kan die dele as sodanige ongewens wees" (PAB Case of *Magersfontein* [77/77] 3; cf. also *Report of the Publications Appeal Board 1977* 2).
74. "die ydellike gebruik van die Here se Naam iets is waaroor die Christelike bevolkingsdeel gevoelig en hierdie faktor moet by die peiling van die gemeenskapsopvatting beslis in ag geneem word" (PAB Case of *Magersfontein* [77/77] 7).
75. The PAB had stipulated that the "median of standards in the community" was represented by "the average decent-minded, law-abiding, modern and enlightened citizen with [C]hristian principles; not the libertine or the ultra-modern, nor the prude or ultra conservative, but that of the man of balance with a tolerant view in regard to the view of others . . . such a man who is prepared to make some allowance for deviations and who is aware that he may be wrong in his own views and allows for it" ("Minderheidsuitspraak *Magersfontein*" 3; cf. also "Appèlraad" 74; Silver, "Sex," especially 126ff; J. Snyman 196–97, 200; van Rooyen, "Aspekte" 129–30; van Rooyen, "Review" 30).
76. "kumulatiewe effek" (5).
77. As said, secs. 47 (2) (*a*) and (*b*) of the new act were exact copies of secs. 5 (2) (*a*) and (*b*) of the old one: "For the purposes of this Act," the new act read, any publication or object, film, public entertainment or intended public entertainment

shall be deemed to be undesirable if it or any part of it—

(*a*) is indecent or obscene or is offensive or harmful to public morals;

(*b*) is blasphemous or is offensive to the religious convictions or feelings of any section of the inhabitants of the Republic. (PA, 1974 61)

78. That is to say, it was not considered to be "bring[ing] any section of the inhabitants of the Republic into ridicule or contempt" (sec. 47 (2) (*c*)); nor to "[be] harmful to the relations between any sections of the inhabitants of the Republic" (sec. 47 (2) (*d*)); nor to "[be] prejudicial to the safety of the State, the general welfare or the peace and good order" (sec. 47 (2) (*e*)) (PA, 1974 61).
79. It seems quite clear that he had drawn up the minority judgment, not Fuchs (cf. McDonald, *Literature Police* 271).
80. "'n ernstige prosawerk wat romankundig 'n eie woordwêreld tot stand bring" ("Minderheidsuitspraak *Magersfontein*" 1).
81. "roman as roman" (2).
82. "die elemente hiervan, (die taal, die beelding, die dialoog, die hele satiriese inslag daarvan) kan nie buite konteks beoordeel en veroordeel word nie" (2).
83. "sal alle elemente kontekstueel sinvol en verdedigbaar wees, en woorde wat buie konteks as onguur of aanstootlik kan geld, sal binne die konteks hulle aanstootlikheid verloor" (2).
84. "die feit dat ons hier met 'n literêre werk van hoë gehalte te make het [is] van groot belang in die poging van die Appèlraad om die reaksie van die mediaan-persoon te voorspel" (2).
85. "[d]aar is al deur die Appèlraad toegegee dat die redelike persoon groter verdraagsaamheid aan die dag sal lê in sy reaksie op 'n ernstige boek as in die geval van 'n ligte, oppervlakkige of nie-literêre geskrif" (2).
86. This very much in contrast to the majority, who held the group to consist primarily of men of letters (cf. 5 et passim). Incidentally, the minority's remark that the thirty-five reports represented the reaction of a heterogeneous group of people (a group that seemingly consisted of men of letters, ministers, educationists, journalists, housewives—white and non-white, English- and Afrikaans-speaking); indeed, that the group was to a great extent representative of the community (cf. *Magersfontein: Die Dokumente* 54), clearly revealed the apartheid logic under-

lying part of its reasoning. For apparently, the sections of the population that spoke African languages did not really signify.

87. "Dis 'n hoogs relevante feit was onses insiens net nie deur die Appèlraad in sy peiling van die gemeenskapsopvatting geïgnoreer kan word nie" (3).

88. "Gesien die algemene strekking van die bepalings van art. 47 (2) (a) wat nie voorskrifte bevat om die ondersoekingsveld van die Appèlraad te beperk nie het die Appèlraad . . . regstrydig besluit dat met betrekking tot art 47 (2) (a) by die bepaling van die gemeenskapsopvatting die waarskynlike leser nie in ag geneem mag word nie" (846, cf. also 847).

89. "aard of strekking" (850).

90. "in sy geheel geneem en met inagneming van die konteks waarin die woorde daarin gebesig word" (850).

91. "Hoe die waarskynlike leser dit sal verstaan is nie ter sake nie en dit sou regstrydig wees om die oortuigings en gevoelens aan die hand van die waarskynlike leser te bepaal en strydig wees met die bepalings van art 47 (2) *(b)*" (850).

92. The committee consisted of Dr. Elize Botha, D. J. Coetzee, Prof. L. C. Eksteen, Prof. W. E. G. Louw, P. R. T. Nel, Dr. C. E. Pretorius, C. F. Rudolph, Prof. N. J. G. Sabbagha, Dr. L. Strydom, Prof. P. J. H. Titlestad, Dr. A. P. van der Colf, Prof. H. van der Merwe Scholtz, Dr. R. Wiehahn (PAB Case of *Donderdag of Woensdag* [70/78] 2).

93. "[bevredig] die menslike gevoel van regverdigheid" (Kannemeyer 372).

94. "deur 'n agterlike beheer- of sensuurstelsel grondeloos verneder is" (372).

95. "die keerpunt . . . waarop . . . skrywers, literatore en almal vir wie . . . Afrikaanse literatuur van belang is, so lank reeds wag" (372–73).

Part IV

Decisive Legal Recognition, 1980–2010

Chapter Five

(The Road to) Constitutional Autonomy

As mentioned in the previous chapter, no trials involving literary works have been held in South Africa since the 1978 case concerning Leroux's *Magersfontein*. Our discussion of the post-1980 era will thus be limited to examining the PAB's approach to literature, the relevant legal enactments and the concomitant discussions, particularly juridical ones, of this period. An important decision in a high-profile literary case, namely the 2002 case of Salman Rushdie's *The Satanic Verses*, handled by the successor of the DOP, the Film and Publications Board, will also be scrutinized. As our focus is on the legal regulation of literary texts on the basis of acts specifically designed for this purpose, we will not address the work done by the Truth and Reconciliation Commission or the South African Human Rights Commission.[1]

For the purposes of our discussion, it is adequate to distinguish three distinct phases in the period 1980–2010: (1) the period 1980–1990; (2) the interim period 1990–1994; and (3) the period 1994–2010. The first period was characterized by a marked (semi-)legal autonomization of literature. In this period, literature was, however, still overseen and assessed in terms of the (apartheid) legal framework that the PA provided, and occasional bans under PAB jurisdiction still occurred on moral, religious, or political grounds. The second period was a period of transition, in which the monitoring of literature came to an almost complete halt. In fact, instead of monitoring literature, decisive efforts were being made on the level of the DOP to release as many books "of merit" as possible. Probably because of the quite drastically expanded semi-legal space for literature, the need to appeal to the PAB against decisions on literary works seemed to diminish. Only one appeal against a decision on a work of literature seems to have been made to the PAB in this period—which had a quite interesting outcome however, as we will see below. Moreover, intensive discussions were being held during this interim period about the place of publications regulation in a Bill of Rights society, which South Africa was rapidly evolving into. The third period, finally, was marked by statutory changes that greatly altered the legal status of literature. At the beginning of this period, i.e., on the same day as the first ever non-racial democratic elections took place in South Africa, the Interim Constitution, adopted in 1993 (see Constitution of the Republic of South Africa, Act 200 of 1993), came into effect. The beginning of this period further witnessed efforts at drafting an act to replace the PA. In 1996, the Interim Constitution was replaced by a definite Constitution (see Constitution of the Republic of South Africa, No. 108 of 1996), and, moreover, the draft replacement of the PA was passed by Parliament, thus becoming the Films and Publications Act, 1996.[2]

Let us in the following three sections examine these three consecutive periods. In the closing section we will then recapitulate the main observations and draw a general conclusion regarding the post-1980 era.

THE PUBLICATIONS APPEAL BOARD AND THE LITERARY FIELD, 1980–1990

After the 1978 amendments and up to 1990, the statutory and common legal situation, at least as far as literature was concerned, remained virtually unaltered: no amendments were made to the PA during this period that really changed the statutory guidelines regarding literature regulation and no decisions of the PAB were taken to court for review either. As of 1980, the semi-legal regulation of literature started to change fairly dramatically, however.

One could have sensed that change was in the air when, after the *Magersfontein* controversy, the new Minister of the Interior, Alwyn Schlebusch, had taken the initiative to amend the PA so as to enable the literary field to play a greater part in the decision-making process once again. With Snyman still in place and unwilling to alter the course of the PAB, Schlebusch's measures did not, however, have much effect, as we observed in the previous chapter. In fact, the situation deteriorated even further, because of Snyman's disregard of the great amount of literary expert evidence that had been produced in the *Donderdag of Woensdag* case. It turns out that after this case, Snyman was entreated by the Minister, albeit off the record, to give more weight to the opinions of literary Committees of Experts in the future—in other words: to be more considerate of the literary field. Snyman refused as a matter of principle, stating that he would give just as much weight to such committees as he, as a judge, deemed "to be in the interests of justice" (van Rooyen, *Censor's Tale* 56–57). Yet Snyman's tenure was coming to an end, and not very surprisingly, considering the discrepancy between Schlebusch's and

Snyman's stances, the retired judge was not given a second five-year term as chairman of the PAB. Instead of giving him a new term, State President Marais Viljoen[3] chose to appoint the thirty-seven-year-old J. C. W. (Kobus) van Rooyen, the PAB's deputy chairman during the period 1975–1980, as chairman for the next five years (van Rooyen, *Censor's Tale* 57–59). Van Rooyen, who was reluctant to take up the position at first, fearing that his young age might hinder his acceptance as chairman by all members of the board—all of whom were over fifty—was finally convinced by Schlebusch, and assured, moreover, "that the literary establishment would back [him]" (van Rooyen, *Censor's Tale* 60).

Considering the wider political context of appointing van Rooyen at the expense of Snyman, it does not seem coincidental that this appointment was made. There had been drastic changes at the ministerial level: a political scandal, the so-called Information Scandal,[4] had catapulted P. W. Botha into power in 1978 and had led to the end of the political lives of former Prime Minister and, later, for a short period of time, state president, John Vorster and of the Minister of the Interior Connie Mulder. The changes at the ministerial level heralded the coming of a new political paradigm. Snyman had been a longtime friend of hardliner Vorster (Bizos 24; van Rooyen, *Censor's Tale* 49; cf. also Rickard), but since his friend was no longer in power, since his own PAB policy had apparently run out of allies, and since he refused to cooperate with Schlebusch, it was only logical that he would be replaced. When Snyman left the board in 1979, J. C. W. van Rooyen stated retrospectively, "he told us, his colleagues, at a farewell dinner that he had not succeeded in his task of cleansing literature from its dirty-mouthed authors. A task, he said, Prime Minister John Vorster had given him when he was appointed as chair in 1975" (van Rooyen qtd. in Rickard). It seems quite plausible that Snyman would have said such a thing: van Rooyen always remained quite loyal to his former mentor (cf. van Rooyen *Censor's Tale* 57 et passim), to whom he even dedicated his first monograph on South African censorship (see van Rooyen, *Publikasiebeheer* iii). It appears equally likely that the staunchly conservative Vorster would have given such an assignment to his former colleague.[5] It might further be noted that Snyman's own analysis of his period in office was rather accurate: His attempt to curb the autonomy of the literary field on the basis of a conception of literature that, judging from van Rooyen's paraphrase, seemed quite coherent with the Platonic positions adopted by the Cronjé Commission, the majority in the AD trial of Smith's *Lion* and Justice van Wyk in the trial of Brink's *Kennis*, had indeed failed. Schlebusch had already begun to take legal measures by means of which a considerable degree of literary autonomy could be guaranteed, and he, Snyman, had not been reappointed.

When, in late 1979, van Rooyen took over as acting chairman,[6] he quickly began implementing new guidelines for publications control in general and the handling of literature in particular—apparently to the relief of Minister Schlebusch, who very much wanted the concept of the literary committee to work and the PAB to be "reasonable" (van Rooyen, *Censor's Tale* 59). With his new line of approach, van Rooyen was effectively continuing the tradition that had begun with the majority judgment in the CPD case of Smith's *Lion* and continued in the judgment on Themba's "The Fugitives," the dissenting opinions of Rumpff and Williamson in the AD case of *Lion*, the judgments of Diemont and Steyn in the Cape trial of Brink's *Kennis* and the Transvaal decision on Leroux's *Magersfontein*. Van Rooyen determinedly departed from the interventionism that had characterized Snyman's approach—and that of Cape Justice van Wyk and the majority of the Appellate Justices in the AD trial of *Lion* before Snyman's time. As van Rooyen himself put it in a 1982 statement in which he set forth the guidelines for publications control: "One who is in control of publications . . . cannot prescribe to the community. He can only assess what the community's or a section of the population's degree of tolerance is" (van Rooyen, "Guidelines" 28). It was quickly signaled within both the legal and the literary field that literature was being granted a considerably greater degree of autonomy under van Rooyen than it had been under Snyman (Marcus, Rev. of *Censorship* 210; Silver, "Banning" 485; Silver, "Publications Appeal Board" 273; Unterhalter 782), although some did not immediately recognize this (cf. e.g., Brink, "Censorship" 44ff; A. Coetzee qtd. in Marcus, "Reasonable Censorship?" 349; J. Coetzee 192 et passim; Gordimer, *Telling Times* 348ff). Let us proceed to examine the most notable features of the approach that the new Appeal Board took toward literature on the basis of a number of key decisions and separate statements of the principles guiding the new approach that were delivered throughout van Rooyen's tenure.

Immediately at the outset of his first five-year term, van Rooyen was given the opportunity to set some paradigmatic precedents and provide a clear signal that the system was in the process of being reformed. When it became clear that the tide was changing since the PAB had gotten a new chairman, the rate of appeals started to grow dramatically (van Rooyen, *Censor's Tale* 61),[7] as a result of which the board could set all the major parameters of its approach in a relatively short period of time. Most crucially, the board established a number of general guidelines that were to be applied when dealing with literature.

Literary Merit

Continuing along the lines of the precedent that had been set by his predecessor Snyman, van Rooyen declared that "literary merit" was to be considered a "mitigating factor" (van Rooyen, "Guidelines" 6). However, van Rooyen went further than his predecessor when it came to establishing the implications of this kind of merit being a "mitigating factor." He declared that when it came to this issue, the guiding principle was: "[t]he higher the literary merit of a book the less is the likelihood of its being found undesirable" (23). Indeed, in his 1987 monograph *Censorship in South Africa*, he wrote:

> The legislature has deemed it fit to give recognition to the minority rights of literature, art and drama; therefore, even if a member of the general public might arguably [*sic*] find the language in a work of literature with a limited likely readership offensive, and even if a substantial number of such readers might have similar objections the recognized literary or dramatic value of the work as a whole could save it from a finding of undesirability. (89–90)

As this quote demonstrates, the implications that van Rooyen's board attached to the factor "literary merit" effectively instituted a quite far-reaching institutional autonomy for literature.

The Likely Reader

On the basis of the judgment that had been delivered by the Transvaal Bench in the *Magersfontein* case and also on the basis of the judgments that Diemont and Steyn had delivered in the trial of Brink's *Kennis* (see van Rooyen, *Censorship* 50), van Rooyen introduced the concept of the likely reader as an instrument for the PAB. On the basis of a 1976 AD trial that had not involved any works of literature,[8] the board stated that the likely readership of a work was to be taken as "a mitigating or aggravating factor" (6, 23). The basic dichotomous scheme that underlay the board's concept of the likely reader—just as it had done in the other era in which the likely reader had played a crucial role in publications control, i.e., during the period 1963–1975—was that of a limited, sophisticated readership versus a wide, non-sophisticated readership. Literature was held to attract but a limited readership; one that, furthermore, consisted of sophisticated readers. This latter fact was vital, because the board postulated that the sophisticated reader would not be offended and incited as easily as the non-sophisticated reader (van Rooyen, "Guidelines" 8, 14, 23; cf. also Silver, *Guide* 64, 92). Indeed, the general principle regarding likely readership was also that "[t]he more sophisticated or intellectual the likely reader of a book is the less is the chance of its being found undesirable" (van Rooyen, "Guidelines" 23). Conversely, it was a guiding principle, especially where the religious and political clauses of the act were concerned (cf. 8, 10, 23), that "the more popular the material [wa]s the more likely it [wa]s to be undesirable"—hence the potential "aggravating" effect of likely readership (10). Van Rooyen employed the provision of the Publications Amendment Act of 1978 that made it possible to allow books to be distributed under certain conditions as a means of guaranteeing the literary socialized reader a considerable freedom of choice. For it held that the legislature's intention with this provision had been to "recognize [...] the interests of the likely reader" (van Rooyen, *Censorship* 9).

Literary Expertise

For establishing the degree of "literary merit" of a given work, interpreting the work and determining what kind(s) of person would make up its likely readership, the PAB, as a matter of principle, fell back on the opinions of literary experts, that is to say, on the advice that it was given by the literary committees of experts generally convened in cases concerning supposed literature. Indeed, in the 1979 appeal case concerning André Brink's novel *'n Droë Wit Seisoen* (Brink's own translation in English is titled *A Dry White Season*), the first literary case that the board handled under van Rooyen's guidance—he operated in the capacity of acting chairman at the time—the board stated that "[a]lthough the Appeal Board also has experts on this area, it, as a body, is more heterogeneously composed. If it gets to deal with a literary work, however, it realizes that this is a special field of knowledge and that the opinion of a committee of men of letters weighs heavily."[9] In the 1980 appeal case of *Magersfontein*, the board again expressly professed that following the case of *S v McBride*,[10] it "w[ould] not lightly reject the opinions of ... specialist witnesses" (PAB Case of *Magersfontein* [7/80] 7–8). In attaching such considerable weight to literary merit, likely readership and literary expert evidence—in fact, to theoretically underpinned literary analysis and exegesis (of alleged literary works)—(see PAB Case of *'n Droë Wit Seisoen/A Dry White Season* (81–82/79) 5; PAB Case of *Magersfontein* (7/80) 12), the board was in line with the precedent that had been set in the trial of Brink's *Kennis*. For, as we saw in chapter 3, all three judges in this trial had gone beyond the precedent that had been set in the *Lion* trial with regard to admissible evidence. In the latter trial it had been declared that literary expert evidence might only be allowed when it came to establishing "objective," "factual" evidence, not for establishing "subjective," "opinion" evidence (cf. *PCB v Heinemann* 147). In the *Kennis* trial, all three judges had for the first time employed literary expert evidence for establishing facts about the text itself, not just about the text's likely readership. Van Rooyen's board, in effect, followed this precedent. Yet its principal justification for doing so seemed to lay in the fact that the Publications Amendment Act of 1978 had made provisions to include committees of literary experts in the decision-making process. As van Rooyen stated in his *Censorship in South Africa*: "By introducing this advisory body the legislature has given recognition to the minority rights of literature, art and language" (9). That van Rooyen's PAB recognized expertise to be a quite indispensable instrument for guiding the board through "special field[s] of knowledge" was further underpinned by its 1983 ruling that in dealing with African/South African literature written by blacks, evidence given by black literary experts that were not on the ministerial list—apparently there were no black literary experts on the list at that time—might also be admitted (see PAB Case No. 79-81/83). The recognition of black literary expertise went hand in hand with the recognition of a conception of literature that was dominant among black literary actors in South Africa, as we will see below. Evidently, the general recognition of the presence of a homology between the literary field and the political field now also pertained to blacks.

The Contextual Approach

On the basis of both Ogilvie Thompson's judgment delivered in the 1972 case of *PCB* v *Republican Publications* and Rumpff's dissenting opinion in the AD trial of Smith's *Lion* (see van Rooyen, *Censorship* 49; van Rooyen "Guidelines" 22–23), van Rooyen declared that a contextual approach had to be applied. In a 1982 statement in which he set forth the guidelines for publication control, he wrote that "[p]arts m[ight] not be judged in isolation"; "if [and only if] a part or parts are so scandalous as to taint the whole book . . . the part or the parts [should] be regarded as sufficient for a finding of undesirability" (22; cf. also 28). Although the contextual approach was to be applied for adjudicating publications in general, it was apparently "especially applicable in the case of a novel where the parts must be read in the light of the whole" (van Rooyen, "1963–1988" 344; van Rooyen, *Censorship* 49, 89).

Tolerance

On the basis of *inter alia* Bok's judgment in the 1932 case of *R* v *Meinert*, the dissenting opinions of Rumpff and Williamson in the AD trial of Smith's *Lion* and the opinion of Ogilvie Thompson in the *PCB* v *Republican* case, the board came to attribute "strong meanings" to basically all concepts of the act that underlay the adjudicatory tests to be applied in order to determine whether a publication contravened any of the act's moral, religious, or political provisions—e.g., the concepts of offensiveness, ridiculing, and bringing into contempt (see van Rooyen, *Censorship* 54, 100; van Rooyen, "Guidelines" 8, 9, 10, 25, 26, 27, 28, 29). In doing so, the board ensured that a "generous" interpretation would always be given to a text or parts of it (cf. van Rooyen, "1963–1988" 344). Indeed, the board emphatically professed that its basic philosophy was that "matter should be prohibited only when it [wa]s 'absolutely necessary' to do so" (van Rooyen, "Guidelines" 26). This last aspect of its policy was applicable to all publications and objects that would be placed before the board; not just, or "especially" to works of literature.

On the basis of these guidelines a considerable series of domestically and foreign produced works deemed to be of "literary merit" were unbanned by the PAB in the course of the 1980s. However, when it came to applying the act's three categories of provisions—moral, political, and religious—the board did not grant literature an equal amount of freedom. It appears, indeed, that the board held that the law, as it stood in the 1980s, granted literature the greatest degree of autonomy in the moral and political spheres. Conversely, van Rooyen's board felt that it had to be more restrictive when it came to religion. Let us examine how it dealt with literature in terms of the separate categories.

Literature vis-à-vis the Act's Moral Provisions

It is somewhat ironical that one of the areas in which the PAB seemed to be granting literature the greatest degree of autonomy was in the moral terrain, since of the three kinds of issues that apartheid censorship addressed, the moral kind seems to have been the most important one in the initial period of its existence (cf. van Rooyen, "1963–1988" 348). Indeed, as we saw in chapter 2, cultural expressions regarded to be obscene seemed to have formed the very reason why, in the 1950s, the first apartheid government—that of Prime Minister Malan—started to design a new censorship law in the first place. In the 1980s, however, the PAB felt that literature could be granted considerably more space than previously when it came to moral issues, and so the board deemed it justified to unban a whole series of works that in the past had been considered morally offensive. For instance, it lifted the ban on Leroux's *Magersfontein* (see PAB Case No. 7/80), Brink's *Kennis* (see PAB Case No. 131/81), D. H. Lawrence's *Lady Chatterley's Lover* (see PAB Cases No. 62/80 and No. 100/81), John Cleland's *Memoirs of a Woman of Pleasure* (also known as: "*Fanny Hill*"; see PAB Cases No. 149/83 and No. 207/85), and Philip Roth's *Portnoy's Complaint* (see PAB Case No. 199/83).[11] In order to put these unbannings, and the "tolerance" of the board, into relief, one should note, however, that the board did find it justified to uphold the ban on William Styron's *Sophie's Choice* and Alberto Moravia's *Time of Desecration*, even though it recognized, on the basis of the opinion of the committee of experts convened in these cases, that both were works of considerable literary merit (see PAB Cases No. 105/79 and 100/80). Notwithstanding, it should be acknowledged that these decisions were made very early in van Rooyen's tenure, and that the degree of autonomy that, according to the PAB, literature could be allowed in terms of section 47 (2) of the PA—the section containing the moral, religious, and political provisions—gradually increased in the 1980s: this is *inter alia* evidenced by the fact that some literary works were only released after a second appeal to the PAB.[12]

Literature vis-à-vis the Act's Religious Provisions

When it came to religious issues, it appears that the board held that the amount of literary autonomy allowed by the law was smaller than regarding moral matters.[13] Yet, here too, "tolerance" was the key word (cf. van Rooyen, "Guidelines" 7, 8, 23). And so the board deemed it justified to unban Leroux's *Magersfontein* and Brink's *Kennis*—although the latter only in the second instance[14] and with restrictions regarding distribution and age, so as to try and keep the book, *inter alia*, out of children's hands (see PAB Case No. 131/81 19–20). The board also saw fit to unban the novel that had formed the central focus of that other very controversial case of the 1970s: John Miles's *Donderdag of Woensdag* (see PAB Case No. 27/83). Yet when it came to religion, the amount of "tolerance" that could legally be justified in the board's view had its limits: a Publications Committee's decision that Anthony Burgess's *Man of Nazareth* was offensive to religious convictions or feelings and, therefore, undesirable was upheld by the PAB on two occasions: once in 1979 and once in 1984, at a time when the "tolerance" of the PAB seemed to have reached a high point that would not be surpassed in the remaining years of van Rooyen's tenure (see PAB Cases No. 72/79 and No. 128/84). Indeed, it held the book to be of such an undesirable nature that it did not want to release it under age and/or distributional conditions, as it had done with Brink's *Kennis*, for instance. As in the Styron and Moravia cases, the two decisions that Burgess's novel was undesirable were reached even though the PAB acknowledged that the work in question had considerable literary merit. Thus, although van Rooyen's PAB had substantially increased the institutional autonomy of literature through its guidelines, this guarantee had its limits.

Religion seemed to remain a somewhat tricky field both for literary actors and institutions and for the PAB, which clearly attempted to demonstrate that since van Rooyen had taken office, an era of "reasonable" censorship had begun (cf. van Rooyen, "Guidelines" 1). Indeed, as late as 1988, van Rooyen, in his capacity as chairman of the PAB, could still be found to be making the following statement: "We do find . . . that religious sensitivities are very acute, and this is an area where we make our way very carefully" (van Rooyen, "1963–1988" 343). It should be noted though, that van Rooyen might have been thinking first and foremost of films and other mass media when making this remark (cf. 343), not so much of literature. The fact of the matter is that no cases involving literary works found to be undesirable in terms of the religious section 47 (2) (*b*) appear to have been brought before the PAB after the Burgess novel. One can thus not tell at what point the board's scales would have tipped in favor of religion during van Rooyen's second term in office. Yet one might wonder how, in terms of the PA, the board would have judged a work like James Kirkup's poem "The Love that

Dares to Speak its Name,"[15] or, indeed, Salman Rushdie's *The Satanic Verses*, a work that was effectively banned by a Publications Committee in 1988, but that was never brought before the PAB (van Rooyen *Censor's Tale* 94).[16]

Literature vis-a-vis the Act's Political Provisions

As far as the political provisions of the act were concerned, and section 47 (2) (*e*) dealing with state security, in particular, the board seemed to gradually come to grant literature a degree of autonomy comparable to the degree it came to award the medium vis-à-vis the moral provisions of the law. In applying the political sections 47 (2) (*c*) to (*e*) of the act, "toleration" was, once more, the main slogan. Indeed, the board employed "strong" tests when applying any of the three political sections. Among other things, it adopted a "real danger" test for assessing works in terms of section 47 (2) (*e*) (van Rooyen, "1963–1988" 346), inspired by the American "clear and present danger" doctrine, which with its main aim of protecting the First Amendment creates a vast space for freedom of speech, primarily in the political sphere.[17] On the other hand, however, the board was not always as "tolerant" as it professed when it came to publications that, in its view, were of a communist, or other revolutionary nature, particularly in the early 1980s (cf. PAB Case of *Two Thousand Seasons* [24/80]; PAB Case of *Fire Flames* [2/81]). In this respect the board was quite in line with the Botha administration's vehemently anti-communist notion of the "total onslaught" and, in a wider context, with the logic of the Cold War, in the first years of van Rooyen's tenure.

For instance, it decided to uphold the ban on Ayi Kwei Armah's *Two Thousand Seasons*, even though the Directorate of Publications motivated its appeal against the Publications Committee's decision that the novel was undesirable by stating, among other things, that Armah's novel "ha[d] literary value" and formed "an important contribution to Black Africa by a well-known black writer" (PAB Case No. 24/80 2). The PAB also upheld the ban on Oswald Mtshali's volume of poems *Fireflames* (1980) despite its recognition that Mtshali was a "renowned black poet" (PAB Case No. 2/81 1) and that the work in question had been favorably received by, for instance, Es'kia Mphahlele, who at the time was the foremost black critic in South Africa (McDonald, *Literature Police* 81). A remarkable aspect of the board's decision was that it here considered literariness, i.e., poeticality, as an aggravating factor, in apparent contrast to its literary-protective approach: it stated that "it also had to be kept in mind that the black languages are particularly rich in imagery, that poetry as a consequence hereof has special resonance with the black man and that he will be incited more easily thereby than by prose."[18] One might indeed hear an echo in this racialized poetological—and institutional—position of the remarks that Justice Bok made in Meinert's case about "immature, uneducated and uncivilised persons" and Earl Buxton's observation that the Bantu peoples of Africa represented the "child races" of the Empire—observations which we encountered in chapter 1.

Yet, as indicated above, the general degree of autonomy that literature could be granted vis-à-vis the law according to van Rooyen's PAB increased as the decade advanced. When it came to the application of the political provisions of the law this was also due to the fact that the guidelines regarding the application of the political stipulations were adapted rather significantly during van Rooyen's first term (cf., e.g., PAB Case 79-81/83 8; PAB Case No. 100/85 2). The banning of the works by Armah and Mtshali thus seemed to have been the (early) exception to the otherwise indeed fairly freedom-oriented, or rather: *artistic* freedom-oriented, approach of van Rooyen's Board (cf. van Rooyen, *Censorship* 16). In the majority of cases the usual mitigating factors—literary merit, likely readership, context, "strong" tests—were applied to guarantee the autonomous space for literature that the law—both statutory and case law—had created in the board's view. And, indeed, when in 1984 Armah's novel was brought before the PAB for a second time, it was no longer considered to be undesirable; this mainly because the new guidelines had at that point been applied during the adjudication (see PAB Case No. 79-81/83).

These new guidelines had a markedly poetological dimension. Indeed, at some point during the early eighties, the PAB started to expressly legitimize what it termed "protest literature," whenever it came to judge literature in terms of the political sections of the act. With this notion, van Rooyen's Board seemed to be signifying works that were sharply critical of the government and/or sympathetic to black liberation movements and/or communism (Silver, *Guide* 69, 199ff; cf. also van Rooyen, *Censorship* 16, 115). Although the board's (semi-)legal legitimization of pragmatic literature (*sensu* Abrams) cohered with Justice Steyn's defense of "engaged" literature in the trial of Brink's *Kennis*, van Rooyen's board appeared not to have based this new aspect of its approach on Steyn's opinion. Apparently, it developed the notion on its own authority. The philosophy behind the notion was that "it [wa]s often in the interests of state security to permit the expression of pent-up feelings and grievances" (van Rooyen, *Censorship* 16); in the board's view, "protest literature" could represent a "useful safety-valve" for such "feelings and grievances" (van Rooyen, *Censorship* 115), or "a means of communication with the authorities" (van Rooyen, "1963–1988" 346). Yet while the board might have introduced the notion on the basis of these considerations regarding state security, the introduction in effect had another result on a quite different level: by legally legitimizing the kind of pragmatic literature the notion was referencing—a legitimation which in effect consolidated Steyn's earlier standpoint on "engaged" literature—and by legally sanctioning the poetological legitimations of such literature by (black) literary experts, the board further expanded the degree of literary autonomy vis-à-vis the law that had already been established. Now it not only recognized the autonomist conception of literature that had been dominant within Afrikaans literary circles and that, furthermore, had always formed the foremost poetological fundament for judging literature within the different levels of the censorship bureaucracy, PAB included (cf. McDonald, *Literature Police* 38ff), but also recognized the pragmatic poetics that was adhered to by another part of the literary field, namely, first and foremost, by black literary actors.

By referring both to its general outline regarding literature and its specific guidelines regarding the political stipulations of the act, the PAB started to unban works that had previously and newly been banned on the basis of the political provisions of the act right from the point when van Rooyen took over as chairman. It continued doing so throughout the 1980s—although in the second half of the decade, the number of appeals against works banned under the political sections of the act started to decrease. Thus, it unbanned, for instance, Nadine Gordimer's *Burger's Daughter* (see PAB Case No. 64/79), André Brink's *'n Droë Wit Seisoen/A Dry White Season* (see PAB Case No. 81-82/79), Mothobi Mutloatse's *Forced Landing* (see PAB Case No. 45/80), Wessel Ebersohn's *Store Up the Anger* (see PAB Case No. 101/80) and his *Divide the Night* (see PAB Case No. 60/81), various issues of the literary magazine *Staffrider* (see PAB Cases No. 70/80, No. 122/80 and No. 206/83), Harry Bloom's novel *Transvaal Episode* (see PAB Case No. 49/82), and a whole series of other works of literature.

THE REGULATION OF LITERATURE IN TRANSITIONAL SOUTH AFRICA, 1990–1994

In 1990, van Rooyen's second term came to an end. He was not reappointed for a third term. According to McDonald this was due to government concerns that reappointing van Rooyen, who was known among more reactionary Afrikaners to be an overly liberal reformer, might effectuate a decrease in support from this part of the electorate (*Literature Police* 82). Thus, for the remainder of the time that the PA was in force, the period 1990–1996, the PAB was led by two other chairmen, namely Louis Pienaar, an advocate (1990–1992) and Dan Morkel, a professor of law (1992–1996). Coetzee remained Director of Publications until 1996, the year in which the act that replaced the PA, the Films and Publications Act, 1996, came into force.

As of 1990, when far-reaching political change started to occur—witnessing, among other things, the unbanning of the ANC and other clandestine political parties as well as Mandela's release from prison—Coetzee started an active campaign of releasing previously prohibited works. Coetzee's effort led to over four thousand works being unbanned (McDonald, *Literature Police* 82; Westra 11). While this fact already appears to indicate that the policies regarding publications in general, or literature in particular did not really change under the respective chairmanships of Pienaar and Morkel, there do not seem to be other indications that they did either.[19]

It seems as if the PAB only once had to deal with a literary case during the period 1990–1994, namely, for the third time since 1979 with Anthony Burgess's *Man of Nazareth*. The decision that the board, at this point already chaired by Morkel, came to was essentially the same as previous ones. It held that the book was "of considerable [literary] merit" (PAB Case No. 35/92 6). This assessment was informed, among other things, by the report that the literary committee of experts had drawn up in the first PAB case regarding the book. Yet, because of its theme, and despite its literariness, the board declared, its likely readership would not be limited (to literary socialized readers) but "wide," further declaring that this "wide" readership would consist of "[m]any devout Christians" (7). As the latter part of the novel's likely readership would be "shocked and offended" (7) by certain passages in the book that referred "to the sexuality of Christ" (6), the book had to be considered undesirable within the meaning of section 47 (2) (*b*). The only real difference between the previous two decisions of van Rooyen's Board and the decision of Morkel's PAB—and herein the latter board proved itself to be slightly more autonomy-oriented than even van Rooyen's board—was that the new decision allowed "bona fide" libraries (excluding school libraries) to keep copies of Burgess's work and lend it out (7–8). Morkel's PAB thus decided against prolonging the "total" ban on the book that had been in force during the van Rooyen era. However, this modest exemption notwithstanding, the board's decision goes some way toward demonstrating that the institutional autonomy of the literary field was still weakest when it came to religious matters in early 1990s South Africa. Observations made by others regarding the sensitivity of religious issues in South Africa at this time seem to confirm this (see van Rooyen, "Dignity"; van Rooyen, "Does" 1127, 1132; *Report of the Task Group* 71; Westra viii, 75).

Indeed, when negotiations began in the early 1990s regarding the future of publication, film, and theater regulation in a Bill of Rights society, religion was among the central issues. Yet there were of course many more issues brought to the fore by parties that had a stake in the discussions—some of the most prominent of which were the government, the South African Law Commission, the ANC's Department of Arts and Culture (DAC), the National Arts Initiative (NAI), and the South African Institute for Librarianship and Information Science (SAILIS). While there was a consensus among these organizations about the need to guarantee freedom of expression, a vexing problem was the question as to what limitations should be placed on this right. Other major questions were whether there should be a statutory body for regulation, or whether there should rather be self-regulation; in which areas control should be maintained (in the moral sphere? the religious sphere? the political sphere?); and, if any administrative regulation should remain, what should fall under this kind of control, and what under the jurisdiction of (criminal) courts. Recurring themes in the negotiations were, among others, the already mentioned theme of religious sensitivities, as well as hate speech, pornography, the protection of children, free choice for adults, incitement to violence, problems of racial friction, the right to equality, to dignity, and so on. A central question was also that of artistic freedom, or the institutional autonomy of the arts.

THE REGULATION OF LITERATURE IN DEMOCRATIC SOUTH AFRICA, 1994–2010

Legal Developments

There were several legal developments in 1994 that were of great relevance to the regulation of publications in general, and literature, specifically. First of all the amendments to the PA as brought about by the Abolition of Restrictions on Free Political Activity Act 206 of 1993 came into effect (cf. Westra viii). These amendments were quite substantial: the act completely repealed the political sections 47 (2) (*c*) and (*d*) of the PA (see Abolition of Restrictions on Free Political Activity Act, 1993). These sections had provided that any publication should be deemed undesirable if it, or any part of it, "[brought] any section of the inhabitants of the Republic into ridicule or contempt" (47 (2) (*c*)) or "[was] harmful to the relations between any sections of the inhabitants of the Republic" (47 (2) (*d*)). The only political provision that was maintained was the one stipulating that any publication should be deemed undesirable if it, or any part of it, "[was] prejudicial to the safety of the State, the general welfare or the peace and good order" (47 (2) (*e*)). Apparently, the reason for the repeal was that the government of F. W. de Klerk felt that provisions 47 (2) (*c*) and (*d*) might have hindered the political debates that were so vital in the transitional phase that South Africa was in (cf. van der Poll 219–20). In terms of our investigation, the repeal not only meant greater freedom of political expression, but also greater institutional autonomy for literature vis-à-vis the law.

Secondly, on the same day as the first ever non-racial democratic elections in South Africa, i.e., on April 27, 1994, the Interim Constitution, which had been adopted in 1993 (see Constitution of the Republic of South Africa, Act 200 of 1993), came into effect. Most importantly, for the regulation of literature, this Constitution provided in section 15 (1) of Chapter III, which was titled "Fundamental Rights," that "[e]very person shall have the right to freedom of speech and expression, which shall include freedom of the press and other media, and the freedom of artistic creativity and scientific research" (Constitution of the Republic of South Africa, 1993). As of April 27, 1994, a constitutional *exceptio artis* pertaining *inter alia* to literature, comparable to that of the German constitution thus came into effect. None of the freedoms mentioned in section 15 (1) of Chapter III amounted to an absolute freedom: they were kept in check by section 33 (1) of the same Chapter, which stipulated the limitations that might be placed on every right formulated in the Chapter. In this sense also, the South African constitutional *exceptio artis* resembled the German one (cf. Grüttemeier, "Law" 188–89).

Third and lastly, the newly appointed Minister of Home Affairs, Mangosuthu Buthelezi, appointed a Task Group on Film and Publication Control in August 1994 to draw up a report about the constitutional validity of the PA. Quite in line with the pragmatic and reconciliatory politics that was so characteristic of the Mandela administration, Kobus van Rooyen was appointed chairman of the Task Group. Braam Coetzee, the director of publications from 1980 to 1996, was also selected to join the group. The Task Group published its report on December 1, 1994. On the basis of, *inter alia*, section 15 of Chapter III of the Interim Constitution, which it had taken as its point of departure, it concluded that the PA was no longer valid (cf. *Report of the Task Group* 1: 2, 11–12). Importantly, the Task Group concluded, among other things, that the act "[did] not place sufficient emphasis on the freedoms of artistic expression and of scientific research which are guaranteed by the Constitution" (*Report of the Task Group* 1: 11–12). As the Task Group held that the act was flawed to such a degree that statutory amendments could not salvage it, it decided to draw up an entirely new bill. This new bill would instigate a control structure based on classification of material and demarcation of age restrictions, the fundamental philosophy behind it being that since "South Africa has moved into a new, free democratic order . . . it would be in conflict with the spirit of this order unreasonably to limit artistic expression and freedom of choice. The emphasis should, as far as possible, be on regulation and management of the problem, and not on prohibition" (*Report of the Task Group* 1: 15–16). The group felt that only the prevention of "clearly perceived harm" would justify placing limitations on the rights that the Constitution meant to protect (1: 15–16). Thus, whereas the Bill would be aimed at promoting "the optimum amount of freedom for adults," it would at the same time be directed at protecting children against "what is harmful and disturbing" (1: 23). In this sense, the bill would be aimed at continuing a tradition that had begun as early as 1932 with Bok's judgment in the case of *Rex* v *Meinert*.

The bill that the Task Group drafted provided for the creation of an infrastructure that greatly resembled the one that had been created through the PA. It stipulated that a Film and Publication Board[20] and a Film and

Publication Review Board[21] be established—indeed, basically the equivalents of, respectively, the old DOP and PAB—and, furthermore, that there should be a possibility to appeal to the Supreme Court against decisions of the Review Board (cf. *Report of the Task Group* 2: 2–3). As had been the case during the period 1963–1975, the highest arbiter would thus again be the judiciary. Despite the similarities between the envisioned new bureaucracy and the old one, there were also some significant differences between the two: the new bodies would be far more representative of South Africa's multiracial and multicultural population; the functions that the respective bodies were to have would change in some important ways; and the new bureaucracy could only be set in motion through complaints from the public—the old one also started working as soon as it was given a notice from customs or police.

As had been the case under the old act, the FPB was to convene committees that were to classify publications and so on and, when necessary, impose age restrictions—both of which could either be accepted by the FPB or appealed against to the FPRB. Four distinct classifications were to apply to publications: XX, X18, R18, and F18. The first two would be the most restrictive. The classification XX would amount to an absolute ban (cf. van der Poll 219). X18 would limit distribution to persons of eighteen years or older. XX classifications would be reserved for publications that contained visual representations of extreme forms of pornography, notably child pornography, and "extreme violence likely to create a substantial risk of such violence" (*Report of the Task Group* 2: 16), or that, "judged as a whole, promote[d] hatred against the religious convictions of a section of the Republic" (2: 25). X18 classifications should be given to publications that, "judged as a whole," "predominantly and explicitly" described extreme pornography, or "extreme violence likely to create a substantial risk of such violence," or contained visual presentations of non-extreme pornography (2: 17).

In quite principled fashion, the Task Group advanced in its report, and stipulated in its bill, that the classifications XX and X18 should not apply to works of art and science, however (see *Report of the Task Group* 2: 10, 20, 25). Indeed, in its view, an absolute art exemption should be introduced into the new law: "We have come to the conclusion," the Task Group wrote in its report,

> that there is no compelling and substantial government interest in denying absolute protection to art and science in so far as adults are concerned. Artistic expression is, like political speech, central to the cultural and political vitality of a democratic society. Although "art" is an elusive concept, we believe that once the Board, or Review Board, having heard expert evidence, is convinced that a publication or film amounts to art or literature, it should find in its favour despite its content....

> Canada, Great Britain, the USA and Germany all exempt the arts from control. Whilst the rather enticing proposition is to regard art only as a factor to be weighed against other factors, we have come to the conclusion that if the preponderance of expert opinion classifies a film or a publication as *bona fide* art or literature, any measure taken by the State to limit its distribution or display to adults would be disproportionate to the slight, if any, possibility of harm. (80–81)

The only restrictions that should be allowed to be imposed, the Task Group stated, were restrictions on sale and display so as to protect children (81). The group's proposed absolute exemption was, however, only to be granted on the level of the envisioned new act; in terms of the Constitution, the exemption could never be absolute, as on that level the right to artistic freedom would always have to be weighed against other fundamental rights. The fact that in the group's proposed dispensation the institutional autonomy of literature could only be limited on the level of the Constitution, i.e., by other constitutional rights, again recalls the German constitution, where this is also the case (cf. Grüttemeier, "Law" 188–89).

Expanding on the statement quoted above, the Task Group emphasized that the term "bona fide" should not be understood "to be based on the purpose of the writer from his or her point of view" (81). It was not the task of the adjudicators to try and determine whether it had been the purpose of the author to write a work of literature. On the contrary, the Task Group declared that in dealing with an alleged literary work, "[o]bjective appraisal by experts should be the test and the publication or film itself should be the object of appraisal" (81). It added to this that "[i]t would obviously not be wrong to allow the artist or author a voice, but his views should be borne out objectively by the work" (81). In this sense, too, the envisioned new act would be aimed at continuing a long tradition in the legal regulation of literature within the nation.

In its draft bill, the Task Group made sure to devote a separate section to "Art and Science Exemption for Publications" (*Report of the Task Group* 2: 20). In this section, it emphatically stated that a contextual approach was to be applied, thereby ruling out the isolated-passage criterion:

> The XX or X18 classification shall not apply to a bona fide technical, professional, educational, scientific, documentary, literary or artistic publication or any part of a publication which, judged within the context of the publication, is of such nature. (*Report of Task Group* 2: 20)

As seen above, the Task Group also made sure to provide for the adoption of a contextual approach in the sections that pertained to XX and X18 classifications. The incorporation of the contextual approach into the bill represented yet another means through which continuity could be guaranteed.

In sum, the bill that the Task Group had drawn up would for a large part ensure continuity in the regulation of literature within the nation. However, through its guarantee of absolute protection for art it also went a decisive step further than the law had previously done. Yet of course this latter step had been prompted by—and could be legitimized by referring to—the constitutional *exceptio artis* that had been established in 1994. In 1996, some two years after the Task Group had published its report, the group's bill was accepted by Parliament without any substantial amendment having been made to it, thus becoming the Films and Publications Act, 1996[22] (cf. van Rooyen, "Dignity"). It came into effect on November 8, 1996.

Some nine months earlier, on February 4, 1996, to be exact, the Constitution of the Republic of South Africa, which replaced the Interim Constitution, had also come into effect. Two sections of this final Constitution are of particular importance for the regulation of literature: section 16 and section 36 of Chapter 2, i.e., the Chapter containing the Bill of Rights. Section 16, which is titled "Freedom of expression," reads as follows:

1. Everyone has the right to freedom of expression, which includes—

    a. freedom of the press and other media;
    b. freedom to receive or impart information or ideas;
    c. freedom of artistic creativity; and
    d. academic freedom and freedom of scientific research.

2. The right in subsection (1) does not extend to—

    a. propaganda for war;
    b. incitement of imminent violence; or
    c. advocacy of hatred that is based on race, ethnicity, gender or religion, and that constitutes incitement to cause harm. (Constitution of the Republic of South Africa, 1996)

Whereas section 16 (2) already limits the institutional autonomy of the arts, the Constitution provides for another possibility to curtail it, namely through its section 36, the so-called limitation clause.[23] This section provides that the freedom of artistic creativity and all other rights mentioned in the Bill of Rights may be limited, provided that this is done only "to the extent that the limitation is reasonable and justifiable in an open and democratic society based on human dignity, equality and freedom" (Constitution of the Republic of South Africa, 1996), and by taking into account certain other specific conditions. The institutional autonomy of literature thus remains but a relative one in the new constitutional dispensation—as seems to be the case in every legal system that provides for an *exceptio artis*.

The Case of Salman Rushdie's *The Satanic Verses*

Since the definitive Constitution and the FPA have become operational, only one literary case seems to have been put before the FPB (cf. McDonald, *Literature Police* 349; van Rooyen, *Censor's Tale* 95), namely that of Salman Rushdie's *The Satanic Verses*. The decision reached in this case is a very interesting one though, especially concerning its institutional dimension. Moreover, despite the fact that the final decision in this case was given on the administrative level, namely that of the FPB and not on the quasi-judicial level of the FPRB or the proper judicial level of the Supreme Court, an appeal was never made against the decision, which makes the decision appear quite valid, legally speaking. In a recent analysis of the decision, J. C. W. van Rooyen, who not only has three decades of experience as a law professor and more than three decades of experience with the (semi-)legal control of publications and other media in South Africa,[24] but who also was one of the principal architects of the new act, called the decision "a wise one, given the strong feelings of Muslims against the book" (*Censor's Tale* 96). Let us therefore proceed to examine the case.

In January 2002, the FPB published a notice indicating that Rushdie's novel was no longer banned—it had been banned by a Publication Committee in 1988. In response to this notice, the board received a large number of complaints, mainly from members of the Muslim community, the substance of which apparently was that *The Satanic Verses* was "blasphemous, an insult to Islamic integrity and dignity and a denigration of the character of the Prophet Mohammed" (FPB Decision on Salman Rushdie's *The Satanic Verses* qtd. in van Rooyen, *Censor's Tale* 170). The complainants all expressed the wish that the ban on the novel be reinstated.

The FPB appointed a committee to consider the case. Among the adjudicators were a number of literary experts.[25] The FPB fully accepted the conclusions that the committee came to (351). In the FPB's decision, it was stated that the FPA's stipulations dealing with hate speech based on religion were not applicable in this case, because "*The Satanic Verses* is without argument a bona fide literary work by a leading international literary figure," and, moreover, "it does not in fact advocate hatred against Islam or indeed against any other religion or faith system" (FPB Decision on Salman Rushdie's *The Satanic Verses* qtd. in van Rooyen, *Censor's Tale* 172).

The board did, however, decide to apply an X18 classification, because it could not "ignore religious sensibilities and the sense of profound outrage and hurt which the majority of Muslims feel towards this novel" (172). It stated that it was "aware of the fourteen-year history of Islamic opposition towards *The Satanic Verses*" and that it was "sympathetic to the representations which were received from distinguished Islamic groups in South Africa, as well as from very many individual members of the Muslim community" (172). Moreover, it declared that since in its estimation, X18 would "not satisfy the concerns of the complainants" (171), it had decided

> in accordance with section 36 of the Constitution which allows for "limitations to freedom of expression," [to] modify the "X18" restrictions as follows: *The Satanic Verses* is restricted from all forms of commercial public distribution in retail outlets, except to the libraries of all bona fide universities, technical colleges or other tertiary institutions, and to all South African legal deposit libraries. (172–73)

The novel should be available at these institutions, the FPB added, "to any scholars and members of the public of any age, who wish to read it" (173). There would be no restrictions on personal possession or personal importation of the novel, whether in person or by means of postal delivery, the board further added, nor would there be on commercial importation of copies for sale or distribution to the mentioned libraries.

Summing up the crux of the decision, the board stated that "[t]he decision given here is an attempt to satisfy the theological and religious concerns of the South African Muslim community while allowing for the crucial principle of right of access and freedom of expression within a controlled context" (173).

Unfortunately, considering the purposes of this study, the question whether the FPAB or the Supreme Court would have held the judgment of the Committee/FPB to be legally valid remains open, because it was not contested by any party. With the decision being upheld in this way, a broad ban on the distribution of Rushdie's novel also remains intact in democratic South Africa.[26] Thus, while it appeared that a far-reaching freedom of artistic activity had been promulgated through the Constitution and the FPA, practice seems to reveal that the institutional autonomy of literature is still liable to limitation, especially when it comes to religious issues.

Recent Legal Developments

There is further issue that may lead to a limiting of the institutional autonomy of the medium. For the Films and Publications Amendment Act, 2009 reversed literature's exemption from the FPA's provisions aimed at combating child pornography (cf. van Rooyen, *Censor's Tale* 175). The exemption clauses of the act concerning literature now read: "unless, judged within context, the publication is, *except with respect to child pornography*, a *bona fide* documentary or is a publication of scientific, literary or artistic merit or is on a matter of public interest" (Films and Publications Amendment Act, 2009 20; my emphasis).

It is clear that fighting child pornography represents one of the highest priorities in post-apartheid film and publication regulation. Since coming into effect in 1996, the act has already been amended three times in order to more effectively combat this form of pornography (see Films and Publications Amendment Act, 1999; Films and Publications Amendment Act, 2004; and Films and Publications Amendment Act, 2009). Yet whereas the first two amendment acts seemed mainly aimed at altering the infrastructure established by the FPA, the third amendment act brought a clear change to the superstructure that the act represents too. This latter aspect of the 2009 amendments did not go unnoticed in South Africa: a recent report of the FPB observes that the Films and Publications Amendment Bill No. 27 of 2006, which was first introduced by the Department of Home Affairs in 2006 and subsequently signed into law by President Jacob Zuma on August 28, 2009, "created uproar and contestation within the media industry which viewed it as a hindrance to the freedom of expression" (*Appeals Tribunal Decisions 1998–2008*, 119).

Necessarily, the 2009 Amendment Act had an impact on the institutional autonomy of literature. For whereas literature had previously enjoyed absolute exemption on the level of the FPA and was only limited on the level of the Constitution, the 2009 amendments introduced limitations on the level of the act as well. The question remains to what extent the new statutory state of affairs would affect literature's autonomy vis-à-vis the law in practice. One might indeed wonder how the Film and Publication Board, the Film and Publication Appeals Board,[27] or the Supreme Court would deal with a novel accused of representing child pornography. The question is to what extent these tribunals would confirm van Rooyen's observation, made a year before the last amendments were issued, that in the new South Africa, "art is protected where it is overwhelmingly present even in offensive forms" (van Rooyen, "Law Faculty"). Yet considering, firstly, the century-long tradition of the legal treatment of literature in South Africa, a tradition that slowly but steadily—albeit with temporary setbacks—progressed toward the *exceptio artis* which was established in 1994 by the Interim Constitution and consolidated two years later by the final Constitution and the FPA; and considering, secondly, the way in which the FPB dealt with Rushdie's *Satanic Verses*, it is highly unlikely that the autonomy of literature vis-à-vis the law would be curbed so much as to make possible a total ("XX") ban on a work labeled "objectively"—that is, by literary experts—a work of literature. It is improbable that the administrative or judicial bodies entrusted with the task of regulating literature would go further than to impose certain restrictions on the distribution of a work of literature, just as the FPB did in the Rushdie case. Therefore, it appears that McDonald is not entirely correct when he observes in the conclusion to his *Literature Police* that "there can be no guarantees that South Africa's democratic literary guardians will always succeed where their repressive predecessors repeatedly failed," and that although "there are good grounds for being confident about the future of literature in a democratic South Africa," the fact that "it is impossible to predict who the literary will strike next, or where its historic association with the 'daring experiment' of free speech will lead" means that "it will always pay to remain, following the now familiar adjuration, 'eternally vigilant' as well" (353).[28] In fact, when surveying a century-long history of legal treatment of literature in South Africa and especially the latter half thereof, McDonald's observations appear unduly anxious. The recognition of a relative institutional autonomy of literature has simply become too firmly rooted in South African law over the past fifty years for any graver sanctions than a limitation of distributional rights to be imposed on a work of literature. Besides, existing research suggests that once an *exceptio artis* is established in a parliamentary democracy, it will not easily disappear from the legal—let alone constitutional—stage: it is far too robust for such a thing to happen (cf. Grüttemeier, "Law" 186–89, 191–92).

CONCLUSION

With van Rooyen taking over from Snyman, first as deputy chairman of the PAB in 1979 and then in 1980 as chairman, the board started to consistently emulate the approach towards literature taken by the Supreme Court during the period 1965–1978. In fact, van Rooyen legitimized the line of approach that he came to implement by explicitly referring to the precedents set by the Supreme Court during this period. Thus, van Rooyen's board came to guarantee a fairly high degree of institutional autonomy for literature through the instruments of the contextual approach, the concept of the likely reader and a fundamental tolerance regarding the written word. Also coherent with the approach of the Supreme Court, but grounded in van Rooyen's own interpretation of the Publications Amendment Act of 1978, was the board's consistent recognition of literary expertise. Moreover, again on the basis of van Rooyen's interpretation of the latter Amendment Act, the board increased the degree of autonomy that had been granted to the literary field during the period 1963–1975—the period before the Vorster Cabinet and Snyman's rollback efforts—through its particular application of the adjudicating factor of literariness. The board further expanded the institutional autonomy of literature by consolidating the recognition that Justice Steyn had given to pragmatic literature (*sensu* Abrams) in the trial of Brink's *Kennis*. For it not only extended the (semi-)legal recognition that the autonomist-pragmatic conception of literature of the disciples of van Wyk Louw had long since enjoyed, but, on the basis of its own concept of protest literature, it also gave recognition to the pragmatic conception of literature that was dominant among black literary actors. In effect, the van Rooyen's approach, with its crucial explanation of the concept of literariness, amounted to the establishment of a quite far-reaching institutional autonomy—one might indeed say *exceptio artis*—for literature. Van Rooyen legitimized his autonomy-oriented approach by referring first and foremost to the amendments made to the Publications Act in 1978: as he declared, these amendments had been aimed at acknowledging what he termed the "minority rights" of literature.

In his pioneering study *The Literature Police*, Peter McDonald borrows the term "repressive tolerance" from the leading black publisher Jaki Seroke to characterize van Rooyen's approach (see 77).[29] Seen from within an institutional framework, it appears however more adequate to describe his approach as decisively autonomy-oriented. Indeed, at the very outset of his tenure, van Rooyen effectively established a quite far-reaching institutional autonomy for literature. Moreover, he not long thereafter expanded the arsenal of acceptable conceptions of literature through his concept of protest literature—a policy that implied a further expansion of the already established institutional autonomy of literature. The institutional autonomy that was effectuated by van Rooyen's board did have its limits though, certainly when it came to religion. The fate that Anthony Burgess's novel *Man of Nazareth* befell in the van Rooyen era represents a clear demonstration of this.

During the interim period 1990–1994, the autonomy-oriented approach of van Rooyen was continued and the relatively precarious position of literature vis-à-vis the religious stipulations of the PA was underlined once more when Burgess's *Man of Nazareth* was again brought before the PAB in 1992. For the third time, the board declared the novel to be undesirable, and it did so basically on the same grounds as it had in 1979 and 1984. As in these earlier cases, the board acknowledged, *inter alia* on the basis of the literary expert opinions that had been voiced in the 1979 case, that the book had considerable literary merit. Yet it argued that the book's likely readership would not be limited to literary socialized readers because of the theme it dealt with. Rather the book's likely readership would be fairly wide and, moreover, include pious Christians who would be gravely affronted by the book's descriptions of the sexuality of Christ.

The period 1994–2010, finally, demonstrates how literature is being regulated in the new, democratic South Africa. The way in which this is being done cannot be regarded as an absolute break with the past. The infrastructure set up for regulating literature and other media through the FPA largely resembles that which was in place under the PA since 1975. The statutory superstructure guiding the regulation of literature did change quite drastically, however. First and foremost, an explicit *exceptio artis* pertaining, *inter alia*, to literature was instituted on the constitutional level. Moreover, on the lower level of the FPA, some quite significant statutory changes were effectuated also. For the first time in South African legal history, the contextual approach was prescribed statutorily. Furthermore, literature was granted absolute exemption from the act's stipulations regarding XX and X18 classification.

These statutory novelties were, however, not entirely new to literature regulation in South Africa. Both of them had been implemented before: the contextual approach by the judiciary, and the literature exemption—albeit in rudimentary form—by van Rooyen's PAB in the 1980s. Indeed, the new statutory superstructure stands firmly in the nation's century-long tradition of literature regulation. This is borne out by other evidence too: The FPA's spirit of promoting "the optimum amount of freedom for adults," while at the same time protecting children against "what is harmful and disturbing" (*Report of the Task Group* 1: 23) continues a tradition that had begun as early as 1932 with the Bok's judgment in the *Rex* v *Meinert* case. Likewise, the insistence of the FPA's draftsmen that in dealing with an alleged literary work, "[o]bjective appraisal by experts should be the test and the publication or film itself should be the object of appraisal" (81) continues a long tradition in the nation's legal regulation of literature. The new statutory dispensation thus largely brought continuity in the regulation of literature within the nation, although the establishment of a constitutional *exceptio artis* and the guarantee of absolute protection for art on the level of the FPA each effectuated a proper legal ratification to van Rooyen's merely semi-legal art exemption. Furthermore, the Constitution and FPA's respective ways of protecting literature effectively expanded the art exemption that had been established by van Rooyen: Whereas literary merit had been given but a relative protection on the level of the PA during the van Rooyen era, it had now been given absolute protection on the level of the FPA. What is more, literature had now been given relative protection on the level of the sovereign Constitution.

It turned out, however, that the protection given on the level of the FPA was perhaps not as absolute as it seemed. The 2002 FPB case of Rushdie's *Satanic Verses* indeed demonstrated that the principle of absolute exemption established by the act did not hinder the FPB from imposing sanctions on Rushdie's work based on a combined reading of both the act and the Constitution. Whereas the FPA explicitly granted literature absolute exemption from the act's stipulations regarding XX and X18 classification, the board gave an X18 classification to the book anyhow, even augmenting this with further restrictions. This despite the fact that the FPB, on the basis of *inter alia* the judgments of literary experts, held the book to represent a work of "bona fide" literature. As a result of the board's decision, a far-reaching ban on distributing Rushdie's novel remains intact in today's South Africa—a ban not so different from the one imposed in 1988. Apart from the fact that the Rushdie case appeared to reveal that literature in practice did not enjoy absolute protection on the level of the FPA, it seemed also to be evidencing that the institutional autonomy of literature as it is being recognized through the Constitution and the FPA is still most likely to be restricted on the basis of religious issues.

In recent years, legal recognition of the institutional autonomy of literature has been subjected to a certain degree of erosion. The far-reaching protection that literature was given on level of the FPA was reduced to a certain extent through the Films and Publications Amendment Act of 2009. When it comes to child pornography, literature is no longer exempted from the act's stipulations. However, considering both the century-long tradition of the legal treatment of literature in South Africa and the way in which the FPB dealt with Rushdie's *Satanic Verses*, it is highly unlikely that the 2009 amendments could practically result in the curbing of the autonomy of literature vis-à-vis the law to such an extent as to render possible a total ("XX") ban on a work "objectively"—that is, by literary experts—labeled a work of literature.

NOTES

1. Interesting as this work—and most notably the controversy around an oral submission to the South African Human Rights Commission of Inquiry into Racism in the Media by the ANC on April 5, 2000, in which Coetzee's *Disgrace* was linked to contemporaneous white racism (see e.g., Attwell, "Race"; Peter D. McDonald, "*Disgrace* Effects")—might be from certain literary theoretical perspectives—e.g., from a "law-as-literature," narratological, or literary historical perspective (see e.g., Clarkson; Krog; Sanders)—it would contribute little to our current analysis.
2. Hereafter, FPA.
3. The PA stipulated that the chairman of the PAB should be appointed by the state president (see PA, 1974 49).
4. Also called Muldergate, after the 1972–1978 Minister of the Interior, and one of the central figures in the scandal, Connie Mulder.
5. The two had worked together as advocates at the Johannesburg Bar (Rickard; van Rooyen, *Censor's Tale* 49).
6. After the informal meeting between Schlebusch and Snyman had taken place, the former did not waste any time replacing the latter: Snyman appears indeed to have been "gently eased out of office early" (McDonald, *Literature Police* 75), within a month or so after the meeting had occurred (cf. van Rooyen, *Censor's Tale* 56–59).
7. Not only did the number of appeals to the PAB increase significantly, but also the review requests made to the DOP. Many applications to the DOP were made by the South African Library and by the Ad Hoc Committee on Banned Books of the South African Institute for Librarianship and Information Science (SAILIS), which was established in 1978. In the late 1970s, and especially during the 1980s, both made a systematic effort to apply to the DOP to have "important" books, "fiction as well as nonfiction" (Westra 63), that had been banned for two years or longer, reconsidered. (As noted already in the previous chapter, sec. 15 of the PA provided that after a period of two years had lapsed since a publication or object had been declared undesirable, any person could make that such publication or object would be examined *de novo* by a committee [see PA, 1974 21].) It seems telling of the climate within the censorship system at the time that the DOP cooperated fully in this: it did not even charge these organizations the usual fee that was required for resubmitting a work (Westra 63).
8. Namely the case of *Mame Enterprises (Edms) Bpk* v *Raad van Beheer oor Publikasies* 1976 (1) SA 429 (A). The case had centered on a number of photographs that had appeared in a calendar.

9. "Alhoewel die Appèlraad ook deskundiges op hierdie gebied het, is hy as liggaam meer heterogeen saamgestel. Indien hy egter met 'n letterkundige werk te doen kry, besef hy dat dit 'n besondere kennisveld is en dat die mening van die Komitee van Letterkundiges swaar weeg" (Appeal Case No. 81-82/79 4–5).

10. A case in which the opinion of psychiatric experts had been obtained (see Appeal Board Case No. 7/80 8).

11. For brevity's sake, the bibliographical details of the reports of the PAB cases referenced in this section are not given in the list of works cited at the end of this study. It suffices to say that the reports are all archived in the Western Cape Archives and Records Service, Cape Town, and that details regarding the reports can be found in the Cape Town Archives Repository database that can be accessed on the website of the National Archives of South Africa (see http://www.national.archsrch.gov.za/sm300cv/smws/sm300gi?20130926140354 81E2BE06%26DB%3DKABE).

12. For example, Ayi Kwei Armah, *Two Thousand Seasons* (see PAB Cases No. 24/80 and No. 79/83) and André Brink's English translation of his novel *Kennis van die Aand, Looking on Darkness* (see PAB Cases No. 64/80; 131/81; and 87/82).

13. Van Rooyen himself retrospectively also observed that this had been the case (see van Rooyen, "Censorship" 29).

14. When a new ban on the novel instigated by a Publication Committee was appealed in 1980, the PAB upheld the ban.

15. The poem was judged to be blasphemous in a 1977 English Central Criminal Court case, a judgment that was subsequently upheld on appeal, firstly, by the Court of Appeal in 1978 and, after that, by the House of Lords in 1979. The case was finally brought before the European Commission of Human Rights in 1982, where the judgment that the poem was blasphemous in terms of English law was validated for the third time. For an analysis of these cases, see Moran.

16. As we will see later on in this chapter, some fifteen years after it was first published, Rushdie's novel would still confront the successor of the DOP, the Film and Publication Board, with a great legal dilemma.

17. According to Cheh, the South African variant was far more interventionist than its American counterpart though (see 30–31).

18. "Ook moet in gedagte gehou word dat die Swart tale besonder ryk is aan beeldspraak, dat poësie gevolglik besondere weerklank by die swartman vind en dat hy makliker daardeur aangevuur sal word as deur prosa" (PAB Case No. 2/81 3). With the term "prose," the Board probably meant to signify *non-literary* prose (cf. de Lange 24, 29).

19. Cf. Asmal 58; Brink, "Literature" 48-49; B. Coetzee 65, 68; Van Rooyen, "Censorship" 41n18; Westra viii, 11, 63.

20. Hereafter: FPB.

21. Hereafter: FPRB. It was later renamed Film and Publication Appeal Board.

22. Hereafter FPA.

23. For a juridical discussion of how and under what circumstances the freedom of artistic creativity should be limited, see Oosthuizen and Russo.

24. Van Rooyen was Professor of Criminal Law at the University of Pretoria from 1971 to 1998, and apart from having been, consecutively, Deputy Chairman and Chairman of the PAB from 1975 to 1990 and having chaired the Task Group: Films and Publications from 1994 to 1996, he has also served *inter alia* as chair of the Press Council from 1991 to 1997 and as Chairperson of the Broadcast and Complaints Commission of South Africa since 1993.

25. The FPA allows for the FPB and FPRB to appoint literary experts to assist in their deliberations (FPA, 1996 10, 16). As to the identity of the members of the committee: this may not be disclosed until 2022.

26. Decisions of the FPB have the force and effect of law (*Appeals Tribunal Decisions 1998–2008*, 5).

27. The Film and Publication Review Board was at some point renamed Film and Publication Appeals Board (*Appeals Tribunal Decisions 1998–2008*, 2).

28. McDonald is borrowing the term "eternally vigilant" from the 2002 book *Eternally Vigilant: Free Speech in the Modern Era*, ed. Lee C. Bollinger and G. R. Stone. The editors in

turn took the concept from the judgment delivered by Justice Oliver Wendell Holmes in the 1919 case of *Abrams* v *United States*, as McDonald points out (*Literature Police* 389n32).

29. De Lange also uses this term to describe van Rooyen's policy (see de Lange 132).

Conclusion

Long Walk to Artistic Freedom

Our investigation into the judicial—and semi-judicial—treatment of literature in South Africa in the period 1910–2010 reveals that the 1994 establishment of the constitutional *exceptio artis* pertaining, *inter alia*, to literature did not represent an unprecedented novelty in the nation's law. Rather, it formed the constitutional culmination, and crystallization, of a process that had already been set in motion in the period 1910–1955. For although no works were put on trial in this period that would have been characterized by literary experts or the literary socialized public as representing works of literary merit, the judiciary did come to introduce a number of concepts and procedures that would go on to play a crucial role in the autonomization of literature within the nation. Indeed, the concepts and procedures it came to introduce—i.e., the contextual approach; the admissibility of testimonies regarding an incriminated work; and the requirement that adjudicators would, as a matter of principle, observe tolerance with respect to changing societal norms regarding certain themes—effectively prepared the ground for a future recognition of a relative institutional autonomy of the South African literary field by the nation's judiciary. Moreover, in the 1932 case of *Rex* v *Meinert*, Justice Bok, the judge hearing the case, demonstrated to be in favor of what might be termed a colonial *exceptio artis*, i.e., a quite high degree of institutional autonomy vis-à-vis the law for imported modern literature—albeit one with racial implications.

In the early 1960s, a new censorship act was introduced to guide, *inter alia*, the regulation of literature: the Publications and Entertainments Act of 1963. Whereas South Africa had previously kept in step with the laws of its former motherland England when it came to regulating literature, this new law clearly evidenced that it now determinedly chose to go its own way. While in England the recently introduced Obscene Publications Act, 1959 had instigated an explicit *exceptio artis* pertaining to literature through its four fundamental instruments of the (mandatory) contextual approach, the likely reader test, the public good test and the admissibility of expert evidence, just one of these was incorporated into the PEA: the concept of the likely reader. Yet the new South African Act, although not making the contextual approach *mandatory*, did not rule out this approach either. Rather, it appeared to be leaving it to the Courts to either apply the contextual or the isolated-passage approach—the latter made it possible to judge a publication on the basis of a single passage rather than judge incriminated passages in the light of the whole, as the former approach did. Furthermore, the new act also contained sections that provided for literary experts to take up positions within the new censorship bureaucracy—which they, effectively, did: on the administrative level, literary experts were *de facto* in control of literature from 1963 to 1975 (see McDonald, *Literature Police*), when the PEA was replaced with a new censorship act.

When one examines the first trials that were held during the period when the PEA was in force, the 1965 Cape trials of Wilbur Smith's *When the Lion Feeds* and Can Themba's "The Fugitives," one can discern that the majority of the Cape Court was of the opinion that a certain degree of institutional autonomy should be granted to the literary field. In the trial of Smith's work, both the majority and dissenting opinions contained critiques of the new act: both lamented that literature had not been given enough protection under the PEA and that the act did not bear a greater resemblance to the English Obscene Publications Act of 1959. Yet notwithstanding the fact that only one of the fundamental instruments of the English Act had been incorporated into the PEA—the concept of the likely reader—the majority of the Cape Court appeared to employ a number of the means it had at its disposal to nevertheless guarantee a certain degree of institutional autonomy for literature. They found a way to demand that the contextual approach be applied and a publication thus be judged as a whole and not on the basis of isolated passages, and they appeared to be applying both the concept of freedom of expression and the likely reader test as means to grant literature a certain degree of autonomy vis-à-vis the law. The unanimous Cape judgment in the case of Can Themba's "The Fugitives" cohered with the judgment concerning Smith's *Lion* in that it secured a considerable degree of autonomy for the intellectual reader. Yet in the Appeal Court trial concerning Smith's *Lion* a quite different position was taken. The majority judgment delivered in this Court reversed many of the measures that the Cape Court had taken to grant literature some institutional autonomy. Indeed, for the majority of the Appeal Court, the PEA was clearly aimed *inter alia* at combating contemporary sexually explicit literature. With their judgment, they therefore provided the judiciary with a number of instruments enabling them to do this.

Some ten years later, the Cape trial of André Brink's *Kennis van die Aand* reversed much of the heteronomy-oriented approach that had been laid down by the Appellate Division in the *Lion* case. True, one of the three judges hearing the *Kennis* case, Justice van Wyk, adopted a position that for the largest part cohered with the position of the majority in the *Lion* appeal case. Yet, very much unlike the majority in this latter case, van Wyk showed that he recognized the value of literary expert evidence. Indeed, he determinedly underpinned his opinion with some of the literary expert evidence that had been adduced in the case. The opinions of the other two judges—Diemont and Steyn—were much more autonomy-oriented. Both allowed the literary field a quite significant degree of autonomy vis-à-vis the law, *inter alia* through their particular application of the concept of the likely reader, through their principled recognition of the (judicial) value of literary expertise, and through their application of arguments advanced by the literary experts in their testimonies. Yet although both adopted a position that established a considerable degree of autonomy for literature vis-à-vis the moral and political provisions of the act, this autonomy clearly remained precarious when it came to religion: both judges felt that Brink's *Kennis* violated the act's religious provisos and that the ban should, therefore, be upheld.

As had happened in 1965, the new autonomizing impulse given by the Cape Court was again rolled back almost immediately—this time not at the hands of the Appellate Division but through actions of Parliament. For the Publications and Entertainments Act of 1963 was repealed and replaced with the Publications Act, 1974. This new act scrapped the only two instruments with which literature could be granted a certain degree of autonomy from the statute books: it got rid of both the concept of the likely reader and of the stipulation that allowed individuals to be appointed as censors by virtue of their "special knowledge of art, language and literature." Moreover, the right to appeal to the Supreme Court against censors' decisions was also abolished. A semi-judicial body called the Publications Appeal Board was set up to deal with such appeals instead, and the only role left for the Supreme Court to play was to review decisions of this PAB when it was called upon to do so. Censorship thus became an entirely executive affair—an affair that was indeed firmly in the hands of the Minister of the Interior.

Indeed, the approach toward literature taken in the initial phase of the PAB's existence, the period 1975–1978, considerably reduced the autonomous space that had been created for literature over the years. Chaired by former Supreme Court Justice J. H. Snyman, the board took a number of measures to ensure that the act was being applied as the interventionist tool he took it to be—a tool aimed at curbing the institutional autonomy of literature rather than promoting it. The policy of the PAB also revealed that

Snyman et al. did realize that the literary field had become a societal factor that could not be ignored, however. The board made sure to carefully stress that literary merit was a factor that had to be taken into account when adjudicating works in terms of the PA and that functionality, i.e., the functionality of textual elements within the entire text, was also a factor that had to be taken into consideration. Furthermore, the board admitted evidence from literary experts, and in principle it did indeed leave the establishment of the literary merits of an incriminated work entirely up to them. In practice, this ostensible recognition of a certain amount of institutional autonomy of the literary field did not prevent the work of even a foremost Afrikaans author like Etienne Leroux from being banned.

However, the most fundamental features of the PAB's approach to literature were invalidated by the Transvaal Provincial Division of the Supreme Court when it was called upon to review the board's decision on Leroux's novel *Magersfontein, O Magersfontein!* Indeed, the Court's judgment delivered a quite crucial contribution to shoring up the degree of institutional autonomy—which, by Western standards, of course represented but a modest amount—that the literary field had come to attain in the period before the executive started its rollback efforts. The bench underpinned its judgment by extensively referring to some of the opinions handed down in the trials of Smith's *Lion* and Brink's *Kennis*. Yet although the Transvaal Bench quite clearly evidenced respect for the (modestly) autonomy-oriented course that the Supreme Court had come to take over the years, it did choose to disregard a very important precedent that had been set by the majority of the judges—namely by Justices Diemont and Steyn—in the case of Brink's *Kennis*. These two judges had in effect—through a particular application of the likely reader concept—expanded the degree of autonomy that literature enjoyed vis-à-vis the religious and political stipulations of the law. The Transvaal Court chose not to follow this precedent, but instead to adopt the more heteronomist position that van Wyk had taken on the issue in the same trial. Thus, although the judgment of the Transvaal Court effectively shored up the institutional autonomy of literature in very significant ways, at the same time it did not alter the precarious position of literature vis-à-vis the religious stipulations of the act. As a consequence of its principled position on this issue, the Court had to uphold the PAB's judgment that Leroux's *Magersfontein* constituted an undesirable work in terms of the PA and that therefore it should be banned.

The autonomy-friendly parts of the Supreme Court's judgment in the *Magersfontein* case turned out to represent a crucial fundament on which Snyman's successor, Kobus van Rooyen, built his autonomist-oriented PAB approach during the 1980s. Indeed, the case heralded the end of the rollback that had been instigated in 1975. The battles fought over the case both inside and outside of court prompted the newly-formed Botha government to amend the PA so as to grant literature a more autonomous position vis-à-vis the law. The Publications Amendment Act of 1978 made it possible in principle to again grant literary socialized readers more freedom of choice by allowing the board to release books under an age and/or distributional restriction. Moreover, the act arranged for literary experts, who had effectively been written out of the statutory regulations regarding censorship through the PA, to again receive a more prominent role within the system. Minister of the Interior Schlebusch made sure that Snyman was replaced, and with van Rooyen taking up the baton, the new measures quickly took effect. The new board started to consistently apply the approach toward literature taken by the Supreme Court during the period 1965–1978. Van Rooyen's board came to guarantee a fairly high degree of institutional autonomy for literature through the instruments of the contextual approach, the concept of the likely reader, a fundamental tolerance toward the written word and a consistent recognition of literary expertise. Moreover, through its particular application of the adjudicating factor of literariness—an application that was justified through van Rooyen's interpretation of the Publications Amendment Act of 1978—the board increased the degree of legal autonomy that the Supreme Court had granted the literary field. Yet although in the decade of its existence van Rooyen's board consistently granted literature a relatively high degree of autonomy, literature's position vis-à-vis the religious provisions of the PA remained as (relatively) precarious as it had always been—a situation that would remain unaltered in the transitional period 1990–1994.

The way in which literature has been regulated since 1994, i.e., since South Africa became a non-racial constitutional democracy, cannot be regarded as an absolute break with the past. The infrastructure set up for regulating literature and other media through the Films and Publications Act of 1996 largely resembles that which had been in place since 1975 under the Publications Act. The statutory superstructure guiding the regulation of literature did change quite drastically, however. First and foremost, an explicit *exceptio artis* pertaining, *inter alia*, to literature was established on the constitutional level. Moreover, on the level of the FPA, some quite significant statutory changes were also effectuated. For the first time in South Africa's legal history, the contextual approach was prescribed statutorily. Furthermore, literature was granted far-reaching exemption from the act's stipulations regarding XX and X18 classification. These statutory novelties were not entirely new in the nation's history of literature regulation at large, though. Both of them had been implemented before: the contextual approach by the judiciary as early as 1910, and the art exemption—albeit in rudimentary form—by Justice Bok in the 1932 case of *Rex* v *Meinert* and, half a century later, by van Rooyen's PAB in the 1980s. Indeed, the new statutory superstructure stands firmly in the nation's century-long tradition of literature regulation. This is borne out by other evidence too: The FPA's spirit of promoting freedom of choice for adults, while at the same time protecting children against harm continues a tradition that had begun as early as 1932 with Bok's judgment in the *Rex* v *Meinert* case. Furthermore, the insistence of the FPA's draftsmen that in dealing with an alleged literary work the literary merits of such a work should be assessed "objectively" by literary experts on the basis of a text-oriented approach also continues a long tradition in the nation's legal regulation of literature. The new statutory dispensation thus to a large extent brought continuity to the regulation of literature within the nation, although the establishment of a constitutional *exceptio artis* and the guarantee of far-reaching protection for art on the level of the FPA of course both effectuated a proper legal ratification to the merely semilegal art exemption that van Rooyen's PAB had instigated. Moreover, the exceptional legal status that literature has thus received is of course far more robust than the kinds of protection it was given before 1994. Nevertheless, as the 2002 case concerning Rushdie's *Satanic Verses* demonstrates, the institutional autonomy of literature in the new, democratic South Africa seems still most vulnerable to limitation when it comes to religion.

As it appears, conceptions of literature also played an important part in the long and gradual—though not linear—development toward the establishment of a constitutional *exceptio artis* in 1994. As early as 1955, one can discern up-to-date conceptions of literature penetrating the political field: the Cronjé Commission's recommendations for a new censorship act contained clear references to the formalist poetics that had recently been introduced in South Africa. Obviously, however, its report also contained crucial elements of Platonic poetics. As it turned out, Platonic poetics appeared to play a fundamental role in the rollbacks that were effectuated by the Appeal Court through the case of *Lion* in 1965 and by the PAB's policy in the second half of the 1970s. Platonic poetics also seemed to form one of the pillars on which van Wyk's opinion in the 1974 case of *Kennis* was built. Yet in the latter case, conceptions of literature that had legitimacy within the contemporaneous literary field also found their way into judicial opinion—namely into the opinion of at least Justice Steyn. As of 1980, such conceptions of literature, moreover, became a crucial component of the semi-judicial regulation of literature: in the day-to-day operations of van Rooyen's PAB they were employed to determine the literary merit of incriminated works. In practice, this meant that an autonomist-pragmatic conception of literature emanating from the Afrikaans subfield and a pragmatic poetics (*sensu* Abrams) that was adhered to by another part of the literary field, namely, first and foremost, by black literary actors, became important elements of literature control.

Judging from the above-described institutional and poetological dimension of the legal regulation of literature in twentieth- and twenty-first-century South Africa, it appears that the formation of a(n) (relatively) institutionally autonomous literary field (*sensu* Bourdieu) in this nation occurred in the

1960s and 1970s. Rather clearly autonomist-oriented positions were already taken in the trials of 1965. However, more heteronomist opinions—opinions that, moreover, appeared rooted in a Platonic conception of literature—rolled back the institutional autonomy that was granted to the literary field in the first instance. A decade later, the judiciary revealed itself to be giving a significantly higher degree of recognition to the literary field than it had in 1965: this was mainly evidenced by the strong consensus that appeared to exist in the judiciary about the judicial value of literary expertise. Indeed, all three judges dealing with the case of Brink's *Kennis* determinedly employed expert evidence and, indeed, up-to-date literary theoretical arguments, to underpin their respective opinions. Furthermore, the more heteronomist position appeared to have become a minority position in judicial circles by that time. Parliament was, however, able to uphold the dominancy of the more heteronomist position for a few more years through its establishment of a new super- and infrastructure for regulating *inter alia* literature. Its effort was short-lived though: the literary field appeared to have reached such an advanced stage that it could not be pushed aside that easily. The major protests which the 1978 *Magersfontein* case gave rise to—protests which emanated not just from the literary elite and progressive circles, but also from more conservative circles—bore witness to this. With the curtain falling on Snyman's PAB, the curtain seemed also to fall on the judicial—and semi-judicial—life of Platonic poetics in South Africa. On the poetological level, the legal regulation of literature has solely been guided by more up-to-date poetics ever since the exit of Snyman around 1980.

When one examines the available data regarding the South African literary field that are to be found in existing research, this observation pertaining to the barometer function of judicial recognition seems to be confirmed. The available data indeed seem to suggest that in the 1960s and 1970s, the English and Afrikaans subfields reached such a stage of development that one might speak of relatively autonomous subfields, or of a relatively autonomous literary field (*sensu* Bourdieu) in South Africa.[1] It should be repeated though, that no systematic research into the South African field has been carried out yet and that the suggestion that it emerged in the 1960s and 1970s is thus not underpinned by sufficient evidence. A more definite confirmation or rejection of the hypothesis that the judicial recognition given to literature in these two decades signals, and rounds off, the formation of an institutionally autonomous literary field in South Africa would require a more solid underpinning of the hypothesis regarding the internal development of the South African field.

Yet apart from the fact that more evidence is needed with respect to the internal development of the field, the results of this study would also gain precision and depth if they were juxtaposed with data regarding other players comprising South Africa's cultural field and its field of power. If, in line with

Dorleijn, Grüttemeier and Korthals Altes, we define the institutional autonomy of literature as autonomy vis-à-vis (1) economic forces (the market); (2) political forces, i.e., "political parties, state power and authorities grounded in political power" (xiv); (3) religious and moral forces; and (4) concurrent medial forces such as journalism, this study has only mapped out the relationship between South Africa's literary field and a part of the nation's "political forces." Of course, the forces that it describes—laws as crystallized parliamentary politics and the practice of the application of laws as a (practical) continuation of parliamentary politics—represent the most powerful of these forces, but the picture that it thus produces is not complete. The "political" field also comprises less powerful forces, such as the *administrative* forces of censorship. As McDonald's *Literature Police* so clearly demonstrates, these forces did not necessarily always comply with what was ordained at the top levels of South African political force. Moreover, "religious and moral forces" also played an important role in South African society, both previous to, during, and after apartheid, as some of the cases discussed in this study evidence in a quite direct manner. These forces certainly also impacted the autonomy of the literary field, and the same obviously goes for the "economic" and "concurrent medial forces" present in South African society in the researched period. To come to as precise a picture as possible, all of these dimensions should be taken into account. It goes without saying that many methodological hurdles would have to be overcome when setting out to sketch as complete a picture as possible of the institutional autonomy of South African literature in the scrutinized period—or any other literature of this period, or any other length of time, for that matter. One only has to think of the phenomenon of self-censorship, a phenomenon that was doubtlessly very prevalent in apartheid South Africa.[2] Other complexities of the South African situation, such as the multiracial, multicultural, and multilingual character of its literary field, could make one question the methodological feasibility of such an endeavor even further. Certainly, the notion of autonomy is a complex, multidimensional one that is "to be handled with care" (Dorleijn, Grüttemeier, and Korthals Altes ix). And as mentioned in this study's introduction, the barometer function that the judicial treatment of literature arguably has is necessarily somewhat crude. It only enables us to more roughly measure the overall amount of institutional autonomy that a literary field has reached at a certain time and the societal reach that poetological positions might have. It is not an instrument that can be applied to describe the many dimensions of literary autonomy in a detailed manner.

But apart from its shortcomings, the method of "literature in law," i.e., the method of analyzing literary trials so as to come to hypotheses regarding the institutional development of literary fields, also has its strengths. One of its strengths lies in its comparatist potential. Coming back to our earlier expectation that the legal treatment of literature in twentieth- and twenty-first-century South Africa might display some similarities with the way in which the medium was legally treated in nineteenth- and—particularly—twentieth-century Belgium, France, Germany, and the Netherlands, it appears that we must conclude that the legal autonomization of South African literature largely unfolded along different lines than it did in the other countries. The art exemption that was established in South African law was for the largest part established through different parameters than it was in these European nations. This is undoubtedly due to the South African orientation toward English and U.S. law, instead of the continental legal tradition.

Yet as South African law began to go its own way in the 1950s, the particular parameters it came to set with regard to literature regulation cannot entirely be explained by its orientation toward the latter two legal systems. Since Parliament was revealed to have been heavily inspired by Australian and, particularly, Irish law when developing its Publications and Entertainments Act in the 1960s and its Publications Act in the 1970s, it might prove fruitful to compare the legal treatment of literature in South Africa to the way in which it was regulated in these further two countries. It appears, indeed, that the commonalities in the legal infra- and superstructures implemented for governing literature regulation in these countries—not to speak of the shared roots of these nation's respective legal systems in English law—do not provide the only rationale for undertaking such an endeavor. The fact that the institutional autonomy of literature in South Africa has been revealed to be relatively precarious when it comes to religion might provide further grounds for doing so, as religion also seems to play an important role in the censorship histories of Australia and Ireland (see Kennedy; Moore). The fact that these two nations appeared to have been quite restrictive in their legal dealing with literature compared to other Anglophone nations, just as South Africa was, provides yet another reason for comparing the three countries. Perhaps, indeed, systematic comparative research into the legal treatment of literature in these three nations will reveal that their literary fields underwent a markedly "postcolonial" process of institutional autonomization—a process that represents a relatively "long walk" to artistic freedom indeed.

NOTES

1. For data regarding the institutions realizing both the material and symbolic production as well as the distribution of literature in South Africa, see Cronjé 25 et passim; Driver 387ff; Johnson 827ff; McDonald, *Literature Police* 166ff et passim; McDonald, "Book" 807ff; 810ff; Willemse 429–30, 446). The African language subfield appears to have always been dominated by heteronomist forces: until the mid-twentieth century it was under the influence of missionary presses, and as of the 1950s under that of Afrikaner-owned publishing houses, some of which had direct links to the Afrikaner political elite (Kunene 301–2; McDonald, *Literature Police* 89, 96; McDonald, "Book" 804ff; Swanepoel 607ff). This situation would remain unaltered throughout apartheid (McDonald, "Book" 806–7). Today, African languages seem first

and foremost to represent a medium for schoolbooks and religious books (cf. le Roux, Struik and Labuschagne 44 et passim; Masilela 337; Swanepoel 619–28; van der Waal 50).

2. A 1997 study by Margreet de Lange focuses on this subject (see de Lange).

Bibliography

Abolition of Restrictions on Free Political Activity Act 206 of 1993. *South Africa Government Online*. Government Communications (GCIS), n.d. Web. 5 Mar. 2013. http://www.info.gov.za/view/DownloadFileAction?id=71079.
Abrams, M. H. *The Mirror and the Lamp: Romantic Theory and the Critical Tradition*. 1953. Oxford: Oxford University Press, 1975. Print.
Aedilis Curulis. "When the Lion Feeds the Press." *Standpunte* 19.1 (1965): 17–19. Print.
Akyeampong, Emmanuel K., and Henry Louis Gates Jr., eds. *Dictionary of African Biography*. 6 vols. New York: Oxford University Press, 2012. Print.
"Another Raid." *The New African* 3.4 (1964): 73. Print.
Anschütz, Gerhard. *Die Verfassung des deutschen Reichs von 11 August 1919*. Darmstadt: Wissenschaftliche Buchgesellschaft, 1960. Print.
Antonissen, Rob. *Die Afrikaanse Letterkunde van Aanvang tot Hede*. 2nd ed. Cape Town: Nasionale Boekhandel, [c. 1960]. Print.
Appeals Tribunal Decisions 1998–2008. Johannesburg: Film and Publication Board, n.d. Print.
"Appèlraad oor Publikasies." *De Rebus Procuratoriis* 98 (1976): 73–76. Print.
Asmal, Kader. "Freedom to Read and a Bill of Rights: Looking Ahead." Pieter E. Westra, ed. *Freedom to Read: Papers Presented at a Seminar on the Future of Publications Control and the Free Flow of Information in South Africa on 11 June 1993*. Cape Town: South African Library, 1994: 57–61. Print.
Attwell, David. "Race in *Disgrace*." *interventions* 4.3 (2002): 331–341. Print.
———. "South African Literature in English." F. Abiola Irele and Simon Gikandi, eds. *The Cambridge History of African and Caribbean Literature*. Vol. 1. Cambridge: Cambridge University Press, 2004: 504–29. Print.
Attwell, David, and Derek Attridge, eds. *The Cambridge History of South African Literature*. Cambridge: Cambridge University Press, 2012. Print.
Barnett, Ursula A. *A Vision of Order: A Study of Black South African Literature in English (1914–1980)*. Amherst, MA: University of Massachusetts Press, 1983. Print.
Beekman, Klaus, and Ralf Grüttemeier. *De wet van de letter: Literatuur en rechtspraak*. Amsterdam: Athenaeum—Polak & van Gennep, 2005. Print.
Bevinding van die Komitee van Deskundiges [Finding of the Committee of Experts]. 1980. TS. Publications Appeal Board Case of *Magersfontein, O Magersfontein!* (7/80). P77/1/97. Western Cape Provincial Archives and Records Service, Cape Town.
Biko, Steve. *I Write What I Like*. London: Bowerdean Press, 1986. Print.
Bizos, George. *No One to Blame?: In Pursuit of Justice in South Africa*. 3rd ed. Bellville: Mayibuye, University of the Western Cape, 2000. Print.

Bourdieu, Pierre. *The Field of Cultural Production: Essays on Art and Literature*. Ed. and introd. by Randal Johnson. 2008 ed. Cambridge: Polity, 1993. Print.

———. *The Rules of Art: Genesis and Structure of the Literary Field*. Trans. Susan Emanuel. 2008 ed. Cambridge: Polity, 1996. Print.

———. *Schwierige Interdisziplinarität: Zum Verhältnis von Soziologie und Geschichtswissenschaft*. Ed. Elke Ohnacker and Franz Schultheis. Münster: Westfälisches Dampfboot, 2004. Print.

Boyer, Paul S. *Purity in Print: Book Censorship in America from the Gilded Age to the Computer Age*. 2nd ed. Madison: University of Wisconsin Press, 2002. Print.

Brandwagpers (Edms) Bpk v Raad van Beheer oor Publikasies 1975 (2) SA 32 (D). Durban and Coast Local Division of the Supreme Court of South Africa. 1975. *The South African Law Reports (1947 to date)*. Juta Law, n.d. Web. 27 Oct. 2012.

Brink, André. "Antwoord aan Smit." *Kol* 1.3 (1968): 4–6. Print.

———. "Censorship and Literature." Theo Coggin, ed. *Censorship: A Study of Censorship in South Africa by Five Distinguished Authors, Johan van der Vyver, André Brink, Allan Boesak, Ian McDonald and André du Toit. Introduction by Geoff Budlender*. Johannesburg: S.A. Insitute of Race Relations, 1983: 37–54. Print.

———. *Kennis van die Aand*. 2nd ed. Cape Town: Human & Rousseau, 1983. Print.

———. "*Kennis* Verbode." André P. Brink. *Waarom Literatuur?* Cape Town: Human & Rousseau, 1985: 90–96. Print.

———. "Literature and Control in a Future South Africa." Pieter E. Westra, ed. *Freedom to Read: Papers Presented at a Seminar on the Future of Publications Control and the Free Flow of Information in South Africa on 11 June 1993*. Cape Town: South African Library, 1994: 45–56. Print.

———. "Op soek na Afrika." *Standpunte* 28.8 (1973): 1–9. Print.

———. Preface. Kobus van Rooyen. *A South African Censor's Tale*. Pretoria: Protea, 2011. Print.

———. "Tussen Sestig en Sewentig." *Kol* 1.1 (1968): 2–5. Print.

Bronstein, Carolyn. *Battling Pornography: The American Feminist Anti-Pornography Movement, 1976–1986*. Cambridge: Cambridge University Press, 2011. Print.

Brooks, Peter. "Literature as Law's Other." *Yale Journal of Law & the Humanities* 22 (2010): 349–67. Print.

Burchell, E. M., and J. R. L. Milton. "Criminal Law: Publications Act 42 of 1974." P. Q. R. Boberg et al., eds. *Annual Survey of South African Law 1974*. Cape Town: Juta, 1975: 331–32. Print.

Buren Uitgewers (Edms) Bpk en 'n Ander v Raad van Beheer oor Publikasies 1975 (1) SA 379 (C). Western Cape Provincial Division of the Supreme Court of South Africa. 1975. *The South African Law Reports (1947 to date)*. Juta Law, n.d. Web. 17 Feb. 2011.

Burns, Yvonne Marie. "An Analysis of the Publications Act 42 of 1974." MA thesis. University of South Africa, Pretoria, 1979. Print.

Cape Committee of the Publications Control Board. "Kontrolering van Ongewenste Publikasies." Internal memo directed to the full-time and part-time members of the Publications Control Board. Ref. no. 1/14/1. N.d. TS. BCS vol. 22, ref. M1. Western Cape Provincial Archives and Records Service, Cape Town.

Casanova, Pascale. *The World Republic of Letters*. Trans. M. B. DeBevoise. Cambridge, MA: Harvard University Press, 2004. Print.

Castagna, JoAnn E. "Glyn, Elinor (1864–1943)." *Oxford Dictionary of National Biography*. Oxford: Oxford University Press, 2004. Online. Jan. 2008. Web. 15 March 2014. http://www.oxforddnb.com/view/article/33428.

Cheh, Mary M. "Systems and Slogans: The American Clear and Present Danger Doctrine and South African Publications Control." *South African Journal on Human Rights* 2 (1986): 29–48. Print.

Clarkson, Carrol. *Drawing the Line: Toward an Aesthetics of Transitional Justice*. New York: Fordham University Press, 2013. Print.

Cloete, T. T. "Gerrit Dekker, Pretoria 11 november 1897–Pretoria 10 april 1973." *Jaarboek van de Maatschappij der Nederlandsche Letterkunde te Leiden, 1974–1975*. Leiden: Brill, 1976. *Digitale Bibliotheek voor de Nederlandse Letteren*. Web. 20 Oct. 2011.

———. "Na Hoër Hoogtes." *Dekades in die Afrikaanse Letterkunde: 'n Reeks Praatjies Uitgesaai in die Afrikaanse Diens van die Suid-Afrikaanse Uitsaaikorporasie*. Johannesburg: SAUK, n.d. Print.

———. "Sensuur: Prinsipieel en Prakties Besien." Studiestuk nr. 67. Potchefstroom: Instituut vir Bevordering van Calvinisme, Potchefstroomse Universiteit vir Christelike Hoër Onderwys, n.d. Print.

Coetzee, Braam. "Options for the Future." Pieter E. Westra, ed. *Freedom to Read: Papers Presented at a Seminar on the Future of Publications Control and the Free Flow of Information in South Africa on 11 June 1993*. Cape Town: South African Library, 1994: 64–69. Print.

Coetzee, J. M. *Giving Offense: Essays on Censorship*. Chicago, IL: University of Chicago Press, 1996. Print.

———. "Into the Dark Chamber: The Writer and the South African State (1986)." J. M. Coetzee. *Doubling the Point: Essays and Interviews*. Ed. David Attwell. Cambridge, MA: Harvard University Press, 1992: 361–68. Print.

———. "Jerusalem Prize Acceptance Speech (1987)." J. M. Coetzee. *Doubling the Point: Essays and Interviews*. Ed. David Attwell. Cambridge, MA: Harvard University Press, 1992: 96–99. Print.

Coggin, Theo, ed. *Censorship: A Study of Censorship in South Africa by Five Distinguished Authors, Johan van der Vyver, André Brink, Allan Boesak, Ian McDonald and André du Toit. Introduction by Geoff Budlender*. Johannesburg: S.A. Insitute of Race Relations, 1983: 37–54. Print.

Comaroff, Joan Laura. *The Appellate Division and Transvaal Bench, From 1943 to 1970: A Bio-Bibliography Compiled by Joan Laura Comaroff*. Johannesburg: U of the Witwatersrand Department of Bibliography, Librarianship and Typography, 1972. Print.

Constitution of the Republic of South Africa, Act 200 of 1993. *South Africa Government Online*. Government Communications (GCIS), n.d. Web. 5 Mar. 2013. http://www.info.gov.za/documents/constitution/93cons.htm.

Constitution of the Republic of South Africa, No. 108 of 1996. *South Africa Government Online*. Government Communications (GCIS), n.d. Web. 5 Mar. 2013. http://www.info.gov.za/documents/constitution/1996/a108-96.pdf.

Conter, Claude D., ed. *Justitiabilität und Rechtmäßigkeit: Verrechtlichungsprozesse von Literatur und Film in der Moderne*. Amsterdam : Rodopi, 2010. Print.

Corder, Hugh. *Judges at Work: The Role and Attitudes of the South African Appellate Judiciary, 1910–50*. Cape Town: Juta, 1984. Print.

Craig, Alec. *The Banned Books of England and Other Countries: A Study of the Conception of Literary Obscenity*. Westport, CT: Greenwood, 1977. Print.

Cronjé, G., et al. *Verslag van die Kommissie van Ondersoek insake Ongewenste Publikasies*. Pretoria: Government Printer, 1957. Print.

Davis, D. M. "Judicial Appointments in South Africa." *advocate* 23.3 (2010): 40–43. Print.

Davis, Geoffrey V. *Voices of Justice and Reason: Apartheid and Beyond in South African Literature*. Amsterdam: Rodopi, 2003. Print.

Dean, Barry. "Censorship in South Africa: Censorship and the Law." *Philosophical Papers* 5.1 (1976): 34–52. Print.

Dean, W. H. B. "Judging the Obscene: A Critical Analysis of the Criteria Used for Determining What Are Undesirable Sexually Explicit Materials in South Africa." B. Beinart, Wouter de Vos, J. D. Thomas, eds. *Acta Juridica 1972*. Cape Town: Juta, 1973: 61–150. Print.

———. "O Tempora! O Mores!" *The South African Law Journal* 92.1 (1975): 1–12. Print.

Debatte van die Volksraad (Hansard). Tweede Sitting—Tweede Parlement. Republiek van Suid-Afrika. 18 Jan.–28 Jun. 1963. Vols. 5–8. Pretoria: Government Printer, n.d. Print.

Debatte van die Volksraad (Hansard). Vierde Sessie—Derde Parlement. 31 Jan.–21 Jun. 1969. Vols. 25–7. Pretoria: Government Printer, n.d. Print.

de Grazia, Edward. *Girls Lean Back Everywhere: The Law of Obscenity and the Assault on Genius*. New York: Random House, 1992. Print.

Dekker, Gerrit. "Advies oor *Die Ysterkoei Moet Sweet* deur B. Breytenbach. Ms. deur die Uitgewers, A.P.B., Johannesburg voorgelê." Internal memo directed to the full-time and part-time members of the Publications Control Board, 14 Sep. 1964. TS. BCS 841/64. Western Cape Provincial Archives and Records Service, Cape Town.

———. *Afrikaanse Literatuurgeskiedenis*. 9nd ed. Cape Town: Nasou, [c. 1958]. Print.

———. "Die Calvinisme en die Kuns." *Standpunte* 7.3 (1953): 1–13. Print.

———. Inaugural Address. N.d. [November 1963]. TS. BCS vol. 17, ref. B1. Western Cape Provincial Archives and Records Service, Cape Town.

———. Letter to van Wyk, Vice-Chairman of the Publications Control Board. 11 Nov. 1963. MS. BCS vol. 17, ref. B1. Western Cape Provincial Archives and Records Service, Cape Town.

———. Reader's Report on André P. Brink, *Miskien Nooit*. C. J. D. Harvey et al. Report of the Decision of the Publications Control Board on André P. Brink, *Miskien Nooit*. 9 May 1968. TS. BCS 52/68. Western Cape Provincial Archives and Records Service, Cape Town.

de Klerk, W. A. *The Puritans in Africa: A Story of Afrikanerdom*. London: Rex Collings, 1975. Print.

de Lange, Margreet. *The Muzzled Muse: Literature and Censorship in South Africa*. Amsterdam: John Benjamins, 1997. Print.

Diemont, Marius. *Brushes with the Law*. Cape Town: Human & Rousseau, 1995. Print.

Dorleijn, Gillis J. "Autonomy and Heteronomy in the Dutch Literary Field around 1900." Gillis J. Dorleijn, Ralf Grüttemeier, and Liesbeth Korthals Altes, eds. *The Autonomy of Literature at the Fins de Siècles (1900 and 2000): A Critical Assessment*. Leuven: Peeters, 2007: 121–44. Print.

———. "Niet de knikkers maar het spel, of: De poëziecriticus als symbolische producent: Een institutionele close reading." *Neerlandica Extra Muros* 44.2 (2006): 2–13. Print.

———. "De plaats van tektstanalyse in een institutioneel-poëticale benadering." *Nederlandse Letterkunde* 14.1 (2009): 1–19. Print.

Dorleijn, Gillis J., Ralf Grüttemeier, and Liesbeth Korthals Altes. "'The Autonomy of Literature': To Be Handled with Care: An Introduction." Gillis J. Dorleijn, Ralf Grüttemeier, and Liesbeth Korthals Altes, eds. *The Autonomy of Literature at the Fins de Siècles (1900 and 2000): A Critical Assessment*. Leuven: Peeters, 2007: ix–xxvi. Print.

Dorleijn, Gillis J., and Wiljan van den Akker. "Literatuuropvattingen als denkstijl: Over de verbreiding van normen in het literaire veld rond 1900." Dorleijn, Gillis, and Kees van Rees, eds. *De productie van literatuur: Het literaire veld in Nederland, 1800–2000*. Nijmegen: Vantilt, 2006: 91–122 Print.

Dorleijn, Gillis, and Kees van Rees, eds. *Literatuuropvattingen in het perspectief van het literaire veld*. The Hague: NWO, 1999. Print.

———. *De productie van literatuur: Het literaire veld in Nederland, 1800–2000*. Nijmegen: Vantilt, 2006. Print.

Driver, Dorothy. "The Fabulous Fifties: Short Fiction in English." David Attwell and Derek Attridge, eds. *The Cambridge History of South African Literature*. Cambridge: Cambridge University Press, 2012: 387–409. Print.

Dubow, Saul. *A Commonwealth of Knowledge: Science, Sensibility, and White South Africa 1820–2000*. Oxford: Oxford University Press, 2006. Print.

———. *Scientific Racism in Modern South Africa*. Cambridge: Cambridge University Press, 1995. Print.

du Toit, André. "The Rationale of Controlling Political Publications." Theo Coggin, ed. *Censorship: A Study of Censorship in South Africa by Five Distinguished Authors, Johan van der Vyver, André Brink, Allan Boesak, Ian McDonald and André du Toit. Introduction by Geoff Budlender*. Johannesburg: S.A. Insitute of Race Relations, 1983: 80–129. Print.

Dyzenhaus, David, Sophia Reibetanz Moreau, and Athur Ripstein, eds. *Law and Morality: Readings in Legal Philosophy*. 3rd ed. Toronto: University of Toronto Press, 2007. Print.

Eckard, C. F. "*Functus Officio* ten aansien van Verbanne Publikasies?" *Tydskrif vir Hedendaagse Romeins-Hollandse Reg/Journal of Contemporary Roman-Dutch Law* 34 (1971): 175–81. Print.
Edelman, Bernard, and Nathalie Heinich. *L'art en conflits: L'œuvre de l'esprit entre droit et sociologie*. Paris: La Découverte, 2002. Print.
Ehlers, D. L. "Sensuur op Binnelandse Publikasies." *South African Libraries* 22.2 (1954): 40–41. Print.
Ehmeir, Walter. *Literature in Time with History: South African Literature in English and Political Change in the 1960s*. Essen: Die Blaue Eule, 1995. Print.
Entertainments (Censorship) Act, 1931. *Statutes of the Union of South Africa 1931*. Pretoria: Government Printer, 1931: 132–43. Print.
Films and Publications Act No. 65 of 1996. *Government Gazette* 8 Nov. 1996: 2–35. Print.
Films and Publications Amendment Act No. 34 of 1999. *Government Gazette* 30 Apr. 1999: 2–9. Print.
Films and Publications Amendment Act No. 18 of 2004. *Government Gazette* 2 Nov. 2004: 2–19. Print.
Films and Publications Amendment Act No. 3 of 2009. *Government Gazette* 28 Aug. 2009: 2–39. Print.
Forsyth, C. F. *In Danger for their Talents: A Study of the Appellate Division of the Supreme Court of South Africa from 1950–80*. Cape Town: Juta, 1985. Print.
Fowler, Roger, ed. *A Dictionary of Modern Critical Terms*. London: Routledge & Kegan Paul, 1973. Print.
"Freedom of Speech and the Press: The Publications Act 42 of 1974." P. Q. R. Boberg et al., eds. *Annual Survey of South African Law 1974*. Cape Town: Juta, 1975: 32–40. Print.
"Freedom of Speech and the Press: Publications Act 42 of 1974." P. Q. R. Boberg et al., eds. *Annual Survey of South African Law 1975*. Cape Town: Juta, 1976: 19. Print.
Galloway, Francis, and Rudi M. R. Venter. "Book History, Publishing Research and Production Figures: The Case of Afrikaans Fiction Production during the Transitional Period 1990–2003," *South African Historical Journal* 55 (2006): 46–65. Print.
Gardner, John. "The Many Faces of the Reasonable Person." *Law Quarterly Review* 131 (2015): 563–84. Print.
Geldenhuys, Pieter B. *Obseniteit en die wet op publikasies en vermaaklikhede, 1963*. Bloemfontein: U.O.V.S., 1974. Print.
———. *Pornografie, Sensuur en Reg*. Johannesburg: Lex Patria, 1977. Print.
General Law Amendment Act, 1973. *Government Gazette* 27 June 1973: 2–35. Print.
Giliomee, Hermann. *The Afrikaners: Biography of a People*. London: C. Hurst, 2003. Print.
Goeie Hoop Uitgewers (Eiendoms) Bpk v Central News Agency and Another 1953 (2) SA 843 (W). Witwatersrand Local Division of the Supreme Court of South Africa. 1953. *The South African Law Reports (1947 to date)*. Juta Law, n.d. Web. 27 Oct. 2012.
Gordimer, Nadine. *Telling Times: Writing and Living, 1950–2008*. London: Bloomsbury, 2010. Print.
Grüttemeier, Ralf. "Interdisciplinariteit als participerende objectivering: Over de erkenning van de institutionele autonomie van literatuur in het recht in Nederland rond 1920." *Nederlandse Letterkunde* 16.2 (2011): 65–84. Print.
———. "Law and the Autonomy of Literature." Gillis J. Dorleijn, Ralf Grüttemeier, and Liesbeth Korthals Altes, eds. *The Autonomy of Literature at the Fins de Siècles (1900 and 2000): A Critical Assessment*. Leuven: Peeters, 2007: 175–92. Print.
———. "De omgang van de rechtspraak met literatuur in België aan de hand van Jef Geeraerts' *Black Venus*." *Spiegel der Letteren* 55.1 (2013): 35–49. Print.
———. "De rechter en de 'autonomiedoctrine': Over institutionele en poeticale autonomie in literaire processen." *Vooys* 28.3 (2010): 42–52. Print.
———. "'Zo schrijft hij en zo doet hij': Literatuur als bewijsmateriaal in strafzaken tegen schrijvers." *Nederlandse Letterkunde* 14.2 (2009): 155–79. Print.
Grüttemeier, Ralf, and Ted Laros. "Literature in Law: *Exceptio Artis* and the Emergence of Literary Fields." *Law and Humanities* 7.2 (2013): 204–17. Print.

G. W. Hardy v Rex. Supreme Court of Natal. 1905. *All South African Law Reports 1828 to 1946*. LexisNexis South Africa, n.d. Web. 27 Oct. 2012.

Hamilton, Carolyn, Bernard K. Mbenga, and Robert Ross, eds. *The Cambridge History of South Africa*. Vol. 1. Cambridge: Cambridge University Press, 2009. Print.

Harvey, C. J. D. Reader's Report on André P. Brink, *Miskien Nooit*. C. J. D. Harvey et al. Report of the Decision of the Publications Control Board on André P. Brink, *Miskien Nooit*. 9 May 1968. MS. BCS 52/68. Western Cape Provincial Archives and Records Service, Cape Town.

Harvey, C. J. D. et al. Report of the Decision of the Publications Control Board on Wilbur A. Smith, *When the Lion Feeds*. 21 Apr. 1964. TS. BCS 649/64. Western Cape Provincial Archives and Records Service, Cape Town.

Hepple, Alex. *Censorship and Press Control in South Africa*. Johannesburg: n.p., 1960. Print.

Hood, B. G. Introduction. "Literary Censorship and the South African Librarian: A Symposium by B. G. Hood, D. L. Ehlers and D. H. Varley." *South African Libraries* 22.2 (1954): 39–40. Print.

Huber, Ernst Rudolf. *Deutsche Verfassungsgeschichte seit 1789*. Vol. 1. Stuttgart: Kohlhammer, 1957. Print.

———. *Zur Problematik des Kulturstaats*. Tübingen: Mohr, 1958. Print.

Human & Rousseau Uitgewers (Edms) Bpk v Snyman NO 1978 (3) SA 836 (T). Transvaal Provincial Division of the Supreme Court of South Africa. 1978. *The South African Law Reports (1947 to date)*. Juta Law, n.d. Web. 27 Oct. 2012.

Hupe, Katharina. "Belgische Literatur vor Gericht: Über die Autonomie literarischer Texte in Gerichtsverfahren." Diss. Carl von Ossietzky U of Oldenburg, 2011. Print.

Janssens, A. L. J. M. "Strafbare belediging." Diss. U of Groningen, 1998. Print.

Joch, Markus, and Norbert Christian Wolf, eds. *Text und Feld: Bourdieu in der literaturwissenschaftlichen Praxis*. Tübingen: Niemeyer, 2005. Print.

Johnson, David. "Literary and Cultural Criticism in South Africa." David Attwell and Derek Attridge, eds. *The Cambridge History of South African Literature*. Cambridge: Cambridge University Press, 2012: 818–37. Print.

Jordan, Radford. "Withdrawal of Ban by Publications Control Board." *The South African Law Journal* 89 (1972): 349–53. Print.

Kader, David, and Michael Stanford, eds. *Poetry of the Law: From Chaucer to Present*. Iowa City: University of Iowa Press, 2010. Print.

Kahanovitz, S., and N. Manoim. *Radically Undesirable*. N.p.: n.p., [c. 1979]. Print.

Kahn, Ellison. "The 'Dirty' Books that We Have Banned." *Standpunte* 20.4 (1967): 33–42. Print.

———. "Freedom of Speech and the Press: Publications and Entertainments Act, No. 26 of 1963." H. R. Hahlo, Ellison Kahn, Ian B. Murray, Arthur Suzman, R. S. Welsh, eds. *Annual Survey of South African Law 1963*. Cape Town: Juta, 1964. 46–53. Print.

———. "Publications and Entertainments Act, No. 26 of 1963." P. Q. R. Boberg et al., eds. *Annual Survey of South African Law 1965*. Cape Town: Juta, 1966: 36–45. Print.

———. "*When the Lion Feeds*—and the Censor Pounces: A Disquisition on the Banning of Immoral Publications in South Africa." *The South African Law Journal* 83.3 (1966): 278–336. Print.

Kannemeyer, J. C. *Geskiedenis van die Afrikaanse Literatuur*. 2nd ed. 2 vols. Pretoria: Academica, 1984. Print.

Katz, Al. "Free Discussion v. Final Decision: Moral and Artistic Controversy and the Tropic of Cancer Trials." *The Yale Law Journal* 79.2 (1969): 209–52. Print.

Kayman, Martin A. "Literature vs. the Law: Modernity, Modernism, Postmodernity." Gillis J. Dorleijn, Ralf Grüttemeier, and Liesbeth Korthals Altes, eds. *The Autonomy of Literature at the Fins de Siècles (1900 and 2000): A Critical Assessment*. Leuven: Peeters, 2007: 193–211. Print.

Kearns, Paul. "The Judicial Nemesis: Artistic Freedom and the European Court of Human Rights." *Irish Law Journal* 1 (2012): 56–92. Print.

Kemp, Sandra, Charlotte Mitchell, and David Trotter. *Edwardian Fiction: An Oxford Companion*. Oxford: Oxford University Press, 1997. Print.

Kennedy, Brian P. *Dreams and Responsibilities: The State and the Arts in Independent Ireland.* Dublin: The Arts Council, 1990. Print.
Knies, Wolfgang. *Schranken der Kunstfreiheit als verfassungsrechtliches Problem.* Munich: C. H. Beck, 1967. Print.
Kohler, Gun-Britt. "Feld und Nation: Perspektiven für die slavische Literaturwissenschaft." Oldenburger Universitätsreden Nr. 189. Oldenburg: Carl von Ossietzky U of Oldenburg P, 2009: 29–49. Print.
———. "Institutional Autonomy 1840 versus Aesthetic Autonomy 1900? Moments of Tension in Croatian Literature with Respect to the Idea of 'Nation' in the Poetic Self-Positionings of Authors." Gillis J. Dorleijn, Ralf Grüttemeier, Liesbeth Korthals Altes, eds. *The Autonomy of Literature at the Fins de Siècles (1900 and 2000): A Critical Assessment.* Leuven: Peeters, 2007: 1–27. Print.
———. "National Disposition and the Author's Trajectory: Reflections on Polish and Croatian Literature." Gillis J. Dorleijn, Ralf Grüttemeier and Liesbeth Korthals Altes, eds. *Authorship Revisited: Conceptions of Authorship around 1900 and 2000.* Leuven: Peeters, 2010: 11–38. Print.
Krog, Antjie. *Country of My Skull.* London: Vintage, 1999. Print.
Kruger, J. J. "The Publications Control Board: The Rules by Which It Works." *Suid-Afrikaanse Biblioteke/South African Libraries* 38.4 (1971): 236–37. Print.
Kruger, J. T., et al. *Report of the Commission of Inquiry into the Publications and Entertainments Amendment Bill (A.B. 61—'73).* Pretoria: Government Printer, 1974. Print.
Kruger, J. T., et al. *Report of the Select Committee on the Publications and Entertainments Amendment Bill.* Pretoria: Government Printer, 1973. Print.
Kulhoff, Birgit. *Bürgerliche Selbstbehauptung im Spiegel der Kunst: Untersuchungen zur Kulturpublizistik der Rundschauzeitschriften im Kaiserreich (1871–1914).* Bochum: Brockmeyer, 1990. Print.
Kunene, Daniel P. "African-Language Literatures of Southern Africa." F. Abiola Irele and Simon Gikandi, eds. *The Cambridge History of African and Caribbean Literature.* Vol. 1. Cambridge: Cambridge University Press, 2004: 289–305. Print.
LaCapra, Dominick. *"Madame Bovary" on Trial.* Ithaca, NY: Cornell University Press, 1982. Print.
Ladenson, Elisabeth. *Dirt for Art's Sake: Books on Trial from* Madame Bovary *to* Lolita. Ithaca, NY: Cornell University Press, 2007. Print.
Leavis, F. R. *The Great Tradition: George Eliot, Henry James, Joseph Conrad.* 1948. Harmondsworth: Penguin, 1972. Print.
Leerssen, Joep. *The Cultivation of Culture: Towards a Definition of Romantic Nationalism in Europe.* Amsterdam: Opleiding Europese Studies, University of Amsterdam, 2005. Print.
le Roux, Beth, Willem Struik, and Margaret Labuschagne. *Annual Book Publishing Industry Survey Report 2010. Publishers' Association of South Africa.* Publishers' Association of South Africa, 2011. Web. 2 June 2013. http://www.publishsa.co.za/downloads/industry-statistics/Survey_2010_Report.pdf.
Leroux, Etienne. *Magersfontein, O Magersfontein!* 8th ed. Cape Town: Human & Rousseau, 1989. Print.
Lewis, Felice Flanery. *Literature, Obscenity, and Law.* Carbondale, IL: Southern Illinois University Press 1976. Print.
Lockey, Brian. *Law and Empire in English Renaissance Literature.* Cambridge: Cambridge University Press, 2006. Print.
Lockhart, William B., and Robert C. McClure. "Censorship of Obscenity: The Developing Constitutional Standards." *Minnesota Law Review* 45.5 (1960): 5–121. Print.
MacDonald, I. A. "Censorship: Some Philosophical Issues: The 'Offence Principle' as a Justification for Censorship." *Philosophical Papers* 5.1 (1976): 67–84. Print.
Magersfontein: Die Dokumente. Cape Town/Johannesburg: Human & Rousseau, 1990. Print.
Magerski, Christine. *Die Konstituierung des literarischen Feldes in Deutschland nach 1871: Berliner Moderne, Literaturkritik und die Anfänge der Literatursoziologie.* Tübingen: Niemeyer, 2004. Print.

Magubane, Bernard. "From Détente to the Rise of the Garrison State." South African Democracy Education Trust. *The Road to Democracy in South Africa*. Vol. 2. N.p.: U of South Africa P, 2006: 37–97. Print.

Malan, Charles, and Martjie Bosman. *Sensuur, Literatuur en die Leser:* Donderdag of Woensdag *as Toetsgeval: Verslag van 'n SENSAL-ondersoek*. Pretoria: Raad vir Geesteswetenskaplike Navorsing, 1983. Print.

Mame Enterprises (Edms) Bpk v Raad van Beheer oor Publikasies 1976 (1) SA 429 (A). Appellate Division of the Supreme Court of South Africa. 1976. *The South African Law Reports (1947 to date). Juta Law*, n.d. Web. 27 Oct. 2012.

Marais, J. F. "Regsaspekte van Literêre Sensuur." *Standpunte* 13.6 (1960): 49–53. Print.

Marcus, Gilbert. "Reasonable Censorship?" Hugh Corder, ed. *Essays on Law and Social Practice in South Africa*. Cape Town: Juta, 1988: 349–60. Print.

———. Rev. of *Censorship and Public Morality*, by P. R. MacMillan. *The South African Law Journal* 104 (1987): 210–11. Print.

Masilela, Ntongela. "New African Modernity and the New African Movement." David Attwell and Derek Attridge, eds. *The Cambridge History of South African Literature*. Cambridge: Cambridge University Press, 2012: 325–38. Print.

McDonald, Peter D. "The Book in South Africa." David Attwell and Derek Attridge, eds. *The Cambridge History of South African Literature*. Cambridge: Cambridge University Press, 2012: 800–17. Print.

———. "Brief Biographies of Some Key Censors." *The Literature Police: Apartheid Censorship and Its Cultural Consequences*. N.p., 2009. Web. 11 Oct. 2011.

———. "Disgrace Effects." *interventions* 4.3 (2002): 321–30. Print.

———. *The Literature Police: Apartheid Censorship and its Cultural Consequences*. Oxford: Oxford University Press, 2009. Print.

———. "Old Phrases and Great Obscenities: The Strange Afterlife of Two Victorian Anxieties." *Journal of Victorian Culture* 13.2 (2008): 294–302. Print.

Merrett, Christopher. *A Culture of Censorship: Secrecy and Intellectual Repression in South Africa*. Macon, GA: Mercer University Press, 1995. Print.

Meyer, Bernard S., Burton C. Agata, and Seth H. Agata. *The History of the New York Court of Appeals, 1932–2003*. New York: Columbia University Press, 2006. Print.

"Minderheidsuitspraak: *Magersfontein, O Magersfontein!*" [Minority judgment: *Magersfontein, O Magersfontein!*] Publications Appeal Board Case No. 77/77. 1977. TS. P77/1/97. Western Cape Provincial Archives and Records Service, Cape Town.

Mix, York-Gothart. "Wahre Dichtung und Ware Literatur: Lyrik, Lohn und Kunstreligion und Konkurrenz auf dem literarischen Markt 1760–1810." Markus Joch and Norbert Christian Wolf, eds. *Text und Feld: Bourdieu in der literaturwissenschaftlichen Praxis*. Tübingen: Niemeyer, 2005: 109–35. Print.

Moore, Nicole. *The Censor's Library: Uncovering the Lost History of Australia's Banned Books*. St. Lucia: University of Queensland Press, 2012. Print.

Moran, Leslie J. "Dangerous Words and Dead Letters: Encounters with Law and The Love that Dares to Speak its Name." *Liverpool Law Review* 23 (2001): 153–65. Print.

Murray, A. H. "Kommentaar op Professor Kahn: When the Lions Feed and the Censor Pounces." Internal memo directed to the full-time and part-time members of the Publications Control Board. N.d. TS. BCS vol. 22, ref. M1. Western Cape Provincial Archives and Records Service, Cape Town.

Nabers, Deak. *Victory of Law: The Fourteenth Amendment, the Civil War and American Literature, 1852–1867*. Baltimore, MD: Johns Hopkins University Press, 2006. Print.

Ndebele, Njabulo S. *Fine Lines from the Box: Further Thoughts about Our Country*. Houghton: Umuzi-Random House, 2007. Print.

———. *Rediscovery of the Ordinary: Essays on South African Literature and Culture*. Johannesburg: COSAW, 1991. Print.

Newman, Roger K. *The Yale Biographical Dictionary of American Law*. New Haven, CT: Yale University Press, 2009. Print.

"A Note on South African Legislation concerning 'Objectionable Literature.'" *South African Libraries* 22.2 (1954): 46–47. Print.

"Notice 840 of 1972: Summary of the Report of the Interdepartmental Committee of Inquiry into the Application of the Publications and Entertainments Act, 1963." *Government Gazette* 22 Dec. 1972: 1–23. Print.
"A Nun's Passion: A Xmas Story." *The Ringhals* 30 Dec. 1933: 4. Print.
Nussbaum, Martha C. *Hiding from Humanity: Disgust, Shame, and the Law*. Princeton, NJ: Princeton University Press, 2004. Print.
"'n Wêreld vol Dinge..." *Keur* (1953): 22–25, 39. Print.
Obscene Publications Act, 1892. Hercules Tennant and Edgar Michael Jackson, ed. *Statutes of the Cape of Good Hope, 1652–1895*. Vol. 3. Cape Town: Juta, 1895. Print.
Obscene Publications Act 1959. *legislation.gov.uk*. HM Government, n.d. Web. 13 Oct. 2011.
"Obscenity and the First Amendment: The Search for an Adequate Test." *Duke Law Journal* 7 (1958): 116–26. Print.
"'Obscenity' on Trial: The New African Case." 4.1 *The New African* (1965): 2–3. Print.
Olson, Greta, and Martin A. Kayman. "Introduction: From 'Law-and-Literature' to 'Law, Literature, and Language': A Comparative Approach." *European Journal of English Studies* 11.1 (2007): 1–15. Print.
O'Neil, Robert M. "Artistic Freedom and Academic Freedom." *Law and Contemporary Problems* 53.3 (1990): 177–93. Print.
Oosthuizen, I. J., and C. J. Russo. "A Constitutionalised Perspective on Freedom of Artistic Expression." *South African Journal of Education* 21.4 (2001): 260–63. Print.
Peters, Bas. *Op zoek naar Afrika: Over het verbod op* Kennis van die Aand *van André P. Brink*. Leiden: SNL, 1996. Print.
Peters, Julie Stone. "Law, Literature, and the Vanishing Real: On the Future of an Interdisciplinary Illusion." *PMLA* 120.2 (2005): 442–53. Print.
Petersen, Klaus. *Zensur in der Weimarer Republik*. Stuttgart: Metzler, 1995. Print.
Pienaar, G. J. "Histories-Juridiese Aspekte van Sensuur in Suid-Afrika." *Suid-Afrikaanse Biblioteke/South African Libraries* 38.4 (1971): 238–49. Print.
———. "Sensuur: Histories en Juridies Besien." 1972/1973. Studiestuk nr. 66. Potchefstroom: Instituut vir Bevordering van Calvinisme, Potchefstroomse Universiteit vir Christelike Hoër Onderwys, n.d. Print.
Polak, Ernest. *De artt. 240 en 451bis W.v.Sr. beschouwd in hunne verhouding tot kunst en wetenschap*. Amsterdam: Amsterdamsche Boek- en Steendrukkerij, 1912. Print.
"Publications Act 42 of 1974." P. Q. R. Boberg et al., eds. *Annual Survey of South African Law 1978*. Cape Town: Juta, 1979: 33–35. Print.
Publications Act No. 42 of 1974. *Government Gazette* 9 Oct. 1974: 2–67. Print.
Publications Amendment Act No. 79 of 1977. *Government Gazette* 15 June 1977: 2–11. Print.
Publications Amendment Act No. 109 of 1978. *Government Gazette* 30 June 1978: 2–13. Print.
Publications Amendment Act No. 44 of 1979. *Government Gazette* 9 May 1979: 2–3. Print.
Publications Amendment Act No. 60 of 1986. *Government Gazette* 25 June 1986: 2–29. Print.
Publications Amendment Act No. 90 of 1992. *Government Gazette* 1 July 1992: 2–13. Print.
Publications and Entertainments Act No. 26 of 1963. *Statutes of the Republic of South Africa 1963*. Part 1, nos. 1–60. Pretoria: Government Printer, n.d.: 276–301. Print.
Publications and Entertainments Amendment Act No. 85 of 1969. *Government Gazette* 4 July 1969: 2–4. Print.
Publications and Entertainments Amendment Act No. 32 of 1971. *Government Gazette* 12 May 1971: 2–8. Print.
Publications Appeal Board Case of *The Dawn Comes Twice* (144/76). 1977. TS. P84/10/48. Western Cape Provincial Archieves and Records Service, Cape Town.
Publications Appeal Board Case of *Donderdag of Woensdag* (70/78). 1978. TS. P78/5/59. Western Cape Provincial Archives and Records Service, Cape Town.
Publications Appeal Board Case of *Magersfontein, O Magersfontein!* (77/77). 1977. TS. P77/1/97. Western Cape Provincial Archives and Records Service, Cape Town.
Publications Appeal Board Case of *Magersfontein, O Magersfontein!* (7/80). 1980. TS. P77/1/97. Western Cape Provincial Archives and Records Service, Cape Town.

Publications Control Board v Republican Publications (Pty) Ltd 1972 (1) SA 288 (A). Appellate Division of the Supreme Court of South Africa. 1972. *South African Appellate Division Reports (1910 to date). Juta Law*, n.d. Web. 1 Nov. 2011.

Publications Control Board v William Heinemann, Ltd and Others 1965 (4) SA 137 (A). Appellate Division of the Supreme Court of South Africa. 1965. *South African Appellate Division Reports (1910 to date). Juta Law*, n.d. Web. 17 Feb. 2011.

Queen v de Jong 11 S.C.R. 326. Supreme Court of the Colony of the Cape of Good Hope. 1894. *All South African Law Reports 1828 to 1946. LexisNexis South Africa*, n.d. Web. 27 Oct. 2012.

R v Hicklin (1868) L.R. 3 Q.B. 360. *Wikisource*. Wikimedia Foundation, 24 Oct. 2010. Web. 13 Oct. 2011.

Reader's report on Etienne Leroux's *Magersfontein, O Magersfontein!* in terms of the Publications Act, 1974 by "Leser A" [Reader A]. MS/TS. P77/1/97. Western Cape Provincial Archives and Records Service, Cape Town.

Reader's report on Etienne Leroux's *Magersfontein, O Magersfontein!* in terms of the Publications Act, 1974 by "Leser B" [Reader B]. MS/TS. P77/1/97. Western Cape Provincial Archives and Records Service, Cape Town.

Reader's report on Etienne Leroux's *Magersfontein, O Magersfontein!* in terms of the Publications Act, 1974 by "Leser C" [Reader C]. MS/TS. P77/1/97. Western Cape Provincial Archives and Records Service, Cape Town.

"Report of the Commission on Undesirable Publications: Memorandum Sent by the Council of the S. A. Library Association to the Hon. Minister of the Interior." *South African Libraries* 25.4 (1958): 113–15. Print.

Report of the Publications Appeal Board and of the Directorate of Publications for the Calendar Year 1977. TS. National Library of South Africa, Cape Town Campus.

Report of the Task Group Film and Publication Control to Dr M G Buthelezi Minister of Home Affairs of the Republic of South Africa. 3 vols. Pretoria: Government Printer, 1994. Print.

Report on Etienne Leroux's *Magersfontein, O Magersfontein!* in terms of the Publications Act, 1974 by the ad hoc committee appointed by the Directorate of Publications. 1977. MS/TS. P77/1/97. Western Cape Provincial Archives and Records Service, Cape Town.

Republican Publications (Pty) Ltd v Publications Control Board 1970 (1) SA 577 (C). Western Cape Provincial Division of the Supreme Court of South Africa. 1969. *The South African Law Reports (1947 to date). Juta Law*, n.d. Web. 19 Jan. 2015.

Republican Publications (Pty) Ltd v Publications Control Board 1971 (2) SA 1 (D). Durban and Coast Local Division of the Supreme Court of South Africa. 1970–1971. *The South African Law Reports (1947 to date). Juta Law*, n.d. Web. 19 Jan. 2015.

Republican Publications (Pty) Ltd v Publications Control Board 1971 (2) SA 162 (D). Durban and Coast Local Division of the Supreme Court of South Africa. 1970–1971. *The South African Law Reports (1947 to date). Juta Law*, n.d. Web. 19 Jan. 2015.

Republican Publications (Pty) Ltd v Publications Control Board 1971 (2) SA 243 (D). Durban and Coast Local Division of the Supreme Court of South Africa. 1971. *The South African Law Reports (1947 to date). Juta Law*, n.d. Web. 19 Jan. 2015.

Republican Publications (Pty) Ltd v Publications Control Board 1971 (3) SA 399 (D). Durban and Coast Local Division of the Supreme Court of South Africa. 1971. *The South African Law Reports (1947 to date). Juta Law*, n.d. Web. 19 Jan. 2015.

Republican Publications (Pty) Ltd v Publications Control Board 1972 (3) SA 562 (D). Durban and Coast Local Division of the Supreme Court of South Africa. 1972. *The South African Law Reports (1947 to date). Juta Law*, n.d. Web. 19 Jan. 2015.

Republican Publications (Pty) Ltd v Publications Control Board 1973 (4) SA 549 (D). Durban and Coast Local Division of the Supreme Court of South Africa. 1973. *The South African Law Reports (1947 to date). Juta Law*, n.d. Web. 19 Jan. 2015.

Republican Publications (Pty) Ltd v Publications Control Board 1974 (2) SA 55 (D). Durban and Coast Local Division of the Supreme Court of South Africa. 1973. *The South African Law Reports (1947 to date). Juta Law*, n.d. Web. 19 Jan. 2015.

Rex v Meinert. High Court of South-West Africa. 1932. I. Goldblatt and R. E. G. Rosenow, eds. *The South African Law Reports [1927] South-West Africa: Decisions of the High Court of South-West Africa. January to December, 1927*. Cape Town: Juta, 1928. Print.
Rex v Shaw. Cape Provincial Division of the Supreme Court of South Africa. 1910. *All South African Law Reports 1828 to 1946. LexisNexis South Africa*, n.d. Web. 27 Oct. 2012.
Rex v Webb 1934 AD 493. Appellate Division of the Supreme Court of South Africa. 1934. *All South African Law Reports 1828 to 1946. LexisNexis South Africa*, n.d. Web. 27 Oct. 2012.
Rickard, Carmel. *Thank You, Judge Mostert!* Johannesburg: Penguin, 2010. Print.
Robertson, Geoffrey. *Obscenity: An Account of Censorship Laws and their Enforcement in England and Wales*. London: Weidenfeld and Nicolson, 1979. Print.
Ross, Robert, Anne Kelk Mager, and Bill Nasson, eds. *The Cambridge History of South Africa*. Vol. 2. Cambridge: Cambridge University Press, 2011. Print.
Roth v United States 354 U.S. 476 (1957). *FindLaw*. FindLaw, n.d. Web. 8 July 2013. http://caselaw.lp.findlaw.com/scripts/getcase.pl?court=US&vol=354&invol=476.
Sachs, Albie. "Art and Freedom." Bronwyn Law-Viljoen. *Art and Justice: The Art of the Constitutional Court of South Africa*. Parkwood: D. Krut, 2008: 17–36. Print.
———. *Justice in South Africa*. Berkeley, CA: University of California Press, 1973. Print.
Sanders, Mark. *Ambiguities of Witnessing: Law and Literature in the Time of a Truth Commission*. Stanford, CA: Stanford University Press, 2007. Print.
Sandwith, Corinne. *World of Letters: Reading Communities and Cultural Debates in Early Apartheid South Africa*. Scottsville: University of KwaZulu-Natal Press, 2014. Print.
Sapiro, Gisèle. *La guerre des écrivains, 1940–1953*. Paris: Fayard, 1999. Print.
———. "The Legal Responsibility of the Writer between Objectivity and Subjectivity: The French Case (Nineteenth to Twenty-First Century)." Ralf Grüttemeier, ed. *Literary Trials: Exceptio Artis and Theories of Literature in Court*. London: Bloomsbury Academic, 2016: 21–47. Print.
———. "The Literary Field between the State and the Market." *Poetics* 31 (2003): 441–64. Print.
———. *La responsabilité de l'écrivain: Littérature, droit et morale en France (XIXe–XXIe siècle)*. Paris: Seuil, 2011. Print.
Schalkwyk, David. *Hamlet's Dreams: The Robben Island Shakespeare*. London: Bloomsbury Academic, 2013. Print.
Schmidt, Siegfried J. *Die Selbstorganisation des Sozialsystems Literatur im 18. Jahrhundert*. Frankfurt: Suhrkamp, 1989. Print.
Schneck, Peter. *Rhetoric and Evidence: Legal Conflict and Literary Representation in American Culture*. Berlin: De Gruyter, 2011. Print.
Senekal, Burgert A. *Canons and Connections: A Network Theory Approach to the Study of Literary Systems with Specific Reference to Afrikaans Poetry*. Washington, DC: New Academia Publishing, 2014. Print.
"Senior Judge Admits to Having Been a Member of the Broederbond." *ANC Daily News Briefing*. 12 Oct. 1998. 12 Nov. 2012 http://www.e-tools.co.za/newsbrief/1998/news1014. Web.
Silver, Louise. "Banning Future Editions of a Periodical Publication." *The South African Law Journal* 97 (1980): 482–85. Print.
———. "Criticism of the Police: Standards Enunciated by the Publications Appeal Board." *The South African Law Journal* 95.[2?] (1978): 580–83. Print.
———. *A Guide to Political Censorship in South Africa*. Johannesburg: Centre for Applied Legal Studies, University of the Witwatersrand, 1984. Print.
———. "The Publications Appeal Board: A Closer Look at Nudity." *The South African Law Journal* 99 (1982): 272–83. Print.
———. "Sex, Nudity and the Average Man." *The South African Law Journal* 97 (1980): 125–37. Print.
———. "The Statistics of Censorship." *The South African Law Journal* 96 (1979): 120–26. Print.
———. "Trends in Publications Control: A Statistical Analysis." *The South African Law Journal* 100 (1983): 520–30. Print.

———. "Who Are the Custodians? A Closer Look at Publications Control." *The SouthAfrican Law Journal* 98 (1981): 105–11. Print.
Smith, Wilbur A. *When the Lion Feeds*. London: Heinemann, 1964. Print.
Smuts, J. P. "Die Tydperk van Waterskeiding: Die Sestigers." *Dekades in die Afrikaanse Letterkunde: 'n Reeks praatjies uitgesaai in die Afrikaanse diens van die Suid-Afrikaanse Uitsaaikorporasie*. N.p.: SAUK, n.d.: 71–76. Print.
Snyman, J. H. "Die Wet op Publikasies 42 van 1974." *Tydskrif vir die Suid-Afrikaanse Reg/Journal of South African Law* 1976: 190–201. Print.
Snyman, N. J. "Misvattinge oor die Literatuur in Afrikaans soos Weerspieël in Vier Polemieke: 'n Historiese Oorsig." MA thesis University of Pretoria, 1969. Print.
Sova, Dawn B. *Banned Books: Literature Suppressed on Sexual Grounds*. Rev. ed. New York: Facts on File, 2006. Print.
St. John-Stevas, Norman. *Obscenity and the Law*. 1956. New York: Da Capo, 1974. Print.
Stockhorst, Stefanie. "Feldforschung vor der Erfindung der Autonomieästhetik? Zur relativen Autonomie barocker Gelegenheitsdichtung." Markus Joch and Norbert Christian Wolf, eds. *Text und Feld: Bourdieu in der literaturwissenschaftlichen Praxis*. Tübingen: Niemeyer, 2005: 55–71. Print.
Strauss, S. A., M. J. Strydom, J. C. van der Walt. *Die Suid-Afrikaanse Persreg*. 3rd. ed. Pretoria: J. L. van Schaik, 1976. Print.
Strydom, M. J. "Besit van Verbode Publikasies." *Standpunte* 18.6 (1965): 65–69. Print.
———. "Ne Bis in Idem . . . ? Hersiening deur Publikasieraad van Sy Eie Beslissings." *Tydskrif vir Hedendaagse Romeins-Hollandse Reg/Journal of Contemporary Roman Dutch Law* 28 (1965): 51–56. Print.
———. "Die Wet op Publikasies en Vermaaklikhede, 1963." *Tydskrif vir Hedendaagse Romeins-Hollandse Reg/Journal of Contemporary Roman-Dutch Law* 26 (1963): 195 205. Print.
Suzman, Arthur. "Censorship and the Courts: The Suggested Abolition of the Right of Appeal to the Supreme Court from Decisions of the Publications Control Board." *The South African Law Journal* 89 (1972): 191–206. Print.
S v Insight Publications (Pty) Ltd and Another 1965 (2) SA 775 (C). Western Cape Provincial Division of the Supreme Court of South Africa. 1965. *The South African Law Reports (1947 to date)*. Juta Law, n.d. Web. 26 Oct. 2011.
Swanepoel, Christiaan. "Writing and Publishing in African Languages since 1948." David Attwell and Derek Attridge, eds. *The Cambridge History of South African Literature*. Cambridge: Cambridge University Press, 2012: 607–32. Print.
Tafira, Hashi Kenneth. *Black Nationalist Thought in South Africa: The Persistence of an Idea of Liberation*. New York: Palgrave Macmillan, 2016. Print.
"The Judiciary: Judges' Remuneration and Pensions Act 14 of 1975." P. Q. R. Boberg et al., eds. *Annual Survey of South African Law 1975*. Cape Town: Juta, 1976: 536–37. Print.
Themba, Can. "The Fugitives." *The New African* 3.3 (1964): 51–3. Print.
———. *Requiem for Sophiatown*. Johannesburg: Penguin, 2006. Print.
Unterhalter, David. Rev. of *A Guide to Political Censorship in South Africa*, by Louise Silver. *The South African Law Journal* 101 (1984): 780–82. Print.
van Blerk, Adrienne E. *Judge and Be Judged*. Cape Town: Juta, 1988. Print.
van Coller, H. P. "The Beginnings of Afrikaans Literature." David Attwell and Derek Attridge, eds. *The Cambridge History of South African Literature*. Cambridge: Cambridge University Press, 2012: 262–85. Print.
van Coller, H. P., and B. J. Odendaal. *The Emergent Canon: Case Studies of Phenomena in the Afrikaans Literary System and its Relationships with Other Systems*. Forthcoming.
van der Merwe Scholtz, H. Reader's Report on André P. Brink, *Miskien Nooit*. C. J. D. Harvey et al. Report of the Decision of the Publications Control Board on André P. Brink, *Miskien Nooit*. 9 May 1968. TS. BCS 52/68. Western Cape Provincial Archives and Records Service, Cape Town.
van der Poll, Letetia. "The Constitution of Pornography." Diss. University of Stellenbosch, 2001. Print.

van der Vlies, Andrew. "South Africa in the Global Imaginary." David Attwell and Derek Attridge, eds. *The Cambridge History of South African Literature*. Cambridge: Cambridge University Press, 2012: 697–716. Print.

van der Vyver, Johan. "General Aspects of the South African Censorship Laws." Theo Coggin, ed. *Censorship: A Study of Censorship in South Africa by Five Distinguished Authors, Johan van der Vyver, André Brink, Allan Boesak, Ian McDonald and André du Toit. Introduction by Geoff Budlender*. Johannesburg: S.A. Institute of Race Relations, 1983: 9–36. Print.

van der Waal, Margriet Christien. "The Battle over the Books: Processes of Selection in the South African Literary Field." Diss. University of Groningen, 2006. Print.

van der Westhuizen, J. B. "Pornografie en die Reg." *De Jure* (1976): 57–64. Print.

van Rees, Kees. "How Conceptions of Literature Are Instrumental in Image Building." Klaus Beekman, ed. *Institution & Innovation*. Amsterdam: Rodopi, 1994: 103–29. Print.

van Rees, Kees, and Gillis J. Dorleijn. "The Eighteenth-Century Literary Field in Western Europe: The Interdependence of Material and Symbolic Production and Consumption." *Poetics* 28 (2001): 331–48. Print.

———. *De impact van literatuuropvattingen in het literaire veld: Aandachtsgebied literatuuropvattingen van de Stichting Literatuurwetenschap*. The Hague: Stichting Literatuurwetenschap, 1993. Print.

van Rensburg, F. I. J. "'n Literator kyk na die Publikasiewet." *Tydskrif vir die Suid-Afrikaanse Reg/Journal of South African Law* (1986): 153–63. Print.

van Rooyen, Kobus. "Aspekte van die Wet op Publikasies." *De Jure* Oct. 1975: 122–32. Print.

———. "Censorship in a Future South Africa: A Legal Perspective." Pieter E. Westra, ed. *Freedom to Read: Papers Presented at a Seminar on the Future of Publications Control and the Free Flow of Information in South Africa on 11 June 1993*. Cape Town: South African Library, 1994: 24–44. Print.

———. *Censorship in South Africa, Being a Commentary on the Application of the Publications Act*. Cape Town: Juta, 1987. Print.

———. "Dignity, Religion and Freedom of Expression in South Africa." *HTS Teologiese Studies/Theological Studies* 67.1 (2011): n. pag. Web. 5 Mar. 2013. http://www.hts.org.za/index.php/HTS/article/viewFile/1030/1514.

———. "Does the Offence of Blasphemy Have a Future under the South African Constitution?" *HTS Teologiese Studies/Theological Studies* 51.4 (1995): 1127–33. Print.

———. "Guidelines with Regard to Section 47(2) Act 42 of 1974." Addendum to Publications Appeal Board Case of *Heartland* (43/82). 1982. TS. R82/2/130. Western Cape Provincial Archives and Records Service, Cape Town.

———. "1963–1988: From Absolutism to Differentiation: An Analysis of the Changing Perceptions Informing the Work of the Publications Appeal Board." *The South African Law Journal* 106 (1989): 340–49. Print.

———. *Publikasiebeheer in Suid-Afrika (Publications Control in South Africa—Summaries in English)*. Cape Town: Juta, 1978. Print.

———. "Review of Recent Cases." *De Rebus Procuratoriis* 97 (1976): 30–32. Print.

———. *A South African Censor's Tale*. Pretoria: Protea, 2011. Print.

———. "University of Pretoria Centenary Law Faculty: Ninety Years." *University of Pretoria*. Web. 5 Mar. 2013. http://web.up.ac.za/default.asp?ipkCategoryID=7263&ifkModuleID=21&cx=004332890790385142604%3Aqyccuatg3pc&cof=FORID%3A11&q=centenary+law+faculty&sa.x=0&sa.y=0.

———. "Die Wet op Publikasies: 'n Christelike Lewensbeskouing?" *De Jure* 23.1 (1990): 354–57. Print.

Varley, Douglas H. "Trends Abroad: South Africa." *Library Trends* 19.1 (1970): 139–51. Print.

Viala, Alain. "Bourdieu, wiedergelesen mit den Augen Boileaus." Markus Joch and Norbert Christian Wolf, eds. *Text und Feld: Bourdieu in der literaturwissenschaftlichen Praxis*. Tübingen: Niemeyer, 2005: 45–53. Print.

———. *Naissance de l'écrivain. Sociologie de la littérature à l'âge classique*. Paris: Minuit, 1985. Print.

Visconsi, Elliott. *Lines of Equity: Literature and the Origins of Law in Later Stuart England.* Ithaca, NY: Cornell University Press, 2008. Print.
Visser, D. P. "As Durable as the Mountain: The Story of the Cape Town Law School since 1859." *Consultus* 5.1 (1992): 32–40. Print.
Welsh, David. "Censorship in South Africa: Censorship and the Universities." *Philosophical Papers* 5.1 (1976): 19–33. Print.
Westra, Pieter E., ed. *Freedom to Read: Papers Presented at a Seminar on the Future of Publications Control and the Free Flow of Information in South Africa on 11 June 1993.* Cape Town: South African Library, 1994. Print.
Wiechers, M. "Enkele Gedagtes oor die Wet op Publikasies 42 van 1974." *De Rebus Procuratoriis* 86 (1975): 59–63. Print.
———. "Publications Control Board v. William Heinemann Ltd., 1965 (4) S.A. 137 (A): Wet op Publikasies en Vermaaklikhede, No. 26 van 1963—Appel van die Raad van Beheer oor Publikasies en Vermaaklikhede, na die Hof." *Tydskrif vir Hedendaagse Romeins-Hollandse Reg/Journal of Contemporary Roman-Dutch Law* 29 (1966): 70–72. Print.
Wiehahn, Rialette. *Die Afrikaanse Poësiekritiek: 'n Histories-Teoretiese Beskouing.* Kaapstad: Academica, 1965. Print.
Wilkins, Ivor, and Hans Strydom. *The Broederbond.* New York: Paddington, 1979. Print.
Willemse, Hein. "Afrikaans Literature, 1948–1976." David Attwell and Derek Attridge, eds. *The Cambridge History of South African Literature.* Cambridge: Cambridge University Press, 2012: 429–51. Print.
William Heinemann Ltd and Others v Publications Control Board 1965 (2) SA 258 (C). Western Cape Provincial Division of the Supreme Court of South Africa. 1965. *The South African Law Reports (1947 to date). Juta Law,* n.d. Web. 15 Sep. 2011.
Williams, Bernard, et al. *Report of the Committee on Obscenity and Film Censorship.* London: Her Majesty's Stationary Office, 1979. Print.
Williams, J. E. Hall. "Obscenity in Modern English Law." *Law and Contemporary Problems* 20 (1955): 630–47. Print.
Williams, Raymond. *Culture and Society: 1780–1950.* London: Chatto and Windus, 1958. Print.
———. *The Long Revolution.* London: Chatto and Windus, 1961. Print.

Index

Abrams, M. H., 92, 119n33. *See also* theory of literature
absolute approach to publications control, 148, 149. *See also* relative approach to publications control
academic field of South Africa, 39, 44
academic law schools in South Africa, 44n2
Acts of Parliament (England): Customs Consolidation Act, 1853, 23; Obscene Publications Act, 1857, 24; Obscene Publications Act, 1959, 53, 55, 56, 59, 60, 63, 64, 80, 132; South Africa Act, 44n1; Statute of Westminster, 32, 44n2
Acts of Parliament (Ireland): Irish Censorship of Publications Act, 1946, 52
Acts of Parliament (South Africa and South-West Africa): Abolition of Restrictions on Free Political Activity Act, 1993, 178; Criminal Law Amendment Act, 1909, 24, 37; Customs Act, 1872 (Cape Colony), 23; Customs Act, 1955, 60, 83n20; Customs Consolidation and Shipping Act, 1899 (Natal), 23; Customs Management Act, 1913, 23, 38, 39; Customs Management Ordinance, 1902 (Transvaal), 23; Entertainments (Censorship) Act, 1931, 39, 53, 82n2; Films and Publications Act, 1996, 165, 176, 182, 183, 184, 185, 187, 188, 190n25, 197; Films and Publications Amendment Act, 1999, 184; Films and Publications Amendment Act, 2004, 184; Films and Publications Amendment Act, 2009, 184, 185, 188; Obscene Publications Act, 1892 (Cape Colony), 24, 25, 26, 31; Obscene Publications Suppression Ordinance 5, 1926 (South-West Africa), 32; Police Offences Ordinance, 1902 (Orange Free State), 24; Post Office Act, 1911, 44n6; Post Office Act, 1958, 44n6; Publications Act, 1974, 118, 127–132, 156, 161n77, 165, 166, 176, 178, 179, 187, 188, 189n3, 189n7, 195, 196, 197, 201; Publications Amendment Act, 1977, 158n25; Publications Amendment Act, 1978, 152, 156, 169, 170, 186, 196; Publications and Entertainments Act, 1963, 23, 53–57, 59, 60, 63, 64, 67, 69, 72, 74, 75, 76, 80–81, 82n14, 83n20, 83n29, 85, 98, 102, 108, 116, 127, 130, 131, 135, 157n2, 193, 194, 195, 201; Publications and Entertainments Amendment Act, 1969, 118n1; Publications and Entertainments Amendment Act, 1971, 118n1; Status of the Union Act, 1934, 44n2. *See also* moral provisions of the Publications Act, 1974; moral

217

provisions of the Publications and Entertainments Act, 1963; political provisions of the Publications Act, 1974; political provisions of the Publications and Entertainments Act, 1963; religious provisions of the Publications Act, 1974; religious provisions of the Publications and Entertainments Act, 1963
aestheticism, 115
aesthetic novel, 92
aesthetics: *Dertigers*, 115; idealist, 3, 15, 51, 144; N. P. van Wyk Louw, 115, 124n109, 138, 186; Platonic, 51, 79, 81, 93, 102, 116, 167, 198; *Sestigers*, 128. *See also* conception of literature; poetics; theory of literature
African National Congress (ANC), 28, 176, 189n1; Department of Arts and Culture (DAC) of, 177
Afrikaans literature, 68, 88
Afrikaner nationalism, 5, 115
aggravating factor, 169, 174
Aktie Morele Standaarde (Action Moral Standards), 135
Alexander the Great, 38
A. M. Gardner & Co., 30
Antigone, 86
anti-vice organization, 31, 158n36
"A Nun's Passion: A Xmas Story", 36
apartheid censorship, 2, 172
Apostolic faith, 67
argument of the classics, 27–29, 33, 38, 74
Armah, Ayi Kwei, 175; *Two Thousand Seasons*, 1, 190n12. *See also* Publications Appeal Board case of Armah, Ayi Kwei, *Two Thousand Seasons*
art exemption, 52, 180, 181, 188, 197, 200. *See also exceptio artis*
artistic freedom. *See* freedom
artistic merit, 52, 184
Attorney General, 24, 56, 65
Austin, Alfred, 114, 115, 124n106
authors' rights, 7
autonomist work of literature (Abramsian sense). *See* theory of literature
autonomization: external, 17; internal, 17; of the American literary field, 26, 28; of the Canadian literary field, 26; of the Dutch literary field, 28; of the English literary field, 19n2, 26; of the French literary field, 19n2; of the German literary field, 19n2; of the literary field, 7, 19n8, 55; of the South African literary field, 43, 44, 132, 146, 150, 155, 193, 200
autonomous pole of the literary field. *See* pole of restricted production
autonomy, 6, 8, 10; aesthetic, 10–12; external, 8–9; institutional, 3, 5, 8, 11, 13, 17, 44, 88; internal, 8, 9; of American literature, 45n14, 53; of Dutch literature, 15, 26; of English literature, 53, 55; of German literature, 15; of intellectual/literary socialized readers, 34, 70, 80, 104, 154, 156, 194; of literature, 3, 5, 17, 18; of South African literature, 18, 44, 55, 56, 64, 73, 78, 80, 81, 98, 99, 102, 106, 107–108, 111, 112, 113, 114, 115–117, 131–132, 141, 143, 145–146, 150, 151, 152, 154–156, 167, 169, 172, 173, 174, 175, 177, 178, 181, 182, 184, 185, 186, 187, 188, 189, 193, 194, 195, 196, 197, 198, 199, 201; poetological, 8, 12
avant-gardism, 115
average, civilized, decent, reasonable and responsible inhabitants of the Union, 52
average man, 143, 145, 146, 154, 161n75
average member of the South African community, 140
average reader, 62, 71, 72, 75, 78, 79, 91, 137, 147, 148
average reasonable person, 137, 138–139

Bantu peoples of Africa, 35, 174
Barbusse, Henri, 15; *L'enfer*, 15
Barnard, Chris, 88
barometer function of literary trials, 3, 5, 18, 199
Battle of Magersfontein, 134
Beekman, Klaus, 14
Beukes, D. P. M., 87, 88
Beyers (judge). *See* judges
Bill of Rights, 182
bills: Films and Publications Amendment Bill, 2006, 184; Publications and

Entertainments Bill, 1960, 53;
Publications and Entertainments Bill,
1962, 53; Undesirable Publications Bill,
1961, 53
binding precedent. See stare decisis
black liberation movements, 175
black literature in English, 68, 70
blasphemy, 2, 3, 36, 37, 38, 54, 55, 57, 89,
90, 106, 111, 134, 153, 183, 190n15
Block, J. N., 65, 67, 68
Bloemfontein, 65, 71
Bloom, Harry, *Transvaal Episode*. See
Publications Appeal Board case of
Bloom, Harry, *Transvaal Episode*
Board of Censors, 39, 40
Bok, Curtis. See judges
Bollinger, Lee C., 190n28
Booth, Wayne C., *The Rhetoric of Fiction*,
95
Boshoff (judge). See judges
Botha, Elize, 162n92
Botha, P. W., 167
Bourdieuian theory, 8, 20n14, 30;
Francocentricity of, 9
Bourdieu, Pierre, 2, 3, 6, 7, 9, 12, 17, 19n4,
88, 107, 117, 198
Breytenbach, Breyten, 5
Brink, André, 87, 92, 102, 134; *A Dry
White Season*, 170; *Kennis van die
Aand*, 1, 36, 128, 173; *Lobola vir die
Lewe*, 79; *Looking on Darkness*, 128,
190n12; *'n Droë Wit Seisoen*, 170. See
also Publications Appeal Board case of
Brink, André, *'n Droë Wit Seisoen/A
Dry White Season*; Publications Appeal
Board case of Brink, André, *Kennis van
die Aand*; trials
British Empire, 4, 29
Broadcast and Complaints Commission of
South Africa, 190n24
Brooks, Cleanth, *The Well-Wrought Urn*,
50
Buren Uitgewers, 87, 88
Burgess, Anthony, 177, 187; *Man of
Nazareth*, 1, 173, 187. See also
Publications Appeal Board case of
Burgess, Anthony, *Man of Nazareth*
Buthelezi, Mangosuthu, 179
Buxton, Earl, 35, 174

Byron, Lord, 29

Caldwell, Erskine, 46n21
Calvinist Churches in South Africa,
118n10, 135
Calvinists, 106
Cape Colony, 23, 24, 30
Cape Presbytery, 67
Cape Province, 44n3
cases (England): *Regina v Hicklin* (1868),
29, 33, 46n20, 74; *R v Bradlaugh*
(1878), 46n20; *R v Penguin Books Ltd*
(1960), 53
cases (South Africa and South-West
Africa): *Buren Uitgewers (Edms) Bpk
en 'n Ander v Raad van Beheer oor
Publikasies* (1974), 45n8; *Goeie Hoop
Uitgewers v Central News Agency and
Another* (1953), 25, 40, 41–43, 44,
45n8, 49; *G. W. Hardy v Rex* (Natal,
1905), 25, 27–30, 33, 34, 45n8, 74, 75,
81; *Human & Rousseau Uitgewers
(Edms) Bpk v Snyman NO* (1978),
45n8; *Mame Enterprises (Edms) Bpk v
Raad van Beheer oor Publikasies*
(1976), 189n8; *Publications Control
Board v Republican Publications (Pty)
Ltd* (1972), 85, 112, 149, 150, 155, 171;
*Publications Control Board v William
Heinemann, Ltd and Others* (1965),
45n8; *Q v de Jong* (Colony of the Cape
of Good Hope, 1894), 25–27, 31, 45n8;
Rex v Meinert (South-West Africa,
1932), 25, 32, 36, 38, 44, 45n8, 63, 104,
171, 174, 179, 188, 193, 197; *Rex v
Shaw* (1910), 25, 30–32, 33, 34, 38, 43,
45n8, 131, 150; *Rex v Webb* (1934), 25,
36–39, 40, 42, 44, 45n8, 45n17; *S v
Insight Publications (Pty) Ltd and
Another* (1965), 45n8, 65; *S v McBride*,
170
cases (United States): *Abrams v United
States*, 190n28; *Commonwealth of
Pennsylvania v Gordon and Others*
(1949), 42; *Roth v United States* (1957),
53
censor: literary, 50, 88, 134
censorship: administrative, 1, 2, 23, 44n4,
46n19, 52, 53, 56, 129, 195, 199; bill of

Cronjé Commission, 49; in Australia, 201; in Ireland, 201; in South Africa, 1–3; judicial, 2, 3, 40; of domestically produced literature, 2, 23, 24, 40, 49; of imported literature, 2, 23, 40, 49, 82n2; self-, 199. *See also* apartheid censorship
censorship board, 2
censorship committee (ad hoc), 129, 130; judgment on Etienne Leroux, *Magersfontein, O Magersfontein!*, 134–135
C. F. Albertyn Publishers, 91, 109
Chaucer, Geoffrey, 29
Cheh, Mary M., 190n17
child pornography, 180, 184, 185, 189
child races, 35, 174
Christ, 36, 37, 38, 177, 187
Christianity, 108, 117
Christian section of the South African population, 143
Christian view of life, 132
Cilliers, S. A., 136, 137, 139
classic literature, 28, 29, 44, 74, 75, 83n25, 135
classics argument. *See* argument of the classics
clear and present danger, 174
Cleland, John, *Memoirs of a Woman of Pleasure*. *See* Publications Appeal Board case of Cleland, John, *Memoirs of a Woman of Pleasure*
Cloete, T. T., 82n15, 88, 91, 92, 101, 105, 114
CNA Award, 135, 147
CNA chain of bookstores, 135
Cockburn, Alexander. *See* judges
Coetzee, Ampie, 87, 88, 108
Coetzee, Braam, 176, 179
Coetzee, D. J., 162n92
Coetzee, G. J., 93, 119n34
Coetzee, J. M., *Disgrace*, 189n1
Cold War, 174
Colony of Natal, 27, 30
Colony of the Cape of Good Hope, 26
Commission of Inquiry into Undesirable Publications, 49–53
committee of experts, 152, 153, 166, 167, 170, 172, 177
common law, 24, 25, 157n15

Commonwealth of Nations, 1
communism, 175
community standards, 33, 38, 59, 71, 72, 77–78, 131, 136, 140, 143, 145, 149, 161n75
comparison of incriminated work with other books, 59, 74–75, 77–78, 81, 83n25, 97, 142, 145, 154
Comstock, Anthony, 31, 45n8, 158n36
conception of literature, 5, 7, 10, 11, 13, 17, 19n9, 51, 117, 141, 187, 198; autonomous, 15, 96, 128, 144, 157n6, 175. *See also* aesthetics; poetics; theory of literature
conforming literature, 114, 115
constitution: of the Federal Republic of Germany (1949), 14, 178, 181; of the Republic of South Africa (1961), 68; of the Republic of South Africa (1993), 1, 165, 178, 179, 181, 182, 185; of the Republic of South Africa (1996), 83n28, 165, 182, 183, 184, 185, 188; of the Weimar Republic (1919), 14, 41; Paulskirche (Germany, 1849), 41
contempt, 54
contextual approach, 26–27, 28, 31, 38, 41–42, 43, 52, 55, 56, 60, 64, 66, 73–74, 80, 85–86, 95, 112, 132, 139, 142, 143, 144, 150, 155, 171, 175, 181, 186, 187, 188, 193, 194, 196, 197
continental legal tradition, 200
control of publications. *See* censorship
copyright. *See* law
court's opinion. *See* opinion of the court
court system: Republic of South Africa, 23; Union of South Africa, 23
crimen laesae venerationis, 45n17
criminal cases centering on literary authors, 5
Cronjé Commission, 53, 55, 56, 79, 81, 93, 127, 167, 198. *See also* Commission of Inquiry into Undesirable Publications
Cronjé, Geoffrey, 49, 82n1
Court of Appeal (England), 190n15; case of James Kirkup, "The Love that Dares to Speak its Name", 190n15
cultural field, 11, 199
cultural nationalism, 20n13

defamation, 2, 3
de Jong (lawful proprietor or editor of *Worcester Advertiser*), 26
de Klerk, F. W., 157n5, 178
de Klerk, J., 54
de Lange, Margreet, 191n29, 202n2
Department of Arts and Culture (DAC). *See* African National Congress
Department of Coloured Affairs, 119n34
deprave and corrupt, 57, 74, 76
Dertigers (Writers of the Thirties), 68, 138, 146. *See also* aesthetics
Die Burger (newspaper), 160n54
Diemont, Marius. *See* judges
Die Schönheit (magazine), 32
Directorate of Publications, 129, 130, 134, 135, 143, 157n18, 160n68, 165, 174, 179, 189n7
dirt for dirt's sake test, 26. *See also* contextual approach
dominant effect test, 26. *See also* contextual approach
dominant theme test, 26, 59. *See also* contextual approach
Dominion, 4
Dorleijn, Gillis, 8, 9, 10, 12, 19n11, 20n12, 199
Drum (periodical), 65
du Plessis, I. D., 93, 105, 119n34
Dutch Reformed Church, 106. *See also* Nederduitse Gereformeerde Kerk

Ebersohn, Wessel. *See* Publications Appeal Board case of Ebersohn, Wessel, *Divide the Night*; Publications Appeal Board case of Ebersohn, Wessel, *Store Up the Anger*
Eksteen, Louis, 88, 162n92
engaged literature, 110, 112, 113, 175
engaged novel, 92, 114
English Central Criminal Court, 190n15; case of James Kirkup, "The Love that Dares to Speak its Name", 190n15
Enlightenment, 4, 16
erotic fiction, 28
eternally vigilant, 185, 190n28
European Commission of Human Rights, 190n15; case of James Kirkup, "The Love that Dares to Speak its Name", 190n15
evidence, 17, 59, 67, 69, 71, 72, 73; objective, 72; subjective, 72. *See also* literary expert evidence
exceptio artis, 3, 14, 15, 19n1, 38, 41, 137, 182, 185; colonial, 32–35, 44, 193; constitutional, 1; in Belgian law, 14; in Canadian law, 181; in Dutch law, 14, 15, 41, 82n5, 121n47; in English law, 53, 64, 80, 181, 193; in French law, 121n47; in German law, 14, 15, 19n5, 41, 178, 181; in South African law, 34, 40, 44, 55, 56, 64, 143, 178, 182, 185, 186, 187, 193, 197, 198; in United States law, 53, 181; pertaining to literature, 7, 17. *See also* artistic freedom
exceptio scientiae: in Dutch law, 41; in German law, 41; in South African law, 36–39, 40, 41–42, 44, 56, 143
expert. *See* literary expert
expert evidence, 59, 64, 73, 77, 79, 80, 102, 105, 108, 110, 116, 141, 146, 180. *See also* literary expert evidence
expressive work of literature (*sensu* Abrams). *See* theory of literature

Farrell, James, 46n21
Faulkner, William, 46n21
Federasie van Afrikaanse Kultuurvereniginge (Federation of Afrikaans Cultural Associations), 118n11
field: juridical, 17; of power, 199. *See also* literary field
field theory, 6–12
Film and Publication Appeals Board, 185, 190n27
Film and Publication Board, 165, 179, 180, 183, 184, 185, 190n16, 190n25, 190n26; case of Salman Rushdie, *The Satanic Verses*, 165, 183–184, 185, 188, 189, 197
Film and Publication Review Board, 179, 180, 183, 184, 190n25, 190n27
First Afrikaans Language Movement, 159n42
First Amendment, 46n21, 174
Flaneuse, *The Grip*, 30

Flaubert, *Madame Bovary*. *See* trial
formalism, 50, 51, 198
Fowler, Henry: *A Dictionary of Modern Critical Terms*, 158n32; *A Dictionary of Modern English Usage*, 136
freedom: academic, 182; of art, 14; artistic, 1, 14, 15, 177, 181, 201; of artistic creativity and scientific research, 178, 179, 182, 184, 190n23; of expression, 62–63, 64, 77, 80, 177, 178, 182, 184, 194; of political expression, 178; of religion, 111; of speech, 14, 45n17, 77, 103, 108, 111, 113, 114, 115, 122n77, 135, 174, 178, 185; of the press and other media, 178, 182; of thought, 45n17; political, 113; to print, 77, 103; to receive or impart information or ideas, 182. *See also exceptio artis*; liberty
Fuchs, C. D., 140, 144
functionality, 95, 106, 112, 134, 135, 136, 137, 139, 141, 143, 154, 195
fundamental rights, 178, 181

General Synod of the Dutch Reformed Church, 128
general welfare, 54
Genootskap vir die Handhawing van Afrikaans (lit.: Association for the Maintenance of Afrikaans), 88
genre. *See* literary genre
Gericke, J. S., 88, 118n11
Glyn, Elinor, 30
government: of P. W. Botha, 174, 196; of F. W. de Klerk, 178; of Paul Kruger (Transvaal Republic), 124n107; of D. F. Malan, 49; of Nelson Mandela, 179; of J. G. Strijdom, 53; of H. F. Verwoerd, 53; of B. J. Vorster, 186
Government Gazette, 57, 157n18
Grové, A. P., 88, 91, 101, 119n31, 140, 144, 153
Grüttemeier, Ralf, 8, 10, 14

Hardy, G. W., 27
harm to relations between sections of the population, 54
hate speech, 177, 183
Hertzog, J. B. M., 84n40

Hertzog Prize, 79, 139, 153, 159n51
heteronomous forces, 8, 9
heteronomy, 97, 99, 145, 154, 155, 156, 195, 196, 198, 201n1
Hicklin's case, 30, 33, 46n20, 74
Hicklin test, 33, 34, 55
high brow literature, 68, 76
High Court of South-West Africa, 32
Highet, Gilbert, *The Autonomy of Satire*, 136
Hillier (attorney of G. W. Hardy in *G. W. Hardy* v *Rex*), 28
Holmes, Oliver Wendell. *See* judges
homology, 7, 9, 170; between juridical and literary field, 7, 107, 117; conceptual, 117; structural, 7, 39, 117
House of Lords, 190n15; case of James Kirkup, "The Love that Dares to Speak its Name", 190n15
Human, J. J., 147
Human & Rousseau, 87, 119n34, 133, 136, 141, 145, 147
Humboldt, Wilhelm von, 15
Hupe, Katharina, 14

idealist aesthetics. *See* aesthetics
"immature, uneducated and uncivlised persons", 33, 34, 174
incest, 52
"indecent or obscene" pubications, 23, 37, 39, 40, 44n6, 54, 55, 59, 64, 67
Information Scandal, 167
Ingarden, Roman, *Das literarische Kunstwerk*, 50
Insight Publications, 65
institutional analysis, 1, 12–13, 14, 17, 20n12
institutional autonomy. *See* autonomy
institutional context, 13
institutional reading, 12, 19n11
institutional research, 12
institutional valences, 19n11
intellectual classes of the community, 70
intent, 38, 96, 100
intentional-oriented approach. *See* subjective approach to literature regulation
internal necessities test, 26. *See also* contextual approach

irony, 134, 136
isolated-passage criterion, 25–27, 31, 42, 46n20, 55, 60, 64, 66, 74, 85, 86, 112, 149, 150, 181, 193

James, Henry, 113
Jameson Raid, 114, 124n107
Jesus. *See* Christ
Joubert, Gideon, 140
Joyce, James, 45n14; *Finnegans Wake*, 138; *Ulysses*, 32, 42
judges: Beyers (Cape Provincial Division of the Supreme Court), 61, 63, 64, 75, 77, 83n22; Bok (High Court of South-West Africa), 33, 63, 171, 174, 179, 188, 193, 197; Bok, Curtis (Supreme Court of Pennsylvania), 46n21; Boshoff (Transvaal Provincial Division of the Supreme Court), 148; Cockburn, Alexander (Chief Justice of England, 1875-1880), 29, 30, 33, 46n20, 74, 77; Diemont, Marius (Cape Provincial Division of the Supreme Court), 60, 61, 64, 65, 83n19, 83n22, 83n24, 97, 99, 103–108, 110, 116, 117, 118, 121n53, 122n59, 151, 155, 167, 169, 195, 196; Hall (Cape Provincial Division of the Supreme Court), 84n31; Holmes (Appellate Division of the Supreme Court of South Africa), 71, 76; Holmes, Oliver Wendell (Supreme Court of the United States), 190n28; Marais, J. F. (Transvaal Provincial Division of the Supreme Court), 24; Myburgh (Transvaal Provinvial Division of the Supreme Court), 148; Ogilvie Thompson, Newton (Chief Justice of South Africa, 1971–1974), 85, 86, 112, 143, 149, 150, 155, 171; Potgieter (Appellate Division of the Supreme Court of South Africa), 71, 76, 97; Price (Witwatersrand Local Division of the Supreme Court), 41, 42; Rumpff, F. L. H. (Appellate Division of the Supreme Court of South Africa), 71, 73, 74, 75, 77, 78, 79, 84n35, 94, 103, 108, 149, 150, 160n64, 167, 171; Steyn (Cape Provincial Division of the Supreme Court), 97, 108–116, 117, 123n81, 123n90, 123n94, 137, 151, 155, 167, 169, 175, 186, 195, 196, 198; Steyn, L. C. (Chief Justice of South Africa, 1959–1971), 57, 71, 72, 74, 75, 76, 79, 97, 102, 108, 128, 160n53; van der Walt (Transvaal Provincial Division of the Supreme Court), 148; van Heerden (Appellate Division of the Supreme Court of South Africa), 66, 84n31; van Wyk (Cape Provincial Division of the Supreme Court), 97–102, 103, 104, 105, 108, 110, 112, 113, 114, 116, 121n53, 149, 151, 155, 167, 195, 196, 198; van Zyl (Cape Provincial Division of the Supreme Court), 60, 61, 63, 64, 75, 77; Williamson (Appellate Division of the Supreme Court of South Africa), 71, 72, 73, 74, 75, 78, 94, 130, 167, 171; Woolsey (District Court for the Southern District of New York), 45n14
judicial review, 157n15, 166; of Publications Appeal Board judgment on Etienne Leroux, *Magersfontein, O Magersfontein!*, 1, 148–152, 167, 169, 196
juridical field, 68
Juvenal, 29

Kahn, Ellison, 62, 79, 83n24
Kannemeyer, J. C., 88, 134, 153
Kirkup, James, 173; "The Love that Dares to Speak its Name", 173. *See also* Court of Appeal case of James Kirkup, "The Love that Dares to Speak its Name"; English Central Criminal Court case of James Kirkup, "The Love that Dares to Speak its Name"; European Commission of Human Rights case of James Kirkup, "The Love that Dares to Speak its Name"; House of Lords case of James Kirkup, "The Love that Dares to Speak its Name";
Korthals Altes, Liesbeth, 8, 10, 199
Krige, Uys, 68, 128
Krijnauw, P., 139
Kriterium (periodical), 119n34
Kruger Commission, 128
Kruger, J. J., 82n15, 91, 109, 128

Kruger, J. T., 128
Kruger, Paul, 124n107

La Guma, Alex, 5
l'art pour l'art, 11, 128
law: Anglo-American, 42, 43, 53, 74; Australian, 201; civil, 3; copyright, 3, 41, 43; Dutch, 14, 121n47; English, 1, 2, 23, 26, 27, 45n8, 73, 74, 80, 95, 114, 137, 190n15, 200, 201; French, 96, 121n47; German, 14; Irish, 201; penal, 3; positive, 2; South African, 2, 137, 193, 199, 200, 201; United States, 1, 2, 73, 74, 80, 95, 114, 200. *See also* Acts of Parliament; artistic freedom; cases; constitution; *exceptio artis*; *exceptio scientiae*; literary trials; obscenity trials; trials
law-and-literature, 3
law-as-literature, 3, 19n3, 189n1
law-in-literature, 3, 19n3
Lawrence, D. H., *Lady Chatterley's Lover*, 53. *See also* Publications Appeal Board case of Lawrence, D. H., *Lady Chatterley's Lover*; trials
Leavis, F. R., 113
Leerssen, Joep, 20n13
Leroux, Etienne, 128, 133, 139, 146, 159n51, 195; *Magersfontein, O Magersfontein!*, 1, 173, 198; *Sewe Dae by die Silbersteins*, 79, 159n51. *See also* judicial review of Publications Appeal Board judgment on Etienne Leroux, *Magersfontein, O Magersfontein!*
Lewis, Felice Flanery, 28, 75
liberty, 77; of the printing press, 73; political, 77
likely reader, 55, 56, 59, 61, 64, 66, 69, 71, 72, 75–76, 79, 80–81, 91, 93, 94, 98–99, 100, 102, 104–106, 107, 108, 110, 116, 117, 131, 141, 145, 146, 147, 148–152, 153, 154, 155, 169, 170, 175, 177, 186, 187, 193, 194, 195, 196
likely reader test, 55, 61, 64, 69, 75, 80–81, 117, 131, 193, 194
limitation clause, 182
Lindenberg, Ernst, 93, 105, 119n34, 153
literariness, 93, 141, 174, 177

literary academic, 7, 153
literary censor. *See* censor
literary elite, 7
literary expert, 7, 23, 31, 40, 50, 53, 55, 56, 59, 72, 82n13, 83n29, 116, 132, 136, 156, 160n68, 170, 175, 183, 185, 187, 188, 189, 190n25, 193, 195, 196
literary expert committee. *See* committee of experts
literary expert evidence, 17, 53, 64, 72, 73, 80–81, 91, 93, 96, 99, 102, 105, 108–109, 116, 136, 141, 146, 147, 154, 166, 170, 193, 195, 198
literary expertise, 7, 17, 40, 43, 59, 71–73, 107, 116, 117, 141, 170, 186, 195, 196, 198
literary field, 6, 11; Belgian, 3; Dutch, 3; emergence of, 2, 3, 12, 17; French, 3; German, 3; postcolonial, 9; "small", 9; South African, 4, 17–18, 19n6, 20n14, 20n16, 44, 199. *See also* subfield
literary genre, 6–7, 135, 137, 141
literary merit, 40, 43, 53, 59, 64–65, 67, 78, 141, 146, 152, 154, 165, 168–169, 170, 172, 173, 175, 177, 184, 187, 188, 193, 195, 197, 198
literary socialized reader, 34, 43, 55, 91, 93, 99, 104, 105, 106, 110, 117, 131, 141, 154, 156, 169, 177, 187, 193, 196
literary taste, 76
literary trials, 200; civil, 4; criminal, 4; in Belgium, 3, 7, 200; in France, 3, 7, 200; in Germany, 3, 7, 200; in South Africa, 45n8; in the Netherlands, 3, 7, 200
literary value, 78–79, 82n15, 91, 128, 135, 136, 139, 146, 147, 154, 174
literati, 93, 110, 140, 141. *See also* literary socialized reader
literature-in-law, 3, 14–15, 19n3, 200
littérature engagée. *See* engaged novel
Lobard (theologian), 111
London, 18, 57
Louw, Anna, 134, 153
Louw, W. E. G., 162n92
loyal resistance ("lojale verset"), 115, 146. *See also* aesthetics N. P. van Wyk Louw

magistrates: Magistrate for the Division of Cape Peninsula, 66, 68, 69, 70; Magistrate of Windhoek, 32; Resident Magistrate for Cape Town, 31; Resident Magistrate of Worcester, 26
Magistrates' Court, 23, 56; of Cape Town, 65; of Durban, 27; of Johannesburg, 36
Mahabane, Z. R., 28
Malan, D. F., 49, 172
Malan, Etienne, 134
Mandela, Nelson, 176
Marais, Eugène, 138, 159n42
Marais, J. F., 24. *See also* judges
Marxist theory of art, 6
McDonald, Peter D., 2, 46n19, 176, 185, 190n28; *The Literature Police*, 2, 46n19, 185, 187, 199
median person, 137, 139, 145
meta-perspective, 11, 12
Miles, John, 88; *Donderdag of Woensdag*, 153, 173. *See also* Publications Appeal Board case of Miles, John, *Donderdag of Woensdag*
Miller, Henry, *Tropic of Cancer*, 53. *See also* trial
Milton, John, 29
mimetic work of literature (*sensu* Abrams). *See* theory of literature
minority rights : of literature, 169, 170, 186; of the intellectual/literary socialized reader, 117
miscegenation, 83n26
mitigating factor, 160n64, 168, 169, 175
moral provisions of the Publications Act, 1974, 139, 148–150, 161n77, 172
moral provisions of the Publications and Entertainments Act, 1963, 54, 68, 69, 70, 72, 73, 76, 89, 93, 97, 102, 107, 112
Moravia, Alberto, *Time of Desecration*. *See* Moravia, Alberto, *Time of Desecration*
Morkel, Dan, 176, 177
Mphahlele, Es'kia, 174
Mtshali, Oswald, 175; *Fireflames*, 1. *See also* Publications Appeal Board case of Mtshali, Oswald, *Fireflames*
Muldergate. *See* Information Scandal
Mulder, P. C., 88, 135, 156, 167, 189n4
Müller, H. C. T., 88

Muslim community, 183, 184
Mutloatse, Mothobi, *Forced Landing*. *See* Publications Appeal Board case of Mutloatse, Mothobi, *Forced Landing*
Myburgh (judge). *See* judges

Napoleon, 115
Nasionale Boekwinkels (National Bookshops), 119n34
Nasionale Party (National Party), 5, 49, 84n40, 128
Natal, 23, 24, 44n3, 44n5, 45n7, 57
National Arts Initiative (NAI), 177
Nederduitse Gereformeerde Kerk, 118n10, 118n11, 154. *See also* Dutch Reformed Church
Nel, P. R. T., 162n92
neo-Marxist literary sociology, 114
New York, 18
New York Society for the Suppression of Vice, 31, 158n36
Noble anti-censorship petition, 128
Noble, J. N., 157n3
normal and natural, satisfying and right, 139, 160n53

objective approach to literature regulation, 100, 121n47, 197
objective work of literature (*sensu* Abrams). See theory of literature
obscenity, 2, 3, 34, 41, 42, 43, 45n8, 46n21, 49, 53, 54, 55, 57, 59, 60, 65, 74, 82n5, 83n25, 86, 134, 172; test of, 30, 34, 46n20, 55, 63, 74
obscenity trials: in territories of the British Empire, 29; in the United States, 29, 53, 63, 82n8
offence against good morals, 28, 29
Ogilvie Thompson, Newton. *See* judges
opinion of the court, 59, 69, 72, 98, 108
Opmerker (pseudonymous author of "Teekenen des Tyds"), 25
Opperman, D. J., 88, 93, 96, 100, 105, 119n34
Orange Free State, 23, 24, 44n3
Orange River Colony, 30
ordinary man, 30, 34, 45n8, 45n15, 79
ordinary man test, 75, 81, 117
ordinary reader, 75, 93, 104, 105, 110

Pannevis, Arnoldus, 138, 159n42
parliamentary sovereignty, 103, 122n60
participant objectivation, 3
participant observation, 3
Paton, Alan, 128
Paulskirche constitution. *See* constitution
peace and good order, 54
PEN, South African branch of, 53
petitions. *See* Noble anti-censorship petition; Rutter pro-censorship petition
Pienaar, Louis, 176
Platonic poetological principles. *See* aesthetics
poetics, 13. *See also* aesthetics; conception of literature; theory of literature
Poet Laureate of England, 114, 124n106
poetological analysis, 1, 5, 12–13, 14, 17, 20n12
poetological position, 18
poetological position-taking, 13
pole of large production, 7
pole of restricted production, 7
poles that determine literary activity, 7
political field, 102, 106, 116, 153, 170, 198, 199
political provisions of the Publications Act, 1974, 139, 161n78, 174–176, 178
political provisions of the Publications and Entertainments Act, 1963, 54, 89, 93, 97, 101, 107, 112
pornography, 177, 180, 184
possible reader, 55, 61, 75
Potgieter (judge). *See* judges
pragmatic work of literature (*sensu* Abrams). *See* theory of literature
pre-censorship, 50, 142
Presbyterian Church, 67
Press Council, 190n24
Pretorius, C. E., 162n92
Prince (newspaper), 27
Prince of Wales, 114
privacy of the reader, 62
private morality, 62. *See also* public morality
probable reader, 55, 61, 76
production of literature: material, 9, 19n6, 201n1; symbolic, 9, 19n6, 201n1
"profane, indecent or obscene" publications, 24

Prophet Mohammed, 183
protest literature, 175, 186, 187
Prussia, 14
Publications Appeal Board, 45n8, 128, 129–130, 131, 153, 154, 156, 157n20, 157n22, 158n23, 160n68, 165, 166–176, 177, 179, 186, 187, 188, 189n3, 189n7, 190n24, 195, 196, 198; approach toward literature of, 145–146, 152–154; case of Armah, Ayi Kwei, *Two Thousand Seasons*, 174, 175; case of Bloom, Harry, *Transvaal Episode*, 176; case of Brink, André, *Kennis van die Aand*, 172, 173; case of Brink, André, *Looking on Darkness*, 190n12; case of Brink, André, *'n Droë Wit Seisoen/A Dry White Season*, 170, 176; case of Burgess, Anthony, *Man of Nazareth*, 173, 177; case of Cleland, John, *Memoirs of a Woman of Pleasure*, 172; case of Ebersohn, Wessel, *Divide the Night*, 176; case of Ebersohn, Wessel, *Store Up the Anger*, 176; case of Gordimer, Nadine, *Burger's Daughter*, 176; case of Lawrence, D. H., *Lady Chatterley's Lover*, 172; case of Leroux, Etienne, *Magersfontein, O Magersfontein!*, 132, 136–145, 146, 170, 172, 173; case of Miles, John, *Donderdag of Woensdag*, 153, 166, 173; case of Moravia, Alberto, *Time of Desecration*, 172, 173; case of Mtshali, Oswald, *Fireflames*, 174; case of Mutloatse, Mothobi, *Forced Landing*, 176; case of Roth, Philip, *Portnoy's Complaint*, 172; case of *Staffrider*, 176; case of Styron, William, *Sophie's Choice*, 172, 173
Publications Board, 50, 52, 55
Publications Board of Appeal, 50
publications control, 24, 38, 40, 49, 50, 52, 183. *See* censorship
Publications Control Board, 55, 56, 57, 58, 60, 62, 65, 73, 82n15, 83n20, 83n29, 85, 86, 88, 89–93, 127, 128
public good, 63, 114, 115, 116
public good test, 64, 80, 193
public indecency, 27, 28

public morality, 62, 140. *See also* private morality
public morals, 34, 54, 57, 59, 62, 67, 78, 98, 131, 140
public morals test, 62
Public Prosecutor, 67
publishing industry: Afrikaans, 46n23

quasi-judicial, 50, 82n4

Rabie, Jan, 128
Rand Daily Mail, 86
real danger test, 174
reasonable man/person, 34, 45n8, 139, 145
referendum on becoming a republic. *See* South African republic referendum, 1960
regulation of literature. *See* censorship
Reichsgericht, 15
Reitz, F. W., 138, 159n42
relative approach to publications control, 148
reliable narrator, 92
religious convictions, 54, 67
religious feelings, 54, 67
religious provisions of the Publications Act, 1974, 139, 150–151, 161n77, 173
religious provisions of the Publications and Entertainments Act, 1963, 54, 68, 69, 89, 90, 93, 97, 102, 106, 107, 111
Rembrandt, 138; *The Night Watch*, 138
repressive tolerance, 187
Republican Publications, 85
Republic of South Africa, 5
restrictions on distribution, 173, 180, 181, 184, 185
restrictions with regard to age or display, 152, 156, 173, 179, 180, 181, 196
reversed economy, 10
ridicule, 54
right: of access, 184; to enquire into any matter, 63; to publish and disseminate knowledge, 63. *See also* freedom; fundamental rights; minority rights
Robbins, Harold, 46n21
rollback, 81, 186, 195, 196, 198
roman engagé, 101, 119n31. *See also* engaged literature; littérature engagée

Roth, Philip, *Portnoy's Complaint. See* Publications Appeal Board case of Roth, Philip, *Portnoy's Complaint*
Roth standard, 53
Rousseau, Leon, 93, 119n34
Royal African Society, 35
Rudolph, C. F., 162n92
Rumpff, F. L. H. *See* judges
Rushdie, Salman, 190n16, 197; *The Satanic Verses*, 1, 173. *See also* Film and Publications Board case of Salman Rushdie, *The Satanic Verses*
Rutter, G. O., 157n4
Rutter pro-censorship petition, 128

Saayman, Daantjie, 93
Sabbagha, N. J. G., 162n92
Sapiro, Gisèle, 6–7, 9, 15
Sartre, Jean-Paul, *Qu'est-ce que la littérature?*, 50
satire, 134, 135, 136, 137, 141, 158n32
Schlebusch, Alwyn, 152, 156, 166, 167, 189n6, 196
science exemption. *See exceptio scientiae*
Scope (periodical), 85
Second Afrikaans Language Movement, 159n42
Second Boer War. *See* South African War
Security Police, 67
self-censorship. *See* censorship
Seroke, Jaki, 187
Sestigers (Writers of the Sixties), 79, 84n38, 86, 102, 115, 128, 138, 146. *See also* aesthetics
Shaw, C. S. Scott, 67
Shaw, Robert, 31
Skrywersgilde (Writers' Guild), 88
Smit, Bartho, 153
Smith, Wilbur, 71, 72, 83n19. *See also* trial
Snyman, J. H., 130, 131, 140, 141, 145, 148, 152, 153, 157n20, 160n68, 166, 167, 168, 186, 189n6, 195, 196, 198
Social Reform Association, 31, 158n36
societal norms. *See* community standards
sophisticated reader, 102, 106, 169. *See also* literary socialized reader
Sophocles, *Oedipus Rex*, 52
South Africa: court system in. *See* court system

South African Broadcasting Corporation, 144
South African Human Rights Commission, 165, 189n1
South African Institute for Librarianship and Information Science (SAILIS), 177, 189n7; Ad Hoc Committee on Banned Books of the, 189n7
South African Institute for Literature, 50
South African Law Commission, 177
South African Library, 189n7
South African republic referendum, 1960, 53
South African Teachers Union, 128
South African War, 84n40, 134
South-West Africa, 32, 35, 44, 44n6, 45n8
special interest group, 140–141, 148
spiritual poison, 51
Staffrider (periodical). *See* Publications Appeal Board case of *Staffrider*
Standpunte (periodical), 144
Stanzel, F. K., *Narrative Situations in the Novel*, 95
stare decisis, 5, 83n18, 131
state security, 2, 3, 54, 174, 175
Steyn (judge). *See* judges
Steyn, L. C. *See* judges
St. John-Stevas, Norman, 26, 46n20
Stone, G. R., 190n28
Strijdom, J. G., 53
strong reader, 55, 69, 70, 76, 91, 105
Strydom, L., 162n92
Styron, William, *Sophie's Choice*. *See* Publications Appeal Board case of Styron, William, *Sophie's Choice*
subfield: African-language, 17, 19n6, 20n15, 82n12, 201n1; Afrikaans, 17, 19n6, 68, 82n12, 84n40, 93, 116, 128, 137, 146, 153, 198, 199; English, 17, 18, 19n6, 113, 116, 199. *See also* literary field
subjective approach to literature regulation, 100
Suid-Afrikaanse Akademie vir Wetenskap en Kuns (South African Academy for Science and Arts), 88, 144, 153
Supreme Court: Appellate Division of, 23, 37, 45n17, 56, 57, 65, 71, 72, 74, 129; Cape Provincial Division of, 31, 58, 61, 69, 71, 78; of Natal, 27, 74; of South Africa, 2, 56, 68, 73, 179, 183, 184, 185, 186, 195, 196; of the Cape of Good Hope, 26; Provincial and Local Divisions of, 23, 56, 129; Transvaal Provincial Division of, 37, 147, 148, 157n19; Witwatersrand Local Division of, 41
Susann, Jacqueline, *The Love Machine*, 85
Swart, J. J., 88
Swarts (witness), 67
symbolic production of literature. *See* production of literature

Task Group on Film and Publication Control, 179, 180, 181, 182, 190n24
"Teekenen des Tyds", 25
Terblanche (counsel), 66
Terblanche, H. J., 88
testimony, 68, 69
text-oriented approach. *See* objective approach to literature regulation
"The Black Peril", 27
The Classic (periodical), 65
Themba, Can. *See* trial
The New African (periodical), 65, 67
theory of literature : expressive (*sensu* Abrams), 119n33; mimetic (*sensu* Abrams), 92, 96, 100, 101, 102, 107, 110, 112, 113, 116, 119n33, 134; objective/autonomist (*sensu* Abrams), 92, 96, 101, 115, 119n33, 141, 144–145, 157n6, 186, 198; pragmatic (*sensu* Abrams), 92, 100, 101, 115, 119n33, 141, 157n6, 175, 186, 198. *See also* aesthetics; conception of literature; poetics
The Ringhals (newspaper), 36, 37
Tim du Toit and Co., 136
Titlestad, P. J. H., 162n92
tolerance, 171; regarding changing societal norms, 31, 43, 193; regarding evolving norms concerning modern literature, 34
total onslaught, 174
transformation principle, 51, 92, 96, 144
Transvaal, 23, 24, 44n3, 57
Transvaal Colony, 30
Transvaal Republic, 124n107
Treason Trial, 5

Treaty of Versailles, 44n6
trials: Brink, André, *Kennis van die Aand* (South Africa), 1, 36, 57, 85–118, 122n59, 137, 142, 146, 149, 151, 155, 167, 169, 170, 175, 186, 195, 196, 198; Flaneuse, *The Grip* (South Africa), 30–32, 43; Flaubert, Gustave, *Madame Bovary* (France), 96; Joyce, James, *Ulysses* (United States), 32, 42; Lawrence, D. H., *Lady Chatterley's Lover* (England), 53; Miller, Henry, *Tropic of Cancer* (United States), 53; *Scope* (South Africa), 127, 157n14; Smith, Wilbur, *When the Lion Feeds* (South Africa), 1, 45n8, 57–65, 69, 70, 71–79, 80–81, 85, 94, 95, 97, 98, 102, 103, 108, 111, 117, 128, 142, 146, 149, 150, 155, 160n64, 167, 170, 171, 194, 195, 196, 198; Themba, Can, "The Fugitives" (South Africa), 1, 57, 65–71, 80–81, 167, 194. *See also* judicial review
Truth and Reconciliation Committee, 165
Tweede Vryheidsoorlog (Second War of Independence). *See* South African War

undesirable publication, 50, 51, 54, 55, 56, 57, 60, 69, 72, 75, 76, 89, 97, 107, 108, 111, 115, 117, 143, 152
Union of South Africa, 1, 5, 23, 25, 30, 32, 40, 43, 44n6, 84n40
United Party, 128
university: of Cape Town, 119n34; of Potchefstroom, 91; of Pretoria, 49, 82n1, 91, 144, 190n24; of the Witwatersrand, 119n34; Stellenbosch, 118n11, 119n34

van der Colf, A. P., 162n92
van der Merwe, C. N., 88
van der Merwe, Schalk, 128
van der Merwe, W. F., 68
van der Merwe Scholtz, H., 50, 52, 88, 134, 152, 153, 158n32, 162n92
van der Poll, Letetia, 83n24
van der Waal, Margriet, 19n6, 20n14
van der Walt (judge). *See* judges
van Gogh, Vincent, 138
van Heerden (judge). *See* judges

van Heerden, Ernst, 128, 153
van Rees, Kees, 12, 20n12
van Rensburg, F. I. J., 88
van Rooyen, J. C. W., 131, 132, 140, 154, 166, 167, 168, 170, 171, 172, 173, 174, 175, 176, 177, 179, 183, 185, 186, 187, 188, 190n13, 190n24, 191n29, 196, 197, 198; *Censorship in South Africa*, 168, 170
van Rooyen, J. J., 91, 109
Van Schaik Boekhandel (Van Schaik Bookstore), 119n34
van Schaik, J. J., 93, 119n34
van Wyk (judge). *See* judge
van Wyk Louw, N. P., 115, 141
van Zuyl, Eddie, 135
van Zyl (judge). *See* judges
Verwoerd, Hendrik, 53
Viljoen, Marais, 166
Vorster, B. J., 118n11, 127, 167, 186
Vorster, J. D., 88, 118n11

weak reader, 55, 76, 91
Webb (accused in the case of *Rex* v *Webb*), 36
Wellek, René, and Austin Warren, *Theory of Literature*, 50
"Wende zum Kulturstaat", 15, 17, 50
Western civilization, 63
Wiechers, M., 129
Wiehahn, R., 162n92
Wilcocks, D. P., 140
William Heinemann Ltd. (publishing house), 58, 60, 61, 71, 72
Williamson (judge). *See* judges
Willingham, Calder, 46n21
witness, 31, 43
Witwatersrand, 57
Woolsey (judge). *See* judges
Worcester Advertiser (newspaper), 25

X18 classification, 180, 181, 183, 187, 188, 197
XX classification, 180, 181, 185, 187, 188, 189, 197

Youth for Christ Movement, 157n4

Zandberg, T., 67

Zuma, Jacob, 184

About the Author

Ted Laros studied Dutch and comparative literature at Utrecht University (Netherlands) and the University of California, Los Angeles. He took his PhD at the Carl von Ossietzky University of Oldenburg (Germany). He is assistant professor of literary studies at the Open University of the Netherlands, and also teaches at the University of Duisburg-Essen in Germany. He has previously taught at the Radboud University of Nijmegen (Netherlands), and Oldenburg University. He has held visiting positions at the University of Münster (Germany) and the *Vrije Universiteit Brussel* (Belgium). His main research interests are in Dutch and South African literature, sociology of culture, the relationship between literature and the law, and that between literature and politics.